Gender and Survival in Soviet Russia

Library of Modern Russia

Building on Bloomsbury Academic's established record of publishing Russian studies titles, the *Library of Modern Russia* will showcase the work of emerging and established writers who are setting new agendas in the field. At a time when potentially dangerous misconceptions and misunderstandings about Russia abound, titles in the series will shed fresh light and nuance on Russian history. Volumes will take the idea of 'Russia' in its broadest cultural sense and cover the entirety of the multi-ethnic lands that made up imperial Russia and the Soviet Union. Ranging in chronological scope from the Romanovs to today, the books will:

- Re-consider Russia's history from a variety of inter-disciplinary perspectives.
- Explore Russia in its various international contexts, rather than as exceptional or in isolation.
- Examine the complex, divisive and ever-shifting notions of 'Russia'.
- Contribute to a deeper understanding of Russia's rich social and cultural history.
- Critically re-assess the Soviet period and its legacy today.
- Interrogate the traditional periodisations of the post-Stalin Soviet Union.
- Unearth continuities, or otherwise, among the tsarist, Soviet and post-Soviet periods.
- Re-appraise Russia's complex relationship with Eastern Europe, both historically and today.
- Analyse the politics of history and memory in post-Soviet Russia.
- Promote new archival revelations and innovative research methodologies.
- Foster a community of scholars and readers devoted to a sharper understanding of the Russian experience, past and present.

Books in the series will join our list in being marketed globally, including at conferences – such as the BASEES and ASEEES conventions. Each will be subjected to a rigorous peer-review process and will be published in hardback and, simultaneously, as an e-book. We also anticipate a second release in paperback for the general reader and student markets. For more information, or to submit a proposal for inclusion in the series, please contact: Rhodri Mogford, Publisher, History (Rhodri.Mogford@bloomsbury.com).

New and forthcoming

Fascism in Manchuria: The Soviet-China Encounter in the 1930s, Susanne Hohler

The Idea of Russia: The Life and Work of Dmitry Likhachev, Vladislav Zubok

The Tsar's Armenians: A Minority in Late Imperial Russia, Onur Onol

Myth Making in the Soviet Union and Modern Russia: Remembering World War II in Brezhnev's Hero City, Vicky Davis

Building Stalinism: The Moscow Canal and the Creation of Soviet Space, Cynthia Ruder

Russia in the Time of Cholera: Disease and the Environment under Romanovs and Soviets, John Davis

Soviet Americana: A Cultural History of Russian and Ukrainian Americanists, Sergei Zhuk

Stalin's Economic Advisors: The Varga Institute and the Making of Soviet Foreign Policy, Ken Roh

Ideology and the Arts in the Soviet Union: The Establishment of Censorship and Control, Steven Richmond

Nomads and Soviet Rule: Central Asia under Lenin and Stalin, Alun Thomas

The Russian State and the People: Power, Corruption and the Individual in Putin's Russia, Geir Hønneland et al. (eds)

The Communist Party in the Russian Civil War: A Political History, Gayle Lonergan

Criminal Subculture in the Gulag: Prisoner Society in the Stalinist Labour Camps, Mark Vincent

Power and Politics in Modern Chechnya: Ramzan Kadyrov and the New Digital Authoritarianism, Karena Avedissian

Russian Pilgrimage to the Holy Land: Piety and Travel from the Middle Ages to the Revolution, Nikolaos Chrissidis

The Fate of the Bolshevik Revolution, Lara Douds, James Harris, and Peter Whitehead (eds)

Writing History in Late Imperial Russia, Frances Nethercott

Translating England into Russian, Elena Goodwin

Gender and Survival in Soviet Russia, Elaine MacKinnon (trans. and ed.)

Gender and Survival in Soviet Russia

A Life in the Shadow of Stalin's Terror

Ludmila Miklashevskaya

Translated and Edited by
Elaine MacKinnon

BLOOMSBURY ACADEMIC
LONDON • NEW YORK • OXFORD • NEW DELHI • SYDNEY

BLOOMSBURY ACADEMIC
Bloomsbury Publishing Plc
50 Bedford Square, London, WC1B 3DP, UK
1385 Broadway, New York, NY 10018, USA
29 Earlsfort Terrace, Dublin 2, Ireland

BLOOMSBURY, BLOOMSBURY ACADEMIC and the Diana logo are trademarks of
Bloomsbury Publishing Plc

First published in Great Britain 2020
Paperback edition published 2021

Cover design by Tjaša Krivec
Cover image: Saint Petersburg, January 2017 (© Marina Pissarova / Alamy Stock Photo)

A catalogue record for this book is available from the British Library.

A catalog record for this book is available from the Library of Congress.

ISBN: HB: 978-1-3501-3920-6
PB: 978-1-3502-4674-4
ePDF: 978-1-3501-3921-3
eBook: 978-1-3501-3923-7

Series: Library of Modern Russia

Typeset by Newgen KnowledgeWorks Pvt. Ltd., Chennai, India

To find out more about our authors and books visit www.bloomsbury.com
and sign up for our newsletters.

For Aran and Kieran

Contents

Translator's Acknowledgments

It is an honor and a privilege to make available to English-speaking readers this moving account of one woman's struggle for love and family against the backdrop of Stalin's terror. Above all I have to express thanks to Ludmila Pavlovna Eizengardt Miklashevskaya for her courageous action in setting down the story of her life; since reading Ludmila's memoir for the first time, I have wanted to make this work available to a broader audience, though due to space limitations my translation is an abridged version of the original published in Russia in 2007 and 2012. I owe an enormous debt of gratitude to the Epanchin family, who are related to Ludmila Miklashevshkaya's first husband, Konstantin Mikhailovich. I owe special thanks to Michael Epanchin and to his uncle Nikolai Epanchin, who first brought this memoir to my attention and asked me to translate sections of it for their family. I am grateful for Nikolai Epanchin's careful reading of my translation and helpful edits.

I want to thank the Russian publishers of Ludmila's memoir, the journal and publishing house *Zvezda*, for allowing me to publish this English-language edition and for offering me invaluable assistance. The editor, Andrei Iur'evich Ar'ev, graciously granted me the rights to publish my translation. Galina Kondratenko welcomed me warmly to the *Zvezda* office in St. Petersburg and assisted me in multiple ways with my preparation of this manuscript. Also invaluable to this publication is Iakov Gordin, the editor of Ludmila's memoir and the person who carefully safeguarded it from the time of her death in 1976 until it could be published in 2007. He has generously shared with me his memories of Ludmila, which has greatly informed my understanding of a woman I am so very sorry to have never known personally. I also must thank a former writer for *Zvezda*, Valery Zavorotny, for his generous help in arranging for me to meet with his former colleagues, and I am indebted to Donald Raleigh for introducing me to Valery and for his invaluable advice and assistance with this project.

I want to thank the publisher, I.B. Tauris, and Bloomsbury Publishing, my editor Rhodri Mogford, Laura Reeves, and all others involved in the process of preparing this translation for publication. They have helped me find my way through the different stages of publication and have been extremely generous with advice and assistance at every step. I also want to thank Thomas Stoddard for believing in this project and helping to secure this opportunity for me at I.B. Taurus. I want to thank as well the University of Illinois Summer Research Laboratory and all of the Slavic Reference Service and International Studies and Area Studies Library staff for providing me with the opportunity to conduct research that has informed my understanding of Ludmila's life and the individuals closely connected with her. In particular I would like to thank Christopher Condill for his help in identifying sources and guiding my research when in residence at Illinois.

Finally, I owe eternal thanks to my husband Dr. Aran MacKinnon for all of his support through this entire project; he has read drafts and listened to my endless questioning of words and phrases to best convey thoughts from one language to another. I want to thank as well my son, Kieran, for encouraging me and for helping me to grasp just how agonizing it had to have been for mothers such as Ludmila to be separated from their children by the heartless hand of the Stalinist state and its policy of terror.

Translator's Preface

This edition is an abridged translation of Ludmila Pavlovna Miklashevskaya's memoir, *Povtorenie proĭdennogo*. The print edition you are reading focuses solely on her life in Russia and therefore leaves out the section of the memoir detailing her life in Paris from 1924 to 1927. It also omits the appendix of the original Russian edition, which included copies of her rehabilitation documents. Readers who are interested may access the omitted chapter on Ludmila Pavlovna's sojourn in Paris in PDF format through the book's web page on the publisher's website.

In my translation I have tried to be accurate and preserve Ludmila Pavlovna's detailed descriptions of people and places, and her amazing memory of dialogue and the thoughts she had as she went through her remarkable life. But due to space limitations, I have had to leave out material found in the original text and in places convert dialogue into narrative description. When the quoted materials are longer than sixty words, I have kept these indented. I have made modifications to the text to make it more readable. Ludmila Pavlovna did not divide her memoir into individual chapters, but wrote just one continuous narrative. I have divided the narrative into ten chapters, nine of which appear in this edition. The chapter titles are my own. The passages that reflect her thoughts and anxieties as she was writing the memoir are italicized to help the reader discern the change in the time frame of the narrative. I have had to revise the original endnotes from the Russian edition. Some I have retained in their original and some I have revised, some I have omitted, and I have added explanatory endnotes of my own for English language readers. In the text whenever added information included in parentheses are my own explanatory notes, I have indicated this by adding "translator's note."

I have followed the Library of Congress transliteration system, but I have modified it in order to make certain Russian names easier for readers unfamiliar with the Russian language. I am using a more Anglicized version of Ludmila, which if transliterated literally from Russian would read "Liudmila," and of her last name, Miklashevskaya," rather than "Miklashevskaia." Likewise, I am using a modified spelling for the diminutive or pet name she uses for her second husband, Izya, rather than Izia. I have used the more familiar spellings for Russian names of famous persons such as Maxim Gorky, Feodor Chaliapin, Vladimir Mayakovsky, and Ilya Ehrenburg. In deference to the Miklachevsky family, when referring to Ludmila's first husband, Konstantin Mikhailovich Miklachevsky and his siblings, I am transliterating the Russian letter "ш" as "ch," which is how Konstantin Mikhailovich and his family spelled their last name after emigrating to France and to Germany. Otherwise, however, I transliterate "ш" as "sh," and I use this for the spelling of Ludmila Miklashevskaya's name.

Introduction

The preface to the Russian edition of Ludmila Pavlovna Eizengardt Miklashevskaya's memoir begins with an evocative verse from the 1923 poem, "My age, my beast," written by one of Russia's greatest poets, Osip Mandelshtam, who met with a tragic end in a remote Gulag transit camp, a victim of the Stalinist terror. The editor Iakov A. Gordin, a personal friend of Ludmila's, presents Mandelshtam's poetic rendering of the twentieth century as a bloodthirsty beast in tribute to this courageous woman whose life bore its deep scars. Ludmila Pavlovna's memoir is a compelling personal narrative of love, suffering, and survival across decades of war, revolution, and repression. She relives her desperate plight as a mother in Stalinist Russia struggling to keep her family together in the face of terror and persecution. She sheds light into the myriad dimensions of Russian history—Jewish life in the turn of twentieth-century Odessa, the cultural avant garde in Leningrad and Moscow in the 1920s and 1930s, incarceration in the Gulag, and readjustment to life after imprisonment and exile. Ludmila Pavlovna completed the narrative in 1976 but it did not come out in published form until 2007 when it appeared under the title *Povtorenie proĭdennogo. Iz vospominanii* (Reliving the Past. From Memories) as part of the volume *Chemu svideteli my byli: Zhenskie sudby XX vek* (What We Witnessed: Women's Fates in the 20th Century), published by the journal and publishing house *Zvezda*. Its popularity among readers in Russia led *Zvezda* to publish it in a single volume in 2012.

The portrait that emerges from these pages is of a woman possessing remarkable resilience, integrity, and courage. The very writing of this memoir was a monumental achievement of will and stamina. It is not an account of "immediately lived experience," based on a diary or a daily journal. Rather, it is a narrative of Ludmila's "remembered" experiences, composed as a personal journey back through her past. She wrote it during the last year of her life as she battled myasthenia gravis, a severe and painful neuromuscular disease that affected her eyesight. The reader is brought periodically into her treatment experience, and a parallel time frame emerges as she struggles to keep writing amid acute physical pain from her worsening condition as well as mounting emotional distress from her memories. As she relives the tragedies that befell her under Stalin, she reveals both her past and present agony. Close friends encouraged her to tell her story and assisted in preparing the manuscript, particularly the well-known mathematician and professor at Leningrad University, Rem Georgievich Barantsev.

She finished and submitted the memoir to her friend and editor, Iakov Gordin, only days before she died in the arms of Gordin's wife.

Despite her debilitating illness, her prose sparkles with lively and descriptive details of the people and places she encountered. She is a compelling storyteller with a wry sense of humor. Her memoir reveals her keen powers of observation and deep interest in people and in the more quirky sides of life that she managed to find even in the dark abyss of the Gulag. She shares openly and honestly the intimate details of her life, both happy and sad, her successes as well as her mistakes and misgivings. She took in all of her surroundings wherever she was and possessed an uncanny ability to reconstruct dialogues, settings, and situations with such masterful detail that the reader feels drawn into her world at nearly every step.

Ludmila's Story

Ludmila Pavlovna Eizengardt Miklashevskaya lived through three-fourths of the twentieth century. The memoir covers her life from her childhood through 1976, the year she died. Ludmila Pavlovna was born in Odessa in 1899; she was one of three children born to a lower-middle-class Jewish family. Her father was an accountant and her mother, a gifted pianist, gave music lessons. Ludmila attended a girl's gymnasium and enrolled in Odessa's Higher Courses for Women to study history. Her childhood was blemished by her parents' financial struggles and by the fact that being Jewish, her family experienced the traumas of the 1905 pogrom as well as other manifestations of anti-Semitism. Her parents' marriage was often troubled and she came to find refuge in the home of a school friend where intellectualism flourished and books and theater were the common topics of conversation.

Ludmila was a good student and developed a love of culture and philosophy that drew her to a circle of young friends eager to explore new trends, which is how she came to meet the colorful avant-garde playwright, director, and historian of theater, Konstantin Mikhailovich Miklachevsky, who was working in Odessa at the time. He had left Petrograd to bring his dying mother to live in Odessa with his sister. Miklachevsky's family were wealthy aristocrats highly placed at the Russian court. His father, Mikhail Il'ich Miklashevsky, was a member of the State Council and his sister Tatiana had married Prince Anatole Gagarin, son of a Master of the Court and curator of the Imperial Botanical Garden. Konstantin Mikhailovich had served as an officer in the army in the First World War and his older brother was commander of a Guard's regiment. Yet Konstantin Mikhailovich had chosen an unconventional path; he forsook the traditional career laid out for him in foreign service to become an actor, training initially in the Alexander Theater and later under the famous director Vsevolod Meyerhold. At the beginning of his theatrical career, in 1907, he worked in the Starinnii (Ancient) Theater in St. Petersburg (it existed from 1907 to 1912). This was an experimental theater, which aimed at reconstructing on a contemporary stage the theatrical shows from past epochs (particularly from the Middle Ages). He was also the author of a very highly regarded work on theater history, the *Commedia dell'arte, or the Theater of Italian Comedy in the 16th, 17th and 18th Centuries*. After returning from the war in 1916 to Petrograd,[1] he resumed work in the theater. When he went to Odessa in 1919, he began putting on plays with the Chamber (Kamernyi) Theater.[2]

Ludmila met him when her friends invited him to give lectures on theater history; she was 18, very beautiful, and her charm and lively curiosity so captivated him that he proposed marriage to her (he was going through a divorce at that time). Despite a large gap in their ages, Ludmila, dazzled by his creative spirit and amazing intellect, agreed to go with him to Petrograd, where he had been offered a position as co-director of the Peoples' Comedy theater. She left Odessa with few regrets, for she was not close with her parents and she had lost her talented brother Sasha to the Russian Civil War. In Petrograd she stepped into a life and a world far removed from what she had known in Odessa. They moved into the apartment of Konstantin Mikhailovich, which was filled with his family's treasures: expensive jewelry, exquisite china and porcelains, ornate rugs, antique furniture, and lavish furnishings hidden away from the prying eyes of the new Bolshevik regime fully intent on confiscating all such forms of private wealth. They had to spend considerable time and energy inventorying these items, which Ludmila describes delightfully as tedious but very educational for her, and a process that shaped her cultural sensibilities forever after. Eventually they sold or traded these items for more portable valuables to be passed to Konstantin's two brothers and sister who were by then living impoverished lives abroad as émigrés.

Ludmila's life in Petrograd with Konstantin from 1920 to 1924 was marked by economic penury and shortages of food and fuel due to Russia's slow recovery from war, revolution, and Civil War. Yet, for Ludmila, they were exhilarating years culturally and intellectually for, thanks to Konstantin's connections, she met and socialized with leading Russian artists, writers, and scholars. These included such figures as the artist Natan Altman, writers Maxim Gorky and Andrei Bely, the opera singer Feodor Chaliapin, the Serapion Brothers, and poets Alexander Blok, Anna Akhmatova, and Osip Mandelshtam. She enjoyed the romantic attentions of two of early Soviet Russia's most dashing and talented writers, Konstantin Fedin and Mikhail Zoshchenko, as well as a brief affair with the actor Alexei Dikii. Ludmila's descriptions convey the excitement of this early period in Soviet cultural life when the regime supported the arts and encouraged innovative approaches to culture. Creative artistic elites, spurred by radical idealism, strove to refashion human consciousness by cultivating new values of collectivism and egalitarianism. During these years Konstantin Mikhailovich worked in various theaters, as well as giving lectures on the history of theater. He too was engaged in this attempt to construct new forms of artistic expression and communication by writing and directing experimental plays. But fears over his aristocratic origins and concern for his siblings drove him to go abroad in 1924, and despite a serious rift in their marriage due to Konstantin's ongoing affair with artist and theatrical designer Valentina Mikhailovna Khodasevich, Ludmila made the decision to join him.

Officially Konstantin Mikhailovich went to Paris with the backing of the State Institute of Art History in order to do research for a second volume on the history of Italian theater, which he did complete. But he did not intend to return to the Soviet Union, and he looked for work in the fledgling French film industry. The marriage soon disintegrated, but they remained close friends and Ludmila stayed on in Paris for three years, working at the Soviet Trade Commission and socializing with scores of prominent Russian and European cultural figures, including the writer Ilya Ehrenburg, poet Vladimir Mayakovsky, and the artist Ivan Puni. But when she lost steady employment and a romantic love affair took a troubling turn, she decided in 1927 to return to the Soviet Union.

Ludmila started a new life for herself in Moscow as a writer and a typist, armed with the special typewriter Konstantin Mikhailovich had handcrafted with Cyrillic letters and given to her when she left Paris. She had developed a penchant for writing, and with the help of noted writer and critic Viktor Shklovskii, she was able to publish a series of sketches she penned on life in Paris. She also wrote articles for a Central Asian newspaper and worked for a film studio surveying recent literature for potential screenplays. But it was not easy for her, and there were many moments when she regretted leaving Paris. Konstantin Mikhailovich kept urging her in his letters to return and pledged to help her financially, but by the time she was ready to seriously consider it, traveling abroad for ordinary citizens was no longer possible. Then one day during a rainstorm, by chance, she ran into an old acquaintance from childhood, a promising young scholar, four years Ludmila's junior, by the name of Isaak (Izya) Moiseevich Trotsky, who had left Odessa to study history at Leningrad University. This encounter reignited his childhood crush on her, and he began courting her. Before long he convinced her to leave Moscow and move to Leningrad (formerly known as Petrograd but renamed Leningrad in 1924 to honor the deceased Vladimir Lenin), where he was currently living after having graduated in 1924 with a degree in history. He visited Moscow because he was pursuing a doctoral degree in history and working with one of the most prominent Marxist historians of the 1920s, Mikhail Pokrovskii, who was based in Moscow. Izya was not able to complete his studies with Pokrovskii, who died in 1932 from cancer.[3] Nonetheless, in 1935, Izya Trotsky was awarded a postgraduate degree based on his well-respected publications on the ancient Novgorod Republic and the nineteenth-century Decembrist movement.[4]

It was not hard to convince Ludmila to return to Leningrad, for she had never felt at home in Moscow and had longed to return to her beloved city on the Neva River. She and Izya married, though as she reveals in her memoir, she came to feel increasing ambivalence toward her handsome new husband. She felt his photographic memory and knowledge of poetry paled in comparison with the talents of Konstantin Mikhailovich. She focused on her own writing and under the direction of Samuil Marshak, a leading figure in Soviet children's literature, published a children's book on the nineteenth-century Russian radical Nikolai Chernyshevsky. Then in late 1929, she discovered she was pregnant. This was not her first pregnancy; while married to Konstantin Mikhailovich she had undergone at least two abortions at his insistence. This time she was determined to give birth, but Izya resisted. However, circumstances worked in Ludmila's favor and she ended up having the baby in August of 1930. This changed her life forever and brought her what to her was the most meaningful role she would ever have—motherhood. They named their daughter Elena (as is customary in Russia, Ludmila also uses various diminutive forms of her name, including Elenushka, Elenka, and Lenochka), and Ludmila devoted much of her time over the next six years to raising her, though she continued to write and type to supplement their income. She contributed to the major Stalinist history project, the *History of Factories and Plants*[5] and became a member of Leningrad's Union of Writers in the early 1930s.

After 1932, Izya's career as an historian took off, and he was invited to work at the prestigious USSR Academy of Sciences' Historical-Archeographic Institute by its director, S. G. Tomsinskii, and was also offered a position lecturing on history at Leningrad State University.[6] During this time Ludmila's complete and total devotion to her daughter caused friction between her and Izya, and both sought refuge in relationships with other persons, Ludmila renewing her old friendship with the writer Mikhail Zoshchenko. But their daughter's illness in 1936 and the fear generated by growing numbers of arrests brought them back together, though only briefly as fate would have it.

In the spring of 1936, Ludmila took Elena to Ukraine to help her recover her health, but she had to rush back to Leningrad when Izya was arrested on June 2 on the charge of being a member of a counterrevolutionary conspiratorial group (allegedly headed by his former institutional director, S. G. Tomsinskii) aimed at carrying out acts of terror. Ludmila, like countless others whose loved ones had been arrested, spent months waiting in long lines for hours trying to get information; she found herself increasingly isolated as friends and colleagues distanced themselves out of fear. On December 23, 1936, Isaak Moiseevich Trotsky was sentenced to ten years imprisonment in the Solovki Islands forced labor camp, and Ludmila was only given twenty-four hours' notice to get a package of warm clothing ready for him. But soon thereafter, in October of 1937, Izya, along with several hundred others, were brought back to Leningrad (Ludmila knew nothing of this) to be tried by a special secret police organ known as a "troika" for allegedly continuing counterrevolutionary actions in the camp. He was found guilty and at the age of 34 was sentenced to death and shot in early November of 1937.[7] Only years later did Ludmila learn of his death, and even then she was told he died of a "heart attack." As was typical of this period, in 1937, Ludmila was also targeted as the "wife of an enemy of the people" and exiled with Elena north to a remote, isolated village, Semenovskoe, in the Arkhangelsk region. Here she tried to eke out an existence with her daughter, but the tentacles of terror would not let her go. In the early hours of May 1, 1938, Ludmila Pavlovna was arrested, initially for the charge of not having informed on her counterrevolutionary husband, but later the case against her came to include completely false accusations of anti-Soviet agitation and organizing terrorist conspiracies against Soviet power.

Sentenced to ten years in the forced labor camps, Ludmila's only thought was how to secure the safety of her daughter. From the moment of her arrest, she had sought to protect her daughter from the typical fate of children whose parents were arrested as "enemies of the people"—ending up in orphanages and often never reunited with parents or family. Ludmila insisted on the right to send telegrams to relatives, particularly to Izya's brother-in-law, Iosif Moiseevich Tronsky, a gifted and quite prominent classical scholar who lived with his wife on Leningrad's most illustrious street, Nevskii Prospekt (Avenue). Ludmila begged them to come and get Elena, and they sent a servant to bring her to live with them. The entire time she was imprisoned, Ludmila's chief concern was staying in touch through letters with her daughter. It was love for her daughter and a strong determination to return to her that sustained

Ludmila through her incarceration in the Viatka forced labor camps. Her letters from her daughter boosted her spirits, and the packages Elena and her aunt sent provided her with much needed food supplements and items she could barter for extra portions of bread. Ludmila also resourcefully gained for herself the opportunity to train and work as a nurse, which enabled her to avoid dangerously debilitating manual labor tasks and thereby survive her time in the forced labor camps. Her diligent service at a medical clinic earned her an "early" release by several months, but the joy of her reunion with Elena was marred by the fact that she could not live in Leningrad due to her status as an ex-prisoner. Then in 1949, she was rearrested and sentenced to exile in the Krasnoiarsk region, which lasted until Stalin's death. Living in exile afforded her more "freedom" than in the camps, but she once again endured the agony of separation from her daughter and the impossibility of finding anything but menial jobs that subjected her to patronizing harassment from boorish bosses and debilitating physical and mental strain. She found solace again in her daughter's letters, following through them Elena's maturation from university student into a young woman entering into marriage.

Finally, Stalin's death in 1953 made possible her release, and she was able to return to Leningrad, but sadly, she faced many difficulties in trying to rebuild her life and restore her bond with her daughter. Many Gulag returnees began applying for and receiving exoneration from the crimes they had been accused of, a process termed "rehabilitation." Although many were being rehabilitated in 1954–5, Ludmila's application was rejected, and she had to travel to Moscow to ask former friends, members of the Soviet artistic elite who had now won terms in the top legislative body, the Supreme Soviet, to write letters of support for her rehabilitation. The writers Ilya Ehrenburg, Samuil Marshak, and Konstantin Fedin all wrote letters for her and in June of 1956, the Military Collegium of the USSR Supreme Court, the body that in 1938 had convicted her, now "rehabilitated" her by declaring that the charges were dropped because of the absence of any crime. She received certificates of rehabilitation for herself and for Izya, though for him it was posthumous. Rehabilitation brought her some measure of peace and satisfaction, above all because it removed the stigma of being the child of "enemies of the people" from her daughter. But Ludmila's trip to Moscow dealt her one very hard and tragic blow. From Ehrenburg's wife Liuba, who had socialized with Ludmila and her first husband in Paris, Ludmila learned that Konstantin Mikhailovich had committed suicide after the Ehrenburgs had mistakenly told him that Ludmila had been executed during the terror. This devastated Ludmila, who realized that Konstantin Mikhailovich must have blamed himself for her arrest. She and Konstantin had managed to stay in touch through letters, but once 1936 began, their correspondence had ended, and Ludmila knew nothing of his fate until this trip to Moscow.

Rehabilitation brought Ludmila monetary compensation and a new place to live in a section of Leningrad she cherished, but it proved difficult to rebuild a meaningful relationship with her daughter. Ludmila knew that Elena loved her but over the years Elena had grown much closer to her aunt. Ludmila notes ruefully in her memoir how Elena showed more concern for her aunt's impaired health than for her own physical and emotional debilitation as a former prisoner. Pushed by her in-laws, Ludmila worked again as a typist, gradually building a clientele of her own, and she tried to be grateful to her in-laws for raising Elena. Tragically, Ludmila's daughter fell ill and died in 1958 at the age of 28, from an infection caused by an earlier miscarriage. Ludmila spent the rest of her life trying to recover from this terrible loss; she never remarried, though she had a circle of close friends who loved and supported her. She chiefly worked as a typist for much of the year but then in summer would travel to places she found interesting and where she could explore beautiful landscapes. Although she mentions nothing in the memoir's concluding page about her personal circumstances, in her last years she struggled to make ends meet with a meager pension and endured the typical strains of living in a communal apartment. Then, she developed myasthenia gravis and had to undergo the radiation treatments that are described in the memoir. Sadly, the disorder metastasized into her body and caused her death on October 8, 1976.[8]

The Historical Context

To help the reader understand the backdrop for Ludmila's memoir, the following sections provide an overview of the major historical developments that shaped her life. The context for Ludmila's life is Russia's tumultuous twentieth century. As Iakov Gordin stated in his preface to the Russian edition, it is this intersection of Ludmila's personal story with the harsh historical realities of twentieth-century Russia that make this memoir "so uniquely vital for understanding what this 'century of the wolfhound' did to people."[9]

Ludmila Pavlovna was born into a Russia ruled by tsars, absolute monarchs overseeing a vast multinational empire stretching from Poland in the west to the Pacific Ocean in the east. When she died in 1976, she was a citizen of its successor state, the Soviet Union, still a vast empire of over one hundred nationalities divided into fifteen republics covering eleven time zones. Her birth took place as the Romanov dynasty was unknowingly entering into its twilight years, lumbering toward the momentous year of 1917 with its two revolutions that overthrew the tsarist monarchy and began a new era in Russian history. She grew up during a time of rapid and unsettling economic, social, and cultural change; indeed, Russia experienced a remarkable explosion of artistic creativity possibly unmatched anywhere in Europe. She was born in the city of Odessa, a bustling port city on the Black Sea founded as part of Russia's imperial expansion under Catherine the Great, who in the eighteenth century had taken the Crimean Peninsula from the Ottoman Turks. By the time of Ludmila's birth, it was the fourth largest city in the empire, commercially vibrant and diverse in its population. Her parents were both Jewish, though secular in their outlook, and were part of Odessa's sizable Jewish community (encompassing nearly 40% of the city's population). Ludmila shows us, though, that despite decades of Jewish assimilation, Odessa continued to experience outbreaks of violent anti-Semitic pogroms, including the infamous one of 1905 that she personally experienced and describes here, which killed over five hundred persons and destroyed many Jewish-owned properties.

Precipitated by Russia's humiliating defeats in the Russo-Japanese war in 1904, the year 1905 also witnessed a series of revolutionary upheavals as workers, peasants, and middle-class elites sought to overthrow Tsar Nicholas II. The tsarist regime survived thanks to the continued loyalty of the military and minor liberal concessions, including the establishment of Russia's first parliament, the State Duma. But, weak in mind and will, Nicholas II could not accept his role as a constitutional monarch and refused to work with the Duma until changes made in the electoral laws produced more compliant representatives. He wanted Russia to stay politically and socially what it had been for centuries, a society dominated by the aristocracy, but due to modernization there were factory workers and middle-class professionals demanding rights and representation in public affairs. Despite turmoil, however, Russian legislative politics stabilized and the Third and Fourth Dumas managed to carry out significant reforms, particularly in the area of education. But Russia's entry into the First World War proved to be a disastrous decision that brought catastrophic losses, inflation, and breakdowns in public services and transportation. The demands of war strained the empire's resources and exposed the weaknesses of Russia's late economic modernization and industrial growth.

Early enthusiasm for the war quickly dissipated as the casualties mounted (over 4 million by August 1915), along with growing food and fuel shortages. Major defeats in battle led to serious losses of territory and of men. Nicholas II made matters worse when he took over command of the armies and left the government in the hands of his wife, Empress Alexandria, and her disreputable advisor, the Siberian "holy man" Grigory Rasputin. This peasant-born healer had an uncanny ability to control the bleeding of the only son and heir to the throne, Alexei, who suffered from hemophilia. But Rasputin's dissolute reputation and questionable political competence discredited the regime even further. Nicholas II and his wartime leadership alienated every sector of society, including the highest ranks of the Russian military. When the winter of 1916–17 brought continued shortages of food and fuel, unrest began to mount. In January and February tens of thousands of workers went on strike to protest rising prices and stagnant wages. Revolution came at the end of February when women workers spontaneously burst out in frustrated protest.[10] On February 23 women textile workers took advantage of a socialist holiday, International Women's Day, to march through the streets calling for bread and an end to the war. As the day progressed, more and more factories shut down as workers rushed out to join the growing demonstration. Strikes, meetings, and demonstrations swept across the city. By February 26, the third day of protest, there were over two hundred thousand people in the streets, and violence began to break out in accompaniment to cries of "down with the tsar."

What turned these popular street disturbances into a revolution was the mutiny of the soldiers, who on February 26 had been ordered by the tsar to suppress the disorders. At the Tauride Palace on February 27, 1917, a group of Duma leaders proclaimed the formation of a temporary committee to establish authority. The disaffected military commanders supported the Duma and demanded the tsar abdicate, which he did. In a lone train car, Nicholas II, the last tsar of Russia, surrendered his throne, not just for himself but also for his son and heir, Alexei. Power then passed to the Duma leaders, who set up the Provisional Government which committed itself to continue the war while preparing for a democratically elected constituent assembly that would craft a new Russian state. It initiated a series of sweeping reforms, including the release of all political prisoners and the establishment of civil liberties, but it refused to make any major changes in property rights, labor relations, or the war policy until the convening of the much-anticipated constituent assembly. The Provisional Government found itself challenged from the very beginning, however, by a rival institution formed by workers and socialist party activists, the Petrograd Soviet of Workers' and Soldiers' Deputies. This body viewed itself as a necessary overseer of the Provisional Government, which was predominantly gentry and upper middle class in composition. This situation came to be known as "dual power" and it seriously weakened the Provisional Government. Another fatal development for the Provisional Government was its decision to continue fighting in the First World War, which proved just as disastrous a drain on resources and popular support as it had been for the tsar.

Russia's fate was shaped as well by the growth in numbers and popularity of a Marxist-based political party, the Bolsheviks, who adopted policies that gained them increasing popular support. Their founder and leader, Vladimir Il'ich Lenin, had returned to Russia from Swiss exile in April 1917 on a sealed train financed in part by the German government in hopes that he would oppose the First World War upon arrival. The Bolshevik leaders in Russia had been tentatively supporting the Provisional Government, but, once Lenin returned, the party began calling for all power to be transferred to the people in the form of revolutionary councils, or soviets, for land reform and for an end to the war. Over the summer and early fall, despite suffering a setback when the Provisional Government blamed the Bolsheviks for instigating violent protests and accused Lenin of being a German spy, the party attracted growing numbers of supporters as continued economic decline and losses in war radicalized the masses. The reluctance of the Provisional Government to carry out land reform coupled with its continued war effort alienated increasing numbers of peasants and made Bolshevik promises of "Peace, Land and Bread" more appealing. By September the Bolsheviks had won majorities in the soviets of St. Petersburg and Moscow, and they increased their popularity in late August by helping to suppress a poorly organized attempt at a military takeover led by Russian military commander, General Lavr Kornilov. The Provisional Government, now headed by socialist Alexander Kerensky, successfully aborted this coup but had to turn for help to Bolshevik soldiers, sailors, and worker militia units.

These latter forces then turned around and overthrew Kerensky and the Provisional Government in what became known as the Great October Socialist Revolution, which occurred during October 25–27, 1917 (November 7–9). This overthrow of the Provisional Government was not a spontaneous street movement; it was a conscious act set in motion by Lenin and fellow Bolshevik leader Leon Trotsky. More than any other politician in 1917, Lenin was convinced that the First World War, which he called an imperialist war, had created conditions for an immediate socialist revolution and that revolution in Russia would then spark similar movements in more advanced industrialized nations. But there was also mass support for the Bolsheviks to take power because workers, peasants, and soldiers believed that at long last the Bolsheviks would allow them to realize their natural rights of equality, land, and self-rule.

The October Revolution began when in response to an attempt by Alexander Kerensky to shut down Bolshevik newspapers, the Bolshevik-controlled Petrograd Soviet activated its newly formed Military Revolutionary Committee (MRC) to seize control of all means of communication and transportation in the city, including bridges, railway terminals, and postal, telephone, and telegraph offices. Kerensky ended up fleeing the city in a car borrowed from the US embassy, and within months left Russia for permanent exile abroad. The October Revolution in St. Petersburg was virtually bloodless, as were similar seizures of power across Russia, with the exception of Moscow, where there were over a thousand casualties. The Bolsheviks formed a new executive body, which they entitled the Council of Peoples' Commissars, and the new government signed an armistice with Germany; nationalized land, industry, and assets; and held elections for the Constituent Assembly.

But Lenin had no intention of turning over the fate of the revolution and Bolshevik power to this body, particularly because his party lacked a majority in it. He had it dispersed when it met for its one and only session on January 18, 1918 and refused to allow any other leftist or liberal parties to operate. This, along with the March 1918 signing of the Brest–Litovsk Peace Treaty with Germany that ended the war but gave away vast tracts of Russian territory, as well as the execution of Tsar Nicholas II and his entire family in July, prompted a brutal Civil War that lasted until 1921. Lenin's primary goal became the centralization of power in the party apparatus, not empowering workers through factory committees or through soviets, and this trend was not reversed when the fighting stopped. By the end of the Civil War, the democratically elected Congress of Soviets and even the Council of Peoples' Commissars were eclipsed in power by the party organs, the Central Committee and the Politburo. This concentration of power in the hands of the ruling party, the Communist Party (renamed in 1919), remained the essential core principle of the Soviet Union until Gorbachev's political reform in 1990 ended one-party rule.

The Civil War pitted the Bolshevik Red Army against a diverse group of opponents that collectively made up the White Army. It brought enormous suffering to Russian society and a near-complete economic breakdown. Bolshevik economic policies known as War Communism nationalized the economy and forced peasants to give up their grain for the Red Army, which contributed to the famine and deindustrialization that produced the difficult living conditions described by Ludmila between 1918 and 1921. Those from the former tsarist aristocracy and ruling classes were denied civil rights as well as access to rationing cards, which contributed to the privation and suffering that pushed so many into emigration. Ludmila's husband Konstantin Mikhailovich was able to avoid this only because he was a prominent cultural figure, but he remained wary of being persecuted for his aristocratic family origins and for having served as a tsarist army officer during the First World War. The conflict also severely impacted Ludmila's home city, Odessa, which suffered through multiple changes of power from White to Red that wreaked havoc on its economy and the lives of the people. Both sides carried out heinous atrocities against each other and against civilians. The Russian Civil War proved more costly than even the First World War, with over 1.5 million military deaths and up to 12 million civilians who died from cold, hunger, armed attacks, famine, and disease.[11] For Ludmila the Civil War not only disrupted her university studies but, more cruelly, led to the death of her beloved brother Sasha, who was killed by White forces in Constantinople. Her parents never really recovered from the emotional and economic blows dealt by the Civil War and depended for the rest of their lives on whatever help Ludmila could give.

By 1921, the Bolshevik Red Army forces had prevailed over the Whites but faced serious unrest in the countryside, starvation, and abandoned factories. Lenin and the party instituted the New Economic Policy (NEP) as a compromise measure to spur industrial production, stabilize the economy, and restore the alliance with the peasantry by replacing forced state requisitions of grain with a tax in kind. Peasants could now keep their surplus grain and after paying a tax sell it on the open market. The state kept its control of the commanding heights of heavy industry, banking, and transportation, but stepped back from light industry, small manufacturing, and the service sector; private trade was permitted and market relations restored. Ludmila recalls how NEP brought welcome relief from food and goods shortages and helped ease the hardships still lingering from the years of war and revolution. It also allowed her and Konstantin Miklachevsky to engage in the buying and selling of his family treasures as he sought to convert antique heirlooms into cash or goods that could be taken abroad for his penurious émigré siblings.

With Lenin's illness and death in 1924, however, the way forward for the country, and particularly the question of how to build socialism without an industrial economy, became a pivotal issue in the struggle for power in the Communist Party. One of the main figures vying to succeed Lenin was Joseph Stalin, a Georgian Bolshevik who had gained prominence during the Civil War as a commissar who could organize campaigns effectively and get things done, skills which later led Lenin to appoint him as General Secretary for the party's Central Committee. Stalin was able to transform this administrative position into an effective power base and source of patronage that helped him to defeat his rivals, who formed factions known as the Left and Right Oppositions. Stalin triumphed first by supporting a moderate line of fostering development through a continuation of NEP policies, but then abandoned this path to champion a more radical industrial drive that included mass collectivization of agriculture. In 1928, when Ludmila returned from her three years stay in Paris, she observed the last of Stalin's rivals for leadership being defeated by Stalin and his supporters. But she takes little notice of what the political implications of Stalin's triumph are, except that she brings out how when frustrated by her living situation at the time, she thought of returning to Paris but found that all doors out had been shut. Travel abroad was coming to a halt. Stalin's defeat of his rivals opened the way to what he termed in the official newspaper *Pravda*, "the Great Turn of socialist construction"; beginning in 1929, the Soviet state launched policies of forced rapid industrialization and agricultural collectivization aimed at modernizing the economy and building a solid foundation for socialism. Stalin's "Revolution from Above" abolished the NEP and required peasants to give up their land and farming tools to join large communal collective or state farms. Many resisted, slaughtering livestock rather than give them up to the state, but the forced transition to collective agriculture was nonetheless completed by 1936. The cost, though, was high in terms of human losses and drastic reductions in meat and grain supplies. Millions of peasants lost their lives to famine in Ukraine and Kazakhstan or were deported into labor camps or remote settlements where many died from deprivation and exhaustion.[12]

Much of the upheaval that stemmed from Stalin's economic policies touched Ludmila only indirectly, and they receive scant attention from her, for these years coincided with the changes to her personal life due to her marrying Izya Trotsky. Her daughter Elena was her sole focus until 1936, when her fate and that of her family was swept up in Stalin's Great Terror, the period from 1934 to 1939 marked by mass arrests and executions directed against former opponents of Stalin, leading party and state officials, army officers, engineers, scientists, intellectuals, artists, and scholars. Stalin's motives for launching policies of terror continue to be debated. Some argue he acted from personal drives rooted in either paranoia or an obsessive need for power and control; others view him more as a rational actor aware of his country's vulnerability and determined to root out all potential sources of "fifth column" betrayal if hostile powers invaded.[13] Whatever the motive, what ensued was a massive witch hunt for supposed "enemies of the people" that ended up altering Ludmila's life forever, leading to the death of Izya, her own deportation to the Gulag, and a heartbreaking separation from Elena. This state-sponsored terror sought to eradicate all opposition and thereby transform the party-state apparatus into a body completely subordinated to Stalin and his confederates. To carry out these terror operations, Stalin relied heavily on the secret police; this body had been part of the regime since December 1917, when Lenin created the Extraordinary Commission for Combating Counter-revolution, Speculation and Sabotage. Known at first by the acronym Cheka, under Stalin it went through several reorganizations, first designated the State Political Administration (OGPU) and then after 1934, the People's Commissariat of Internal Affairs (NKVD). Stalin increased the powers of the secret police and expanded its role to include management of major economic projects through its oversight of the forced labor camp penal system, known to the world by its acronym Gulag (*Glavnoe upravlenie ispravityelno-trudovykh lagerei i koloniy* or Main Administration of Corrective Labor Camps and Settlements).

The starting point for the Great Terror was the December 1, 1934 assassination of Leningrad Communist Party boss, Sergei Kirov. The lone assassin, Leonid Nikolaev, was tried and executed within a month, but then the state began claiming it involved a much larger conspiracy directed by former Stalinist rivals. Some scholars maintain it was Stalin who ordered the assassination, but direct evidence of this has yet to emerge. However, it is clear that he took advantage of the situation to declare the country under siege from class "enemies" and to justify the arrests and public trials not only of his former rivals—Zinoviev, Kamenev, Bukharin, Rykov, along with their supporters—but also of thousands of persons held to be complicit or supportive of the act. In the immediate aftermath of the Kirov assassination, the government issued an edict ordering accelerated juridical processes and even immediate execution of those accused of counterrevolutionary crimes. In just one month, between February 28 and March 27, 1935, more than eleven thousand persons whose social origins as aristocrats, clergy, tsarist army officers, and officials made them suspect were exiled from Leningrad by the NKVD.[14] Ludmila recalls in a chilling passage her husband's prophetic reaction to Kirov's murder. Izya sensed it could lead to tragic consequences, but neither fully realized how heavy the blow would be. In the waves of arrests that followed, party, state, and educational institutions such as the Academy of Sciences were major targets. Like for so many people in the 1930s, fear became a predominant element in their lives as they watched the arrests and intimidation of friends, acquaintances, and colleagues.

One of the early victims of the expulsions following the Kirov murder was S. G. Tomsinskii, the director of the Institute of Archeography who had invited Izya Trotsky to work there. Tomsinskii had once supported Leon Trotsky's Left Opposition and on this basis was exiled to Central Asia. But then he was brought back to Leningrad in 1936 and accused of creating a counterrevolutionary association directed by Leon Trotsky (who was exiled outside of Russia in 1929) and Grigory Zinoviev to kill Kirov. Tomsinskii was a high-profile target included on lists that came from the highest levels of the Stalinist state, and this is the connection that doomed Izya Trotsky.[15] He was arrested and accused of being a member of this organization and of organizing meetings in Moscow with other conspirators. The basis for his arrest and for millions of others was Article 58, a special section of the Criminal Code defining political or "counterrevolutionary" crimes against the state. The multiple subarticles defined a wide range of actions deemed "anti-Soviet" or "counterrevolutionary." Izya Trotsky was accused of terrorism, Article 58-8, carrying out anti-Soviet propaganda, 58-10, and belonging to an organization aimed at carrying out counterrevolutionary actions, 58-11.[16]

The terror reached its height in 1937–8 under the leadership of Nikolai Yezhov, who headed the secret police from September 1936 to July 1938, after which he himself was executed. In 1937, in Leningrad province alone, Izya was just one of four thousand persons who were shot. Another ten thousand were sentenced to the Gulag.[17] However, exact numbers of those arrested and executed remain elusive and continue to spark debate. One estimate is that during 1937–8, 1.7 million were arrested and 692,000 executed, but others argue that deaths during 1937–8 totaled about 1 to 1.5 million. The Communist Party suffered considerably, with one estimate being that out of the 2.8 million party members in 1934, at least 1 million were arrested. Foreign communists who were living or working in the Soviet Union were also targeted, particularly those fleeing from German and Italian fascism.[18]

In 1938, Ludmila was arrested initially for Article 58-12, as the "wife of an enemy of the people" who had not informed on the counterrevolutionary actions of her husband. But the dynamics of the terror were such that the local NKVD investigators decided to implicate her for more serious charges and build a conspiratorial case around her as allegedly acting on cues from the writer Mikhail Zoshchenko to organize a terrorist organization to kill secret police chief Yezhov. All of these charges were entirely bogus and indicative of the way that the terror operated. Innocent persons got swept up into this nightmare and accused of fantastic crimes often through the quota system— NKVD officials had to meet specified "quotas" of enemies and if they did not, they themselves might become suspect. Each region and republic received numbers of how many were to be shot and how many sentenced to the camps.[19] The terror also allowed people to take advantage of the situation to advance themselves; there was no shortage of petty or ambitious officials, spiteful colleagues and neighbors, or overzealous students and teachers ready to denounce others and affirm guilt to serve their own ambitions or the needs of the state as they understood it. Ludmila's fate was sealed by the false testimonies of a woman she disliked and avoided in exile, Nina Posylkina, who claimed that Ludmila had received a letter from Zoshchenko entreating her to take action against Yezhov, that she railed in public places against Soviet power, and that she organized in her home meetings of counterrevolutionary conspirators. Posylkina's romantic ties with the local NKVD boss ensured her outlandish statements carried weight. Ludmila was able to show effectively both in her interrogations and in her trial that the accusations of Posylkina and others were all completely implausible. But nonetheless she was convicted of multiple subarticles of Article 58 from 58-8 through 58-17. The inclusion of 58-8, terrorism, is what brought her a ten-year sentence in the Gulag.

Many who were arrested went through excruciatingly torturous interrogations, sometimes lasting for months, during which they were subjected to a range of physical abuses designed to induce them to sign confessions of their guilt. Interrogators were known to turn to beatings, starvation, sleep deprivation, rape, and threats against family and friends.[20] It is not known what methods of coercion were used against Izya, but in a series of interrogations in the summer of 1936, he confessed to being involved in counterrevolutionary activities and implicated others as well, though he refused to admit to being a terrorist or to being connected with Leon Trotsky. Like many others who similarly confessed to nonexistent crimes, he undoubtedly hoped that by doing so he would be shown leniency.[21] Ludmila went through a series of interrogations but was never beaten or tortured, and she does not seem to have signed any confession of guilt. She notes one instance when an NKVD official claimed to have arrested her "son," but Ludmila could remain calm because she knew that her daughter was safe; the woman she and Elena had rented a room from in their exile had courageously gotten word to her in prison that someone had come for Elena and taken her to Leningrad. Various juridical and extrajudicial bodies and courts acted to convict people, including NKVD special tribunals known as troikas set up to examine cases and issue sentences without a public trial; during the Great Terror troikas sentenced hundreds of thousands to death, including Izya Trotsky when he was accused a second time of counterrevolutionary actions. There were also military courts set up to try cases of state treason, and it is this judicial body that convicted Izya the first time in 1936 as well as Ludmila.[22]

The history of the Gulag did not begin with Stalin, for the Bolsheviks were setting up concentration camps for political opponents as early as 1919, and already by 1925 the Cheka was considering how to utilize prison labor to extract the mineral wealth of Russia's northern regions. The first major camp complex to emerge was near the White Sea in northern Russia, around Arkhangelsk and on the Solovetskii Islands. Here the inmates included former aristocrats, intelligentsia, non-Bolshevik political parties, White Army officers and soldiers, clergy, speculators and black marketers, engineers charged with "wrecking," and common criminals. But under Stalin the system of camps expanded to unprecedented levels. It was in 1929 that Soviet legislation for the first time referred to "corrective labor camps" as a new type of punishment. On July 11, 1929, a state resolution instructed OGPU to expand such camps into Siberia, the North, the Far East, and central Asia with the aim of "colonizing these regions and exploiting their natural resources with the use of prisoners' labor."[23]

It was Stalin who in 1930 created the official body to oversee the camp system, the Main Administration of Camps. Stalinist campaigns such as collectivization and the Great Terror provided growing numbers of prisoners sentenced as "counterrevolutionaries." The expansion in the numbers of prisoners coincided with the state's decision to transform the camp system into a source of cheap labor and a major component of the state drive for modernization and industrialization.[24] In the following years the camps spread across the entire country. Russian historians have documented the existence of 476 camps, with most having branches and subcamps, and over two thousand labor colonies. There were fifty colonies set up for children and ninety infant homes holding over four thousand five hundred children whose mothers had been sent into the camps.[25] Some estimates hold that in the years from 1934 to 1952, 18 million to 20 million persons were sent into Gulag camps and colonies, one-third of which were political prisoners sentenced under Article 58. With the coming of the Second World War, the numbers swelled with the additional influx of nationalities deported from newly acquired Baltic territories (Lithuanians, Latvians, and Estonians) and those accused of collaboration with the Nazi invaders, including the Volga Germans, the Crimean Tatars, Chechens, and so on.[26] Gulag prisoners worked in nearly every sector of the national economy, including lumber, mining, fuel, textile, and steel manufacturing. They built major canals, roads, railroads, ports, hydroelectric dams and power stations, and towns such as Norilsk and Vorkuta. Ludmila was sent to the Viatlag camp system, located about one thousand kilometers north of Moscow, where the main production was timber cutting and processing. The area was filled with vast swamps and boggy forests, and the treacherous task of uprooting tree stumps, as Ludmila describes, was one of the major forms of labor carried out by prisoners.[27]

Tragically, under Stalin the Soviet Gulag was a place of degradation and death; as historian Oleg Khlevniuk describes it, over time what began in theory as a form of rehabilitation became in practice "an organized system of terror and exploitation of forced labor."[28] Death awaited prisoners at every step in the process, from the torturous interrogations to the unsanitary and crowded transit camps and railway journeys, as well as in the camps themselves, stark, barren compounds laden with hunger, filth, sadism, and powerlessness. The Soviet camps killed through forcing prisoners to carry out manually debilitating physical tasks with minimal food rations, inadequate tools and clothing, and brutal treatment. Prisoners were fed on the basis of their labor productivity, which meant that if they could not fulfill the often impossibly high labor quotas, they did not receive adequate food to sustain themselves. The prison diet consisted mainly of bread, gruel or cereal of some kind, thin cabbage or potato soup that only sometimes had meat or fish heads; prisoners were also to receive weekly or monthly rations of sugar, tea, fat of some kind, but often such goods were not available, particularly in the more remote camps. Daily bread ration ranged from two hundred grams to up to a pound a day, depending on whether one fulfilled the work norms or not. The conditions that prisoners had to endure reduced considerably the chances for their survival, particularly if sentenced to more than five years.[29]

After 1938–9, the scale of mass arrests diminished, but waves of prisoners continued to feed into the Gulag. After the Second World War, prisoners of war from nations defeated by the Soviet Union worked on major economic projects, as did many national groups accused of collaboration with the Germans and persons living in occupied territories during the war. During the period 1948–50, Cold War tensions along with rising anti-Semitism and Stalin's renewed paranoia led to the rearrest of many of those convicted in 1937–8 who had survived to complete their sentences, including Ludmila. A decree in February 1948 called for rearresting "state criminals who were former inmates."[30] Most went into exile rather than back into the camps and remained there until Stalin's death in 1953. Stalin's successor, Nikita Khrushchev, relinquished terror as an instrument of political rule and began dismantling portions of the Gulag and ordering a wholesale review of cases of those still in the camps. The great majority of prisoners were released as a result, including Ludmila, and as in her case, some received "rehabilitation." This was often done posthumously, because, like Izya, so many had died in the camps. However, rehabilitation was a laboriously bureaucratic process and not automatic; as we see in the case of Ludmila, it could be denied and appeals had to be made. Plus, as Ludmila's life after her release shows, returnees from the Gulag faced a great challenge in readjusting to regular life and reconnecting with loved ones they had not seen for many years.

Under Khrushchev and then his successor Leonid Brezhnev, who was the leader when Ludmila died in 1976, life achieved a degree of "normalcy" with gradually improving living standards, greater availability of housing and consumer goods, and increasing opportunities for travel, though few were able to go outside of the Soviet Union. Penal camps and repression still existed, particularly against "dissidents" who criticized the regime or sought to defy the still heavy censorship, but people did not have to fear being randomly targeted by the secret police, now known in its last incarnation as the Committee of State Security, or KGB.[31] Yet, former prisoners such as Ludmila could not speak openly about what had happened to them; public discussion of the camps was permissible only in limited form between 1956 and 1964, during a brief period of cultural liberalization referred to as the "Thaw." Its highlight was the publication of Alexander Solzhenitsyn's path-breaking account of one man's experience in the camps, *One Day in the Life of Ivan Denisovich*. But Khrushchev's ouster from the party leadership in 1964, which brought Brezhnev to power, marked the end of cultural liberalization and public references to the Gulag. So while Ludmila was able to live her remaining years after rehabilitation in relative security, she had to keep to herself the agonizing questions that must have haunted her continually—why did this have to happen to her? What rationale could there possibly have been for her to be persecuted, for her life to be so utterly ripped apart? The state told her she had not been a criminal, and provided compensation, but it could not give her back her daughter, a husband whose life and talents were cut short by an executioner's bullet, or the creative energies she could have applied to cultivating her talents as a writer. In the end, all she could do was to commit to paper both her cherished memories and her tragic journey through the nightmare of Stalinism. She does not engage in political commentary or even condemn the regime that destroyed her family. She just tells her story and lets it speak for itself as an indictment of Stalinism and the toll it took on the human fabric of Soviet society.

Women in Twentieth-Century Russia

Gender shaped Ludmila's life and fate. She was born into an era that was witnessing the breakdown of patriarchal constraints and control, along with growing opportunities for women to achieve education and be socially and professionally engaged outside the home. The Revolutions of 1917 opened new vistas for women by granting them legal, political, and professional equality, followed by mass literacy campaigns that transformed the lives of working-class and peasant women. Yet much of the Soviet ideal of womanhood developed into a blend of revolutionary and traditional notions of women's role. Women fully entered the world of work and social production, but did not leave behind the expectation that their duty lay as well in caring for the home and serving as the primary caregiver for children. Women's emancipation after 1917 did not include liberation from traditional gendered notions of domestic labor as "women's work," which contributed to the infamous "double burden" that Soviet women had to bear.

The Westernizing reforms of Peter the Great had been the first major watershed in Russian women's history, by ending the isolation of elite women and opening doors to public life, providing the means for women to begin obtaining education and exercising greater voice and agency within the household.[32] Subsequent rulers, particularly Catherine the Great, opened up new opportunities for elite women to obtain education, and by the end of the eighteenth century, there were growing numbers of schools for girls in Moscow, in St. Petersburg, and in provincial cities.[33] Not all women in Russia experienced such progress, for women's lives were shaped as much by class, religion, and social status as by gender. During the imperial period, the changes that had the broadest impact with regard to women's opportunities were the Great Reforms of Alexander II, which were designed to transform Russia into a modern state. Its major acts abolished serfdom, created an independent judiciary and new institutions of local government, reformed the military, and spurred major social changes. Most consequentially for women, the loosening of censorship enabled the emergence of public debates over the "women's question." For the first time, there was discussion in public forums about the role and status of women, and whether or not women should contribute to society through more than just their role as mothers and housewives.[34]

Alexander II's reforms also created new educational institutions, including gymnasia for girls, which offered a six-year course of study in Russian language, religion, math, and science. By 1883, there were one hundred gymnasia and they were open to girls from all social backgrounds, which helped spur a greater "blurring of social boundaries."[35] Beginning in 1859, women were allowed to audit university lectures, and then in 1869 the government established a series of special lecture programs for women in St. Petersburg and Moscow, which became known as Higher Women's Courses. They did not offer degrees but did allow women access to university professors and courses of study.[36] The reactionary policies that followed Alexander II's assassination in 1881 brought an end to these programs, but the government reopened in 1889 the Bestuzhev courses in St. Petersburg.[37] In 1895 Nicholas II approved the establishment of the St. Petersburg Women's Medical Institute, and in 1900, the Guerrier Courses in Moscow reopened. In 1903, a special pedagogical institute for women opened in Odessa, and six hundred students entered its doors in the first two years.[38]

The 1905 Revolution spurred further expansion in women's access to higher education, culminating in the momentous decisions in 1911 to allow women to take state exams at universities and receive a degree. Then after 1913 women were allowed to enter universities themselves, and by 1915, women made up nearly one-third of all students in higher education. Enrollment of women in higher education rose to 44,017 in 1915–16, up from 2,588 in 1900. By 1914, eighteen cities had higher course offerings with a total of 23,534 women taking part. Women's entry into higher education was spurred by the continued expansion of secondary educational opportunities for girls. By 1915, there were over nine hundred women's gymnasia, and girls made up about half of all students enrolled in schools at the secondary level. Even lower-class peasant and working-class women were finding greater access to primary education; in 1897, 13.7 percent of rural women and 38.3 percent of urban women were literate. By 1913, of the 5.8 million pupils in government primary schools, most of which were in rural areas, 32 percent were girls.[39]

Debates over women's roles opened the door to critical reevaluation of patriarchy.[40] There were calls to reform the patriarchal family and strengthen women's personal autonomy, establish equality in gender relations, and enable women to find fulfillment outside the home.[41] By the end of the nineteenth century women were becoming politically active at a number of levels, fighting for greater access to professions, higher education, and legal rights. Women joined the growing revolutionary movements aimed at overthrowing the tsarist system and were prominent in the People's Will, which assassinated Alexander II in 1881. Women also played active roles in the illegal Russian socialist parties forming at the turn of the twentieth century, such as the Russian Social Democratic Workers' Party (which after 1903 split into Bolshevik and Menshevik factions) and the Socialist Revolutionary Party. Women participated in the 1905 Revolution; female factory workers, clerical workers, and professionals all took part in strikes, often making demands related to women's issues such as daycare, maternity leave, and nursing breaks. Although the 1905 Revolution did not produce many concrete gains for women, the first union for women emerged, the All-Russian Union for Women's Equality, which called for equality of the sexes and equal rights to land and to education.[42]

Women's lives were also affected by the growing marketplace and expanding culture of consumption emerging in the late nineteenth and early twentieth century. Commercial advertisements as well as popular literature written by female writers encouraged women to be adventurous and pursue their desires; in an unprecedented way they focused attention on women's bodies and on sexuality.[43] The newly emerging world of the cinema did much to shape new ideas about women's fashion, deportment, and behavior; Ludmila recalls in her memoir how enraptured she was by the allure of the movie stars she watched on movie screens, their dresses, and the romantic vistas it opened up in her imagination. By 1914, many trends were in motion that promoted the ideal of a "new woman" in Russian society who was educated, independent, and focused more on her autonomous self than on the needs of family.[44] The First World War also opened up new vistas for women who stepped forward to volunteer in a number of capacities and roles. Women from the upper and middle classes in particular stepped up with patriotic ardor to volunteer as nurses, to roll bandages, sew and knit uniforms, and so on. The First World War saw the formation of at least fifteen all-female combat units, two of which went to the front. Women also stepped into the factories. Already, before the war started, women were one-third of the industrial workforce, but by 1917, their share had risen to 43.2 percent, with over 1 million working outside the home.[45]

Nonetheless, patriarchy and tradition remained strong; despite such sweeping changes, the majority of women still focused their lives on being a wife and mother, and patriarchal relations still served, in the words of Barbara Engel, as both metaphor and model for Russia's political order. Like the Russian tsar, husbands and fathers had "virtually unlimited power."[46] The last civil code before the 1917 Revolutions stated that a wife was "bound to obey her husband as head of the family, to dwell with him in love, respect and unlimited obedience, to show him every compliance and attachment."[47] Wife beating was not grounds for divorce, and a Russian woman could not under tsarist law initiate divorce, could not leave her husband even if he beat her, could not get a job without permission of her husband, and could not have a passport in her own name; women could, however, have control over any property they brought into the marriage.[48]

It took the February and October Revolutions in 1917 to sound the death knell of legal patriarchy. Women themselves played decisive roles in these momentous events. The privations caused by the war—the huge losses, inflation, shortages of food and fuel—had quickly dispelled any patriotic feelings among lower-class women, and by 1915 they had begun to protest the increasing hardships. Women workers, soldiers' wives, and working-class housewives rose up in subsistence revolts, attacking shops and accusing the government of trying to starve them.[49] As noted in the earlier section, it was working-class women who on International Women's Day in February 1917 went out in the streets calling for bread and for peace, and then rallied men in the factories to join them, thus setting off the fateful chain of events that precipitated the February Revolution. When the Provisional Government failed to act on women's rights in its initial program, on March 20, feminist leaders mobilized forty thousand supporters to march to the Tauride Palace where the government was meeting and demand the vote and civil rights. This prompted the Provisional Government to grant women equal suffrage and then in June it passed decrees allowing women to practice law.[50] Working women took part in the continued demonstrations, food riots, and protests that went on until the Bolshevik seizure of power in October and appear to have supported the Bolshevik overthrow of the Provisional Government, though they tended to keep a low profile in political matters and their voices do not always appear in the sources for this period.[51] Substantive support for the Bolsheviks from women is suggested by the large number of women who volunteered to serve in the Red Army during the Civil War. By 1920, between fifty thousand and seventy thousand women had volunteered for the Red Army, comprising 2 percent of its forces. Many saw combat as machine gunners, riflemen, and political commissars, though the majority served as nurses or as support staff.[52] Prominent Bolshevik women included Alexandra Kollontai,

Nadezhda Krupskaya, Inessa Armand, and Konkordiia Samoilova, and they helped influence the party in 1919 to create the Woman's Section, or Zhenotdel, to mobilize and expand support for the party among working-class and peasant women. This was a new step, for Bolshevism had never supported feminism as a separate cause, but argued that the "woman question" had to be subordinated to the cause of revolution for the entire society—only a revolution could liberate women because the source of their oppression lay in the bourgeois capitalist order.[53]

Bolshevik rule quickly engineered important changes in women's status. The very first constitution in July 1918 proclaimed equality for all citizens regardless of gender, race, or nationality. Women enjoyed equal rights to vote and to be elected to the newly constituted bodies, the soviets.[54] The Bolshevik Land Code of 1922 accorded women equality as joint owners in the household.[55] The 1918 and the highly progressive 1926 *Code on Marriage, the Family and Guardianship* ended women's legal subordination to the patriarchal authority of husbands and fathers, allowing them independent and equal rights to work outside the home, sue for divorce, and retain their own names upon marriage.[56] Marriages were secularized, becoming valid only upon registration in a civil registry office, and divorces became easier to attain either through mutual consent or through one spouse applying to a People's Court.[57] This was one of Europe's first examples of "no-fault divorce," and a procedure Konstantin Mikhailovich took advantage of to arrange a quick divorce from his first wife in order to marry Ludmila.[58] One of the most significant changes in women's rights came in 1920 when the commissariats of Health and Justice issued a decree legalizing abortion. Tsarist law had treated abortion as murder and strictly prohibited such a procedure. The Bolsheviks, though, not wishing to encourage abortions, did put certain restrictions in place. Abortions were to be performed "freely and without any charge" but could be done only in Soviet hospitals and only by licensed medical doctors, not midwives. Women had to stay in the hospital for at least three days following the procedure.[59] Bolshevism affirmed reproduction as the major duty of women and sought to protect the right of a woman to be a mother. Work was important but it could not interfere with motherhood, and the regime provided, beginning in 1922, fully paid maternity leave and family benefits for working women.[60]

The new Bolshevik regime pledged itself to the emancipation of women; Bolshevik leaders believed that only through engaging in productive labor outside the home could women find true fulfillment and overcome financial dependence on men. The Bolsheviks expected women to become engaged in socially productive work and presented as an early goal "socializing housework—that is, entrusting household tasks to paid workers," especially cooking, sewing, laundry, and childcare.[61] Lenin railed at how "petty housework crushes, strangles, stultifies and degrades her, chains her to the kitchen and to the nursery, and wastes her labor."[62] For Trotsky, writing in 1923, genuine equality within marriage could only come when washing was done by a public laundry, catering by a public restaurant, and children were educated by good public teachers.[63] During the 1920s, the Communist Party's Zhenotdel worked diligently to establish community kitchens and childcare facilities, as well as to expand literacy among peasant and working-class women.[64]

A number of factors combined, however, to limit the capacity and desire of the regime to fulfill these goals. The party leadership viewed the Zhenotdel primarily as a means to engender support for party policies and provided only minimal support for its broader efforts at emancipation. It was increasingly marginalized and underfunded, and then was abolished in 1930. During the 1920s, the Soviet state lacked the means to provide adequately the public, subsidized services promised to women in order to free them from domestic burdens. Unemployment was particularly high for women, whom employers discriminated against despite the new laws, and the regime did not enforce its commitment to women's equal right to work.[65] This limited women's ability to establish any degree of financial independence and inclined many to oppose regime efforts to liberalize marriage and family ties. In truth there had never been a consensus in the Party as to what the fate of the family should be under socialism, and in the course of the 1920s, initial enthusiasm for weakening it waned, particularly as the regime faced the upheavals connected with the push for modernization and industrialization initiated by the Stalinist leadership at the end of the decade.[66] On the whole, traditional views about women remained strong, and in the course of the 1920s, the ideal of what it meant to be an emancipated Soviet woman evolved into a blend of modern and traditional elements of gender consciousness. As Barbara Evans Clements has pointed out, the image of the new Soviet woman ended up being a "syncretism" between socialist and traditional values.[67] The Bolshevik conviction that motherhood "was a female duty rather than a choice" was not seriously challenged.[68]

Certainly pragmatic demographic and economic imperatives mandated the enlistment of women in social production. The Soviet state faced gender imbalance in the workforce from the beginning due to the ravages of world war, revolution, and the Civil War. In 1926, there were more women than men in the population—76 million to 71 million—and this imbalance was only magnified by the impact of collectivization, the Stalinist purges, and the Second World War. In 1946, there were 100.9 million women to 75 million men, and the imbalance remained even as late as 1979, with 140 million women to 122.4 million men.[69] Stalin's push for rapid industrialization and collectivization also required mobilizing women into production and helped to eliminate the high rates of unemployment among women that had marked the NEP period. Women entered into industry on a mass scale between 1930 and 1937, and then in even greater numbers after the Second World War. By 1932 the number of women working in industry had doubled from 3 million to 6 million, and the number rose to over 13 million by 1940.[70] For the first time, women started working in traditionally male sectors such as metallurgy, chemicals, and mining. Women became welders, construction workers, porters, and crane operators. By fall of 1942, women made up 52 percent of labor in military-related industries;[71] by 1944 they were 40 percent of the workforce in iron and steel industry and over 30 percent of workers in the oil fields.[72] Women had already by the late 1920s been entering into new professions in remarkable numbers, including law, medicine, engineering, academia, and publishing. In 1930, there was no other state in Europe that had as many female lawyers, professors, artists, and judges.[73] The number of women in higher education went from 31 percent in 1926 to 43 percent in 1937.[74] Women's entry into traditionally male industrial sectors continued in the postwar period, especially in machine building and operating and electrical engineering.[75]

This mass participation of women in industrial production and the professions was perpetually hailed by the state as a product of the revolution's emancipation of women, but it was more a product of economic necessity than ideological commitment to a feminist agenda.[76] The Soviet state never made the full emancipation of women a priority.[77] Women's entry into the professional and industrial workforce did not prompt the state to encourage any real change in gender consciousness; instead, under Stalin there was an amplification of a gendered division of labor that remained strong until the end of the Soviet Union itself. New lines of gender division were drawn as certain sectors became designated as female, such as textiles, sewing, the lower and middle levels of white collar and service professions, and positions such as stenographers, cooks, laundresses, and pharmacists.[78]

The 1930s witnessed official proclamation of the family as the core unit of socialist society. The 1936 Stalin Constitution hailed the socialist family as the "strongest and most secure of all families."[79] The Stalinist state not only fully embraced the notion of women as a vital economic asset and a necessary contributor to the collective economy but also affirmed traditional notions that women were biologically suited by nature for domestic tasks and childrearing and therefore necessary as the bulwark for holding the family together.[80] Article 122 of the 1936 Constitution guaranteed women equal right to employment and the right to equal wages for equal work, but also pledged the state to protect the "interests of mother and child" and provide public childcare institutions.[81] Stalin himself proclaimed that a woman must not neglect her duty to the socialist order as a mother, and propaganda projected images of women primarily in domestic settings.[82] Instead of following up on the early promise to liberate women from domestic duties, the regime re-sacralized them, linking them to state goals of building socialism. The new Soviet woman became an ideal wife and mother, as well as "equal citizen and worker."[83] Mounting concerns over falling birth rates, high rates of abortion, and alarming declines in population lay behind the revitalized emphasis upon women's role as mothers and led to new legislation in 1936 and 1944 that prohibited abortion, provided material support to mothers of large families as well as unmarried mothers, and made divorce increasingly difficult and expensive to obtain.[84] The 1936 decree made abortion illegal except in cases when the woman's life or health was at stake or if a serious disease could be transmitted.[85] Contraceptives were also taken from the market, though they had never been widely available.[86] Both laws provided bonuses for women with multiple children, and the 1944 law conferred monthly stipends and honorific titles on mothers whether married or single.[87]

But as in the 1920s, these revised family laws made promises the regime was unable or unwilling to fulfill, such as to expand production of children's clothing, footwear, and hygiene articles. State ministries, local government organizations, and unions were to provide increased housing and childcare, but few steps were taken to construct any such promised facilities. After the war, childcare services did improve, but never expanded to the extent promised. As Greta Bucher has pointed out, while the Soviet state provided more for working mothers in the postwar era than most other countries at the time, including childcare and subsidized housing, what was provided fell far short of what women working full time needed.[88] The failure of the Soviet regime to challenge traditional notions that housework and childrearing were solely "women's work" and to call on men to step in when the state could not provide socialized services meant that women had to "do it all," thus engendering the "double burden" (or "double shift") for Soviet women.[89] The woman engineer who was a leader on the shop floor was also to be the chief caretaker for the domestic hearth, which under the conditions of the Soviet deficit economy, the devastation wrought by the Second World War, the enormous task of reconstruction, and the continued prioritization of heavy industry meant that the chores women had to perform at home took up an inordinate amount of time and energy. Women had to wait in long lines after work for essential items, then cook, clean, wash, and mend clothing by hand, which often took as much of their time as their regular jobs, meaning that Soviet women often had a thirteen- to fifteen-hour workday.[90] Appliances such as washing machines only became available in the early 1950s but were not produced in enough quantity to meet demand. As late as 1976, there were sixty-seven washing machines per hundred families, and only twenty vacuum cleaners.[91]

Consequently, these multiple demands on women's time meant that women's professional development was limited; it was harder for them to get the training necessary to raise their skills or put in the time to achieve a promotion.[92] Women remained largely employed in unskilled, manual labor, tending to fill the lowest paid and often physically hardest jobs. Women predominated in the service sector as typists, salespersons, and telephone operators. Sexual harassment was common, an experience Ludmila describes, as well as verbal abuse and exploitation by male bosses who treated women arbitrarily and assigned them poorly paid and often physically taxing positions.[93] Because salary rates tended to be lower in light and service industries, not areas of high priority for Soviet planners, women on average earned only two-thirds of what men earned, which was not significantly different from their prerevolutionary situation.[94] Nor did women attain high positions of power or supervision in the professions, even those in which they were numerically superior.[95] Likewise, despite attaining high levels of education, women were far less involved in politics and were seriously underrepresented in the highest political organs in the country. Although they made up 24.7 percent of Communist Party membership in 1977, up from 7.4 percent in 1920, only four women ever served in the Politburo, and in 1976, at the twenty-fifth Party Congress, only fourteen of the 426 positions in the Central Committee were held by women.[96]

After Stalin's death some of the more restrictive Stalinist-era legislation was retracted. In 1955 the ban on abortions was repealed and ten years later, the Supreme Soviet passed a decree simplifying divorce procedures and lowering the fees to be paid.[97] The Soviet economy remained heavily dependent on female labor, in part due to the continued demographic imbalance. In 1981, women made up 51 percent of the workforce (they had made up 24% in 1924). Women were 49 percent of the industrial labor force and made up 51 percent of collective farm workers. By the end of the 1960s, 80 percent of Soviet women worked outside the home.[98] The ideal of Soviet women as both emancipated workers and traditional keepers of the domestic hearth, though, remained intact through the end of Ludmila's life. Despite the hardships, most Soviet women appeared not to question the gendered division of labor and the expectation that they should be able to work and provide for their family. Soviet women selflessly devoted themselves to the needs of society and, at the same time, strove to be "loving and maternal, the keeper of the family hearth."[99] Soviet women were truly the twentieth century's first "super moms" expected to be capable of doing it all.[100]

The changes brought to women's lives through modernization and revolution during the twentieth century form the backdrop of Ludmila's life, and her personal experiences intersect with and illuminate many of these developments. Ludmila's life showcases both continuities and differences between pre- and postrevolutionary women's lives. As a girl, she grew up in a family that adhered to traditional gender norms; though her mother gave piano lessons, she did not otherwise work or pursue career goals. Ludmila recalls as a young girl viewing her mother's life as old-fashioned and stunted, especially after she learns from a family friend that her mother had been forced by Ludmila's grandmother into a loveless marriage. Her mother had nonetheless subordinated herself entirely to the needs of her husband and children, particularly the precocious and talented son Sasha. Ludmila describes a difficult relationship with her mother, who though allowing her to pursue education, nonetheless worried more about Ludmila's need to find a husband than to acquire a profession. Yet Ludmila did benefit from the new opportunities for female education. She attended a girl's gymnasia, and after graduation she enrolled in Women's Higher Courses in Odessa. She was eager to be a modern woman; she was an enthusiastic student, dreamed of a career in the movies or on the stage, and hoped to study at the women's courses in St. Petersburg. She pursued her own individual desires and chose impulsively to leave her parents' home to marry a man much older than herself whom she barely knew. Then, after Konstantin Mikhailovich proved unfaithful, she left him to make a life on her own even though she did not have a job or any particular training or skill. She recognized the need for some degree of financial autonomy and sought out jobs to strengthen her independence. Ludmila sought employment through the world of letters and did get published as a journalist and writer. Like many women, though, she ended up working most of her life at a very traditionally gendered occupation for women, typing.

Ludmila's own gender consciousness was a syncretic blending of modern perspectives and traditional values. Even though she defied her mother's desire to arrange a husband for her, Ludmila nonetheless accepted a subordinate role in her two marriages and saw herself primarily as responsible for supporting her husband's career. Although she enjoyed some success and satisfaction as a writer, it is her role as mother that she remembers as the most meaningful experience of her life. Once she gave birth to Elena, motherhood became her primary focus and source of identity, and her life and her memories came to revolve mainly around this. She threw herself so wholeheartedly into her maternal role that she alienated her husband Izya for a time and found herself out of touch with her less domestically inclined peers. Ludmila describes and obviously admired a number of very strong and independent women, but she makes it very clear that she only found true fulfillment in life when she gave birth to her daughter. Ludmila does not question the "double burden," though she certainly expresses some degree of exasperation at times regarding the domestic division of responsibilities, especially with her second husband, Izya, who was much less handy around the house than Konstantin Mikhailovich had been. She also expresses frustration over each of her husband's insistence on controlling the money flow; but rather than confront them, she reveals how in both marriages she had to resort to surreptitious bargaining and dealing on the side in order to have disposable income she could send to her parents or use to buy toys and books for her daughter.

Ludmila's fate is representative as well in her gendered experience of Stalinism. She suffered from one of the most gendered of categories of terror victims, the "wife of an enemy of the people." After her husband's arrest in 1936, she was sent into exile with her daughter as a politically untrustworthy "wife" because under Stalinism, this family relationship made you complicit in the crime. An April 1937 NKVD order called for "wives of enemies of the people" to be sentenced for five to eight years, as well as children over the age of 15 who were "socially dangerous and capable of anti-Soviet actions."[101] Even those not arrested and exiled had problems finding work, friends and neighbors turned away, they often lost their homes, and their children faced ridicule and severe limits to what they could do or aspire to in terms of joining school organizations such as the Pioneers, getting admitted to university, and so on. Unfortunately Ludmila's status as the "wife" of an enemy did not end with her exile but led to her arrest on charges of not having informed on her husband. When her "case" added accusations of terrorism, leading to her sentence of ten years in the Gulag, Ludmila joined a small percentage of women making up the ranks of prisoners in the Soviet Union. During the 1930s, women were generally less than 9 percent of the camp population, though this number increased during the Second World War. At the end of the war women made up 30 percent of the Gulag population, and in 1948 this dropped to 22 percent and then to 17 percent during 1952.[102] Although special camps were set up to house "wives of enemies of the people," such as the Akmola camp in Kazakhstan, Ludmila was never incarcerated in one, probably because of her conviction as a terrorist in her own right.

Gender played a major role in Ludmila's survival in the Gulag. Above all, it was her maternal sense of responsibility that gave her a reason to persevere through all of her trials. She was determined to fulfill the pledge she made to her daughter to return to her, and this led Ludmila to employ a series of successful survival strategies, most importantly securing for herself the opportunity to train and work as a nurse. After her release, the difficulties she encountered in rebuilding a relationship with her daughter dampened any relief or joy at being "free," and she admits to, at times, even feeling as if she had been happier in the camps when she still had the hope of a happy reunion. Her survival became even more bittersweet when her daughter died. The tragic end to her daughter's life that came so soon after her release and rehabilitation dealt her a devastating blow. Life alone, without her daughter, takes up very little space in her memoir. We do not learn much at all about her life after Elena's death. The Stalinist terror had destroyed what meant more to her than any other element of her life—her family and her maternal identity. Her story illuminates one of the harshest facets of women's history in the Soviet Union, having to cope with the damage done to the family, and particularly to children, by such Stalinist policies as collectivization and the terror.

Jews in Russian and Soviet History

Ludmila's life is shaped as well by the fact that she was Jewish, which in the Soviet Union was officially categorized as a nationality rather than as a religion. Although raised in a secular household and not engaging herself in religious practice, Ludmila faced anti-Semitism as a child and as an adult. The history of the Jews in tsarist Russia and in Soviet Russia was marked by deep currents of anti-Semitism, though the legal and civil discriminations characteristic of the prerevolutionary period came to end with the 1917 Revolutions.

Jews in the Russian Empire faced manifest legal and civil prohibitions, periodic pogroms, and officially enforced segregation. Since the time of Catherine the Great in 1791, Jews were required to live in the Pale of Settlement, which included Belarus, Lithuania, Moldova, Ukraine, eastern Latvia, eastern Poland, and western Russia. They could leave only if they converted to Russian Orthodoxy or received special permission. Over time many Jews did assimilate into Russian culture, and after 1827, Jewish males were conscripted for military service. The late tsarist period, however, saw the situation for Jews deteriorate, with severe restrictions on civil rights and rigid quotas for admission to institutions of secondary and higher education and to certain professions. After 1881, multiple waves of violent pogroms devastated Jewish communities and led to widespread emigration. Those occurring between 1903 and 1906, including the one in Odessa in 1905 that terrorized Ludmila and her family, killed over a thousand persons and wounded several times more.

The tsarist regime did little to stop the violence and did not seek to punish those responsible for the pogroms. The Ministry of Justice was complicit in the persecution of Jews and sought to use the reformed tsarist courts as a vehicle for anti-Semitic propaganda. The "Beilis affair" referred to in the memoir by Konstantin Mikhailovich as an issue that alienated him from his aristocratic parents (who expressed belief in Beilis's guilt) was one of the most notorious of these attempts. Menahem Mendel Beilis was a family man and a respected factory superintendent who was arrested for the "ritualistic murder" of a 13-year-old Ukrainian boy Andrei Yushchinskii, despite the fact that Beilis had a solid alibi and the police had determined Yushchinskii was murdered by criminals. After being kept in jail for over two years, Beilis was tried in the fall of 1913 in Kiev, and despite the government's determination to convict him with false testimonies, the jury found him not guilty. The trial became an international sensation and brought much criticism upon the tsarist government.[103] The army was another hotbed of anti-Semitism. Jews faced bias and discrimination from commanders, officials, and fellow soldiers. Jews could not become officers and were under constant suspicion of disloyalty. During the First World War, Jews were suspected of collaboration with the German and Austrian enemy, and Russian armies carried out violent pogroms and deportations throughout the Pale.[104]

The Revolutions of 1917, however, brought significant changes to the situation of Jews in Russia. Both the Provisional Government and the new Bolshevik regime abolished legal restrictions against Jews, including the Pale of Settlement, and outlawed anti-Semitism. Jewish soldiers could enroll in officers' schools, and given the strong currents of anti-Semitism that ran through the White Armies in the Civil War, particularly among Cossack troops, most Jews ended up supporting the Bolshevik Red Army. Indeed, for Jews the new Soviet regime proved at least initially to be very progressive and supportive; they gained access to universities and higher education on a scale unthinkable in the tsarist era. Stalin publicly condemned anti-Semitism as a crime in the 1930s, but after the Second World War, he grew increasingly disturbed by the establishment of the state of Israel and the potential for Soviet Jews to be disloyal. As his paranoia grew, arrests of leading Jewish intellectuals and artistic figures mounted, and beginning in 1948, a campaign in the press against so-called cosmopolitanism became a veiled form of anti-Semitism. Jews from all walks of life were arrested or dismissed from leading positions in government, academia, and science on the charge of "rootless cosmopolitanism." Then in 1952 Stalin declared to the Presidium that "every Jew is a nationalist and an agent of American intelligence."[105]

This rising tide of anti-Semitism peaked in January 1953 when chilling news of the so-called Doctors' Plot, with nine doctors, seven of whom were Jewish, accused of assassinating high-ranking party figures; evidence suggests this was intended to stir up public support for deporting the Jews and to launch a full-scale purge of party-state institutions.[106] After Stalin's death in March 1953, however, his successors quickly disavowed the Doctors' Plot and released the accused doctors. Though anti-Semitism did not again rise to such a prominent level, it nonetheless remained a constant in Soviet life, with unofficial quotas existing for access to universities, to professions, and to state institutions. Beginning in the 1970s, Jewish emigration, particularly to Israel, became an international issue as pressure was put on the Soviet government to allow greater numbers to leave. In total, nearly two million Jews emigrated during the last three decades of the Soviet Union.

In the memoir, Ludmila's Jewish identity is expressed mainly as an ethnic consciousness. Ludmila's Jewish background immersed her in Jewish culture, and this may have influenced her social and personal connections. She had several patrons throughout her life, such as the writers Ilya Ehrenburg and Samuil Marshak, who were Jewish and her second husband, Izya Trotsky, came from a Jewish family. She did not learn Yiddish, however; Ludmila grew up in the confluence between two different generations of Jews in Odessa. Her memories of childhood reveal tensions generated by modernity and desires for assimilation. Her parents did not regularly practice their faith, except on certain holidays and for rituals connected with death. She speaks at length in her memoir about the problems this created for her grandparents, who were more religious and who clearly resented and feared their children's disregard for the faith. She acknowledges more than once that her parents and siblings did not "look Jewish," which enabled them at times to avoid either anti-Semitic violence or the everyday prejudices that underlay Russian attitudes towards Jews before 1917.

What Ludmila Pavlovna remembers most vividly is the persecution that Jews faced in her youth in Odessa. She recalls the horrors of the 1905 pogrom and how she became extremely angry when her older brother Grisha converted to Orthodoxy in the army in order to remove barriers to his promotion and help keep him from the front lines. She viewed this as a betrayal of his people, who continued to suffer from persecution. Her stance created considerable dissension in the family because her parents did not understand her strong reaction. Furthermore, the fact that the Soviet regime improved the legal and civil status of Jews and offered greater opportunities for herself and others like her made an impression on her, and she explains this to Konstantin Mikhailovich as one of the reasons she wished to return to the Soviet Union rather than stay on in Paris. She does not mention, however, ever practicing Judaism and does not further address the situation of Jews in Soviet Russia, except with regard to the Doctors' Plot. She describes how she and two of her friends in exile who were also Jewish suffered terrible anxieties during this period. People looked at them suspiciously, and they realistically feared further persecution and a possible return to the Gulag. This hostility only ended with Stalin's death.

The Autobiography/Memoir in Russian Women's Writing

Ludmila's memoir is part of a rich literary tradition dating back to Russia's eighteenth century. Autobiographical writing was one of the most popular forms of women's writing. Russian and Soviet women used it to explore their self-formation in the face of life's challenges, focusing on such themes as mother/daughter relations, societal limitations on women, revolutionary consciousness and activism, conserving cultural values or heritage, and survival of terror and the Gulag. In their extensive examinations of Russian women's writing, both Barbara Heldt and Beth Holmgren emphasize how traditionally, female memoirists did not present themselves as purely individuals telling a personal story, but seek to serve a larger social cause far more important than their own life.[107] Ultimately, as Heldt points out, a defining feature of female autobiography has been the theme of survival; Russian women's writings about the self have retraced efforts to overcome forced marriage, social or cultural isolation, and imprisonment.[108] Writing about the self in the form of autobiography was also a prominent part of official Soviet culture, harnessed by the party-state as a way of showing one's transformation into a good Soviet citizen. Talking and writing about the self became as politicized as other areas of life and culture, and it was encouraged by the regime as a fulfillment of the mission of transformation. Always in Russian culture, according to Jochen Hellbeck, to be considered worthy of being an "intelligent," you had to show yourself to be a "critically thinking subject of history." Therefore, Soviet intellectuals respected autobiography as a "medium of self-reflection and transformation."[109] Particularly after Stalin's death in 1953, Gulag returnees began writing memoirs that enabled them to co-opt the official Soviet practice of autobiography to expose the injustices of Stalinism and testify to their own and others' ordeal of survival. Although few were published prior to the Gorbachev era, many circulated in underground samizdat publications or appeared abroad. Ludmila's writing links her thus to both nineteenth- and twentieth-century traditions of writing and includes elements drawn from both Russian and Soviet genres of memoir writing.

Multiple themes characterize Ludmila's writing, and it is difficult to categorize it within one single framework of women's memoir. She took the prevalent form of writing about the self that characterized Soviet Russia, yet she used it for her own personal self-examination, not to show her commitment to ideology or revolutionary transformation. She privileges the domestic, private life and makes it clear she was never involved in politics except for the absurd charge made against her in 1938. Her personal biography frames the narrative, but every major stage of her life is richly contextualized and brought to life through detailed observation and description. Early sections of the memoir depict a story of personal transformation through interaction with gifted individuals. Ludmila recounts many of the famous persons she knew and met, and through them she establishes her earned credentials as intelligentsia. She enjoys the memory of her close relationships with noted artists and attributes her maturation from a naïve provincial girl into a more sophisticated and cultured adult to these experiences. Her memoir also taps into a genre of female autobiographical writing that seeks to preserve lost cultural legacies.[110] Ludmila pays tribute to Konstantin Mikhailovich by memorializing his contributions to early Soviet theater and stagecraft, for she knew very well that his life and work had been obliterated from the official histories due to his status as an émigré and then his tragic suicide. She gives a detailed summary of one of his plays that was staged successfully in Petrograd in 1920–1, *The Last Bourgeois*, a lively romp that she suggests could have been a prototype for Mayakovsky's more famous *The Bedbug*.

As a memoirist, Ludmila Pavlovna does not sublimate her individual self into a larger social cause, though certainly her story reveals the tragedies of Stalinism. Her narrative is an individual recovery of her memory.[111] This memoir was a way to come to terms with her life. It served as a form of therapy, allowing her to go back through her life, recovering and sustaining herself through happy memories. She also forced herself to revisit the dark pages. As she wrote, "*I am firmly convinced that each person is responsible for how his or her life turns out. I will write everything, and it will become clear to me and to anyone who might at some time read my manuscript whether I alone bear the guilt for the fact that my life has been hard.*" In her memoir she relives the self-recrimination that plagued her in the camps and then haunted her for a lifetime. What flows through the narrative is her sheer and utter sorrow at the senselessness of what happened. She interrogates herself—could she have done anything to have avoided arrest? She thinks back to her husband's arrest and wonders why she had not at that moment fled south with her daughter. But she reminds herself that she had nowhere to go, no money, and how could she have abandoned Izya, who needed packages and moral support from both of them?

At the same time, Ludmila Pavlovna recognized the historical value of her life experiences and did endeavor to record her story as part of a survivors' collective rewriting of Russian history.[112] She sensed the impact her memoir could have and thereby knew she was serving the cause of history by exposing yet another example of the misery wrought by Stalinism and its politics. To a certain degree, Ludmila was ahead of her time in documenting her own personal experiences as a woman to serve as a lens into twentieth-century history. She courageously wrote this well before Gorbachev's glasnost unleashed a flood of personal writing about the Gulag and before scholars recognized the viability of personal experience as an analytical tool for the study of history. As a survivor of Stalinism, she did write a Gulag memoir, with many of the elements typically found in this genre—descriptions of life before arrest, the state of disbelief and suspicion, endless waiting in lines, interrogations, verdict, the humiliations of prison and transport to the camps, despair and fear, adaptation and survival, and deliverance.[113] She provides a particularly detailed account of how the case against her took shape. She recounts her miserable prison conditions, the interrogation and trial, and shows that she did her best to expose the baseless nature of the charges against her. Like many Gulag survivors, she describes the physical debilitation she suffered in trying to fulfill impossible quotas, and the low point she sunk to before being given opportunities for nonmanual labor, first doing clerical work in offices and then as a nurse. Thus her path to survival is very similar to most Gulag memoirists. She was fortunate to be able to receive packages from her daughter and her in-laws, and items thus procured strengthened her situation and her health. Like two famous Gulag memoirists, Evgenia Ginzburg and Olga Adamova-Sliozberg, motherhood played a key role in her survival, furnishing her with a compelling motive to keep going.

Ludmila, though, departs from standard Gulag memoirs in that she is telling her saga of the Gulag in the context of a larger narrative on multiple chapters of her life. She also does not transform her narrative of self into a testimony for collective wrongs. She describes only a few fellow prisoners and does not emphasize how her interaction with others helped in mutual survival. She pointedly downplays the importance of her Gulag account by saying she does not have much to add to what has already been described about that experience. Instead, she shows how individualistic her commitment to survival made her. She describes moments in which she shrank from reaching out to others, because she feared reprisals might jeopardize her survival. Her narrative is not a chronicle of day-to-day events in the camps; she describes relatively little about her Gulag existence except what she did in order to stay connected to her daughter. When she does provide details about fellow prisoners, it is usually about women like herself, who were separated from a child or who had lost an infant to disease or starvation after their arrest.

Ludmila Pavlovna's narrative also reveals her as a survivor whose "deliverance" did not bring a happy ending. She does not describe meaningful reunions with her family; her in-laws proved distant and even distrustful of her, jealously protecting their bond with Elena. Her one surviving brother, Grisha, married a woman Ludmila considered coarse and rude; he also lived in the vicinity of the camp he had been a prisoner in, which Ludmila found terribly depressing and traumatic when she tried to visit. More happily, she does describe a longtime friend who took special care of her after her return, and she did have a cousin who welcomed her. She felt great joy in seeing her daughter again and cherished any and every contact with her, but their former closeness was gone. Then came the fatal infection that destroyed her daughter and with this went the only reason she had survived the horrors of prison and camp life. Tragically, in her Gulag narrative, beyond her account of her successful fight for rehabilitation, there is little "redemption" to be found.

Writing the Memoir

The writing of this memoir during the last year of her life, while she was experiencing extreme pain, taxed Ludmila physically. But what made it even more difficult was having to relive the circumstances that had irrevocably scarred her life. Ludmila Miklashevskaya was a mother forced by the mechanisms of the Stalinist terror to endure separation from her young daughter, an ordeal that proved to have tragic consequences. Her maternal devotion helped her to survive her time in the Gulag. But what Ludmila had to cope with as she recounted the details of her unjust persecution by the Stalinist regime was the tragic reality that the daughter for whom she survived died young and under circumstances that Ludmila could not help but believe were the result of her imprisonment and forced separation from her daughter's life. What informs her narrative voice is the anguish Ludmila had to live with over the rest of her life, knowing that she did indeed survive the nightmare of Stalinism, but without achieving what she had most wanted, simply to share life with her daughter. It had to have been challenging to "recover and revisit" the events that led to her sad fate and the death of her daughter. Yet she courageously produced a memoir that in its Russian edition reached four hundred pages.

Despite the pain she suffered, she writes buoyantly and with humor when remembering the persons she loved and the friendships she cherished. As Iakov Gordin emphasizes in the preface to the Russian edition, this memoir is above all a love story. Despite the tragedy that had engulfed her and the trauma of writing about it, Ludmila joyously weaves endearing portraits of the two persons she loved most in the world, her first husband Konstantin Mikhailovich Miklachevsky and her daughter Elena. Her stories of life with Konstantin in Petrograd, his unique and eccentric talents and tastes are lively and evocative. She made it clear to Iakov Gordin as she was finishing her manuscript that she wanted it to be published with her last name as Miklashevskaya, to honor the man she had never ceased to love. Likewise, her descriptions of becoming a mother and the times she spent with Elena before the terrible events of the terror convey poignantly the exuberant love she poured into their relationship and the deep satisfaction it brought her.

Yet writing the memoir did invoke intense emotional pain. The hardest part of writing her life story was having to revisit the events that led to her daughter's death. The memoir also reveals a personal dilemma she faced. Ludmila had to reconcile her conflicting emotions regarding the role played by her sister-in-law and brother-in-law. Ludmila keeps reminding herself that she owed them much gratitude for their willingness to raise her daughter, despite the fear and suspicion that such an act provoked during the Stalinist terror. Had her in-laws not taken Elena in, tainted as she was by the label "child of an enemy of the people," she would have been sent to an NKVD orphanage; such institutions tended to be poorly staffed, inadequately provisioned, and sought to sever the children from their "enemy" parents by renaming them and losing or destroying vital personal documents. By accepting responsibility for Elena, Ludmila's in-laws risked their professional standing. Tronsky was a prominent scholar of classical Greek and Latin and a gifted linguist with much to lose by such a connection. The fact that he felt fear was obvious in his changing his last name in 1938 from Trotsky to Tronsky, presumably to avoid the taint of sharing the same name as the demonized Leon Trotsky, but possibly also to prevent being connected to his own arrested brother. Yet he and his wife did not hesitate to take in Elena even when many relatives of terror victims refused to do so, and they adopted her as their own.[114]

To revisit these experiences as a memoirist had to have been torturous for Ludmila, but also cathartic. She did not want to be unfair to her in-laws. Just before her death, Ludmila asked Iakov Gordin in a letter to ensure that it was clear in the memoir that she reconciled with her sister-in-law after Elena's death, and all was forgiven. She noted that it was her sister-in-law who paid for the bulk of Ludmila's eye treatments.[115] Ludmila appreciated their courage in giving her daughter a secure and happy childhood. But Ludmila nonetheless still felt anguish over the petty jealousies of her sister-in-law that had kept her at arm's length and put obstacles in the way of Ludmila rebuilding a close relationship with Elena.

Ludmila Pavlovna was a woman both blessed and cursed, fated to experience the best and the worst that life in Soviet Russia offered. Through her marriage to Konstantin Mikhailovich, she got to experience life in both of Russia's "capital" cities, Leningrad and Moscow. She interacted with some of Russia's greatest artistic talents and gained opportunities to develop her own nascent skills as a writer. She was able to return after the Gulag to her beloved Leningrad, a city which had become a part of her and which she felt spiritually linked her with the man who had introduced her to it, her first husband Konstantin, and with her daughter, who spent her short life there. Ludmila got to do what so many Russians could only dream of—she lived in Paris for three years—and then returned to the Soviet Union, a place she considered her home and could not imagine living apart from as she had seen so many doing. She had strong and enduring friendships and persons who loved and supported her. But Ludmila was also a victim of one of Soviet Union's most tragic periods, the Stalinist terror, which destroyed what she valued the most in life, her family. Her story is a gripping portrait of life and death in the shadow of Stalinism and the deep scars it left. I hope readers will take away from this work an appreciation of her indomitable spirit, her generous heart, and her capacity to endure heartbreaking loss and still be able to write about it in a clear and compelling way. She was an ordinary woman who led an extraordinary life as she navigated through one of modern Russia's most complex and challenging centuries.

1

An Odessa Childhood

My memories begin with our life on Uspenskaia Street, in a building owned by the two elderly Shpringer ladies. It was the only place in Odessa where you could purchase the famous "Shpringer ointment" and "Shpringer plaster" used for boils and other types of sores. Our apartment was located inside the courtyard on the first floor, right across from the Shpringers' back door, which served as their main entrance from the street. Ignat, the building's caretaker, prepared the ointment on an open fire. The black goo boiled and bubbled in a large basin, filling the whole courtyard with the smell of tar. My two older brothers and I tried never to miss this procedure. Other children's mothers did not allow them to be outside when it was going on, but ours believed it to be healthy. Odessa had frequent epidemics of childhood diseases, and she was positive that breathing in the vapors of this tar could kill all contagions. Our mama took other preventative measures as well. When scarlet fever was "on the move" in Odessa, we wore amulets filled with camphor crystals. During outbreaks of whooping cough and chicken pox, we hung little bags filled with crushed garlic around our necks. And, truth be told, we were rarely sick.

Twice we left Odessa and traveled with mama to visit our father in Tiflis, where he worked as an accountant for a mill after being transferred from Odessa. For the train trip, mama bought only one adult ticket, which allowed her one free children's ticket. She gave it to Grisha and he sat next to her. My other brother Sasha and I had to pretend to be children of travelers who did not have kids with them. If there were not any childless adults, then we had to cram ourselves into the upper shelf of the compartment, barricaded behind baskets and packages. All we had to do was lie there quietly, not moving a muscle. People were always willing to help us. Once a man from the Caucasus who was traveling to Tiflis with his son covered me with his felt burka. But the cloak had a very strange smell, and I decided to make a tiny opening for air. In the process, though, I got all tangled up in it. Luckily the ticket collector was delayed in coming. It was very stuffy and scary for me lying there underneath this prickly, thick burka. I did not make a sound, but I tried to get myself out of it using the full force of my arms and legs. I managed to crawl out and dangled my legs down over mama's head; fortunately, this was after the ticket man had already gone out into the corridor. Mama grabbed ahold of me and sat me on her knee. She straightened my dress, which was inside out and up around my head. Mama scolded me for not being patient and making an inappropriate spectacle of myself "in front of everyone." She pointed out that the other little girls in our section were all behaving nicely. I retorted that maybe they were behaving properly because they did not have to hide in a burka.

I was 4 years old at this time. My brother Sasha was closest in age to me and he was 5. Wherever we went, he was everyone's favorite. He was handsome and clever; he loved to recite poems and sing songs, and often presented his own literary creations. On the train people dragged him from compartment to compartment to perform. My oldest brother, who was already 7 years old, enviously accompanied him. He would prompt Sasha if he forgot a line of poetry, but Grisha always remained hidden in the shadow. I could only rejoice in Sasha's success from afar. Mama would not let me go, and all I could do was look out the window.

In Tiflis, the door of our apartment opened out to a wooden balcony that ran along the entire second floor, forming a portico overlooking the courtyard. Like others, we had a table on the portico where we had tea and dined. A tall dark-eyed boy brought us hot lavash bread every morning. I would always run to meet him. How wonderful it was to breathe in the warm scent of the lavash and its golden crust. Papa showed us around Tiflis. The boys got to run ahead but papa held on to my hand. We came to an enormous hill that was covered in bright green grass. Papa told us that this was the hill of King David and that at the top was the grave of Alexander Griboedov.[1] I looked at the green grass and I longed to run through it, but papa held me firmly by the hand. "Grisha," mama asked, "do you know who Griboedov is?" Mama was preparing Grisha for his first year preparatory class in school and had taken him and Sasha to the theater for a matinee performance. "I know," answered Grisha, "he wrote a play that we saw at the theater." "And what was the title of this play?" Mama continued to quiz him hoping that papa would appreciate how smart Grisha had become. But I interfered. "Woe about Fog," I declared, in a hurry to show off my own knowledge. "What do you mean, what kind of fog?" Mama asked indignantly. "Well, the kind that causes trouble, probably a big thick fog." Everyone laughed and I felt embarrassed. It seemed to make sense to me, since in Odessa we had thick fogs, and mama herself sometimes said, "Woe is me, it is the fog again." We stayed with father for several weeks, but then returned to Odessa and waited for his letters. More truthfully, it was the beautiful postcards we eagerly anticipated. Papa sent them frequently, and mama gave us an album for them. The boys received ones with scenes of the roaring sea, sunken ships, battles, hunters, and various breeds of dogs while I got beautiful girls with dolls, flowers, birds, and butterflies.

My mother was beautiful, in fact the most beautiful of all women. All of our acquaintances praised her beauty, as did our neighbors, who ran the pharmacy on our street. I loved going there with mama. Mr. Antonovich, after wrapping up mama's purchases, would always give me a beautiful little box, sometimes covered with silk, and said, "May you grow up to be as beautiful a woman as your mama." Mama was also the best at playing the piano. We listened to music everyday and we could identify the nocturnes and waltzes of Chopin, the sonatas of Beethoven, or Mendelssohn's "Songs without Words." Mama usually played by ear without sheet music. Our mother also could speak French and German and checked out library books in these languages. People who knew her also considered her to have excellent taste and would ask her to help them buy a coat or a hat. On such occasions mama would usually take me with her. I found it torturous. In the market on Alexandrovskii, there were a number of small clothing stores known as "Konfeksion." A friend would come from towns such as Nikolaev or Kherson and Mama would take her from one such shop to the next. At each one mama would have her try on all of the coats. To me, the person could have bought any one of them, but mama always insisted on dragging her friend to shop after shop. Then, finally, they would remember that in the first store, there had been a coat that suited best and was the least expensive. So we would go back. The coat would be purchased, packaged, and the store proprietor would send us off with a smile. Then once we were outside, mama would say that, actually, the coat was excellent, but the buttons were not so nice. Her friend should get different ones for it. So then we had to go to mama's favorite tailoring shop, which was run by Dziubin,[2] who was the husband of her school friend Ida. The shop was small and poorly lit but had plentiful boxes of buttons, thumb tacks, buckles, and bundles of silk braid. Mama liked to buy here a special kind of lace called "brush lace," which she used when hemming skirts. For me Dziubin always prepared a small box with different colored spangles and thin, bright circles (*kruzhochki*), which I collected along with silver five-kopek coins mama sometimes gave me.

Once inside, the coat would be unwrapped and the selection of buttons would begin. Dziubin would not offer any advice, but always deferred to my mother. After long consideration, the buttons were purchased and we left the shop. At this point I would refuse to go any further and beg to sit down on a bench. After several minutes, mama would cry out that we were right next to Ptashnikov's shop,[3] where you could buy the very best and the cheapest calico. So they would pull me along to Ptashnikov's ... Finally after much shopping, we would go home in a tram-carriage. Now this always cheered me up, for I liked riding in the carriage. It had three horses harnessed to it and a trace horse that would run on the side, and I could watch it the entire time. For such visits we would dine better than usual. At three o'clock there would be a soufflé made from egg whites beaten with cherry preserves. Mama used the yolks to make amazing, melt-in-your-mouth sesame seed cookies. This was one of our mother's secret recipes. All of our friends raved over these cookies but no one knew how to make them. Sometimes, mother would reminisce with her friends about her youth (she had grown up in Nikolaev); she would tell her visitor sadly that her life had not turned out the way she had dreamed. Her father had been a wealthy man with his own office, and her older sisters had received fine dowries and married well. But then her father went bankrupt and died soon afterward. Mama had to give music lessons in order to support herself and her mother. Moreover, she was forced to marry an accountant and they were always economizing and counting every penny. Mama thought that we did not understand, but we knew very well what she was saying. We loved our papa and always waited impatiently for his postcards, but we began to sense there was discord within our family.

The second trip to Tiflis was intended to make mama happy. Papa had received a bonus and sent it to her to buy new dresses. He proposed a trip to Baku and Batum, for some wealthy Armenians who lived there wanted to meet mama. The dresses were ordered and arrived at our home one day before our departure. Our "all-purpose maid," as we in Odessa used to call domestic servants, laid them all out in a traveling basket covered with oilcloth. The next morning we left. Our maid, who had been with us about a year, saw us off, crying bitterly. Mother was touched by her devotion. But when we arrived in Tiflis and opened the basket, she saw that all of the new dresses and the elegant scarf (mantilla) with velvet applique had been removed and replaced with logs. Nonetheless, we still went to Batum and Baku. What remains in my memory are the long sofas, the piles of pillows embroidered with woolen thread, and the endless time spent sitting at the table. My brothers got to go off and play with the sons of our hosts, but I had to stay next to mama. Once I left the table and settled myself on a couch. I began to examine and rearrange the pillows. I liked two small pillows so much that I ran with them to mama and said, "Look how beautiful these are!" So our hostess said, "Take them, they are yours." Mama started to protest but father stopped her and later explained that the custom was to give a guest what he or she praised. We carried these pillows to Odessa where they lay on our oilskin couch as an ever present reminder of, as my mother put it, my poor behavior in someone else's home.

At our home in Odessa, mama would do lessons after dinner with Grisha, who was already in the first class at the Iliadi Gymnasium. Then an hour of music would commence. Mama would play our favorite songs on the piano while we sang. Sasha was the best singer among us. Mama said that he had inherited his perfect pitch from her. I had the worst ear for music. I could tell immediately when Grisha sang out of tune, but I could sense that I too was not singing properly. It was around this time, when I was 5 years old, that I first discovered the advantages of lying. Mama played an incredibly sad song entitled "Little Dove, why do you sit so sadly?" The tragedy unfolded: "Someone has taken my nest and my family," narrates the bird. Mama played, Sasha sang with much feeling, and Grisha joined in. Mama looked at Sasha so tenderly and approvingly. I just stood off to the left and started to cry, for I felt that everyone had forgotten about me. Mama loved only her Sasha because he was the musical one. But my crying made mama notice me and she tried to comfort me: "Do you feel sorry for the bird? You have such a good heart. But stop this. It is, after all, just a song." I cuddled up to mama and said, "Of course I am sad, she lost her three baby birds in the nest …" But I knew that I was really crying because I felt sorry for myself, not for the baby birds. But mama wrote to papa about my good heart and told the story to friends.

My parents were not religious. They never went to synagogue, they did not know how to read or write in Yiddish, and we did not have Jewish books or newspapers. We did not cook or eat kosher. We laid out on our table tea sausages and ham, and now and then we even enjoyed Ukrainian country suet—pink and tender, the kind that melts in your mouth. Nonetheless, there was always matzo in our house at Passover. In the days leading up to it, all over Odessa large baskets seemed to float in the air, covered tight with white sheets; they were being carried, filled with matzo, on peoples' heads. And one such basket would alight at our apartment. Aron, who had been a footman in my maternal grandfather's home, would always bring it. Aron liked to recall my grandfather's house at the height of its grandeur, when they had celebrated all holidays in grand fashion. They had special Passover dishes they kept in a special cupboard, for matzo was not to be put on plates that had ever held regular bread. Aron's wife Lukeria was the cook who prepared the Passover meals. Aron loved my mother and he considered it his duty to make sure that we had matzo for Passover, although it horrified him to see that we spread butter on the matzo, placed tea sausage on it, and drank milk. He would turn away from the sight and sigh. Mama paid him well and always invited him to dinner, but he was very strict and never violated Jewish law, certainly not during Passover.

My grandmother, my mother's mother, lived alone. Once a year she came to us, on the eve of my grandfather's death. She was small in stature, taciturn, and came dressed in a black hat with a bouquet of silk violets over her forehead. She would look severely about the room, checking whether everything was in order. But she never ate anything at our house and would only drink tea with lemon. For this mama would take down from the top shelf of our pantry a beautiful glass with a glass saucer and say to her, "Mother, no one besides yourself ever drinks from this." Grandmother would nod approvingly and sip several mouthfuls of tea. In the corner of our dining room stood a fat stearin candle that was nearly an *arshin* in length (nearly 71 centimeters), which on the day of her father's death mama would light in the morning and it would burn for twenty-four hours. Grandmother's visit was intended to check that her daughter was duly honoring her father.

During our walks, our nanny often took us into a church. She would go down on her knees, cross herself, and bow toward the icons while we stood off to the side. It was very beautiful inside, but it was also stuffy and a little frightening. Once, as we were leaving the church, nanny bought us pieces of coconut and said we must not ever tell mama that we went there. It had to be our secret. However, I did spill the beans. This happened because of that enormous candle in the corner of our dining room. I asked one day, "Mama, why is our candle so big, when in churches the candles are so much thinner?" She immediately asked me how I knew what it was like inside a church. Rather than betray our nanny, I said that I had seen inside a church once when we passed by and the doors had been open. Mama stared at me, but said nothing more. We were standing by the burning candle, and mama's face looked very sad. "This candle has to burn for an entire day, because no one knows when my Papa's soul will fly here." This startled me and I asked why he would come. Mama answered, "Papa loved me very much, and he wants to see whether or not I am remembering him." It seemed dreadful to think that a soul would fly into our home in order to check that a candle was burning. I tried to imagine the soul of my long dead grandfather, whom I knew only from photographs. Although it was irrational and scary, I wanted to see what this spirit looked like. Mama, to be sure, said that it was impossible to see grandfather's soul, but it was obliged to come, and we should not be too close to the candle. So I waited until mama went out to give her music lessons, Grisha was at school, Sasha was playing outside, and nanny was in the kitchen. I climbed up onto the couch and sat on one of the Armenian pillows while holding the other in front of me as I watched the tall flame of the candle. Suddenly it flared up, and along the base of the candle ghostly tears rolled down. I froze, then I hid my head behind the pillow. This, of course, was my grandfather's spirit flying in and weeping because mama was not here. If only it had not seen me. Was it still here or had his soul flown away? I could not crawl down and run to nanny, nor could I cry out, because this would alert my grandfather's soul that I was there. I shrank into a ball and trembled in fear. But soon nanny came in, rushed over to me, and grabbed me by the arm: What is wrong my little fish? I could only utter one word: soul ... soul ... Nanny did not understand. She felt my forehead and carried me to bed. Then mama came home. She took my temperature. I did not have a fever but I flatly refused to eat supper and stayed in bed until the next morning. Since mama had spent the evening in the dining room, I decided that the soul would have gone to her there and had no need to come into my room. This was my first real fright.

At last our father finished his work in Tiflis and returned home. We met him at the harbor. In recent months he had been working in Novorossiysk and so he came to Odessa by steamer. There was a thick fog that day and the sirens were blaring through the harbor. Because of the weather, the steamer was late. The boys got to run around the whole time, climbing up the gangplanks leading to the enormous black ships and returning with postage stamps. They always begged people for stamps whenever they could. Mama held me by the hand and I had to go with her. The fog finally began to lift, and far off in the distance a black spot appeared on the horizon. We went to check in the harbor office to see if this was papa's ship, and they said that it was. At the wharf, we watched as the black spot grew larger and larger until we finally saw our father standing on the deck, waving his bowler hat. We rode home in a cab, my first ride in a droshky carriage through Odessa. The boys sat on the folding bench and I sat opposite, between mama and papa. The carriage shook as we went across the cobblestone bridge. The boys could barely hold on to the narrow bench, so papa told them to grasp hold of his cane, which was black and stout with silver inscriptions on it from various friends and coworkers. Papa was very proud of it.

Papa's return livened up our home. Every day there were guests, and mama baked her famous cookies and pretzels. The smell of vanilla and almonds filled our apartment. Papa must have told new guests at least a dozen times about the terrible storm his ship had encountered after leaving Novorossiysk. "I looked death right in the eye" is how he would finish his narrative. Our most frequent visitor was Mama's friend Ida and her son Edia, who was the same age as Grisha and liked to play chess. Edia played silently, knitting his thick dark eyebrows. His face would have seemed sinister, if it were not for his eyes, which always looked merry. He beat Grisha every single time. Grisha would rage and argue, and Edia would tease him, then run home after turning down any refreshment. Mama nicknamed him the "rolling stone." Edia attended a specialized high school (*real'noe uchilishche*), and on his cap there was yellow trim. Gymnasium student caps had white.

Now we had dinner once papa came home from work. But tensions emerged. He would bury himself in the *Odessa News* (*Odesskie novosti*),[4] reading it between each spoonful of soup. This irritated mama, who thought it improper to read at the dinner table. She said nothing, though, and papa did not notice anything. He was too absorbed in the news of the Russo-Japanese War.[5] "Aha," he exclaimed—the Japs are on the run ..." Mama still said nothing. My father could not bear the silent treatment from my mother and was on the verge of exploding. The boys exchanged glances. I did not know what to do, but something had to be said in order to break the silence, so I blurted out, "and Dëmka is smoking!" The boys burst out laughing. "Now, who is this Dëmka?" inquired my somewhat pacified father. "He is the son of the caretaker, Ignat," my mother said. "But why are you telling fibs?" "I am not telling a fib, I saw him ..."

"Well you are forever saying things without any rhyme or reason," mother said, but she thought it was funny as well.

Table etiquette, however, sowed further discord. Mama had begun teaching us proper manners: do not eat or drink loudly; do not slurp your soup, smack your lips, or lean over your plate; and above all, always chew with your mouth shut. Now this was the most difficult for me. That and not being able to soak up gravy with your bread. Mama taught us all this in preparation for papa's return from the Caucasus. But either papa had forgotten his manners or mama had earlier not noticed, but now she visibly shuddered when he slurped his soup and sopped up gravy not only on his own plate but also on the platter of food on the table. Along the edges of the dish there was always some gravy left and papa loved to dip pieces of his roll into it. Mama scolded him for setting a bad example. Papa stopped, went back to his own plate, and ate quickly. But then he used his fork to get more food, and mama flinched. When he took a bone from the soup and began to suck the marrow out noisily, mama threw her napkin on the table and ran to the bedroom. This began what we termed "the scandal." Papa acted insanely. He took the bread knife and, blue with rage, cried out, "I am going to cut my throat, I no longer have the right to eat peacefully in my own home!" Mama was crying quietly but her whole body was shaking, and it all ended with her getting a migraine. Mama lay there chilled, her teeth chattering, her legs numb, and she just moaned. Nanny warmed up her legs with hot water bottles and put a washcloth soaked in vinegar on her forehead. Papa sat next to their bed, sobbing and entreating her to stop crying. The boys hid in their room and Nanny took me out to the kitchen. She felt responsible for having put the "so savory" bones in the soup despite mama banishing them from the table. I understood that papa simply loved bones, but I felt sorry above all for mama. A period of calm followed this drama. Both mama and papa looked after each other and during our dinners there were jolly conversations.

At dusk our whole family would often go out for a walk and end up at the Rozenshtein canteen, which sold seltzer water. We would always stop here and sit and wait to order seltzer water with syrup. Inside the canteen was a small counter where there stood three turntables with glass cylinders of all colors. This was the syrup. You could have a drink with one syrup for two kopeks, but for three kopeks you could create your own combination of any two. Papa ordered "rum-vanilla" and mama had a double lemon drink. The boys ordered "fresh hay," which was a new bright green syrup, and I had double cherry. This brought a unique sensation: the carbonated bubbles tingled my nose while the sharp taste of cherries filled my mouth. Then we would go outside and sit on the bench. Ida Dziubin and Edia would often join us, and the boys would be allowed to run around while I had to just sit and watch the carriages go by.

The most interesting time to be outside was during the many "table days" honoring the tsar and members of his family. Ignat and porters from neighboring buildings would stretch out wires between the acacia trees and hang small lamps of colored glass. Inside the lamps candles burned and from all of the gates enormous tricolored flags fluttered in the wind. I knew that the tsar lived in St. Petersburg in a big palace, where there were more than a hundred rooms. He was very rich, he could do anything he wanted, and everyone had to obey him. I had once seen a full-length portrait of the tsar in the apartment of a wealthy relative, the senior factory inspector Popov, who was married to Sarra Kopp, the sister of my Aunt Anya's husband (Aunt Anya was my mother's younger sister). It was a luxurious apartment with an internal staircase, on the top landing of which hung the portrait of the tsar—he stood dressed as an officer standing on a parquet floor, with a beard and mustache looking much like other officers I had seen. But he was different. He was the tsar and could do anything. He could even buy everything in all of the stores. I liked to play a pretend game—if I were the tsar, what would I buy? First of all, I would buy a fur coat, then I would pick out the biggest doll on sale at Kolpakchi's, the best toy store in Odessa. She could open and close her eyes, and she wore a blue silk dress with lace. She had bloomers, a slip with lace frills, and white kidskin slippers. When mama and I passed by the store, I could not bear to leave the window where the doll stood. Mama said that she cost five rubles, which for us was a lot of money.

But then, a miracle happened. My mother's wealthy cousin, Aunt Sasha, bought me this very doll for my birthday. I immediately named her Daisy and hugged her tight, breathing in the sweet smell of her splendid golden curls. But as soon as Aunt Sasha left, mama took Daisy and locked her in her wardrobe. Mama said that this was a very expensive doll, and I could only play with it when she was there. Now our guests were coming and the doll might get broken or dirty. This was my first great sorrow. My beloved doll Daisy had been taken away from me. The children arrived with their mothers, bringing me gifts of books and dishes. Edia presented me with a stove that had a real oven, but I did not care. I kept looking at my mother's wardrobe—there in the darkness my beautiful Daisy lay sleeping, and I was not allowed to touch her. This torture lasted for nearly a year. I rarely got to play with her, for mama was not at home much. When I did get to hold Daisy in my arms, I trembled, for she seemed an exotic treasure I did not deserve. I did not even play with her but just stroked her curls, her blue bow, and her white shoes. After a year, mama decided that I could finally be trusted with this treasure and even presented me with a bed for Daisy. Three years later my brother Sasha broke her out of spite, but by that time I was no longer playing with dolls.

Terror struck our home in the form of a word I had never heard before—pogrom.[6] One day papa rushed home from work earlier than usual. He was pale and his lips were trembling. "They are smashing up Arnautskaia and Bazarnaia Streets and will soon get to Remeslennaia," he said gasping for breath. This meant they were heading our way. Mama stood there as if frozen, then she grabbed her head and began to rock back and forth. Suddenly the bell rang. It was the elderly lady Shpringer, proprietress of our building. She stood there silently for several seconds. "Do not worry," she said. "They will not dare come into our building. I will make sure of that. Ignat and my nephew will stand guard at the entrance with icons." Almost all of the residents in our building were Jewish. The Shpringer sisters went to each of them to reassure them and entreat them to stay indoors. I saw through the window that Ignat, his wife and Dëmka took all of their icons out to the street. Ignat used a large hammer to drive nails into the wooden gates and then hung the icons to signify that Orthodox Christians lived in this building. Our nanny took out from her bed a small icon with a pink ribbon and hung it out through the dining room window. My father and several neighbors stood guard on the staircase. Papa armed himself with a bronze pestle from the mortar we used to crush rusks and almonds. Mama did not go to bed but stayed near us, completely dressed and shuddering every time she heard steps. We did not turn on the lamp but used only a small night light with a round pale-green cap that reminded me of an unripe apple.

While standing guard, papa heard the latest news and came to reassure mama that self-defense squads were already in action all over the city.[7] Later, though, porters arrived from neighboring streets and told Ignat, who then told papa, that the pogromists were throwing small children out from the windows of three-storey buildings, ripping open the bellies of pregnant women, and destroying personal possessions. My terrified father rushed to share this with mama, unaware that we were not asleep and so heard his frightening account. The pogrom lasted for several days. Mama did not let Grisha go to school, but papa went to work, for truthfully, he did not look Jewish. He was tall and stoutly built with a light beard and many said he resembled a Volga German. Nonetheless he did run into trouble. While returning home one day, two "hooligans" assaulted him. I had never heard this word "hooligan" before, and for many years after the pogrom, Odessans used this term to designate anti-Semites. They would say, for example, that this was a hooligan school, a hooligan newspaper, or that this professor is a hooligan because he fails Jews on exams. People even labeled stores as hooligan where Jewish customers received less attention from salespersons. So, my father was stopped by two drunken hooligans, who grabbed him by the coat and asked: "Are you a Yid or a Russian?" Instead of an answer my father let them have his fist. He knocked first one then the other in the teeth. The drunks fell down and papa, trembling all over, ran home with his right hand terribly swollen. All of our relatives and friends came to know of this feat, for papa went about for a long time with his hand bandaged and considered himself quite a hero.

When the pogrom finally died out, and it was possible to go outside safely, mama took us to the park. We walked up Uspenskaia Street and saw buildings with broken windows. Everywhere there were small clusters of people standing about talking with the porters about which victims were thrown from which windows and about how many elderly were murdered. In one building they had butchered Fania, a dressmaker who sometimes had come to sew for us; the pogromists had also murdered her mother. This was very upsetting to me. I had adored the dressmaker, for she was quiet and affectionate. Friends came over, drank tea, argued, and put all of the blame for it on Kaul'bars,[8] the Odessa governor-general. Our Sasha recited with expression verses that were circulating through Odessa. I only recall the first lines:

The fierce and savage leopard (bars) lives in the forest,
But the one known as Kaul'bars dwells in Odessa.

Everyone showered praise on Sasha and kissed him, telling mama what a brilliant son she had.

The very first time we went to a dacha for the summer it was in Lustdorf.[9] Before this I knew little of the sea. I had only seen it through the lattice walls of the old Turkish fortress in Alexander Park. In the port itself the sea was dirty, garbage floated in it along with watermelon rinds, and it all smelled strongly of tar. There were beautiful beaches in Odessa, such as Lanzheron, Small Fountain, and others, but they were far away and expensive. So, until I was 6 years old, I had not seen nor heard up close the real sea and its surf. But oh, here in Lustdorf it cast such a spell on me. I had started reading at the age of 5, and I knew many stories about the sea; I had seen the sea depicted in many pictures. But none of this could even begin to compare with the enormous swells and roaring surf along the length of our vast beach, and the sound of the tide rolling in and back out again. Our dacha was located in the steppe rather than close to the beach. Mama's lungs were weak and she considered the sea air to be harmful for her. Our dacha neighbors would take me down to the sea, though not all that often. But each time we went it was like a holiday to me. Mama would not allow me to swim. I had to just sit on the hot sand, so finely grained, and admire the sea, listen to it. Sometimes, when the sea was calm, I was allowed to go up to the water's edge and gather sea shells on the beach.

Gradually I grew accustomed to the sea, and it became as familiar to me as Uspenskaia Street. I thought at the time that we would be returning to the sea every summer, but things did not work out that way. My father's affairs changed, he took a different job, and we had to pay a lot for Grisha to attend the gymnasium, so money was scarce. We moved to a different apartment, this time on Remeslennaia Street. Mama began teaching me music. I now had to play scales every day along with the exercises of Hanon.[10] I found it unbearably boring.

Our nanny returned to her family in the countryside. Mama sought to hire a new "all-purpose maid" through the "*faktorsha*," a woman who for fifty kopeks would search for a suitable candidate. The woman visited us wearing a bright satin dress and assured mama that she had a girl of such quality that even "Countess Platovskaia" herself would hire her if she lived here in Odessa. Where this countess actually lived, or whether she even existed, was not important; the name itself was synonymous with the height of luxury, nobility, and exactness. One who was hired through this process was Polia, who worked for us for quite a long time. Her husband was a stoker on a vessel in the merchant marine and went away on long voyages. When he was in Odessa, he was allowed to sleep with Polia on the mezzanine level. His name was Phillip, and he was tall, handsome, and strong. My brothers worshipped him. Polia was coarse in her manners but did everything that mama wanted her to do. This made mama willing to put up with her grumbling, especially since she did so in her native Ukrainian, which amused mama. But after two voyages Phillip secured a position as stoker for one of the Odessa bathhouses (*banya*) and was allowed to live in one of the back rooms there, so he took Polia from us. After Polia, the "all-purpose maids" we hired changed quite often, for mama was demanding and fastidious.

The time came for Sasha to enter the preparatory class. My parents decided to send Sasha to the public secondary school, the tuition for which was significantly lower than for the private gymnasia. But this school had a quota and would not accept more than two to three Jewish boys to each year's class. Mama counted on Sasha's talent for reading poetry and, indeed, on his charm. And, he did get accepted, even ahead of wealthy boys whose parents had "such important connections ..." But in class Sasha behaved worse than anyone else: he was disruptive, acting as the class clown, and mimicked the teacher and even the head of school. They warned mama that such behavior would not be tolerated within the walls of the institution. Papa twice whipped Sasha with a belt. He bawled and promised to behave better, but after several days he forgot everything he had promised. It was easy for Sasha to learn. He could read and write at an advanced level, he knew his multiplication tables, and he could recite more verses and fables than were required. But he was expelled from the school even before the end of the school year. Mama cried and papa scolded her: "Look at what your precious darling has done …" They decided to start him in the first class at the real school and hired a tutor. He easily got in there. He made it through the first year and advanced to the second class, but was then expelled for a prank. Sasha was not allowed to enroll in any school after this.

I, on the other hand, could not wait to start school, for I was bored. Everyone I knew was already in school but mama had decided to keep me home until I was old enough for the third class. She said that I could be exposed to "bad influences." But the main reason was that we could not afford the tuition. So, before dinner I would often be alone with our "all-purpose maid." Several of them were very good girls. They told me about their village and their family. I especially loved hearing about the forests. Around Odessa there was only the steppe, so I knew about forests only from books. I also amused myself by going out on the balcony whenever an organ grinder came into the courtyard. Some had a parrot on their shoulder that would pull out a "good fortune" from a hat, a piece of paper rolled up inside a tube with a prediction written on it, costing three kopeks. Others brought boy acrobats or wives with mandolins and tambourines. One organ grinder had a girl about 13 years of age. She moved even our maid to tears when she sang with anguish in her voice, "My mother loved me, respected me as a beloved daughter, but that daughter ran off one rainy fall evening with her sweetheart."[11] She also sang the popular song "Marusia poisoned herself, the ambulance took her away to the hospital."[12] But I preferred real concert music to street performers, which I considered to be more a spectacle than an art form. The organ grinder was always trying to induce people to throw more money. If there was a lag he would order the girl to sing again, and although turning blue from the strain, she would sing at the top of her voice "You are parted from me, parted, you are on the other side, no one can separate us but Mother Earth." It was, however, only rarely that I watched such events from the balcony. Mostly I read a lot and played about two hours of piano each day.

During the summers when we could not go to a dacha, we would go for walks in Alexander Park. There, not far from the apple tree planted by Tsar Alexander II, was an enormous flower garden, surrounded by a wide gravel pathway. My brothers would quickly round up other boys who were there to play "cops and robbers." The girls would gather more slowly and carefully, and then we formed two ranks. After clasping arms, one line would stomp their feet and move toward the other, singing energetically, "We have sown, we have sown the millet, we sowed, Oi Did-Lado, we have sown, we have sown!"[13] The song was long, and we would sing it all the way to the end, with its tempo constantly speeding up and with our stomping growing more and more frenzied until our faces burned. Worn out from our galloping, we formed a circle, and one of the girls would get in the middle while everyone sang plaintively, slowly rocking back and forth: "Tell us, my dear, tell us, golden one, how, how, how do you sow?" Last was the game "The Golden Gates," with these tender words: "I am an orphan of God, I will open the gate with a key-locket and my silk handkerchief." We played as if intoxicated, enraptured by our games, but we scattered whenever "Baron Lipse" appeared. Although he was not aggressive, I was still more afraid of him than of the other Odessan "eccentrics." His bald bare skull was the color of chocolate from being sunburnt, and he draped an old blanket over his stooping back. He walked slowly, holding in his hand a packet of notepaper with writing on it. He would stop where people were sitting, stare right at them, and thrust his "letters" with illegible writing on them into their hands. He would not go away until you gave him money, even if it was just a kopek. He would also walk among the well-dressed crowds on Deribasovskaia Street. What frightened me was his sullen, penetrating stare.

I was 10 years old when Dunia came to work for us. She was agile, fast, and dressed fashionably. Maybe she sought revenge on mama for her frequent nagging or maybe she derived some pleasure from our conversations, but it was she who revealed to me all the secrets of sexual relations. I had already asked mama where children came from; mama had gotten angry and said I was too young to be asking such questions. Grisha brought information on this from his school, and he and Sasha whispered together, sniggering and looking at me in a strange way. This was still the time when my Daisy lived in mama's wardrobe. Sasha, taking advantage of a moment when it was only the two of us at home, said that he could make me a live doll if I would undress. "You want me to take off everything, really?" I asked. "Everything," Sasha answered. While I was starting to take off my clothes, mama came home. She asked me why I was undressing in the daytime, and I explained. Sasha got a whipping. My bed was promptly moved away from the boys, and my brothers began calling me a "tattletale." It was after this that Dunia put everything into place for me. I found it all frightening but terribly interesting. "Does this mean that papa and mama also do it?" I asked. "Of course," Dunia answered with a laugh.

A wealthy family lived on the floor below us and I made friends with their daughter Tsilia, who was already in school. After dinner we played hide and seek outside with other girls. After Dunia had talked with me, I took Tsilia aside and shared with her my shocking insights. She laughed and said that she had known this for a long time, but proper girls did not talk about such matters. That evening her mother came over when I was already in the bath. She talked quietly with mama in the dining room. Papa was not at home. Then mama, looking very agitated and flushed in the face, came to me and said: "You are no longer allowed to play with Tsilia, you are a spoiled little girl, you told her filthy things. Do you realize what position you have put me in, where on earth did you get all this from?" I told her that I heard it outside in the courtyard. I felt betrayed. I declared that I did not say anything dirty, but had only talked about how babies are born. At this point mama decided to offer me half-truths in hopes of distracting me. She explained, "When a girl marries, then a baby begins to grow in her tummy, and by the end of the ninth month the skin on it has become so thin, well, it is like dough that has been stretched out, that all the midwife has to do is to cut it with scissors and pull out the baby. You probably have noticed that the midwife always has scissors in her bag." I did not trust these last words, but I knew now that I had to play along. I hung my head and said I understood and that I would not speak to Tsilia nor play with her. I believed Dunia, though, not mama. I started to feel disgust toward my own parents. Mama had said that what I had told Tsilia was filthy. But she and papa were doing it. This made both of them seem nasty to me, and I felt alienated. In the end, Dunia was dismissed. Mama did not ask me about it again but she had figured out who had enlightened me on the subject of sex.

All of these disturbing yet intriguing conjectures were soon erased, engulfed even by a real upheaval—my first encounter with death ... Yes, I knew that people die; I remembered the horrors of the pogrom and its atrocities. I had read obituaries about the death of an "unforgettable" father or mother, and so on. I had seen parade-like funeral processions going through the streets. But none of this had directly involved me. Now, however, for the first time in my life I came face to face with a dead person, and I attended a funeral of someone related to me. I saw my grandmother, my father's mother, lain in her grave. Out of all my father's relatives, my mother loved only one person, his mother. She spoke very little Russian, but she was so friendly, kind, and gentle that you could understand her immediately even without words. Grandfather, though, was a scary old man, especially when he was praying. He would throw a prayer shawl over his shoulder—a cream-colored cape with black stripes—and pray plaintively while swaying over burning candles. He did this in his own room, but for some reason he would not close the door and you could see everything. He was tall, severe in manner, and his angry, penetrating eyes quickly bore into us when we came to visit grandmother. He never greeted us, but either kept praying or left the house immediately. Grandmother had been paralyzed for two years and all she could do was drag her right arm along the wall, leaving a dark semicircle on the wallpaper. Besides us, her daughters visited her, my Aunt Nina and Aunt Tanya. The latter was very industrious and diligent, and would wash and dress her mother plus prepare food for her. But Aunt Nina came only rarely and would only bring a few small apples that were sometimes rotten. Papa seldom visited his mother, for he disliked his father, whom he knew had a second family on the side. Grandfather abhorred my mother because of her "apostasy"—she did not keep a kosher kitchen.

Mama took us to the funeral. First we went to my grandmother's apartment on Malaia Arnautskaia Street, where an enormous black box stood near the entrance door, which mama explained was the coffin. The door was open, and in the first room, where my grandmother's bed stood, a large figure lay on the floor, rolled up tightly in black calico. The bed was empty. I asked mama in a whisper, "Where is grandmother?" Mama bent down over the black figure and began to cry. I then realized that this was my grandmother. Aunt Tanya's son, my older adult cousin Misha, whispered to me that until they put my grandmother into the coffin, you could hear what her spirit was saying about the other world. If you lay down and put your ear to the floor, then you could find out everything, even when you yourself would die. He started to push me down toward grandmother's legs. I began to cry, and mama held me to calm me down, for she thought that I was upset over grandmother as did everyone else, who all looked approvingly at me. Just then a black hearse entered the courtyard. Men dressed in black carried in the coffin and then two women, after ushering us out, unrolled the body and placed it in the coffin, with no onlookers. As they carried the coffin into the courtyard, my aunts began to wail and lament; we went out last, and as I looked back, I saw that all that remained of my grandmother was the dark semicircle on the wall by her bed.

In the courtyard my aunts threw themselves on the coffin and began to pound furiously on the lid with their fists, calling for their mother. This scared me, though I noticed that Aunt Nina was looking out of one eye, trying to see if the neighbors were noticing how she was such a devoted daughter. We went by carriage to the Jewish cemetery located far away on the "Chumka" hill (The Plague Hill).[14] It frightened me when they placed grandmother's coffin into the ground and shoveled the dirt in, which made a rattling sound. This was my first time in a cemetery; it was a city of the dead, Sasha whispered to me. It really seemed like it, with its street-like alleyways, but instead of homes there were tombstones. Fear haunted me for a long time, and at home, especially in the evenings, I saw in every corner my grandmother swaddled in black, gradually disappearing into a hole.

At home my father cried, laid his head on mama's shoulder and sobbed "I no longer have a mother …" Mama declared that as the only son, he had to sit "Shiva";[15] his father would never forgive him if he did not. Mama at least knew all of the rules even if she did not follow them herself. They placed a small bench in the corner of the dining room and covered it with a Caucasian rug. Papa had to take off his boots and sit in this corner for a week. He was heavy and stout, so mama thought he would be more comfortable sitting on the bench than on the floor, which was the custom. Misha dropped by the very next day, probably, according to mama, so he could verify to grandfather that his son was sitting Shiva. Papa, though, found it boring and spent the whole day eating because he had nothing else to do. Inactivity made him feel weak, as if he were coming down with an illness. He kept bothering mother to give him something, "anything," to help fortify him. All of his food had to be served to him in this corner, for he was not even allowed to sit at the dining table. All of this caused havoc in the household, particularly the fact that bread, butter, and other foods were running out at an alarming rate. So on the third day mama announced, since papa was not religious, he had sat "Shiva" long enough to honor the memory of his mother and it was time for him to go back to work. My father happily agreed and everything in the household went back to normal. A fear of death, however, stayed with me for a long time. The dead instilled in me an indescribable horror. I had to turn my head away if we passed by a funeral parlor, and if I had to attend the funerals of relatives or close friends, their frozen faces and the smell of decay, which no amount of flowers could cover up, would remain fixed in my memory, especially in the evenings and during the still of the night. I was too embarrassed to admit this to anyone, but I was traumatized.

Not long after this, summer came and we were able to go to a dacha, this time one in the area of Big Fountain, at the sixteenth station. Although papa's affairs had improved, it was beyond our means both to rent a dacha and pay for a city apartment. So we moved out of the apartment and transported all of our furniture, crockery, winter clothing, and so on to the dacha. We hired wagons for the move. Motia, our new maid, sat in one and had to hold on to wobbly bundles the whole way. At our dacha there were many girls whom I knew, all of them older than me. We all went swimming together and had daring conversations. These quite proper girls knew more than even Dunia had been willing to tell me. They especially liked to talk about prostitutes and had read Alexander Kuprin's novel on this theme, *Yama* (The Pit).[16] They bragged about knowing on what street corners such women frequented. I knew now that I needed to pretend that I was hearing all of this for the first time and that I should not show particular interest. But I listened greedily and remembered everything.

Our dacha was owned by a Pole, an officer and landowner by the name of Shabel'skii. He was friends with the writer Kuprin, who was staying not far from us at the luxurious dacha of Alexander Fedorov,[17] also a writer, along with many visitors from St. Petersburg. They would often gather at Shabel'skii's two-storied dacha to carouse. Shabel'skii and his elderly aunt, from whom I took music lessons, lived above us on the second floor. One time the partying went on through the entire night, with tremendous clatter, lots of singing and shouting, and the din of falling chairs. Papa was away on business and mama declared that it was "quite alarming to have to live under such conditions." The landlord's aunt gave us her word that such antics would not happen again. We occupied two rooms with a large terrace covered in wild grapes. The kitchen was separated from the terrace by a large barn, where the landlord kept a carriage. Now instead of nightly drinking bouts there were daily binges in the barn. Shabel'skii's man-servant dragged boxes of wine and beer there, and then the landlord would arrive with Kuprin and two or three other drinking buddies. They would seal the enormous barn doors and drink in the semidarkness. Once when we were dining on the terrace, the doors of the barn opened slightly and someone stuck his head out and said, "Something smells tasty." Motia the maid approached with a dish of stuffed squash in her hands. The doors opened wider and then someone reached out and grabbed her along with the dish. Motia squealed but the barn doors slammed shut. We saw all this happen through the branches of the grape vine. Mama turned red, the boys laughed into their napkins, and I declared naively, "They must be very hungry." So on that day we did not get to eat our beloved squash with tomato sauce. Motia ran out after several minutes angry and disheveled, and she threw herself at mama, crying out for the entire dacha to hear "What sort of officers are these, they are nothing but tramps; I am a decent girl and I will not stay here!"

The summer came to an end. Grisha had to start school soon and so mama had to start looking for a new apartment. She would be gone the entire day; the boys got to stay at the dacha but I had to go with her. It was torturous walking up and down hot streets. Finally on the third day mama signed the papers to rent an apartment on Koblevskaia Street, not far from the New Bazaar. This was a new district. Earlier we had lived in the area of the Old Bazaar, densely populated with Jews, but here the people were predominantly Russian. This apartment was near to Grisha's school and to the school I would attend the following year. But that fall mama was often ill. She coughed a lot and had to stop giving music lessons. We spent a lot of money on doctors, who prescribed for her a high-calorie diet. She often suffered from hemoptysis, which meant she would spit up blood. No one wanted to utter the word "*chakhotka*" (consumption), so they would say that she had weak lungs. Papa was again out of work. He was a good employee, honest and conscientious, but he was hot-tempered and did not always get along well with his bosses. So there were periods in which we could not afford servants, and I would dust and do the sweeping. When she was able, mama cooked the meals and I washed the dishes. Floors were now cleaned weekly, not daily, and once a month the laundress Kazimira came to do a big washing. I often had to go to the New Bazaar to buy what we needed. Our limited means meant I had to shop around for what was cheapest. I would walk slowly down the rows where they sold kosher poultry. Mama bought red meat only from Russian butchers, but she insisted on buying chicken from the Jewish market women; perhaps this was because they would sell chicken parts separately such as giblets, legs, and chicken quarters, based on how much money you had. Russian poultry sellers would not cut up the chickens.

Generally speaking, my mother's extreme fastidiousness regarding food made it difficult to please her. I kept that in mind while walking along the marble tables piled high with mountains of amber chicken fat. The market women pulled out chicken gizzards and livers and tossed them onto the blood-stained marble tops, loudly squabbling with neighbors all the while. I was like a hunter, trying to track down who had more chicken livers or who would sell me fifteen to twenty pieces at the cheapest price. On meager days our dinner was meatless borscht and omelette with chicken livers and onion. Shopping for cheap tomatoes for the borscht was more pleasant, because there was no smell of fat, blood, or intestines, and you were under an open sky. There were stacks of blue eggplant, heaps of red peppers, baskets of cheerful, light green cucumbers, and entire walls made from corncobs. And all of this smelled heavenly. After inspecting a mountain of huge tomatoes and pointing out to the seller that there were some already spoiled, I received the entire stack for a penny. Then I bought eggplant, onions, parsley, as well as other items, and returned home in triumph with an impressive amount of change from the thirty kopeks I had been given. My relationship with my mother was evolving. There was a certain equality between us, as we were both trying to cope with difficult circumstances. Although we never said this in words, we knew that our men neither understood nor valued our efforts.

Now a teacher began coming three times a week to our home to prepare me to enter the third class at the girl's gymnasium. Learning was easy for me. I was an avid reader and from the age of 6 had memorized the multiplication table just from listening as my brothers crammed for lessons. I mastered arithmetic functions without anyone noticing and played division games with Sasha. Mama's health began to improve, and we were again listening to Chopin and Mendelssohn. But then one day Grisha came home early from school after being told he was to stay at home until he could bring in the payment for the second semester. The building manager kept reminding us that we had not paid rent for two months. Papa searched for work all over Odessa, but came up with nothing. So he decided that we had to sell the piano. He assured mama that as soon as things got better they would buy a new piano or at least rent one. Mama refused until the manager threatened to call the police if he did not receive the rent money in three days. So the piano was sold, and Grisha was able to return to school. The dining room seemed sad and empty, but all of our debts were paid.

My music lessons had ended, but now Madam Mandro stepped in to fill the void. She was an elderly French woman who had long ago taught French to mama and her sister. Mama ran into her by chance and proposed that she come and do lessons with me three times a week in exchange for lunch. Madam Mandro was indigent and readily agreed. Now I was very busy with a teacher coming three times a week to give lessons in all subjects and the remaining days there was Madam Mandro. I was now 11, and I did not yet have friends. I kept a diary and poured out all of my sorrows into it: my parents' unhappy relationship, our financial situation, mama's illness and her having to live without music. A rotten thing happened, however. Sasha opened my diary and transcribed it all into verse, which he recited at dinner with angelic expression. This angered me; it was an act of treachery. I destroyed the diary and did not speak to Sasha for a long time.

Sasha now became an even greater problem for my parents. They tried to hire teachers to tutor him, but no one could cope with his antics, playing the fool and neglecting his lessons. At the age of 12, he began hanging out backstage at the nearby Sibiriakov Dramatic Theater.[18] Mama tried to keep him at home, even pulling off his pants and hiding them when he tried to leave, or on cold days locking his coat in her wardrobe. But this did not deter him. He ran off without his coat, and if the weather was warm, he went out donned in his underwear, with mama's old silk scarves draped over him and long johns hiked up above his knees. Then an accident happened. One day mama had to go to see her friend Margarita Genrikhovna and left us at home. As she left, mama locked Sasha's pants and his shirt in her cupboard. She ordered Grisha to keep the front entry key with him and not let Sasha use it. Sasha could not stand to be treated like this. Grisha locked himself in the bathroom with the key and drew a bath. We lived on the third floor, and the window of our kitchen opened up to a very narrow pier; next to it was a taller building. Sasha threw on mama's scarf, took a stepladder and placed it on the window sill, with the top slanted toward the wall of the neighboring building, and rested it against the cornice of the roof. The window sill in our kitchen was narrow and slightly slanted. I broke my vow of silence and shouted to my brother: "What are you thinking? You are going to fall …." "Nonsense," Sasha cried back, pleased that I was finally talking to him and that I would witness his daring and ingenuity. Without waiting for a response, he scampered to the top step. All he had to do was to grab onto the edge of the roof and pull himself up on to it. But he could not resist turning back to say to me: "I am going down the water pipe and will not come back until evening, let them know that …." This sentence disappeared along with Sasha. The stepladder slid back into the kitchen as Sasha went flying from a height of nearly four floors. The stepladder knocked me down, but then I rushed to the bathroom, banging on the door and screaming at Grisha to give me the key so I could go and call an ambulance: "Sasha fell out the window …." After a fruitless exchange of words with my hapless older brother, he finally opened the door and handed me the key. I ran to our neighbors who had a telephone. I told them what had happened and they immediately called an ambulance, at that time a carriage driven by horses. I explained where my brother had fallen from and I ran to where he lay. He looked completely gray but his eyes were open. The ambulance arrived very quickly, and the neighbors brought the doctor and the attendants to us. They put Sasha on a stretcher and took him to the hospital. I had to run and tell mother, who was at Torgovaia Street, not far from us. My face must have looked grim because mama immediately jumped up, asking, "What has happened?" We all went together to the hospital. Sasha was already in a ward, but mama was allowed one minute with him; the doctor said that he had suffered a hemorrhage in both lungs and this made it hard for him to speak.

But generally speaking, he had not broken anything and did not get a concussion. He thought it remarkable that Sasha "fell from that height and is alive."

After this the police came to our home along with a reporter from the newspaper; they looked at the broken glass, at the roof of the neighboring building, and asked how it had happened. They seemed surprised and full of doubt, not realizing that our Sasha was not like everyone else. Ten days later he was home and feeling great. After this Sasha's escapades grew even bolder. Mama stopped locking him in or undressing him. She tried to use persuasion to influence him, as well as tears. Sasha could not bear to see mama cry, and he would promise "to buckle down" and renew his studies, but it never lasted. My father accused mama of spoiling him, and she said it was his fault for failing to provide a strong masculine influence. But the troupe at the Dramatic Theater loved having Sasha backstage and gave him small errands to run while plying him with sweets. Soon he got himself into the famous Odessa Opera Theater.[19] He was an extra in crowd scenes, though Sasha lied and claimed he had been promised a main role. Mama then put Sasha into a private dramatic school, but he did not even last there very long. He was rude and composed indecent epigrams.

My older brother also brought little joy, for he was lazy and dishonest. He created a fake daily report card and got mama to sign for grades of B and A (*chetverki* and *pyaterki*). But when his quarter grades were low, mama went to school for an explanation and came back in a fury. She took Grisha by the shoulder and shook him, yelling "How dare you!" He, though, instead of repenting, blurted out, "If only you had not married papa, maybe I could have been born into a wealthy family and I would have tutors in every subject!" Now I knew how right Edia had been. At some point I had run into him on the street, and I asked him why he did not come and visit us anymore. "The reason is, he responded, is that your Grishenka is a jerk."

I, however, did well on my entrance exams for school. The seamstress sewed me a green cashmere uniform and a dark apron with wide shoulder straps and a bib that had a pocket for my student ID card. Duly attired, I started school in the third class. At first I had a hard time. I was the new girl, and all of the other girls had been together since preschool. They knew how to fit in, and each had their own special friends. For the first days they all watched me. During lunch they made a circle around me when I took out my basket and laid out the sandwiches mama had prepared for me. My lunch made a good impression and was taken as a sign that my family was well off, as did the fact that papa, who had amazing handwriting, had wrapped my new textbooks in multicolored lacquered paper adorned with calligraphy. Little did these curious, sharp-eyed girls know that mama had had to pawn her gold watch, the only item of value in our home, in order to buy my uniform, textbooks, and so on. Fortunately, the scrutiny soon ended. I earned A's, and so they started sitting with me before class or during breaks to copy my work. I did not give them my assignments directly to copy. Usually I wrote assignments for two or three girls in different ways, and then they copied the responses in their own handwriting. For this they would come home with me. Later I did this with compositions as well. It even happened once that the teacher gave me a B on my composition, but another girl, whose composition I had written, received an A. I found it funny but hurtful when that happy classmate taunted me, "You see, I write better than you." After this I no longer helped her.

I passed the third level with high marks. Papa finally got a long anticipated job working for an American company that manufactured harvesting machines. Papa was hired to be a salesman since he knew well all of the clients leasing machines in the Kherson and Podolsk regions. The pay was much better, and we were now able to rent a dacha. On the very next Sunday mama decided to go out in search of one, and wanted to take me with her. Papa pleaded with her "not to torture the child" and promised he would spend the whole day walking in the park with us. Mama relented. But papa had his own plan. He really did spend the whole day with us, though not in the park. He took us to the velodrome, behind the park. We watched the bicycle races and got to see the famous cyclist Sergei Utochkin.[20] At first the wild din deafened me, but once the races began I was captivated. "Look, look, there is Utochkin," papa pointed out with his cane the ginger-haired, pale-complexioned cyclist, who seemed to be pedaling phlegmatically, willingly allowing others to pass him. Papa urged patience but his eyes betrayed his own frustration. The velodrome had a rather steep ramp but the racers just flew around the smooth track. During the first and second laps, Utochkin rode quite leisurely, but on the last one he began to speed up and by its midpoint he was already in third. Then he screamed wildly, the leaders turned around, and he went flying down the slope with his head almost on his handlebars, his entire body extended over the frame of his bicycle. Before we knew it, he had broken through the ribbon first, decently ahead of the remaining finishers. The Odessa crowd screamed; papa yelled as well and waved his black cane up in the air. There were many heats and each time Utochkin invented a new tactic to end up unexpectedly in front of everyone. The crowd's enthusiasm peaked when Utochkin, having won all of the heats, completed the final lap without holding on to the handlebars and leaning back on the seat as if he were reclining on an invisible armchair. Papa knew the names of all the cyclists as well as interesting tidbits about Utochkin. But what was most amusing to us was the very fact that papa knew such information, which told us that he was not always at the office, especially on Sundays when he was supposedly "updating" accounts. We now knew that this was just a pretense for deceiving our mother. But we laughed and promised not to tell. Our outing ended at Emaevich's, a confectionary shop that had the best cakes in all of Odessa, and they sold them to gymnasium students for three kopeks instead of four. Grisha and I had our student ID cards, but not Sasha. But Grisha used his card to get two *trubochki* (tube-shaped pastry) with cream and gave one to Sasha. Papa ate two "napoleons" and allowed us to have a second pastry as well. Such a feast was unprecedented. Mama thought that children should never have more than one pastry treat.

This time mama found a dacha to rent in a magical spot—behind the Uspenskii Monastery, at the beginning of the road to the renowned "dacha of Kovalevskii."[21] Our dacha was newly built with a garden so young that its foliage offered no shade, but extremely close by, just across the road, was a shady walkway to the sea and a steep precipice overgrown with lilac immortelles and bear's ear (mountain cowslip) that were soft and springy. Here and there magnificent old oak trees towered over you. Although mama told me not to go very far, the very next day I ran there, and to this very day I consider the view of the sea from that precipice to be the most beautiful I have ever experienced.

Sasha insisted we walk to the monastery shore. We passed through the garden and cemetery of the Uspenskii Monastery and went on down to the beach. There, right in front of us, stood fishermen's barges, filled with nets that were strung out for drying. Sasha quickly made friends with the fishermen and they promised to take him out to sea with them. We returned along the same pathway and stopped at the church to listen to the singing. The monks noticed us. We spoke Russian fluently, our hair was straight and light in color, with Sasha being completely blond while mine was chestnut colored with golden tints. Sasha warned me that if I wanted to see the monk's cells, I could not interfere if he told a lie. So first Sasha made friends with the monastery's porter, who was also the bell ringer. Sasha begged him to let us see the bell. I almost went deaf from the thunderous boom, but I was fascinated to watch how quickly this smallish, dried-up monk sorted through the ropes while pressing simultaneously on the wooden pedals to which the ropes were attached. The bell ringer stopped and we returned down the steep spiral staircase. Then Sasha began to lie. He made our father out to be a ship captain and our mother a noblewoman. We lived in Odessa in our own private home. The monk took us to his cell with its narrow trestle bed. A dirty sack lay on it that was thinly stuffed with straw. In the corner stood a homemade altar with the Gospel sitting open, presided over by an icon and an icon-lamp.

The next time we came we brought the bell ringer several cabbage pies, which he enjoyed. He promised to tell the priest Father Afanasy about us. Curious, Father Afanasy had us come to his cell. There stood a rocking chair upholstered in red velvet and a small cupboard with bronze decorations. He pulled out a small decanter of homemade cherry liqueur and gave us some in small glasses. His bed was covered in a white pique bedspread and in the corner was an icon case, in front of which was a large icon-lamp made of garnet-colored glass hung on massive chains. He let us look at it and said that "All this has been a gift of the faithful." He was curious about our parents. He asked if he could meet our mother and wondered which service she attended, the morning or evening one. Sasha continued to lie, saying that mother was intending to make a donation to the monastery on the day our father returned safe from his voyage. We gradually made our way out of the monastery, but Sasha insisted that we not go home. He had noticed that the bell ringer was following us. After reaching the tram station, we returned home through the steppe. The monastery saw no more of us.

I spent much of this summer alone. Sasha was out for entire days with the fishermen, and we did not have any close neighbors besides the proprietor and his family. The latter was a colonel named Lesli with a haughty wife and daughter much younger than me. I would take a book and go to the sea or take long walks. I often met writers on the road: Fedorov, Kuprin, and Ivan Bunin. I recognized Kuprin immediately because he always wore a skull-cap and a bright traditional shirt known as a *kosovorotka* tied with a thin silk strap. Bunin dressed strictly in an urban style despite living in his dacha all summer long. Past Fedorov's dacha there was a marvelous shaded alleyway leading to a precipice. After running along the steep path, I would turn a little to the right and throw myself into the grass, where it was always cool under the dense shadow of an old oak. This was my special spot, where there were never any passers-by. After I finished reading, I would go down to the water, where there were many large stones. Two broad but not very tall rocky outcroppings created a swimming area for me. I floundered about as if I were between two screens, and I examined the jellyfish, which were rose-colored, blue, milk-white, and completely transparent. I even picked them up but let them go immediately for fear of being stung. I never wanted to go home for dinner, but did not have a choice. In the evenings we walked with mama between grain fields and enjoyed the sunsets, which were boundless, filling up the enormous horizon of the steppe sky. During the entire summer my father came only once and then just for a short time. This glorious summer passed by quietly and peacefully.

2

Growing Up during War and Revolution

In the fall of 1913, I entered the fourth class. Our course on ancient history fascinated me, as did the teacher Ksenia Vladimirovna who was slender and shapely, with light-colored hair. We thought she was the most beautiful of our teachers. She dutifully wore the strict teacher's navy-blue dress, but her lace collar and a small lorgnette made from carnelian beads gave her an individual flair. What really made her special, though, was that she spoke plainly and willingly answered all of our questions, no matter how embarrassing they were. I looked forward to her class as if it were a holiday and could not take my eyes off her. On other days I would hang around in the corridor near the teachers' common room during the recess in hopes of seeing her.

At home, though, Sasha's escapades caused further trouble. My textbooks along with Grisha's went missing. Small change left on the sideboard disappeared, followed by papa's good boots. Sasha had turned 16 and was spending his days wandering the streets of Odessa. The luxurious abundance displayed in stores tempted him. So he began to take things from home, flog them helter-skelter on the street, and then used the money to buy what he wanted. But even this did not satisfy him. In Theater Lane, next to the Opera Theater, where he often hung out backstage, there was a famous restaurant, Severny (Northern). We were not even allowed to mention this late-night restaurant, for mama considered it improper. It was a cabaret, and foreigners caroused there, along with Odessan dandies from rich families. Well, somehow Sasha gained entry to this restaurant. A cabaret singer by the name of Tomskaia fancied him, though she was a diva not exactly in the first bloom of her youth. Sasha composed couplets for her and began to go home with her. Mama knew nothing about this. Mama was sick much of the time with a severe cough. Then one day in the spring, when I was doing homework and mama was lying down, Sasha arrived with his arms filled with packages and wearing a brand new morning coat, striped trousers, patent leather shoes, and a bowler hat. He sat down at the table and began to lay out oysters (never before seen in our household), salmon, sturgeon fillet, and caviar; all were of the finest quality. He made several sandwiches and took them to mama. Upon seeing him in this attire, mama was upset and asked him where he had gotten these clothes. Sasha claimed that he had received an honorarium for composing verses and had decided to begin dressing like a man. Mama took him at his word and even ate some caviar, but then, refusing the oysters, she told him to take off these ridiculous items and put on his regular clothes. Sasha retorted that he had left his old stuff at the store and would never again wear such rubbish. The next day, however, a police investigator came and took Sasha away with him. A sordid tale came to light. Tomskaia claimed that she had made Sasha her personal servant, and as such had asked him to wash her rings and brooches. But he then stole one of the rings. Sasha insisted that she had given it to him as a "token of love." The coat, trousers, shoes, and hat went back to the store, and Sasha was tried in juvenile court. He chose to present his response to the judge in the form of verse. It was entered into the record of the trial, which the journalist Zhabotinskii[1] published in the newspaper, including Sasha's verses. Sasha had the audacity to go to the newspaper office and demand royalties. The court released him to mama's custody and appointed an official guardian who came every week to talk to Sasha. Sasha had no choice but to stay at home because he had thrown out his old clothes and mama refused to buy him anything new. He just lay around in his one set of underwear and accused mama of cruelty. Papa came home, and there began an endless pattern of melodramatic scenes accompanied by hysterics. Moreover, Grisha had to retake his exams, and so my parents had to hire a tutor for the entire summer. But papa's financial affairs at least allowed us to return to the same dacha as the previous summer.

Sasha's delinquency, which strained relations between my parents, and the official guardian coming weekly to our dacha—all of this was a disgrace. I felt deeply unhappy and avoided making any new friends. Thankfully, no one from my class spent the summer in this area. All I had were my books and Grisha's tutor, whose name was Vol'f Iakov. He was quiet and mild-mannered. He usually joined us on walks to watch the sunset; he was often attentive and would look at me for a long time. His dark eyes showed sympathy, as if he understood my situation. Sometimes he started up conversations about how a person must not live solely in the narrow world of his or her own experiences. There is a bigger world and bigger matters out there. This was new and interesting to me. I now looked forward to our evening tea, after which Vol'f would take us for a walk.

I regularly headed to my favorite old oak tree and to my stones and rocky outcroppings on the deserted beach. There I hid books that mama did not allow me to read. On one sultry day I took out from my hiding place *Anna Karenina* and lay down beneath the tree to read. I was so engrossed in my reading that I lost track of the time. I realized I would be late for dinner and set off in a hurry. The path was steep and hilly, and I was hot. My mouth felt parched. Halfway to the rise, the cliff hung out like a half circle over the sea and here there were many bushes of yellow acacia. From a distance I noticed a white sheet hung over the bushes like a tent. Under it were sitting two young ladies wearing light-colored dresses and two men whose jackets were lying on the bushes. On the grass was a tablecloth spread with all kinds of food. All I could think was "how can you have a picnic in this heat?" One of the men was playing quietly on his guitar while the other got up and blocked my path. "Where have you come from, my lovely child? You must come and dine!" I was a little taken aback. It was a Caucasian accent. The women were laughing, but they nonetheless felt sorry for me and entreated him to get me something to drink, "don't you see she is feeling the heat!" The other man abandoned his guitar, went down to the sea, and brought back a bottle.

He poured almost an entire glass and gave it to me. The water tasted sour and I figured they had poured vinegar into it. They let me pass, but after several steps I felt a strange sense of lightness; I realized that I had drunk white wine! I had never before drunk wine because my family did not keep it in the house.

What was I to do—I could not go home drunk! I went down to the beach, splashed water on my head and washed my face. I felt better. At home, though, no one paid me the slightest attention. Mama did not even ask me why I had not come home for dinner. She was sitting on the veranda just staring in front of her. Vol'f Iakov was packing his suitcase in the boys' room. Sasha was wearing one of Grisha's suits. I asked what had happened. Grisha answered, "War. Mobilization." Vol'f and Sasha came out to the veranda to say goodbye. I asked why Sasha was leaving, and he said he was volunteering. I flung myself at mama, but she just said, "It is the only answer. Either he becomes a man, or ..." Sasha ran to the wicker gate, followed by Vol'f and Grisha. Mama did not cry, but only moaned quietly. I stayed with her. Grisha came back looking morose. He envied Sasha. "I would have gone as well, if it were not for school and my exams." But I did not believe this. I knew Grisha was a coward.

After several days Sasha came back in his uniform to say goodbye. Fully immersed in his new role, he acted as if he were an experienced warrior. The next day we all went to see him off. There was a throng of people at the station. The soldiers had already loaded onto the freight cars, and their wives, mothers, and children were all crying out at once. We went along the train and finally saw our Sasha, who smiled cheerily, winked at me, and shook his fists. The horns and whistles sounded and the train started to move. The cheerful expression suddenly vanished from my brother's face. He looked pale and on the verge of tears.

It was only that fall when I began the fifth class that I made a real friend, and her name was Ania. This friendship lasted until my departure from Odessa. And even longer ... *But is it worth it to race ahead in time? In a general sense, I will need both to rush forward and to look back, if this attempt at laying out my colorful life is to be successful. I am now 75 years of age, and the task before me is large and laborious. I hope that I have the time and the strength for it. Maybe, I should begin at the end? No, I do not think so. Let my story swim with the current, just as I myself plowed through these three-fourths of our incredible twentieth century.*

So, Ania. We had much in common. Both of us strove to make A's and we shared a love for literature and history. Ania knew German better than me, but I read French more fluently. We lived in the same district and often came home from school together. Ania lived in a beautiful building on Khersonskaia Street. Her family was wealthy and owned a paint and varnish factory; her mother ran the enterprise, for her father was already dead. Their apartment had seven rooms, expensive furniture, and dazzling starched table linen. You were met at the door by a chambermaid in a lace head dress and starched apron. Such luxuries neither surprised nor intimidated me, for I had wealthy relatives. But what did surprise and at first intimidated me was the intellectual atmosphere of their home. Ania's aunt, a physician, lived in the same apartment along with her husband, who was a public figure and a journalist for the newspaper *Odessa Sheet (Odesskii Listok)*. At mealtime there were always substantive conversations about literature, world events, the theater, and so on. Ania and her brother, who was two years younger and a student at the gymnasium, participated on an equal status in these and heatedly debated with their uncle, aunt, and even their mother. This marked a turning point in my life. I began spending all of my free time with Ania. I would not dine with them, though I sometimes did on Sundays if we went together to the theater.

Ania was a strange girl. She was very talented and met quickly any challenge she faced. In front of the class she answered questions in all subjects honestly, but somehow too slowly and deliberately. There was a touching awkwardness about her; she walked with her body bent forward as if she wanted to lift up something from the ground. But her face was perfect. We had endless conversations about everything under the sun, including out dream to go to St. Petersburg and enroll in the Bestuzhev courses.[2] In this way, I began experiencing a completely different life, and I was almost never at home. This went on year after year. Ania's brother was very well-read, witty, and good-natured. We went together to the Illusion, which is what we called the cinema in Odessa at this time. I watched with avid excitement actors such as Vera Kholodnaia,[3] Natalia Lisenko,[4] Ivan Mozzhukhin,[5] Ol'ga Gzovskaia,[6] Vladimir Maksimov,[7] and Vitol'd Polonskii.[8] My earlier revulsion at the thought of physical love dissipated. On the screen beautiful women in fabulously extravagant attire kissed amid flowers, in luxurious boudoirs, in a fairy tale-like garden under the moon, or on the shore of the sea with equally beautiful men who were irresistibly in love. With eyes open wide and long eyelashes fluttering, Vera Kholodnaia would fall as if dying into the embrace of Maksimov or Runich.[9] It seemed to me that nothing on earth was more beautiful. A ballroom pianist, bouncing on his chair, would play *Ochi chernye* (Dark Eyes) at a furious tempo, and my heart would pound in my temples and in my ears. I worried that right then and there the lights would come on in the hall and everyone would see how agitated I was with my face all aglow. The lights frequently came on because the film was forever tearing.

I began to dream about the movies. Ania would listen to me and just smile enigmatically. I had often been told that as I got older, I was looking more and more like my mother. I recall a strange incident that occurred. Ania and I were sitting on the boulevard, and across from us there was an elderly lady on a bench who was reading but kept looking up at me. Then she stood up, placed her book into her large handbag, and came over to ask: "Are you the daughter of Mani Shvarts?" Shvarts was my mother's maiden name. This surprised me, and when I asked her how she knew, she said: "I knew your mother when she was a young girl, and you have her same face. We lived in neighboring buildings in Nikolaev. I was always very fond of your mother." Then the lady left without telling me her name. When I told mama about this, she was pleased, though she pointed out that my nose was much less attractive, but that I had nicer hair. My hair was a great source of pride for my mother. She took care of it and would wash it only with egg yolk, for she considered soap to be too harsh. With light movements of her fingers, mama massaged the egg yolks into my hair until they foamed. She rinsed it with vinegar, and all this made my hair lustrous and silky. My two thick braids went down all the way to my knees. No one in our school had braids such as mine. From all sides I kept hearing over and over again that I had the right looks, and that I resembled Francesca Bertini[10] and even Lisenko a little. All this made my head spin. Without even knowing whether or not I had any dramatic talents, I began dreaming about success, fame, travel, and seeing myself up on the screen. But, when I returned home to our rather wretched apartment and hung up the one dress I owned other than my school uniform (it was forbidden to wear your uniform to the cinema), I would come to my senses: where would I get even one-tenth of the fur coats and shawls and ballroom dresses which Vera Kholodnaia changed in and out of in every picture? So, I continued to study hard and to tutor first-level pupils, and I spent all of my free time at Ania's.

The birthdays of Ania and her brother were magnificent occasions and introduced me to new friends. Elegant mothers brought their sons and daughters, all from wealthy families of physicians, lawyers, and bankers. The daughters were pretentious and flirty; they looked down condescendingly at my cherry-colored blouse with its chenille bows. The boys, though, were mature and smart, always spouting quotations from Immanuel Kant, Arthur Schopenhauer, and Friedrich Nietzsche. Big Boris stood out in particular—he knew everything, had read everything, and talked about everything authoritatively. Ania would listen to him with her mouth open. His friend Little Boris was no less educated but was more modest and quiet. He did not say a lot, but when he did speak it was profound. He was the son of a well-known lawyer, and they lived not far from our apartment. We often ran into each other in the neighborhood but we just said hello to each other. Big Boris, though, got into the habit of coming to see me and we would have long conversations in my room. (During my last two years at school I enjoyed having my own separate room, small and dimly lit though it was.) He spoke so loudly and incessantly that my mother had no worries about his intentions. Boris would bring me the works of new poets. Thanks to him I had slim volumes of Konstantin Bal'mont,[11] Alexander Blok,[12] Igor Severianin,[13] R. Tagore,[14] and even *Thus Spoke Zarathustra* by Nietzsche. Boris was not good looking; his face was covered in pimples, and he was lanky and awkward. Nothing besides his mind was attractive to me. Our relationship was built solely around all of these books.

Meanwhile the world war continued. In Odessa we were not really touched by it except for one alarming night when the city awoke to the distant sound of Turkish cannon fire. You encountered many soldiers on the streets, and sometimes you saw the wounded on crutches. In school we picked lint from old sheets brought from home. Our class put on a concert in a field hospital with poetry recitation and choral singing. My hair even had a role to play. I was draped in white muslin and made to lie on a tall bench with my hair let down so that it touched the floor. One of the girls, dressed in her brother's velvet suit and wearing a hat with a feather, stood at my feet with one knee bent and arms extended. All of this was depicting a scene from Pushkin's fairy tale "The Sleeping Tsarevna," while behind the scenes a teacher read aloud the corresponding lines. Other vignettes had patriotic themes.

In truth, Odessa was booming. Many people were coming here from Moscow and St. Petersburg. Fashions were changing. Dresses grew shorter. Taffeta became particularly stylish. At the heart of the city, at the City Garden in Cathedral Square, but especially on the corner of Deribasovskaia and Ekaterinskaia Streets, the flower girls displayed in their enormous enameled basins bundles of roses and carnations; alongside in tall clay jugs were lilies and tuberoses. A thick, rather intoxicating aroma rose from this cornucopia of flowers. Many women strolled along the boulevard carrying in the crook of their arm a large bouquet of roses or lilies, just like what Vera Kholodnaia did on the movie screen.

The terraces of the two best cafes in Odessa, the Robina and the Fanconi, exuding their sumptuous aromas of coffee, cakes, and almond buns, were always overflowing with people. At Fanconi's the wealthy strollers occupied only the left side of the terrace while on the right were the wheelers and dealers. Sometimes when I was out walking with Ania, I would see my father there. He was out of work again and it was forbidden to travel to border towns, so he was trying his hand at various commercial exchanges going on in the city. The older and more experienced brokers brushed him off but he somehow succeeded in pulling out something for himself at least some of the time. At home we alternated between periods of absolutely no money and weeks of abundance. When he had secured a favorable deal, my beaming papa came home literally covered in parcels of the most tasty items imaginable. There would be packages hanging from the buttons of his jacket, tied up in colored string and containing candy, marzipan and Malaga, a sweet wine mama particularly loved. We would feast at such times, but mama kept a close account of our pawnshop receipts, and there were many in our cupboard. During the difficult periods even our pique bedspreads, tablecloths, and many other items were taken out for pawning. We would redeem one portion, live calmly for a time, but then there would be a breakdown. Once more the bedspreads and tablecloths found their way to the pawn shop.

Grisha volunteered for the front during the second year of the war. He had excellent handwriting and so became a scribe for an officer but only under one required condition, that he convert to Russian Orthodoxy. My parents were fine with this but I was not. Endless arguments ensued between me and my parents, who said this saved his life. I countered that to convert for personal profit was morally despicable when such forms of discrimination still existed as the Pale of Settlement, quotas for Jews, and pogroms. I declared that I would no longer write letters to Grisha and would not speak to him when he came home on leave. Relations with my parents grew tense. My mother said that I had changed and was living in their home as if I were a mere tenant. I said nothing. Mama was right. Home had become unpleasant and alien to me. I wanted to go and study in another city. But I knew this to be impossible. I continued to give all the money I earned from tutoring to mama, but I tried to stay away from home as much as possible.

Sasha's tenure in the active army turned into a revolving spectacle. He came back on leave several times and each time wore a different uniform: first he was a cavalryman, then a Hussar wearing a fur-trimmed cape (*mentik*) flung across his shoulder. Once he came in a felt cloak (*burka*) and a large sheepskin Caucasian hat (*papakha*) and proudly announced that he was now serving in the "Savage Division."[15] Twice he suffered slight wounds and was in the infirmary in St. Petersburg, where he performed in concerts. By now he had established himself as an excellent high baritone. He claimed, and perhaps he was lying, that he had been favored with the attentions of a great princess and by her recommendation had gotten into the Hussars. He had not bothered to be baptized but had managed to alter his documents. He had grown up in the course of the war, was irresistibly handsome, and sang all day. During one of our better periods, papa had fulfilled his promise to mama and she again had a piano. Sasha would break into song while mama accompanied him on the piano, and people would gather on the street under our windows, listening and clapping. But his leaves only lasted a few days and then Sasha would vanish for long periods of time.

Then Sasha retuned home as he had left it—as a simple infantryman, but now with a bandaged leg and a stick. He had lost two toes on his left foot and was demobilized. He demanded that our parents outfit him in the manner he deserved, but there was no money for it. So he spent his days lounging on the window sill and gazing outside. I felt sorry for him, but nonetheless was troubled by my doubts, fearing that he had been wearing uniforms of men who were killed in battle without ever being in any of the regiments he claimed. I told no one about my apprehensions but feared the military was going to catch him and put him on trial. He, however, just wrote poems without a care in the world. He would read them to me, then get angry and pout at me when I critiqued them. As soon as his foot had fully healed and my parents were able to buy him a suit and some boots, he disappeared and for a long time we heard nothing from him.

Father once again found work and now he traveled out to Zhmerinka and Berdichev.[16] It was just the two of us, mama and I; papa only came home twice a month and then went off again. My relationship with my mother changed at this point, largely thanks to mama's friend Margarita Genrikhovna, who came for a visit every day. We all loved her and referred to her as our "second mother." One summer evening she asked me to walk her home. She lived nearby with her son, who was a student; she was widowed and had not remarried. We sat for a long time under the acacia trees in the courtyard garden, and she told me the story of mama's life.

Mama had spent her childhood in Odessa and was in the same class as Margarita, but then mama's family moved to Nikolaev. After her father's death, mama had to give music lessons. In Nikolaev she was well known as a pianist and was invited to do charitable concerts. She willingly performed and it was during these concerts that my father first set eyes on her. Mama, though, was not interested in him. She loved and was loved by someone else, Mark Moiseevich, the son of a wealthy man who forbid his son to marry a dowerless girl. In order to tear his son away from this undesirable fiancée, the father sent him abroad to complete his education. Before his departure, Mark Moiseevich made mama promise to wait for him and vowed to return after a year to elope. Mama waited, but Mark did not return, nor did he write. One evening an officer brought mama home in his carriage after a concert. Grandmother stood by the window, saw her arrive thus, and greeted her with a slap in the face, for she considered this to be disgraceful behavior for a proper Jewish girl. She forbid further concerts and began to search for a husband to wed mama, who was already 24 years old, an old maid by the standards of that time.

Somehow my father found out about my mother's situation and began to get on the good side of grandmother. Mama, though, kept on waiting. Finally, she was forced to give in to her mother's pressure. My father had a decent job in a large grain operation and he promised to support both women. So mama did not marry for love. Mark Moiseevich did finally return, when Grisha was already a year old. He had not married, and he was grief-stricken, but it was too late. He only asked that he be allowed to visit us. I remember when we lived on Uspenskaia Street how he would sit by the window and listen to my mother's music. Then in Tiflis he showed up on our doorstep and brought us chocolate balls wrapped in silver paper. He and papa got along very well. My parents knew that Mark Moiseevich was ill. Sometimes when speaking about him with our friends, papa would point with his index finger to his head and sigh. Later Mark Moiseevich was placed into a care facility. Mama visited him there and once took me with her because he had asked her if I could come. He loved me very much.

I was deeply saddened by these revelations and felt a strong sense of guilt. My mother had kept all of this drama inside her. She was always more concerned about us and denied herself everything. Sasha had brought her so much grief, and yes, even Grisha had been a disappointment. With father there were endless arguments, and now I had become estranged from her. I gave my word to Margarita that I would not betray our conversation but that I would gradually repair my relationship with my mother. Our reconciliation began with the piano. I played poorly but read the notes fluently. I asked mama to play duets with me on light pieces. I began remaining at home more in the evenings, which made mama happy. I was in the seventh class and almost completely grown up. Final exams were approaching and Ania and I decided to study together. Most often I went to her home, but sometimes we studied at mine. Our studies were very interesting. We read Caesar in translation, studied the hexameters of Ovid, quickly mastered the logarithm tables, and still had sufficient energy for a new passion—the theater. New interests also emerged. Boris brought us books and we read radical tracts of Alexander Herzen and Peter Kropotkin.[17] We often got together at Ania's. During one of our conversations, Ania's uncle, the journalist, was present. He considered himself to be liberal-minded, but he was cautious and suggested that it might be better to give up these topics. If we were still fired up, we should instead occupy ourselves with studying the Great French Revolution. This was an interesting theme and a safer one. Ania and her brother tried to argue, but all of the adults teamed up against us and we were forced to concede.

All the while, the war raged on. Everyone grew weary of it, but there was no end in sight. Papa stopped traveling and worked instead in an office, and at dinner he would read aloud the speeches of Kerensky[18] in the Duma. In the evenings he would go out to the Fanconi café and bring back the latest news. One night he came rushing back, bursting with the news about the abdication of the tsar. The city buzzed, trembled, and shook with the frantic rush of people to and fro in the streets. Newspaper boys ran up and down Sadavaia, Deribasovskaia, Rishel'evskaia Streets shouting out the titles of the articles. Right after the abdication, our class, along with some older students, demanded that the portrait of the tsar hanging in the hall be taken down. The head of the school, Mrs. Pashkovskaia, at first balked, but then allowed it to be taken down after school, when none of us were there. No one knew what happened to it, though the rumor spread that the director, just to be safe, had taken it home to hide. Now Odessa came alive with meetings from morning until late at night. Papa got pulled into this maelstrom. We practically never saw him. Grisha returned from the front and enrolled in the Cadet Academy to fulfill his dream of becoming an ensign. He could do this now because he was Orthodox. I still refused to speak to him. My parents scolded me but I was obstinate. Ania and I completed the eighth class, received our diplomas, and applied to the History-Philology Department of the Higher Women's Courses. People poured into Odessa from Moscow and Petrograd hoping to get necessities. In the north the food situation was worsening, but we continued to enjoy abundant supplies. Little known artists from Moscow and Petrograd opened and closed theatrical and dance studios. Cabarets, casinos, and cafes came and went.

At the beginning of spring I fell ill and had to miss about a month of classes. I fell very far behind in all of my subjects, especially in Latin. I needed a tutor, and Boris recommended one of his friends, a student in the eighth class at the public gymnasium. He knew Latin very well and agreed to tutor me for three rubles a month. This is how Nikolai entered my life. He was tall, stately, dark-complexioned, somewhat gloomy but with a surprisingly gentle look in his large dark eyes. Our sessions began to go longer than the designated time, then we began to take walks together, and soon he introduced me to his closest friends. I went with them to the theater to see a play of Leonid Andreev, *He Who Gets Slapped*. After this Nikolai's friend Alexander proposed that we act out this play. I, of course, was given the female role of Consuelo, Nikolai was He (Tot), and we stirred quite a commotion with our antics.[19]

My nascent passion for Nikolai quickly faded, for I was becoming infatuated with the amazing and thrilling Alexander. Sarcastic and resolute, he seemed to me to be the strongest person I had ever met. He was reserved in manner, even withdrawn, yet he was the instigator of all of our excursions and amusements. He knew such a massive amount, and he had read, it seemed to me, every book in the world. He gave me the writings of Vasilii Rozanov[20] and then Pavel Florensky's book *The Pillar and Ground of the Truth*.[21] Only with some difficulty did I master this mystical work. I was not sure what to say to Alexander, for I did not want to discredit myself in his eyes, but all of this mysticism was alien to me. After Florensky there were books by Elena Blavatskaia[22] and Annie Besant,[23] but theosophy[24] did not interest me in the slightest. I tried to make intelligent comments but Alexander was cunning and saw through me. He would impatiently interrupt me and once he said to me, "Boy, you really are just a Consuelo!" In these words lay his critique of me, that I was too mundane, incapable of flying up to the heavenly heights of theosophy.

One day Nikolai convinced me to go for a walk with him, only the two of us. We ended up in an old Orthodox cemetery, and we sat down on a bench next to a neglected gravestone. Nikolai spoke to me about his love, about how cruel I was, and he was almost in tears. I began to feel sorry for him. I stroked his stiff, black hair and said that I had not yet loved anyone but that I cherished our friendship. He started kissing my hands and tried to hold on to me, but I pushed him away and ran home. Then the next day he walked me home from the theater. We went along Konnaia Street, past Bazaar Square. The moon was shining bright. He suggested that we go into the shadow of the covered market and from there look up at the moon. But when we got there, he grabbed me and began to kiss me. Good lord, here were my first kisses, but why did they have to come in this market, right next to the fishmongers' row with its stench of rotting fish? The moon in such a spot was wasted. I broke loose from him and said that all this was disgusting. I ran home, which was only one block away. Although nothing serious had happened, I still felt offended. One of Nikolai's friends, Zhenia, came with a note. Alexander was insisting that we meet as a group and he wrote mysteriously that we were still far from the last act. But I was suffering from a toothache, and my cheek as well as my upper lip swelled up. This ill-fated abscess strengthened my resolve not to go, and truly, I could not go out looking like this. I asked mama to say that I was ill. Mama applied poultices made from flaxseeds and after several days I was able to return to classes. When I got back home, I saw Alexander at our gate. He looked askance at me and was silent. He was the last person I wanted to talk to at the moment. I knew that Nikolai was susceptible to his influence and I suspected that the scene at the bazaar had been inspired by him. Alexander had often claimed the majority of people are just marionettes who only need experienced hands to work their strings.

"Did you come to see me?" I finally asked. "Yes, if you please, I need to see you. Nikolai shot himself; the cemetery watchman found him this morning by an old neglected grave." Then he left. I barely had the strength to make it to our apartment and ring the doorbell. Mama opened the door with a kitchen towel in her hand, for she had been cooking dinner. There was not much light in the entryway. The door to the kitchen was on the left, and my room was to the right. We parted ways. Mama called me to dinner, but I was still standing there in my room with my coat on and my black school hat with its green velvet bow. Mama came in and I told her everything that had happened. She looked at me with alarm on her face. I calmed her down with assurances that there had not been anything between us, but that he had loved me. She did not want me to go to the funeral, because it would suggest I was involved with him. But I had been involved. What should I do? A person who had so recently been in this very room and sat on this chair now lay dead in the morgue, which stood on our street, near the medical department. I left our apartment and went there. I told the guard that I was the sister of the boy who had killed himself. The coffin was raised up on chains. Nikolai's body did not fit well into his short, narrow coffin; his legs were bent at the knees. His hair fell down over his forehead and his eyes were half-open. I stayed there several minutes and then left. I no longer feared the dead, but I had just wanted to come for a moment to be alone next to him. There was nothing more I could do. I went to the funeral and brought flowers—lilies. But afterward I could not sleep at night. My room terrified me; I could see him sitting there on the chair. Ania came and sat with me in silence.

About two weeks later Nikolai's mother visited in deep mourning attire. She was tiny and thin, but had his same large dark eyes. She greeted my mother and asked her permission to speak with me. Mama brought her to my room and then left us there. I did not know who had pointed me out to her and what had been said about me. She sat in silence for a long time and then she asked me why I had quarreled with her son. I tried to explain that we had not argued. I just could not respond to him in the way he wanted me to. She kept asking me what he had done, and I kept saying nothing; there was nothing he could have done to change my feelings. This was the gist of our entire conversation. She looked at me and at my unsightly room. It was obvious she could not understand why I, being so poor, had rejected her son. After a long silence she asked me a further question: "But if you could do it all over again, would you not act differently?" I said no, that I would still act the same way. She looked at me in horror and left without even saying goodbye.

As was her custom, Ania spent the summer at a dacha in Small Fountain. I, on the other hand, received a proposal. Not far from us was a dye works where we sometimes took items for cleaning. The proprietor had his own dacha-farm with an orchard and garden in the steppe region, beyond the sixteenth station. His daughter needed a tutor to help her prepare to enter the third class in the gymnasium. I leapt at the opportunity to get out of Odessa and rid myself of such oppressive memories. But I ended up spending the summer in the melancholy environment of a petty, narrow-minded household. The sea was far off. Only a few times was I able to convince these unimaginative, impenetrable parents to take their dullish daughter to the beach. But I did have free time after dinner and I had brought with me several volumes of Dostoevsky. I read them nestled into a haystack, amid sheaves of wheat. After rereading *Crime and Punishment*, I tackled for the first time Dostoevsky's *The Devils* (*Besy*). As I was reading, it came over me that indeed the ill-fated Nikolai had been influenced by Alexander, who turned out to be our own version of Dostoevsky's character Stavrogin.[25] Alexander had made fools out of us, taking advantage of our naivete to convince us that there was no one on earth more original, more intelligent, or stronger than he. As a matter of fact, Nikolai had told me that Alexander considered suicide to be the ultimate expression of human will and that it was in suicide that one found the genuine power of the soul. Alexander and I at some point had started such a conversation, but I cut it short, saying that it made no sense to rush the matter and that any amount of suffering was better than death. He had commented sarcastically that I was "horribly prosaic." Had he thought he could set up a club focused on suicide? Yes, there amid the stacks of golden hay, under the boundless steppe sky, it became clear to me. Alexander had taken advantage of Nikolai's depression. He had convinced Nikolai that his awkwardness and stupidity had tarnished him forever in my eyes. I was shallow and craved aesthetics above all else, and the only way he could punish and make me feel guilty was to shoot himself.

After returning to Odessa, I ran into Zhenia and told him about my suspicions. He had not read *Besy*, but he was aware of Alexander's influence over Nikolai. He had listened to disturbing conversations and had even once suggested to Alexander that it might be best for him to set an example by being the first to shoot himself. So I decided to write Alexander a letter. I called him a scoundrel and accused him of being a pathetic and unscrupulous copycat with no respect for creative genius. I placed the letter in the box at the door to his apartment. It fell into the hands of his father, who was a lawyer. He was afraid that my honor had been compromised and demanded clarification from my father. My parents nearly went out of their minds, fearing once again the taint of scandal. But I explained everything to them, and I convinced my father that I had to respond and allowed him to read my answer. In just a few words I spelled out for the lawyer how the malicious and deliberate influence of his son had led an unstable, weak-willed boy to commit suicide, and that my honor was not the issue. I suggested that it would be best for both of them to stop mouthing off. And they did fall silent. Soon Zhenia told me that Alexander had left to stay with relatives in Rostov, and from there was going on to the Caucasus. Our paths never again crossed.

Meanwhile, I began attending daily lectures. Professor Varneke[26] taught Latin and Mandes[27] taught Greek. There were excellent historians, such as Evgenii Nikolaevich

Shchepkin[28] and Petr Mikhailovich Bitsilli.[29] We took notes, went to the library, and sat for examinations. Meanwhile, Sasha finally resurfaced. He claimed to have been working for two seasons in various provincial theaters; he named the city and even showed us a playbill where, sure enough, his name appeared, though in small type. Now he was using a pseudonym, Gordeev, and he had changed his first name to "Sandi." Now as Sandi Gordeev he even managed to make it into an Odessa association of poets known as the "Green Lamp." Our old friend Edia helped him; Edia was no longer going by Dziubin, but now called himself Bagritskii.[30] Our Sasha was not exactly a member of the Green Lamp, far from it, but he possessed a certain originality as a poet. His verses were filled with taverns, brass knuckles, gin, sea breezes, daggers, and so on. Once he invited me to a performance. He came out onto the stage (it was a former school building) dressed in torn bell-bottomed pants, striped sailor's shirt, and pea jacket thrown across his shoulders. As he recited, he brought to life the vagabond sailor at the heart of his verses. The ladies in the audience clapped furiously. He was quite handsome.

Political power in Odessa was now changing hands with kaleidoscopic speed. Much has been written about the Civil War period and depicted both on stage and screen. I find it difficult now to reconstruct the sequence, and anyway, there is no point in focusing on this. All of it is well known and covered thoroughly in history books. There were days when Ania and I had to stay home due to the shooting, and at times it was so bad that our classes were cancelled. But somehow or another we passed to the second year. Studying, though, became increasingly difficult because we lacked a clear goal for ourselves. It was interesting and we were learning a lot. But for what purpose? At this point Ania stunned me when she declared that she now had a brand new goal and knew definitely what she wanted to be. "Well, what is it you want to be?" I asked. She told me to guess, so I began naming all of the specializations that I could think of, going even as far as dentistry. Ania looked at me bitterly and with annoyance. I deliberately did not say "actress." Ania had a speech impediment and could not say either the letter "l" or the letter "r," on top of the fact that she had a hunched-over gait, a husky voice, and awkward manners. Eventually, though, I had to say "actress." Ania beamed and asked why I had not said this profession right away. I answered her honestly, but my comments did not bother her. She insisted that she could correct her diction and that if there is genuine talent, the rest would be part of her unique charm. Sasha, who had previously disappeared from sight, returned to Odessa during the first period of rule by the Reds. He rode a white horse into our courtyard. He was wearing a red bandage on his arm and reported that he was now the adjutant to the commissar of a Red Army unit. He did not live at home, but sometimes he would drop by on his horse to toss a package of sugar, a loaf of round wheat bread or something similar, and then take off. When the Reds left Odessa, Sasha did not leave with them; he was delayed, but soon departed for Turkey on a French cruiser. He came one night to my bedroom window, which faced out onto the courtyard, and told me his plans. I did not actually see him, but only heard his hushed voice.

Our lives became troubled and uncertain. Ever since we were children we were accustomed to seeing a diverse range of people in Odessa. Ships came and went from all over the globe. But now it was not sailors passing through, but governments. A new regime would take over, replacing those in power yesterday, but no one knew for how long—days, or weeks, or months? And the whole time it would be seeking to plunder whatever it could, so "raids" on stores and private apartments became more frequent. Excellent works of literature have described all of this, but it was very hard for those of us living through it. I attended lectures when I could, depending on the situation in the city. I helped mother around the house, and meanwhile she decided to find me a husband. She irritated me by inviting over successful young men who were friends of friends. I usually managed to avoid such prospective "fiancés" by slipping out beforehand and going to Ania's. But if I was caught at home, then I would sit at the table looking so unpleasant and indifferent that the "fiancé" himself would hurry away. Then would come mother's reproaches. I told mama that I was holding out so that she could get a higher price for me. This drove her to tears. I knew that she was simply worried about me.

I had many friends who were always inviting me to the theater and escorting me home. The theaters were all very different. There was the "Crooked Mirror" and Balieva's "Bat" cabaret theater[31] plus various touring artists who stayed on in Odessa, where it was still possible to avoid starvation. One visitor who particularly captivated us was K. M. Miklachevsky,[32] a Petrograd director and historian of ancient theater. Both Big Boris and Little Boris had met this artistic innovator at a private apartment and said that he was very well educated and had a genuine European manner. He was working with our Latin Professor Varneke to stage the comedy "Menekhty" or "Gemini—The Twins,"[33] written by the Roman playwright Plautus. We all went: Ania and her brother, both Borises and I. The show took place in a small rundown hall of the former Miniature Theater on Lanzheronovskaia Street. All of the performers wore large, grotesque masks covering their heads entirely. I had never before seen anything like this. This production made all that I had seen before pale in comparison; I had obviously never seen real theater, but this—this was it, genuine acting artistry! Miklachevsky himself played the role of one twin (*Menekht*). But, in truth, he played both without changing either masks or costume. Yet how different each one was. It looked as if the actor did not have a head, for it was covered, like a mantle, by a multicolored, absurd looking mask. But the mask appeared to change its own expression, and the whole body—the shoulders, legs, feet, arms, fingers, and spine—moved accordingly. From behind the mask came different voices, each with unexpected nuances and modulations.

I had always loved the circus and had seen many acrobats, but I had never witnessed such flexibility and expressiveness in a body. It was miraculous. Without understanding or thinking about what I was doing, I stood up (my seat was on the end) and went toward the stage. Ania's brother grabbed me by the arm, which broke my trance and I sat back down. This was a highbrow production; applause was only allowed at the end of the show, and the audience had been duly warned about this in advance. When it finished, though, there was stormy applause. Miklachevsky came out to take a bow, holding his mask in the crook of his arm. His face was strikingly unattractive, yet refined and intelligent. He was bald, with the nose of a harlequin and a protruding jaw. His elegant lips turned up at the corners, covering a set of teeth that were prominent and horse-like, but nonetheless straight. His forced smile seemed a contrast to the cold, calm look of his small, radiant eyes. Afterward, the five of us were delirious with rapture; we walked about for a long time and sat on the boulevard, arguing incessantly. We were aware that Miklachevsky was both the actor and producer for the show and had designed the costumes and the set decorations. Boris told us that he had written a wonderful book, famous in Europe, and the only one in Russia about the improvisational theater, the *Commedia dell' arte*.[34] Boris right then and there gave us a mini-lecture about this form of theater, which was entirely new to us. I wondered how anyone could study theater under our former teachers when in Odessa there was such a marvel as this. We needed an emissary to go to Miklachevsky and ask if he would give us lectures on the *Commedia dell'arte* so that we could organize our own small improvisational theater.

Little Boris said that he was sure his father would allow them to hold the lectures in their large living room. Joining us were two other classmates of Boris—Lenia Trauberg[35] and his friend Izya Trotsky.[36] Izya was younger, in the sixth class, but was so mature and well-read that he had been accepted into Boris's company of friends. He was unbelievably handsome; in fact they called him "Dorian Gray."[37] I was not attracted to such beauty, and moreover, he was timid and shy, which made it difficult to talk to him. But even he was fired up and said that he would attend the lectures. Several days later Lenia, Izya, and little Boris went to Miklachevsky and got him to agree. He named a very small sum—per lecture—and set the date when the lectures would begin. The boys told us that his wife had opened the door—she was an amazing Jewish beauty, and they lived on Gogol Street in a rented room, and the room was really messy. But the wife did not stay for their conversation.

Thus, on the designated day we gathered on Nezhinskaia Street in little Boris's living room. Miklachevsky arrived in a brown velvet jacket and checkered pants. He proposed that we should begin by trying our own hand at improvisation, for he understood that we did not just want to hear about the history of Italian comedy. But in reality, the boys in our group were thinking less and less of a career in theater. Big Boris said that this was still a long way off. Ania cast an angry glance at him. Miklachevsky noticed everything. He turned to me and asked, "And what about you?" I blushed and muttered something about admiring his acting, his pantomime, and his lifelike ancient mask. He bowed theatrically, everyone laughed, and he began the lecture. He was very upbeat and comfortable as a speaker; he spoke concretely, without abstractions and florid phrases. When we were leaving, he handed me my coat and asked whether he could walk me home. I said that I lived very near. "What a pity," he said, "but may I still accompany you?" I felt awkward in front of everyone, but I answered indifferently, "As you please." On the way he asked me whether I was aiming for a career in theater or whether this was just a passing fad. I said that what interested me was the fact that I knew nothing about this subject, and I enjoyed hearing something new. At the gateway into my building he asked if we could meet prior to the next weekly lecture. I said no, that I was always busy. His attentions confused me: he had a beautiful wife, he was a famous director from the capital, the author of a well-known, original book. What did he want with me? Did he have a penchant for secret intrigues? I had no intention of giving him such an opportunity and decided not to attend any more of his lectures.

After the next one, Ania told me that he had asked about me and wondered why I was not there. But as it turned out, I could not have gone to the lecture under any circumstances, for I was crushed by grief. One day, not long after the first lecture, Edia Bagritskii stopped me on Sadovaia Street, pulling me over to the side. He looked at me straight in the eye, put his hand on my shoulder, and said "We have news of Sandi (Sasha), the Whites shot him in Constantinople. They found out who he was."

"Who did, and how?" I asked.

"Well, everyone knew who he was. When he was here in Odessa riding high and mighty about on his horse, there were Whites in disguise all over the city, and then they also fled. Later, they settled scores …"

It was already 1920, and in Odessa the Reds now had a firm foothold. People were afraid, for raids and searches were going on. I understood that Edia could not tell me who had given him this information. I tried to go, but he restrained me and whispered: the writer Alexei Tolstoy had been in Constantinople at that time and now was in Berlin. He had published a short story entitled "The End of Sandi" in the émigré newspaper *On the Eve* (*Na Kanune*).[38] He described how the two of them had sat together on the shore, looking at the sea, and Sandi had reminisced about his mother. On that same day they executed him. That was all he knew, and then Edia quickly walked away. I had to decide whether to go home and tell my parents. Why do so? Let them continue thinking that he was doing fine somewhere. But nonetheless, everything became known, for in Odessa such news instantly became the subject of gossip. And at home things became even more difficult and miserable. Several weeks later on my way to Ania's, I ran into Miklachevsky. He suggested that we go for a walk. I strolled with Konstantin Mikhailovich down Sofia Lane—this was one of my most favorite spots in Odessa. There was a sculptor's studio, and you could look through the fence and see angel statues lying on the ground and marble busts lacking their heads, which lay cast off to the side. Clearly soldiers from all of the different governments in Odessa had amused themselves here. Miklachevsky talked about Italy and France and asked me to come that evening to the literary club. There was a concert there, and I attended it with him. Our seats were in the theater pit, and next to us sat a large, heavy-set man with a lion-like head. Konstantin Mikhailovich said hello to him and introduced him as Maximilian Voloshin.[39] After this the concert just faded into the background as I listened to the conversation of these two individuals during the intervals. It was an unprecedented experience. I did not dare to say a word. I only listened. While he was walking me home, Konstantin Mikhailovich told me that now he was a producer for the People's Theater. The troupe included Boris Glagolin[40] among others, and they were staging interesting plays, but currently his project was to quickly put together a children's show called "Lully the Musician."[41] Rehearsals were now going on, and he very much wanted me to come to one tomorrow. He had stopped giving lectures—no one really had the time and he could not see the point in continuing them.

And so I began going to the rehearsals. As I sat in the dark empty hall, I watched Konstantin Mikhailovich show the actors how to position themselves and how to move. The cast for the children's matinee was rather weak. In one of the scenes of the play a fairy was to appear and sing poetic verse to Lully, who had fallen asleep in the forest. The actress who was to play the fairy fell ill, and Konstantin Mikhailovich asked me if I would replace her. I said that I had never tried melodic declamation, and I did not even know how this was done. He proposed that I come to his home, where he had a piano, and he could help me. I agreed, and when I arrived, he met me dressed in a velvet jacket and on his head was a Turkish fez with a big black tassel. He held a small flute in his hands, which he said was a "piccolo." We went into a rather small, cramped room, which had several different kinds of tables, including one covered with scattered books and journals, a large bed, and bookcases. His wife was not there. He invited me to sit down in the one armchair that was there, while he leaned against the wardrobe and played some sort of eastern melody, very much in keeping with his Turkish fez.

"But where is the piano?" I asked.

"In the other room. The landlady is on vacation and so I am using the whole apartment."

We went into the large empty room where the piano stood. None of my first tries at melodic declamation were successful, but then I began to listen to the pauses and follow the rhythm, and Konstantin Mikhailovich said that "this would suffice if worst came to worst." Subsequently he brought me coffee, and we went back into his room, but his wife still had not returned. He had prepared the coffee using a kerosene lamp, which he rigged up using wooden brackets with hooks. He had attached wire hinges to the handles of a small saucepan so that its bottom could be held over the glass in such a way as to not accumulate soot. There was no fuel oil to be found in Odessa at this time nor methylated spirits for lamps, and it was very difficult even to get kerosene for a primus stove. But I knew of no one else who had thought to use a table lamp for cooking. Konstantin Mikhailovich said that in the mornings this was how he prepared his hot cereal (kasha). Everything about him was remarkable.

I came another day to practice the fairy's monologue. Konstantin Mikhailovich again made coffee, and we drank a cup. Then, managing to avoid my gaze, he said to me: "Now, listen here, I want you to marry me."

"But you already have a wife, and a beautiful one at that; my friends saw her ..."

"My wife has been in Petrograd for a long time, and this morning I have just sent her a letter asking for a divorce. You know it is quite simple now to get one. This is why I am speaking to you about this ..."

"Maybe so; that is your business, but as for me, I do not love you ..."

"Oh, that is nothing; just allow me to love you ..." Then he began to talk about the situation in Petrograd, and how he was most likely quite poor, because all of his family possessions had been thrown into a new apartment after the February Revolution and almost certainly had been pilfered. But he would work in the theater—he was going to produce plays and act. All that was holding him in Odessa was his ailing mother. His father had died in Petrograd the week before the February Revolution; by that time his mother was already ill with cancer.[42] After his father's death, his sister Tat'iana Mikhailovna, who was married to Prince Anatole Gagarin, had gone at the latter's insistence along with their small daughter to their famous estate known as "Priiutnoe," located near Odessa in the district of Arcadia, where Pushkin had once visited.[43] His older brother Il'ia[44] went there as well; he was a Chevalier Garde married to the Countess Bobrinskaia, daughter of the famous Count Bobrinskii who was featured in a painting by Repin, "Ceremonial Meeting of the State Council."[45] At the first opportunity, this couple left Russia with their three small children[46] and went to France via Turkey. Konstantin Mikhailovich and his younger brother then rented a modest apartment on Mokhovaia Street in Petrograd, "no more than six rooms," and moved all of their possessions there, having boxed up all of the family's china, silver, rugs, and other such items.

Prior to this, they had lived nearby on Sergievskaia Street, where they had an entire floor to themselves. When it became cold in Petrograd, and while the Provisional Government was still in power (February to October 1917), they took their mother to stay with their sister Tatiana in Odessa. But then the Gagarins emigrated to France during one of the several changes in government in Odessa, after leaving their mother in the care of Konstantin Mikhailovich. He resettled her among old acquaintances of hers and went to visit her, but already by this time there was little hope for her survival. It was just a matter of time, but exactly when death would come was what made his immediate plans uncertain. As it turned out, she died several days later, and I attended the funeral.

His frankness astonished me, as well as the fact that he had chosen to work in theater, since this was not considered socially acceptable for someone from his background. He chuckled at this. In fact, his father had all but thrown him out of the house when, after finishing the Alexander Lyceum, he turned down the position procured for him in advance at the Ministry of Foreign Affairs. Instead he had enrolled in the Imperial Theater School, where he studied under Vladimir Nikolaevich Davydov.[47] He also completed a course at the Conservatory in music theory because he thought that a director should know how to write music for his own productions. At their home on Sergievskaia, he had two rooms set apart from the others—reached via an internal staircase—and he rarely went downstairs, especially when his parents had guests. The reason for this was an incident that took place during the time of the infamous Beilis trial: he had caused a terrible scene after dinner. There were guests present, and they were all conversing about the case, and he became enraged at them. He declared to all that he could not understand how people who considered themselves to be cultured could believe such nonsense. After this his father told him that when there were guests, he would have to dine in his own room. Why had he told me this, I wondered. So as to reassure me that he was not anti-Semitic? After all, this was already clear. His former wife was Jewish.

Petrograd ... I had long dreamed of it, with the Hermitage and its theaters. And what prospects did I have in Odessa? I said that I could not decide at that moment, but that if I did go, it would be because I had long dreamed of going to Petrograd, and it would be interesting to see it with him. But that would be the only reason. His face lit up, and he said that he ought to meet my parents. There was no need to keep our acquaintance a secret. Thereafter, he became a regular visitor to our home. He felt it necessary to tell mama about his proposal, and she had mixed feelings. At first she was bothered by the difference in our ages, for he was 17 years older than me. On the other hand (she began to muse) ..., he was a nobleman, he had graduated from a lycèe, he belonged to high society. Maybe, I could somehow realize her unfulfilled dreams; maybe, not all was lost ... When he had a talk with mama and expressed the hope that I would eventually agree to marry him, she posited a condition—it could not be a civil wedding, because of the constant turnover of governments in Odessa. Therefore it had to be a church wedding and she agreed that I should be baptized as soon as possible. But at this point I spoke up and said that I would rather not have a wedding at all if it meant doing something that repulsed me. We were not religious, no one in our family had ever prayed to a God, so why should I suddenly have to be baptized? Konstantin Mikhailovich did not let my mother continue the argument. He said that even if I had not yet accepted his proposal, nonetheless tomorrow he would become a Lutheran. According to his passport he was Orthodox, but any minister for a small sum of money would be willing to change him to a Lutheran. And a Lutheran could marry anyone, even a Negro woman. The last thing he wanted to do was to cause me even the slightest problem.

Truth be told, two days later he showed mama and papa the evidence of his conversion to Lutheranism. Mama was shocked. A real knight in shining armor, she said to me, fully enraptured by his gallantry. But I just thought it was funny. After just two weeks of being acquainted, I had already figured out that his personality contained the most unexpected blending of traits—gentility, eccentricity, and even buffoonery coexisted with the very firm principles of an upright man. Whenever we passed by a flea market, he loved to stop and view the scene unfolding there much as an artist would look at a landscape. If there was an old Jew selling all sorts of small items, Konstantin Mikhailovich would begin to bargain with him using the most common Odessan dialect and matching his gestures and expressions completely to his speech. He had an extraordinary facility for linguistics and was fluent in several European languages. After living in Odessa for only two years, he had already mastered the local dialect; yet I who had lived there all my life did not understand a single word of it. I would just step aside and admire his performance. Before the revolution his family had been very wealthy. His father was a *Hofmeister*;[48] at home they had footmen and chambermaids, and his father refused to hire cooks from anywhere but Paris. Every summer Konstantin Mikhailovich and his two brothers received large sums of money for traveling around Europe. His brothers preferred living it up in the most fashionable holiday resorts, but he would travel third class through France, Italy, Spain, the Balkans, Germany, and Scandinavia. He wanted to observe, listen, and absorb the languages and gestures "typical for each nationality." Everywhere he went he would bury himself in the libraries and study museums and architectural styles. He had told me all this during our walks home from the theater, where I was now going almost daily. He was playing a female role, the widow Quinn, in the play "The Gardener's Dog."[49] And although the incomparable romantic Glagolin and the great beauty Valerskaia had the main roles, Miklachevsky's performance stood out for its uniqueness: when he took off the red-haired wig and revealed his bald spot, the audience roared with delight.

One day in early May, I told him that I had to help out at home and could not go that evening to the theater. The truth was that I needed to wash clothes. So I washed all of my underwear and my summer dresses, and hung them up in the attic. Now quite tired, I lay down earlier than usual to sleep. Around midnight there was a knock on my window, and it was Konstantin Mikhailovich. He asked me if I could come outside for a few minutes. I went out on the porch and he told me the following: the Odessa Cheka was sending several train cars of wheat to the Moscow Cheka as a gift.

A commissar by the name of Davydov[50] was to come from Moscow to escort the load. It so happened that he had authority over the theater, and he was bringing with him an invitation for Miklachevsky from M. F. Andreeva[51] to return to Petrograd and work on his own repertoire of plays. The contingent was set to depart at 5:00 a.m. Everything was in my hands. He would not go without me. In any case, he had already said that he was coming with his wife, and so if I agreed to go, I would have to play the role of a wife. But, he warned me, the trip would be quite dangerous, for on the way we might run into bandits. "Alright, I will come," I said. His last sentence had sealed the deal for me. If I refused, would I not appear to be a coward? Konstantin Mikhailovich kissed my hand and rushed off after telling me that I needed to be ready by 4:00 a.m. that very morning.

3

A New Life in Petrograd

My parents stood there, paralyzed with fear, in the doorway of my room. No one had ever called on me in the middle of the night. I got them to go back to their bedroom and gently explained that I was leaving for Petrograd with Konstantin Mikhailovich (henceforth the abbreviation K.M. will be used as in the original Russian edition). A fantastic opportunity had opened up for him, and he swears he will not go without me. I am not so sure about that, but I have my own reasons for going with him. He is the most interesting person I am ever going to meet, and besides, what will people think if I remain here alone? If I go, everyone will envy me, but if I stay, I will be a laughing stock. This latter argument I crafted especially for mama, who valued such female pride, and she readily acquiesced. But then she reminded me that my newly washed clothing was still hanging wet in the attic. Oh lord, I had forgotten about this. I had to go up to the attic by candlelight and bring down some that were almost dry. Right at 5:00 a.m. K.M. arrived in a truck filled with people. He jumped off and assured my parents that everything would be fine, we would write, but the mail was very slow now, so they should not worry if they did not hear right away. Papa sobbed, and mama kissed me but remained silent.

Riding in the back of this truck, we rushed to Nikolaev to catch up with our train. But a heavy downpour managed to soak us to the skin. So much for my dry clothes. The sun when it rose eventually dried us off, and we arrived to find our train was delayed. After a visit with friends of mine, we went back to the station and soon found our freight car. Inside on both sides there were planks of wood laid down, and up above, in one corner, there was a strange contraption: a wide board made from several planks lay on a tall sawhorse. It was fastened to the ceiling of the car by rope and hooks, and the board was covered in straw and a cloth. This was the bed of Commissar Davydov, who was traveling with a lady friend. The latter, though quite young, was heavy-set and capricious. She had whined the entire way in the truck, reproaching her beloved Davydov as though it were in his power to stop the downpour. A glance from K.M. had told me not to say a word. At the station Davydov was running around with various papers, shouting at the railroad workers and checking the security, which consisted of machine gunners in the head car and even in the locomotive. In our car there were additional passengers: several women with children were traveling to meet up with their husbands, two soldiers, and a fellow by the name of Musia Gol'dberg, who was popularly known at the time as "Argo."[1]

The commissar and his beauty lay on their slightly swaying bed, while we occupied a corner by the exit. K.M. immediately made headrests for us and then laid several pillows on them. Later he nailed a piece of cloth to the corner with thumbtacks and nails from his personal stash, just, he declared, "to keep off the draft." We lay with our heads pointing toward the hustle and bustle of the car. During the entire journey he played the role of a landlord, always tinkering with something and making improvements. He made no attempt to be romantic or intimate; sometimes he played his flute. We behaved like an old married couple long familiar with each other. Halfway through the journey bandits attacked our train. They knew we had grain on board. The women were ordered to lie under the wagon. Argo joined us while the rest of the men went to get rifles. The shooting did not last long. The gang was not a big one and, as the Red Army soldiers put it, "they are now resting quietly."

On the twenty-eighth day, we arrived in Moscow. Davydov put us up in an empty apartment in the center of the city. K.M. immediately took me out to see Moscow, but I was disappointed. To me the city seemed dirty, disheveled, and noisy. We went along Kuznetskii Most and reached the Moscow Art Theater. But even this was not as I had imagined it while growing up in far-off Odessa. Then he took me to the magical Arbat district with its alleyways and side streets, which I did find enthralling. What a captivating storyteller he was, with his infinite store of knowledge! He showed me cozy townhomes, nearly all of which had a story. In these moments I could have listened to him forever.

We spent only one night in Moscow. Davydov issued us train tickets for Petrograd, for the international car. We entered its compartment, and by the window sat a rather short young man who looked somewhat "biblical" to me. I had never seen anyone like him in Odessa. He recognized K.M. and, jumping up, extended his hand. "Natan!" exclaimed K.M. and introduced me. It was the artist Natan Altman,[2] returning to Petrograd from the Kremlin, where he had spent many days sketching a portrait of Lenin. He showed us his album, which half a century later I would see again in an exhibit in Leningrad. He looked a bit startled when K.M. called me his wife. I understood that everyone had known his previous wife and had not heard about the divorce, so it was hard for them to take me seriously. I tried to sit quietly by the window and not take part in the conversation. But then a tall, stocky man who reminded me of an actor burst into the compartment and rushed to embrace K.M.: "Kostia, I heard your voice; what are you doing here?" K.M. beamed. He was clearly very happy to see this fellow. He introduced him to me as "Iakov L'vovich, no, he is simply Zhak, an old friend." Unlike the others, Zhak was not surprised at my being referred to as "wife." He had only been away from Petrograd for several days and so he knew that Tamara Vladimirovna, K.M.'s first wife, had moved in with Moisei Frumkin.[3] Zhak always knew everything about everyone. He informed us that K.M.'s apartment on Mokhovaia Street was secure, and Tamara's family, the Zhukovskiis, were keeping an eye on it. They had been feeding a steady stream of bribes to the caretaker, and he in turn had not allowed any searches, claiming the apartment was empty, and somehow had managed to preserve it. Zhak was very talkative; he was entertaining and cheerful. He looked at me approvingly and even winked at me. Altman lost interest in the conversation and left. I tried hard to memorize the names and the different relationships of the people with whom I would undoubtedly be meeting in Petrograd. Although Zhak was very much at home with the Zhukovskiis, I realized later that he was like this with many people. He even became "one of us" in our family, although I was not so keen on him.

We arrived at dawn. Zhak quickly procured a cart to convey all of K.M.'s books and helped us get home. We knew that Tamara Vladimirovna had allowed the mistress of some married party official to move into the two back rooms. Tamara claimed that this was done for greater security, but we found out later that she received favors from the official in return. We went up to the fourth floor and rang the bell. A plump and rather pretty woman, who looked to be from the Caucasus, opened the door. She only reluctantly let us in and did not seem pleased to find that she was going to have neighbors. But the caretaker was with us and when he confirmed that K.M. was the owner of the apartment, the woman managed a smile.

From the entryway we went into a large, semidark space, which at some time before had been the dining room for a large family. Along all of the walls there were book cases, but you could barely see them with all of the baskets, trunks, and boxes piled up in front of them. The caretaker gave K.M. a key for two large rooms facing onto the street and a small room by the outside door that was also filled with boxes. Rather embarrassed, the caretaker informed us that the two bathrooms could not be used, for the plumbing was not working. The electricity only worked in the evenings for a few hours. The caretaker left, and we went into the large, long room that at first was our only living space and later became my husband's study. But at the moment it was filled with suitcases, crates, and traveling bags, as was the next room as well. K.M. said that he had to go to the Zhukovskii's home to get the keys for all of the wardrobes and cupboards. It took him about three hours. Public transport was unavailable, so he had to walk the whole way to the Zhukovskii apartment on Pushkin Street. I watched him return from the window on the fourth floor, loaded down with bags and parcels of different kinds. When he came up the stairs, he looked worried as he informed me that we were going there for dinner the next day. "They insisted, and I had to say yes." The bags contained a little bit of sugar and tea, a piece of homemade pie, some semolina flour, several eggs, lard, and a hunk of dark bread. Stores were not open, and it was impossible to buy anything. Tamara's kind and attentive mother, Olga Mikhailovna, had given us some of her own reserves, obtained from black marketers in exchange for items of furniture. K.M. said that during the whole of his visit she had been dickering in the kitchen with two or three peasant women. I was not sure what to say or do. I was not thrilled that he had gone to see his ex-wife. K.M laid out the food on the table, and then we went into the kitchen, which was horribly dirty and smelly. Behind it was a large passageway and an exit to the back staircase; large boxes stacked to the ceiling lined the hall. K.M. found some sort of poker, propped open one of the boxes, and then pulled out a bunch of straw. He broke an already wobbly stool into pieces and used this and the straw as fuel for cooking the food.

As we ate we had our first family conversation; he tried to reassure me that we were obligated to go to the Zhukovskii's. If not for their vigilance, then everything would have been stolen. He remonstrated with me—Tamara has a new husband, I have a new wife, so what is the big deal? He noted as well that we would need to see them more than once. They were storing a lot of valuables and it would take time to retrieve them all. I was not happy about going, but I said that I understood. After this we began to examine the items in the apartment. I heard many words for the very first time: empire style; Bull; marquetry; Karelian birch; cloisonné; bisque china; and many others. The family possessions were elegant and fancy and K.M. casually dropped the different period designations: "Paul I," "Catherine," "the beginning of Alexander I," and so on. I had never heard of such terms, but I pretended to understand. Glass-fronted cupboards that had a few figurines, which he called "cabinets," a word new to me, were piled up in a far corner. Next to them, standing along a boarded-up door to an entryway, were pictures in gold frames, with dirty curtains strewn over them, while rolled up rugs lay in another corner. We set about constructing a temporary room for me. He used the bookcases to partition off one part; in the other half he put a writing desk, which he referred to as a bureau (also a new term), a leather couch, and a round table for meals. He dexterously pulled out a wooden bed made of mahogany in the "Elizabethan" style and set it up in "my corner," along with two dressers from the dining room.

In the course of a single hour my corner had become a cozy nook. I got to choose a blanket, pillows, and pillowcases from various trunks and chests. I was stunned by my husband's capabilities—he knew how to do everything, asked for no help, and through it all whistled cheerfully! My own father had never once used a hammer. Such tasks were done by a porter or by a yardman or, if worst comes to worst, by one of the girls who worked for us. And my father certainly did not know any European languages. I had never before encountered anyone like K.M. and without a doubt, I would never meet another like him again. What joy he brought me! Oh, how hard I worked to win his praises, to make him be fond of me. I asked whether he would prefer to sleep on the more comfortable leather sofa. He waved this thought away with his hands. "Oh, we will find some sort of mattress. It is no problem. I was at the front during the entire war, I can sleep well just about anywhere." Until now he had never talked about this. Did this mean that he had been an officer in the tsarist army? And yet he had chosen to come back to Petrograd, instead of following his brothers and sister abroad. This thought made me both happy and frightened at the same time.

We had arrived in Petrograd in June. I was puzzled, for it was evening, yet there was still light. Oh my heavens, I had forgotten—the White Nights! K.M. laughed, knowing that in Odessa at this moment the night sky was pitch black. He suggested that we go for a walk. I took my first stroll along the Neva River. We lived just a couple of steps away from Sergievskaia Street. We went along Gagarinskaia Street to reach the Neva. The Summer Garden took my breath away. We traversed the spacious but dusty Field of Mars and gazed behind it at a grand building with columns, which he said were the barracks of the Pavlovskii guards regiment. We then went down Millionnaia Street to the Hermitage. K.M. showed me the marvelous Miatlev family mansion. He had gone there as a boy for various children's holidays.[4] All along he pointed out small, modest homes which he said represented the Russian style of architecture known as empire. I memorized the details—a triangle over a small balcony, small columns. He would make brief but fully explanatory comments on every street and square, for all manner of buildings, and frequently accompanied them with lines from Pushkin. We walked out on to Nevskii Prospekt and reached the Alexander Theater, where in his youth he had acted for two seasons with Maria Savina.[5] I was delighted with the building. "Oh, no," he said, "let me show you where to find the real charm," and led me behind the theater. "There is no such wonder anywhere else," he said. It was Theater Street, and I could have gazed at it forever. I ventured, "Looking at this is like listening to Bach; I could do so for an eternity." He quickly turned to me and said quietly, "Yes, I can see that I was not wrong about you." I was filled with joy. He had approved my words! We tarried for awhile by the horse sculptures on the Anichkov Bridge and then returned home along the Fontanka River. Although it was late, there was no night sky. This walk through a virtually silent Petrograd, with its rivers, bridges, railings, buildings, streets, and, most importantly, all that K.M. had said, somehow merged into his very being; it became one and the same as K.M. himself. It seemed to me that he was part of all that we had seen, and all that we had seen made up part of him. This was because only such a city as this could have created such an extraordinary person.

We returned home to find the plumbing not working. But before we had left for our walk, K.M. had managed to fill two buckets. I washed up first and lay down, then he came to me dressed in a striped, light bathrobe and wearing his fez. He lay down and I became his wife. There was no other way; I could no longer live without this man. I woke up early, but K.M. was not in our room. I went out through the corridor that led into the kitchen, where I saw my husband from the back. He was bent over the toilet bowl, sleeves rolled up, plunging with an enormous stick. Next to him stood the caretaker and an old man who turned out to be the plumber. From their conversation I discerned that the plumbing on the floor below was working and that ours had simply gotten backed up. I quietly returned to our room, made up the bed, and washed in a very colorful porcelain bowl with the same water as yesterday.

After breakfast, we headed to the Zhukovskii's, but first dropped in at the offices of the state Theater Section so that K.M. could report to Maria Fedorovna Andreeva. We were directed into a small office where a woman of average height stood at the desk, dressed smartly in a dark English suit with an elegant white blouse. She turned, said hello, and then smiled at me. Her face was not young, but she knew how to use makeup to her advantage. Most striking were her eyes, which sparkled and yet also burned with a cold intensity. She had a commanding, proud presence and a firm, no-nonsense voice. Later I would see her from time to time on Kronverskaia Street, where she lived in an apartment along with the writer Maxim Gorky. But no matter how often I saw her, I was always flustered in her presence. Her eyes were wide and radiant, as if a blue flame blazed from within, which made her face appear vibrant and beautiful, despite her fading skin. And such posture—she sat so gracefully in her chair, both majestic and feminine at the same time! She asked K.M. several questions. After learning that our journey had lasted twenty-nine days and that we had arrived only yesterday, she called out softly in the direction of the half-opened door: "Petr Petrovich!" Immediately a short, ruddy-faced man with a pince-nez entered the room. This was Kriuchkov.[6] "My dear Petr Petrovich, here is the situation: this is Konstantin Mikhailovich Miklachevsky, at my bidding he has just arrived with his wife. They are exhausted from the journey and more than anything else they need a rest." Petr

Petrovich agreed right away and said that in two days there would be an excellent room available in the Artists' Rest Home on Kamenny (Stone) Island. "Splendid," said Maria Fedorovna. "You will have a month's reprieve, and then you will start work at the People's Comedy Theater. What a nice coincidence it is that Sergei Ernestovich Radlov[7] is also due to spend this month on Kamenny Island. The two of you are to revive this theater. So, you can get acquainted while you are both relaxing."

As K.M. began to take his leave of her, my first reaction was to curtsey, as if I were in front of a school headmistress. But suddenly Maria Fedorovna stopped us. She wrote down several words on a form and then handed it to me, saying, "Go straight to the state warehouse, child. You deserve to be pampered a bit after such a rough journey." At the depot, I was given two classic French perfumes, *Quelques Fleurs* and Coty, in a blue box lined with satin! I also received very fashionable powder. I had not expected such luxury. We went out onto the street, and K.M. put my treasures into the pocket of his jacket, since I still did not have a handbag. He commented, "They have been requisitioning goods from all over the city, and now you (*vy*) are one of the lucky ones. There are even some actresses who do not get Coty." We were still addressing each other formally; the informal you (*ty*) came out only in our most intimate moments. We walked along Liteinii Prospekt, turned onto Nevskii Prospekt ,and then went up to Pushkin Street, which to me seemed narrow and unpleasant, so different from Pushkin Street in Odessa. We went up to the Zhukovskii's apartment by the back stairway. The door to the kitchen was open, and as we entered we could see that some haggling was going on. The mistress of the house, Olga Mikhailovna, was brandishing a bell decorated with sculpted figurines under the nose of a woman who was selling milk. Olga Mikhailovna was shouting, "You do not understand—this is pure silver, and you are offering only one lousy potato, how about some lard, surely you can offer some lard as well ..." Catching sight of us, and visibly embarrassed, she quickly concealed the bell behind her back. We went on into the next room. Later at home K.M. told me that this bell had belonged to his grandfather. It was from his estate near Kiev where he would use it to summon the servants. In their home on Sergievskaia Street, it had stood on his father's night table.

In the cramped dining room we met the three Zhukovskii sisters—Tamara, Lidia, and Vera. Verochka was still a young girl. Lidia was a bit older, very graceful with blonde hair and blue eyes, looking as if she had just stepped out of one of those English postcards that were so popular before the Revolution. Moreover, she was wearing a brightly colored, striped dress just like the ones in the Kodak photography advertisements. Tamara seemed to me to be a real beauty, though she had already lost her youthful charms. She was around 30, which at the time seemed very old to me. She was quite tall, by no means heavy, with upright posture, not even the slightest hint of a waist, and sagging breasts. Such flaws, though, did not make her any less alluring. She was thoroughly feminine and projected languor, voluptuousness, a desire to please, and a self-assurance that everyone found attractive. I could feel the Zhukovskii sisters' six pairs of eyes giving me the once-over, as were Verochka's fiancé and Lidia's husband Grisha Slanskii, a former naval officer. We were invited to sit down, and as he did so, K.M. pulled out my perfume and powder from his pockets. Tamara's face flushed red and she reached her hand out, but I managed to grab my presents and proclaim: "I have only just arrived in your fair city, and look what gifts I have already been given …" In response to Tamara's questioning glance, K.M. detailed our visit to Maria Fedorovna. Tamara Vladimirovna's face darkened and she said, "Oh, I should have warned you yesterday that we needed to go there together. Her proposal bothers me. The People's Comedy … But you have not agreed to it, have you?" Right at this moment Frumkin, Tamara Vladimirovna's new husband, came in from an adjoining room. He greeted us very cordially, bottle in hand, and proposed a toast to the new arrivals. He was very different from Tamara. Spirited and boorish, with Negro-like black hair, he was a pushy person, a sort of "hail-fellow-well-met type who guffawed loudly and drank heavily." During dinner Olga Mikhailovna went on and on to me about all of the hardships they had endured in order to protect our apartment. I just smiled and nodded my head. K.M.'s face turned to stone and he looked down silently at his plate. Afterward, he announced that in two or three days we were going to the Artists' Rest Home for a month. They invited us to dine with them again in order to, as they put it, "get down to business."

So, we once again went to dine with the Zhukovskii family. After supper Olga put on her glasses and began examining the backs of the chairs; she selected two and said to K.M., "These are the ones." Let me point out that this was in July of 1920. The popular book *The Twelve Chairs*[8] had not yet been written by Ilf and Petrov, but here we were in the exact same situation, with one exception. We did not have to do a search—the chairs in question had faint marks identifying them. Tamara Vladimirovna turned them over with the legs sticking up, laid one on top of the other, and then sat down next to them. She suggested that K.M. tear off the linen covering the springs of the chair. The whole family gathered around, but I stayed in place at the table. K.M. adroitly pulled out the nails and undid the covering, which exposed the inside of the chair. Tamara Vladimirovna began to pull out small packages wrapped up in white cloth. K.M. turned them over and quietly identified them: "Mother's earrings," "Mother's brooch," "Tanya's bracelet." Tamara Vladimirovna got her hands on a rather large package wrapped in a multicolored cloth, which she clasped to her chest and said, "This shall be mine." Tamara Vladimirovna unwrapped the cloth and, keeping her hold on it, showed what it held to everyone. It was a massive gold bracelet with large oval emeralds and a gold brooch with the same. "Mother's cabochon," K.M. exclaimed ruefully, sounding even a bit frightened. Tamara Vladimirovna put the bracelet on her wrist and pinned the brooch to her dress. They then turned their attention to the other chair and from it pulled out many packages containing jewelry. Olga Mikhailovna kept glancing at me and then said: "If you only knew what we have suffered … out of the blue, there might be a search … maybe even an arrest." Tamara Vladimirovna all of a sudden stopped and screwing up her eyes asked me: "Why aren't you over here with us, or are you waiting to look at them at home?" I answered, "I have never owned jewelry, so it has little meaning for me."

We left soon after that. But before we even got to the stairway, my husband reproached me for my "rude" response to Tamara Vladimirovna. She could have taken my words to be an insult and would not forget this. But if it had not been for her, then everything would have been lost. I wondered why she would even ask me such a question, and besides, was it even appropriate for me to be grabbing something for myself. A shadow passed over K.M.'s face and he answered: "She has good taste, she chose the best ones, Mama's most beloved pieces .... But she has a right to them, she saved them ..." I said nothing, for I could see the whole process had been painful. Later, when we were at home, he told me that the table cloth, the lovely tea service, the crystal vases, and many other such items at the Zhukovskii's had been taken from our apartment. But he was fine with this, because in his mind the apartment's possessions belonged not just to him but to his entire family. And he and his siblings were indebted to the Zhukovskii family. Thanks to them, everything had been saved, and so it was necessary to behave tactfully toward them. This was my first reprimand, to be followed by many more. In spite of his long years spent among Bohemian artists, K.M. was pedantic about upholding "social proprieties." It was very humiliating and difficult for me. He demanded that all outward proprieties be observed with people whom even he himself did not respect.

He spent the next few evenings finding hiding places for the jewelry brought back from the Zhukovskii apartment. He hung diamonds, sapphires, and rubies under door joints, baseboards and the tile stove. He did this in a way that even the most trained eye could not detect the modifications. Then he devised an intricate code and marked in various dictionaries the places where he had placed earrings, rings, and a necklace. I just simply memorized everything. And later, when we went to France, I was able to point out where everything was, without a mistake. Then the time came for us to head to the Artists' Rest Home on Kamenny Island. We went to where a battered old automobile was waiting. Sitting in it was the artist Natan Altman, whom I had already met. The car would not start, though, until another man who was there jumped on the hood. Like K.M., he was not handsome, yet his ugliness was attractive. When you looked at this little man, with his bald head, narrow quick eyes, thin lips, and such a sly and intelligent grin, you were immediately frightened: it was as though he could see right through you and know all of your flaws. "Well done, Pushkin, come sit," said Altman, directing him to the place next to him, and then introduced him to us as Viktor Shklovskii.[9] Later on, at the Rest Home, I learned that "Pushkin" was a nickname for Viktor. Almost everyone there had a nickname. The Rest Home was located in a magnificent mansion next to the river. We were given a bright and cheery room on the first floor, well-furnished and with a window looking out into the garden. This place seemed like a dream—it was clean and neat, the plumbing worked, and the lights functioned. In the large dining room, there was a long table, covered with a fine tablecloth set with individual place settings. Right next to this was a veranda and there a woman dressed in a bright orange velvet jacket was sitting at a small table. She was cutting from a large reddish Holland cheese and weighing each slice on a scale. At her side was a tall, well-built man wearing an enormous Mexican sombrero. He helped lay out the cheese on small plates, which already contained butter and round slices of smoked sausage. I assumed that this woman was the head housekeeper, but I was wrong. She was an artist by the name of Valentina Mikhailovna Khodasevich,[10] and the man helping her was her longtime friend, Ivan Nikolaevich Rakitskii. We met them at breakfast, along with Khodasevich's husband, Andrei Romanovich Didrikhs, and Sergei and Anna Radlov. This was the same Sergei Ernestovich that my husband was assigned to work with at the People's Comedy. In addition, there was the former director of this theater, Malyshev, and his young wife Innochka, who was animated, clever, and businesslike. And I had already met Altman and Shklovskii, of course.

Although Anna Radlov, not without reason, considered herself to be a beauty, and Inna Malyshev was a very youthful blond, vibrant and elegant, Valentina Mikhailovna stood out as the most interesting and striking of them all. She had marvelous curly hair light-chestnut in shade and shimmering with gold. Her somewhat elongated face could not be called beautiful, but in it there was so much charm, attractiveness, and volatility that it seemed forever new and unexpected. But what made her so exceptionally original was the way she carried herself, her unique style of dress, and the fact that she possessed both a boyish awkwardness and an irresistible femininity. Plus, both her husband and Rakitskii followed her every word and every glance, and they protected her. I soon learned that she had two nicknames, "*Rozochka* (Little Rose)" and "*Kupchikha* (the Merchant's Wife)." Rakitskii's nickname was "*Solovei* (Nightingale)" and her husband Didrikhs, simply "Didi." We were immediately given permission to use these nicknames.

After lunch Valentina Mikhailovna always rested, and Solovei hung on her door a sign saying "QUIET PLEASE—Rozochka is sleeping." In the evenings, they had convinced her not to go out into the garden and to dress more warmly. She had something wrong with her lungs and suffered frequent bouts of coughing. It soon became clear that she had tuberculosis. Later on a famous doctor cured her, a man by the name of Manukhin.[11] Although all who were staying at the rest home did what they pleased, nonetheless it became obligatory for everyone to pay special attention to "Rozochka." I was captivated by how seamlessly she managed it all—she remained unpretentious, friendly, and seemingly oblivious to the fact that she was the queen bee. Anna Radlov took me under her wing and shared all the gossip. I learned that Valentina Mikhailovna had studied painting in Paris, where she had met both Didrikhs and Rakitskii, who were also young artists. Solovei became her lover, and then Didrikhs became her husband. But Solovei had insinuated himself into this family and now followed them everywhere. Both men had given up painting. Only Valentina Mikhailovna remained an artist. Anna's revealing conversations made my hair stand on end, but I pretended that nothing surprised me so as not to appear "provincial." As I recall, Ivan Nikolaevich Rakitskii preferred to spend his time stretched out on the sofa in his sombrero and Mexican attire and reading Jules Verne's *The Mysterious Island*. I had read Jules Verne as a child, as well as authors such as Mayne Reed[12] and Gustav Emar,[13] preferring them to what I was supposed to be reading—*The Soulful Word* [*for Older Children*] (*Zadushevnoe slovo* [*dlia detei starshego vozrasta*]) and the emotional books of Lidia Charskaya.[14] Solovei would get very excited, as if he himself was reliving all of the action in *The Mysterious Island*. He tried to read several of its pages aloud and then rebuked everyone sitting in the living room for not paying attention to this work of genius. When it became clear that I, as the youngest, was familiar with it, he proclaimed me a comrade-in-arms with a genuine understanding of literature. I dazzled him with my recall of names and events. I was of course deliberately trying to impress him. Never had I been in company such as this—so colorful, so magnificent, and, for me at least at first, so unfathomable. Above all, I was afraid of embarrassing my husband.

My moment came when Solovei decided to stage *The Mysterious Island* and was determined to force even "this dull crowd" to get involved. He tried to give me the role of the boy but I objected, saying that I was a newlywed and that I was not about to play a male role. Everyone sitting in the living room overheard our argument. They all approved of my response and laughed loudly. K.M. was pleased that I did not back down and that I got my way. Solovei thought a bit and found a resolution: in *The Mysterious Island* there is only one creature that is female, some kind of wild hog, called Aguti. In the story the characters find a bullet in its body, which let them know that the island was inhabited. Solovei decided that I would play the role of Aguti. Everyone present liked this idea, and the play ended up being reduced to everyone rushing to find the bullet in me. I tried to kick everyone off from me; the merry scuffle lasted several minutes until we were all exhausted from laughing. From that time forward I was nicknamed "Aguti," which even now is my second name among my close friends from those years.

Sometimes "Duka" came for supper—this was the nickname for the writer Maxim Gorky. In Petrograd Valentina Mikhailovna, Didi, and Solovei all lived in the same apartment as Duka, for they were close friends. Twice the world-famous opera singer Feodor Ivanovich Chaliapin came with Gorky. I must admit that when Chaliapin came, I no longer even noticed Gorky. But even the most famous person would be overshadowed by Chaliapin. The very presence of this man, his gestures and the way he carried himself, was divine; his smile, his grand and easy gait, his facial expressions, his playful romping with his white bulldogs were mesmerizing, more interesting than the most fabulous show. I would just gaze at him, paralyzed by excitement, rapture, and joy; to me he was the most wonderful person in the world. I found even his ordinary conversation at dinner to be irresistibly charming. I would watch with fascination as he tied a napkin around his head and became an old, shrewish peasant woman at the bazaar, and then an instant later was himself again. Of course, at this moment Chaliapin was at the height of his fame. Yet even he was struggling and had to perform for a meal, for millet, and for lard.

Later I would see a lot of Gorky in his apartment on Kronverskaia Street. I would also run into him at Valentina Mikhailovna's studio as well as at the cafeteria during lunch or supper. Of course, he was unquestionably an original: I enjoyed his Volga accent, his lighthearted exchanges with friends at the dinner table, and his engaging reminiscences from time to time of his years spent mastering the art of making bread rolls and pretzels. But as a writer, I did not take to him. At that time I was enraptured with the Symbolists: Merezhkovskii[15] and Andrei Bely fascinated me. I found Gorky's verses to be more parody than true poetry. It goes without saying that I did not mention anything like this at the time, since the whole group worshipped their "Duka."

I am continuing on to TsNIRRI (Central Research Institute of Roentgenology and Radiology, Ministry of Public Health), where I have been transferred from GIDUV (State Institute for Advanced Training of Physicians) for radiation. At GIDUV I had trouble sleeping (I did not sleep for thirty-two days), but here new problems await. Loneliness and desolation are more oppressive than the disease. I cannot read, and it is difficult to write. At this place almost every patient has cancer. But all I have is myasthenia gravis. It is necessary to irradiate my thymus gland; they are convinced that it is overactive and must be suppressed. *They also assure me that there is nothing malignant. But it is not easy living with this condition. The eyes see, but do not obey: my eyelids droop, everything appears double. It does get better at times, but the slightest irritation brings pain. Oh it is miserable ….*

I am ordered to walk, and so I venture out into the snow and see several buildings amid a disturbed forest. I climb through a hole in the wire fence and step cautiously along the slippery path. If you stand with your back to these ordinary-looking buildings, then you see only the compressed lights against the dark sky. And at such moments you feel as if you are facing again that other side of life, the abyss. It is better to walk during the day. Even though you are only supposed to walk along the asphalt road around the buildings, I crawl again through the hole in the fence. I venture forth more boldly, following forest roads until I reach a small river flowing rapidly amid white snowdrifts. I am surprised to find it so beautiful here. There are birches and fir trees, and even a squirrel scurrying about. Well, alright then, if my eyes can still see, I must continue my work.

At the moment I am writing in a notebook, hoping that later I can type it. It is hard to work here. In my ward the women are bitter, for they have cancer of the esophagus and it is difficult for them to swallow their liquid food. They are in great pain. I fully sympathize with them, but they do not trust me. I am guilty of being able to easily swallow apples, meat, a slice of pickled cucumber. Of course I do not eat in the ward, but when they come to the cafeteria for porridge, they see me eating. When I return they warn me, "Just wait until you begin radiation, then you will not be able to swallow and you will completely lose your appetite." I say nothing, and only sigh. I understand that this animus is a product of the evil of cancer, but it will not be pleasant to endure two months or so with them. My only defense is my work. I will continue while I am still able to do so.

I do not have with me the notes I wrote down at GIDUV. Where did I leave off? Oh yes, the Artists' rest home, the new group of friends, who started calling me "Aguti." Chaliapin came as well, with his easy gait, grand gestures, and such confidence in his irresistible charm. Sometimes Chaliapin's wife, Maria Valentinova,[16] came with him. She knew everyone here, but was particularly good friends with Valentina Mikhailovna. Chaliapin and Gorky would go for a stroll around the island, and then Maria Valentinova would go up to see Rozochka in her room with a nice balcony. Here the two ladies would sit talking, perhaps imbibing a bit. One day Rozochka told us an amusing story that Maria Valentinova had relayed about her honeymoon with Chaliapin. They had decided to honeymoon on a boat ride down the Volga. As evening approached, they boarded the steamer at Nizhny Novgorod. Standing on the deck was a young lady anxiously watching all who approached the gangway. But the steamer cast off, and whomever it was that the lady had been expecting had not come. She was crying and took out a handkerchief. Fedor Ivanovich's kind heart was filled with pity. He escorted the young woman to her cabin and returned to his wife, but after promising he would not be long, he ran back to the forlorn woman. It was dawn before he returned. Maria Valentinova had not slept a wink and was sitting there in tears. Feodor Ivanovich sat down next to her and explained that it had been impossible for him to leave this sobbing woman without trying to calm her down. Some scoundrel officer had lured her away from her husband and convinced her to run off with him on this steamer. She had left a letter for her husband and rushed off to catch the steamer, but the officer had not come. Maria

Valentinova reminded him that this had been the first night of their honeymoon and that she too had spent it crying. Fedor Ivanovich then clasped her in his arms and said, "But I am now going to be with you always, but this poor thing has only grief to look forward to …." Maria Valentinova had enough delicacy to manage the situation. She chose not to make a scene, and the rest of their honeymoon went splendidly.

I was overwhelmed by all of these new and vivid impressions—such amazing people and they spoke so freely and easily about everything that popped into their heads. After all, K.M. himself was for me a new and inaccessible world, and now I was dealing with all of these individuals as well. For my husband, of course, they were nothing new. At times he seemed bored; he would get enough of the "chatter," as he liked to call our conversations, and then go off to sleep. But what he most liked to do was to take me down to the river, where he had found a small boat and repaired it. Somewhere he managed to find a paddle, and then we were able to explore along all of the channels, sometimes going as far as Elagina Island. It was not inhabited and was very overgrown with brush, like a jungle. He would lay the oars down in picturesque spots and then while resting would tell me about his childhood at the family estate "Belen'kii" near Kiev, his school years, and his family legends. He wanted me to know everything that had happened to him before we met and this made me so happy. When it was time to leave, we parted cordially with this group of friends, knowing that we would be seeing them often. The People's Comedy was located in the Iron Hall of the Petrograd People's House, which was only a stone's throw away from the building where Valentina Mikhailovna, Didi, and Solovei lived.

Much awaited us at home. K.M. loved his work in the theater and was good at it, and it was impossible for him to put it aside. I was prepared for this and directed all of my energies toward pleasing him, trying not to give him any grounds for complaint. I also worried over how to remain on an equal basis with the diverse and unique individuals in his circle. They valued people only for their ability to be amusing and original. What could I do that would dazzle them? Another challenge was the difficult days that now began of going through the family possessions which until now had been packed into cupboards, drawers, trunks, and baskets. It was not unlike the confusion of war—we were prisoners of a massive invasion of "stuff." K.M. personally owned few belongings. Mostly these were books, which stood in a cupboard and were not subject to inspection, and a small trunk in which he had stored his winter coat, a coat and tails, a dinner jacket, a morning coat, and two suits. Before he had gone to Odessa, he had stored his personal china and other antique items he had been collecting since his school days. All the rest were family possessions. Behind the kitchen, stacked in front of two windows, there stood three rows of boxes with chains wrapped around them, reaching all the way to the ceiling.

The first item on the agenda, K.M. decided, was to get rid of the neighbor whom Tamara Vladimirovna had foisted on us. She was taking up two rooms which looked out to the courtyard, which down the line, K.M. said, would be "my half." K.M. offered that, in exchange for her departure, she could keep her furniture, including a fancy set of chairs with gilded legs, small tables, and footstools belonging to his mother. She agreed and we transferred to her rooms the items from the baskets and trunks; we began to sort out what could be used, what could be put away into storage, and what should be sold, bartered, or discarded. First we tackled the tall dark cupboards that stood along the walls of the dining room and in the entryway. Here there were, as if ghosts from the pasts, his father's honorary dress uniforms (chamberlain and *Hofmeister*), his older brother's Chevalier Garde equipment, and even his sister's lady-in-waiting ballroom attire. Before her marriage, she must have made a spectacular appearance at a court ball, with an immense velvet train of a light coffee color, the whole of it embroidered in silver, styled after the fashion of Catherine the Great's era. Later, during the New Economic Policy (NEP), a businessman bought it as a cover for his piano. All around me the room seemed to fill with the mournful sighs of the dresses, the uniforms, and the three-cornered hats, all lamenting the passing of their epoch. Here before my eyes vignettes of the court and upper aristocracy were coming to life in ways completely unfamiliar to me. Eventually K.M. gave the uniforms, hats, and other paraphernalia to the Alexander Theater. Before he donated them, however, he unstitched his father's enormous beaver collar and cape. He said that this still could be used as currency. By wintertime, this "currency" became a collar for my rather improbable fur coat. I constructed this with silver plush from an enormous curtain, a cover coat, and as wadding (there was none at this time and no stores were open) I stuffed a down pillow into a bag. The end result resembled a silvery-looking bubble with a beaver neck. It was warm and very comical. Of course, I was only using the collar temporarily. It, like everything else piled around us, belonged to all of the heirs. K.M. regarded it as his duty to guard everything and never encroach upon the rights of his brothers and sister. When the New Economic Policy began and stores opened, I got a fully proper coat, and the beaver collar was stored with moth balls. Then in four years when we were getting ready to go to France, it was sold and replaced with items of equal value that were more portable.

There was simply no end to his family's possessions. There were multiple varieties of dinner services—English, French, German, Chinese, the Russian Imperial factory—and after them vases, cups, innumerable figurines, as well as family heirlooms that were particularly treasured by K.M. because they came from the Miklashevsky factory. Oh, this process of examining and sorting out items was tedious; yet it was an education of sorts in concepts completely new to me. I had never known there were so many different types of china, that there were types called "biscuit," that fanciful metallic figurines made with enamel were "cloisonné," that elegant china trays with two cups, a coffee pot, a creamer, and sugar bowl is called a "tête-à-tête." I had never heard of the fine furniture such as "empire," "Karelian birch," "Jacobean," "Bow," "marquetry," and many others. What was even harder than trying to catch the names, though, was to discern K.M.'s attitude toward the items and to not extol something until I knew what he thought about it; his taste became the law for me, not only in fine goods but also in art, architecture, music, and, of course, theater.

The "stuff" just kept coming and coming—silver table services for appetizers, fruit, and sweets consisting of complex ensembles illustrating mythological themes; vases; cooking pans; pitchers; sugar bowls; teapots; and even a porcelain samovar from the Imperial Factory with silver handles and valves. There were table mirrors in massive silver frames, toiletry sets, candlesticks—a deep abyss of expensive belongings which we had to take responsibility for and secure. More items brought new words: "rococo,"

"Baroque," "Art Nouveau." For pieces of furniture, I had to learn how to distinguish accurately "Elizabethan" from "Catherine," "Catherine" from "Paul," and even the end of "Paul" from the beginning of "Alexander I" and the end of "Alexander" from the beginning of "Nicholas I." Luckily for me this was as far as the matter went. The last three tsars were not linked with furniture; they only figured with regard to china and even then it was an indication of decline. I attended my "university" while crawling on the floor amid the shavings, picking up delicate rarities and placing them with great trepidation into their designated places. It took all of my energy, but I never broke a single item.

Dealing with all of these objects exhausted us. It was necessary to sort out what items were jointly owned by the family, what belonged personally to his sister Tatiana Mikhailovna, and what belonged to his older brother Ilia, who was married to Kate Bobrinskii. The items belonging to the latter were the most sumptuous, having been given to the young couple by Kate's father, Count Bobrinskii. K.M. had an excellent memory and knew exactly which items belonged to whom. Most were made from bronze: antique candelabra, mantelpiece clocks, and rather large figurines, many of which dated from the end of the eighteenth century to the beginning of the nineteenth. What were we to do with them? After admiring them for a bit, we put them back into their boxes. The crystal stunned me; there were entire services with carafes, cups, and finger bowls. I had to pick up wineglasses ranging in size from small to tall and examine their patterns so as not to break the set. K.M. was always nearby, but he had the more difficult job—dragging the boxes over, tearing off the iron straps, and unloading them, while I worked silently at the long table. K.M. was usually quiet as well, but sometimes he would whistle; he had perfect pitch.

Soon rehearsals for the People's Comedy Theater began, and so the last row of boxes remained unopened. We resolved to work on the boxes on days off. Sergei Ernestovich Radlov had added several circus artists into the theatrical troupe. He thought that the new audiences, which consisted mainly of sailors and Red Army soldiers, could more easily understand the shows if there were fewer monologues and more somersaults, flips, and other such acrobatic stunts. K.M. laughed at this "departure" from theatrical practice, but he was intrigued by its possibilities. He wrote a script for a play entitled "The Last Bourgeois"[17] in which he himself played the main role. It is my view that K.M. got the idea for such a comedy while we were sorting through his family belongings. I can recall his sly grins and grotesque grimaces as he, whistling all the while, dragged to a far corner a candelabra or a bronze nymph holding in her outstretched hand a clock encased in a bunch of grapes. K.M. wanted to write a play with clearly defined characters, but at the same time leave it open for the actors to improvise their dialogue. Unfortunately, though, since the troupe now had so many acrobats, gymnasts, and musclemen, he was forced to provide all of the dialogue and stage direction. The plot of his play was simple: a formerly wealthy man, elderly and bourgeois in taste and manner, is afraid of being robbed, and so he drags his most valuable possessions into one room. Here he lives all hemmed in by furniture, statues, and crockery. His former servant visits him and brings food, but his main purpose is to check out where everything is, for he has gathered a gang together to rob the old man. To make it more frightening, the robbers dress up in the most fantastic costumes and arrive at night on stilts to his room. Wild dances and stunts ensued, providing the circus performers ample opportunity to showcase their skills. George Delvari played the servant.[18] He was a stocky man, short in stature, and could deftly perform multiple somersaults in a row. He loved to turn his back on the audience and entertain them with bold movements of his body. He had a limited vocabulary and could not improvise dialogue, but he was very successful at expressing himself through pantomimes. He received the most applause and considered himself to be the star of the company, and therefore did not feel obligated to memorize his part.

K.M. did the entire staging of the show himself and also designed the costumes. The set decoration matched the continually growing muddle in our apartment of all of the dishes, bronzes, vases, and what not. For props we dragged to the theater several candelabra and an enormous samovar of fanciful design, as well as silver trays, porcelain vases with gilded necks, and a glazed chamber pot of his father's with a cover decorated in rose buds. My husband played the role of the bourgeois eccentric, well-versed as he was in the situation. He came out on stage dressed in a dark bathrobe with violet cuffs and a nightcap and scurried about among his things, endlessly counting them, moving them from place to place, piling them up, knocking them down, lifting them up, and dropping them. He even did a somersault after tripping over some of the objects. The servant appeared, followed by a stream of reprimands, altercations, and involved movements on stage. Then the servant left, and the old man (K.M.) carefully carried the chamber pot through the proscenium arch and placed it solicitously under the bed. He again counted his things and lay down to sleep. Now began the nighttime dance of the burglars. The old man is cowering from fear and despair as he watches the fantastic dancers carry off his possessions. But at this point a Red Army watchman appears, catching the bandits red-handed, and restores everything to its proper place. Next comes a commissar in a leather jacket, who declares that henceforth the apartment with all of its possessions was to be nationalized and would become an exhibit of the bourgeois way of life. The owner himself would be part of the exhibit and at the same time act as the museum's curator. The show ended with a chorus and the singing of satirical ballads composed by K.M. The only one who did not sing was Delvari, who instead did cartwheels, somersaults, and amused the audience with his antics. The show was cheerful and bright. The burglars danced on stilts and tossed multicolored sofa cushions at each other. "The Last Bourgeois" was a success and ran for a rather long time. I must point out that this play preceded Mayakovsky's "The Bedbug" (*Klop*), which was not written until 1928.[19]

After the rehearsals and the shows, we usually got together with Valentina Mikhailovna Khodasevich at their apartment on Kronverskaia Street. Somehow someone managed to get *samogon*.[20] Everyone drank, and K.M. perhaps more than others. Once he drank so much that he lay down on the floor of Valentina Mikhailovna's studio, barricading himself within a wall of papier-mâché elephants Rozochka had acquired from Siam. He refused to get up, and when they stood him up on his feet, he cried out in a high, falsetto voice, "Do not touch me, I am old man-Samogon." From that point on he had the nickname "Samogon." Solovei did not drink, but would usually spread out on an enormous Ottoman and watch everyone else, often accompanied by Maxim, Gorky's son.[21] Another who came was the actor Brif, who was the romantic "leading man" of the theatrical company as well as being Rozochka's lover. Obviously Andrei Romanovich (Didi) was used to his wife's caprices and pretended not to notice anything. This was the rule—Rozochka was allowed to do whatever she wanted, and those who loved her simply had to put up with it. But the little romance soon dissipated, and full peace resumed. Over time, Rozochka's tuberculosis became more acute and her treatment confined her to the apartment, which made her insist we visit more often. K.M. would only agree to go after the theater, but I could not stay away, even when he insinuated that I was neglecting my duties at home. Everything at the Khodasevich's was so interesting and unusual. Not counting our visits after the theater, I hung out there one or two times a week. Gradually I came to feel at home. I became acquainted with another woman living in Gorky's apartment, Maria Ignat'evna Benkendorf, nicknamed "Titka."[22] In this setting she behaved unpretentiously, laughing often and infectiously, showing off her excellent teeth. You could not consider her beautiful, but she was extremely charming. She was fluent in nearly every European language, well educated, well mannered, and knew how to behave in any company. She usually showed up in bright red silk pajamas and made everyone laugh with her unbelievable puns.

Besides Maria Ignat'evna, Maria Fedorovna Andreeva also lived in the apartment, and next to her was the room of Kriuchkov. Maria Fedorovna received the nickname "MFA" (abbreviation of her first name, patronymic, and surname—Translator's note), though never to her face. Similarly, they called Kriuchkov "Pepekriu" behind his back (also an abbreviation of his first name, patronymic, and surname—Translator's note).[23] Everyone was laughing at their love affair, but not openly. This pair mostly kept to themselves. Gorky, or "Duka," lived in two rooms further down the corridor; his son Maxim also had a room, and additionally there was an enormous, semidarkened dining room along with still more small rooms for longer term guests. Sometimes Rozochka's uncle showed up—the poet Vladislav Felitsianovich.[24] I was afraid of him. He was so thin, and his jaundiced skin pulled so tight on his face that he looked like a walking skeleton. His wife Anna Ivanovna[25] lived in Petrograd at the House of Art on Moika Street, but he preferred to stay in Moscow with Rozochka's father, Mikhail Felitsianovich, and only rarely visited. Practically every evening Friedrich Eduardovich Krimer[26] came, who was nicknamed "Fritz." He was an official in *Vneshtorg* (People's Commissariat for Foreign Trade); Maria Ignat'evna had worked with him as an interpreter and as his assistant. They would go out for automobile rides together, and once, when Fritz invited all of us to a wonderful reception he held for foreigners, Maria Ignat'evna served as hostess. Now, if you add into this mixture of people the figure of Zhak, who was bustling about everywhere, then you can get a pretty good idea of the people sharing the evening tea at the spacious and lovely studio of Valentina Mikhailovna. In this company no one could simply be an observer, for everyone had to be able to entertain others.

I do not know what inspired me to try and amuse these people with Odessa folklore. I was well aware that even though my Odessa friends had regarded me as well-read and intellectually mature, in my present company what I could say about literature or the theater would come across as vulgar and dull. This I understood. So, somehow, in a moment of merriment, I described the Odessa newspaper boys, who would tear along Deribasovskaia Street in fierce competition with each other to thrust the *Odessa Mail* into the hands of passersby, all the while yelling out rhyming ditties (*chatushkas*) on the topical news of the day:

The banks are quite happy and feast on fine cake,
For new Kerensky rubles so deftly they make.[27]

This brought me unexpected success, but now I had to come up with something new. Oh, but where would I get this from, from what corners of my memory could I search? I had not frequented Odessa's cabarets and variety shows. My friend Ania and I had intelligent conversations and we had our passions, but obviously we had only experienced life from the sidelines. Therefore, what I drew from was something ingrained in me from childhood, when my brother Sasha would come home singing the street songs of Odessa. I had not memorized them, I did not sing them, but somehow now, they simply began to come back to me. I happened to recall one of the ditties they had sung in Odessa when the skating rink opened for the first time, which ended in what became a famous last line, "Even if dying, you must do it in style!" This bit of nonsense was a hit, and everyone got a big laugh out of it. I remembered as well some songs of Leni Utësov,[28] who had begun his career in the early movie houses, singing during the intermissions. I recalled the rollicking words of one refrain:

We only go around once in life, no one lives forever,
Why think about tomorrow—
In life we only go around once!

All of this meaningless debris was there in my memory; I just had to hook one tiny end for it to come gushing out, just like the old-fashioned clothing tumbling out from the baskets in our apartment. But for my audience, this was something novel, and I became necessary to them. They would call me, saying they were bored without me, and when I arrived, they would be happy to see me. Of course, it goes without saying that I was not always putting on a show. There were also quiet conversations when there were no guests present. One evening Didrikhs was pottering around with his models, Solovei dozing on the Ottoman, and Rozochka and I quietly chatted. She asked sympathetically how I, being such a young girl, could cope with such a brilliant but unattractive, balding man. I was not comfortable talking about my feelings, but I said that it was his bald spot that I most cherished. "So, you really do love him, Aguti?" "Well, what about it, would you like all the details?" I answered with an Odessa accent and we both had a laugh. From Kronverskaia I would return exhilarated, even intoxicated from my triumph, but also embarrassed by the fact that maybe I was not behaving myself appropriately. If K.M. had been with me, then I would have sat there quiet as a mouse.

Once, an extraordinary event took place in the apartment on Kronverskaia—a reception for the English writer H. G. Wells.[29] K.M. was invited because of his fluency in English. No one living in Gorky's apartment, with the exception of Maria Ignat'evna, knew English. At this time people were starving in Petrograd; dead horses lying in the streets soon vanished, for hungry people ravaged such corpses almost instantly. No stores operated, no markets opened, yet the table was lavishly spread for this festive occasion. Alfred Rode, former proprietor of a supper club and cabaret known as the "Villa Rode,"[30] procured the food. He had been commissioned by Gorky to manage rations for the House of Scholars, which we received once a month: 2–3 salted herring kippers; a bag of stale, mushy dried vegetables; sugar; a handful of barley, either pearl or wheat; and in a good month, one-fourth of a liter of linseed oil. It was an enviable ration for this time period. Yes, Rode knew where to find food. This night there were sardines, various smoked delicacies, a savory pie known as *coulibiac*, and many tasty hors d'oeuvres, abundant vodka and wine. After a performance by the Pevcheskii Court Capella[31] in Valentina Mikhailovna's studio, we sat down to supper. The short and rather stocky Wells, dressed in an ordinary gray suit, sat next to Maria Ignat'evna. Ruddy-faced, exuberant, and attentive, Wells looked around at all of us, at the abundance of food, and kept plying Maria with an endless stream of questions; little did he know then that this witty and sociable lady would later become his wife.[32] Wells's son[33] sat next to me, a thin, handsome youth who looked exactly like the young Englishmen we knew from postcards. I did not know any English, so I risked speaking to him in French; neither of us spoke French well, but we understood each other. He asked me if we always dined like this, and I said no, only when honoring famous guests. Across from us sat a pair of ballet dancers who had been invited by Rode—Lopukhova and Orlov,[34] both dressed in traditional Russian clothing. As supper ended, the dishes were cleared away, and just as we were expecting tea to be served, and perhaps a demonstration of classical ballet, a bayan-player began to play a dance tune.[35] Lopukhova and Orlov floated up to the table like butterflies and began to dance on the white tablecloth. Lopukhova's red leather boots flashed between the wine glasses with such dexterity that one might have thought all she had ever done was dance on tables. Orlov did an unexpected move right under Wells's nose, which caused the writer to jerk back a bit from the table. But it all turned out happily, and afterward everyone gathered in Valentina Mikhailovna's studio and danced to the bayan.

Upon our return home, K.M. and I labeled this supper "A Feast in a Time of Plague." Such a meal was like a holiday for us, but it made us feel uncomfortable. We preferred meals with friends such as Krimer, with simpler fare and no dancing on the tables. K.M. said, though, that we should not accept hospitality without reciprocating. I was elated at the possibility of launching a new venture I had been contemplating. In the large entryway dining room there were containers filled with all kinds of finery and I now succeeded in convincing K.M. that as the caretaker of the family legacy, he was entitled to improve our diet by bartering just a small number of less valuable napkins, kitchen aprons, old tablecloths, and so on. I had been noticing two black market entrepreneurs hanging around our staircase. When I showed one of them a large white damask napkin, she folded it into a scarf, tied it excitedly to her head, and asked how many "batches of eggs" I wanted for it. I said what seemed astronomical to me—five! But without any further haggling, she counted out fifty fresh large eggs. For the other napkin I got a jar of cooking oil. Potatoes now appeared on our table along with bits of lard and, at times, even fresh meat or fish. K.M. jealously tracked the expenditures on these products. However, he always provided lavishly for his guests. Whenever we acquired pieces of suet, meat, or fish, or else a small bag of wheat flour, we immediately invited friends. Rozochka would come with her husband. Krimer and Maria Ignat'evna, Shklovskii, the artist Vladimir Lebedev,[36] and his wife Sarra also joined us. You could not call our fare sumptuous, but there was lots to eat and everything was fresh. K.M. would contrive somehow to get wine or, at the very least, some *samogon*. This led to eccentric shenanigans. Once he delivered a lecture dressed in a fantastic costume about how primordial peoples made alcohol from their own spit. Then he called on everyone to lay down on the rug and drink their portion of liquor from the saucer, to facilitate faster intoxication, which we all did. People loved coming to our apartment. We received them in the large living room, furnished in the strict "empire" style and adorned with portraits of K.M.'s ancestors and cabinets displaying fine china, miniatures, snuffboxes, and so on.

Life basically went on in a constant process of sorting out the family "stuff," finding foods to buy or barter for, cleaning, cooking, and attending rehearsals and shows. But there were moments of exaltation as I continued to meet illustrious figures whose works enraptured me, such as the poet Alexander Blok. The troupe of the People's Comedy Theater included his wife—Liubov' Dmitrievna Basargina, an actress no longer in her prime. She had put on a lot of weight, her face was fleshy, and her voice sounded coarse and shabby. K.M. was rehearsing "The Merry Wives of Windsor" which he had "simplified" for its staging at the People's Comedy.[37] I went to one of the rehearsals. K.M. was giving directions to Basargina,[38] who was stubbornly disagreeing with him. I was sitting in the fifth row of the darkened theater. Suddenly I heard someone come in with a careful step and sit down next to me. I was in the second seat from the aisle, and he was in the end seat. I glanced at his thin profile, high forehead, and downy hair that was no longer as dark as in his youthful portraits. I took a deep breath and looked pointedly at his delicate hands—these were the hands that had composed such poetry! I had never met him and was afraid to look him in the face. If I squinted my eyes down to the right, I could gaze at his hands, without turning my head. I feared he would hear my racing heart, for to me he seemed omniscient. But he must not have cared for their revision of Shakespeare for the new postrevolutionary audiences. He soon left, or rather, he seemed to just fade away in the darkness.

Several weeks later K.M. formally introduced me to Alexander Blok at the House of Art, where he had read some of his work. Blok lightly touched my hand but he was not really looking at me as much as upward. Among people he seemed out of place. I knew that he was doing a lot of translating and was often to be found at the "World Literature" office on Mokhovaia Street; the editor A. N. Tikhonov was often our guest and spoke of him as well as of other writers who worked for him.[39] In August of 1921, I was working at the Petropolis[40] publishing house book store when Blok died. The entire publishing company took part in the funeral, walking behind the coffin. The secretary Nadia Zalshupina[41] and I carried wreaths. At the cemetery, there were not more than forty to fifty people in attendance. The writer Andrei Bely was there. Crestfallen, he hung over the trellis of the neighboring grave and stared without blinking as they lowered the coffin into the freshly dug hole. His eyes looked frightening, for they were completely blank. Blok's wife sobbed silently and shook as she rocked back and forth. She seemed sincere, but I could not help recalling a story Rozochka had told about a rainy day encounter between Liubov Basargina and the wife of her lover George Delvari; the latter attacked her rival with her umbrella. At the time I had been appalled by the thought of this Delvari, who imagined himself to be an artistic genius, having an affair with the wife of a famous poet. What could have attracted her to this dim-witted, narcissistic boor who knew how to turn cartwheels? Everyone on Kronverskaia laughed at me when I expressed my outrage; they told me that I was too young to understand the allure of erotic novelties. I later understood better the origin of her sexual frustration, though not her choice of Delvari. But at that time it just seemed unacceptable for someone honored with being the wife of Blok.

I was now obviously seeing a different side of my new artistic milieu, but I had little knowledge or experience among great artists, poets, painters, to go by. The immodest details of their lives were the subject of after-dinner stories among those close to them, an easy form of entertainment. I had come to accept much but this crossed a line for me. K.M. was sympathetic and explained to me that he considered provincial persons like myself to be purer and more ingenuous, with a higher sense of morality. But in our circles, he said, what was valued most was discretion. Being circumspect, somewhat skeptical and even cynical was valued more highly than provincial effusiveness. Thus, behind the compliment to my provincial purity lay subtle advice to become more cynical. He hoped to engender in me a spiritual rebirth, yet this proved more challenging than learning various architectural styles, furniture, schools of painting, and music. I was aware of the complexity and richness of K.M.'s spiritual world, which placed Italy at its height. He had been there many times and his stories were so vivid that I could picture everything as if I had been there with him. All of this enraptured me, though our sexual relations soon became less frequent. The latter did not at first bother me. I was too inexperienced to realize the problem in our age difference. My husband had led a very vigorous life, with a lot of boozing and affairs with many women, and now he just seemed worn out from all of the work at home and long walks to morning rehearsals and shows in the evening. No, I just thought that this was how relations inevitably developed between people of refined taste, with the habitual closeness killing passionate love. It was insulting that gestures of love surfaced so rarely, but I did not dare go up to my husband and kiss him even on the forehead. I was always a little afraid of him.

In the evenings, when he had finished with my lesson on sorting the family possessions, K.M. would sit down at his desk and immerse himself in Italian, Spanish, or French volumes on art, while I sat at another table and greedily devoured journals on art and architecture, such as *Old Years* and *The Capital and Manor*.[42] I also read Lukomskiii's book[43] as well as excellent monographs that acquainted me with the artistic movements known as the "Wanderers" and the "World of Art." My evaluations of these works almost always coincided with those of K.M., for I was now steeped in his tastes. It was more difficult for me to read monographs on Western art because they were all written in foreign languages, though K.M. happily translated them for me. He would recall in what year he had admired the original of these pictures and would describe their setting. Such evenings were like a holiday to me, and I would fall asleep in my corner content, knowing that K.M. would work until late at night.

K.M. particularly missed having coffee, an item rarely seen at this time. It was from him that I first learned how the writer Balzac worked for twenty-four hours by fortifying himself with coffee. So I began to search for it. I went to a flea market and talked at length with two old women who had the look of former aristocrats. They tended to sell odd items: embroidered collars, cuffs, scraps of old lace, plush frames for photographs, and small coffee cups. But it so happened that they had tucked away stale coffee beans. To obtain this treasure I bartered grains, eggs, or lard. I was so pleased to watch how K.M. treated these beans with ceremony, like a religious rite. First he roasted and then ground them in a long stylish mill shaped like a cylinder, which he had bought in Istanbul. He was a true expert at brewing coffee. K.M. was also adept at preparing fuel for the winter. He went to the Fontanka canal and fished out logs with a boat hook. After drying them in our courtyard, he put them on a makeshift sawhorse, and we sawed short blocks for our small stove and stacked them in the dining room. I did not know how to saw, but I got used to it. K.M. was patient, and he calmly guided and cheered me on.

The man who was the director of the Hermitage Museum at this time was K. M.'s uncle (his mother's brother), Sergei Nikolaevich Troinitskii.[44] He received us very politely in his office. He had a distinguished appearance, handsome and debonair, but what I found most striking was his delicacy of manner and the precise correctness of his speech. And "Uncle Serezha" gave us a special pass for the Golden Storerooms of the Hermitage, which were accessible to only a very few. So, after looking at the picture collection, we went up to this secret place and fell in love with the jewelry displayed there. I remember how once we ran into Aleksandr Nikolaevich Benois,[45] who was there with some friends. I knew him only through his writings and reproductions of his delightful paintings and drawings. To me he was inaccessible, a lofty and important artistic master. But he turned out to be a lively, sociable, witty, and convivial fellow, shorter than I expected, and he made me feel immediately at ease with him. K.M. teased me for not viewing him as a Bohemian but as a "genuine man of the world" who "knows painting better than any of us …."

After leaving the People's Comedy Theater, K.M. went to work at the Musical Comedy Theater of Mardzhanov.[46] Here he staged "The Abduction from the Seraglio."[47] My life at this point was fully occupied with new experiences, meeting remarkable persons, and self-education, learning all that I needed to know as the wife of K.M. I was not thinking about the future nor about the fact that I was not trained for any vocation. And some periods were very difficult, when we went days without speaking and I would think in horror that everything was over. This happened most often when I sinned against "propriety." For example, he had two elderly aunts whose family name was Gagarin and each held the rank of princess. In former days, these two homely maidens had attended dinner parties at the Miklashevsky home. Now they were living in poverty, and K.M. would invite them over in order to feed them. I really put myself out on these occasions to cook cutlets, cheese pancakes, and practically everything that it was possible to make from whatever I had available. These two ladies, Katia and Varia, or, as K.M. called them, "Kat'–Var'" were like two starving birds. Old Katia, somewhat pretentious, looked like an owl with her round eyes and face and gray hair cropped short. Varia looked like a plucked hen, with a long wiry neck and a mouth always half-open and toothless. I did feel sorry for them, though they obviously viewed me an unacceptable match for their patrician nephew. But they felt obligated to be nice because I treated them so politely and because of their own proper, aristocratic upbringing at the Smolny Institute for Noble Maidens. Moreover, I plied them with delicacies that were hard to come by at that time. I kept encouraging them, "Have some more pancakes; here, let me pour you some stronger tea, please, take another pancake while they are still warm." They did eat the pancakes and drank tea, but they kept exchanging glances. Then, after they had left, K.M. sulked in silence. I did not understand: Kat' and Var' had left satisfied and took leftovers with them. So I asked, "What is the matter?" K.M. glanced angrily at me and, shifting to the more formal form of you ("vyi"), asked: "Have you really never heard that it is impolite to say to guests, "*s'esh'te* (eat some more, go ahead, eat up)?"

"So how should it be said?"

"You should say 'skushaite (please, would you like to have something more …?)' "

I tried a bit of Odessan humor to lighten the mood but I could never get K.M. to laugh on such occasions. A heated argument ensued. Thanks to such trifles we could go for days without a word to each other. But then we would make up, and all would be well. I remember two times when Chaliapin reconciled us. K.M. managed to procure second row tickets for the opera "Boris Godunov." He burst in all excited, forgetting completely that we were not speaking and rushing me to get ready. This was my first opportunity to see Fedor Chaliapin on the stage, sitting so close that I did not miss a thing. I watched oh so carefully, but not even in a single gesture or movement of his face did I see any glimpse of Fedor Ivanovich as he was in real life. Of course, to me he was always a tsar among men, but this was different, he was Tsar Boris, with nothing in common with Chaliapin. There was not a single wasted moment in his entire performance. On stage he did not relax like other opera stars did, saving their energies. He kept on acting when others were singing; he never spared himself, as though his energy was inexhaustible. Another time, also after one of our quarrels, K.M. forgot all about it and took me to Pavlovsk. There, at the Pavlov Station, Chaliapin sang. He was dressed in tails, looking brilliant as well as irresistibly handsome. This was his last concert in Pavlov Station, for they stopped holding concerts there. The old era was passing. I saw it fading away and heard its very last gasps.

The poet Vladimir Mayakovsky came to Petrograd from Moscow to read his new work, "The 150 Millions" at the House of Art.[48] The verses were unconventional and the poet larger than life. He stood there tall and strong, stunning the audience with his booming voice and large, penetrating eyes. But it seemed to me that this thundering Hercules was stifling fine harmonious verse and pushing out real poetry by shouting it down. Yet the elemental force of Mayakovsky's lines and his stature made a huge impression on me. Lilia (Lili) Brik had also come with him.[49] As always, Zhak was around; he liked to boast that he was a regular visitor at the Brik home in Petrograd and to insinuate he had his own special relationship with Lilia. Afterward, Zhak introduced me to her. Though she was not what you would call beautiful, even if you only met her once, you would never forget her. She was petite, though her head seemed disproportionately large. She had large, radiant eyes, light brown with golden specks. What did she radiate the most—self-confidence, authority, sensuality, smugness? She had much of each. She was surrounded by so many men and women that one might have supposed that it had been she who had written the poem, "The 150 Millions."

Meanwhile at the other end of the hall Mayakovsky was sounding off amid a cluster of young poets.

I am not going to hold myself to a strictly chronological narrative. I am skipping over much. Were it not for my goal of describing all of the milestones of my capacious life, I would gladly write only about my years in Petrograd with Konstantin Mikhailovich, years that are very dear to me, especially now, when my life has become so wretched. It brings me such joy to linger over these fascinating and oh so happy days, but I cannot allow myself too long of a break. I must hurry and record on paper several events from that time that are still clear in my memory, such as the first time I saw Osip Emil'evich Mandelshtam. It was at the House of Art in 1921. The residents of this building, who were mostly writers and literary critics, decided to hold a masquerade. My husband and I did not dress up, but others did. Dressed in tails, Mandelshtam entered the hall sedately and with an air of importance. With his dark hair disheveled and the stubble of whiskers on his cheeks, his starched shirt front propping up his strong chin, I am not sure who he was trying to be, Pushkin's Onegin perhaps? Alas, he obviously could not get ahold of anything fancy except for a tailcoat that was too wide for him, khaki puttees on his legs, and coarse soldiers' boots. Nonetheless, his expression was proud and even haughty. I had recently read his poems for the first time. His verses, how they came alive—they sang, they pealed forth like bells, they pushed everything else into the background as they took you wherever it was that they wished you to go. Yet this amazing poet did not see how absurd he looked. Only later did I understand that his appearance was meant to symbolize the juncture of time and epochs ....

4

Gathering Clouds: Marital Storms and Emigration

My life was both joyful and difficult. The joy came from my everyday experiences. The hardship stemmed from the constant stress and even fear that I would display bad taste or use a word incorrectly and trigger K.M.'s disapproval. The first year had been the toughest. What helped me was my ongoing exposure to the ultra-rarified group of individuals on Kronverskaia Street and to my husband's boyhood friends from his days in the Alexander Lyceum. Oh yes, interacting with these persons helped me to overcome my provincialism and learn to listen without interrupting people, a common habit among my friends in Odessa. Nikolai Nikolaevich Evreinov,[1] a great friend of K.M.'s, visited often. He came not only to converse about theater, but for warmth and the flatbreads (*lepeshki*) I baked with lard. By winter we had managed to stockpile wooden beams, which we then split into firewood. K.M. custom ordered a small metal stove (*burzhuika*) and multiple knee-shaped pipes. He hammered spikes onto the walls of our room and raised up the stove pipe a meter or two. Then he draped it around the room by bracing it on wire rings hanging from the spikes. Just a small amount of firewood was needed to heat the pipes and retain the warmth for a long time. The wall behind the stove and the kitchen table on which it stood were covered with sheets of iron. My bartering enabled us to get rye flour and lard, which I used to bake flatbread right on the stove. Nikolai Nikolaevich, coming from the frosty air into our nice warm room, would ask, "Might there be any bread today?"

We occasionally got together with the Zhukovskii family. Tamara Vladimirovna could not stand it that K.M. was a noted figure in the theatrical world while she was sitting on the sidelines. She tried to entice him back but to no avail, so she insisted that Frumkin take her abroad, which he did. They ended up in Berlin, where Tamara Vladimirovna made a conquest of Leonid Borisovich Krasin, an old Bolshevik and official for the Commissariat of Trade.[2] A tempestuous love affair ensued, but this is not a subject worth dwelling on. My Odessan friend Lenia Trauberg came up to us in the theater. He had with him a young man with a thin, delicate face whom he introduced as "My friend Grisha Kozintsev."[3] They wanted to show K.M. their designs for theater productions, and he invited them to visit us, which they started to do quite often. They worshipped him and hung on his every word. Once they came to dinner but there was no wine. K.M. recalled a basket in the passageway that had homeopathic medicines belonging to his mother. He poured out the contents into a carafe and insisted that such amounts could not hurt us since, after all, alcohol was alcohol. He then delighted the boys by performing a religious rite with considerable ceremony while dressed as an alchemist with a handmade paper cap. After this, however, the boys made sure to bring alcohol with them whenever they came. Once they brought with them Serezha Iutkevich,[4] and after dinner serious discussions went on, but I did not take part. My turn began when K.M. had to leave. Then we would chatter away merrily. I told them stories about "Wednesdays" at Evreinov's and the personalities who gathered on Kronverskaia Street. They would read to me their satirical epigrams. I remember their mean-spirited parody of Anna Akhmatova:

> I scarcely touched the pens,
> And the poems gushed forth like a river,
> Do you remember, my dear, the bitch
> That ran away from the puppy?
> There is nothing else for me to think about ...
> My God! Your grace.
> Let me retreat from human clatter to the double bed.

At that time Akhmatova lived nearby on the corner of Sergievskaia Street in a semibasement flat. She lived there with the Orientalist scholar Vladimir Shileiko.[5] They were a strange pair. I often ran into them when picking up rations at the House of Scholars. Shileiko was scary and reminded me of a spider with his mop of long hair, full beard, and large wandering eyes. He walked along with a dull, gloomy demeanor, all hunched over while bearing on his back a pack filled with our meager allotments. Thin and pale, with a waxen transparency, Anna Andreevna followed behind him in an old-fashioned silk dress that at one time had been chic but now only inspired a feeling of pity. "Else paler seems my saddened face, Above the silk of lilac glaring" blared in my head.[6] She walked with a certain symmetry, lightly swaying to and fro, and to me she seemed a gypsy who accidentally ended up in a famine-stricken city and sought refuge with a visionary scholar.

My main duty was to be an exemplary housewife. K.M. could not stand clutter and dust on the furniture. I tried to keep things in order. I remember once how my efforts led to a fantastic discovery. I had decided to straighten up the fine mahogany Alexander I writing desk; from a slight groove in the desk I pulled out papers in order to wipe it with turpentine. But I inadvertently snagged my cloth on a small wire nail. When I pulled on it, to my horror, one of the columns popped out. I froze—I had spoiled something that my husband treasured! But right at this moment he came in, saw what had happened, and said, "How foolish of me to have forgotten this hidden box!" He pulled out a narrow container concealed behind the column and extracted little packets wrapped in leather. Quite a collection appeared on the table: a large thick braid of rolled-up strands of select pearls; at its ends were turrets studded with rubies, bracelets, brooches, earrings, rings, necklaces, tiepins and two flat cigarette cases, platinum and gold. He had realized when they had retrieved the jewelry hidden at the Zhukovskii flat that pieces were missing but had not inquired about this. Someone in his family must have hidden this jewelry before leaving Petrograd. He put them back into the box and restored it to its hiding place. Just several days earlier he had received a letter from his younger brother Vadim saying that he was not doing well and that their older brother Il'ia and sister Tatiana were living in Nice in great want.[7] K.M. sighed heavily: his family was starving, yet here lay such riches.

We frequently attended the public debates at the Zubovskii Mansion (in St. Isaac's Square), which now housed the Institute of the History of Art. K.M. was a good friend of Count Zubov,[8] who was at that time politically well connected. Soon Zubov asked him to offer lectures on the history of theater and K.M. happily agreed. I was working in the Petropolis publishing house bookstore. But beyond getting to have frequent conversations with such writers as Alexei Remizov[9] and Fyodor Sologub,[10] it was not very interesting to work here. Sometimes the wife of Sologub, Chebotarevskaia,[11] a strange and tormented woman, came with him. I remember how once she came in by herself and then sat in the shop for half an hour. She finally asked about her husband and left. Several days later we learned that she had disappeared. Sologub hung about in our shop for hours and shuddered whenever the door opened. Not long after this they found her body under the Tuchkov Bridge. To comfort and distract Sologub, Anna Akhmatova and the actress Olenka Sudeikina moved in with him (or perhaps he moved in with them on the Fontanka?).[12] Perhaps this is why Akhmatova and Sudeikina invited us to tea, though K.M. had known Sudeikina and her former husband in the prewar period. I went there in a state of agitation. I do not know what fascinated me more, the verses of Akhmatova or her tragic, tortured beauty. Akhmatova sat at a round table, silently stirring her tea that she drank from an antique teacup, occasionally smiling as she gazed at Sudeikina. Sologub was morose and distracted, our presence more a burden than a comfort. Sudeikina acted as hostess; she was a delicate blond, rather "cutesy" in manner, and she kept trying to amuse us by talking about the absurdity of current songs. We were supposed to find her examples funny and interesting, but we soon left. They politely asked if they could visit us, but we knew this was not genuine. We both wondered why, in K.M.'s words, "these myrrh-bearing women" had invited us.[13] I was grateful, though, to Akhmatova for staying silent. By not speaking a word or making a gesture, she remained fascinating to me. She must have noted how I could not take my eyes away from her.

Although I enjoyed making new acquaintances, my favorite spot remained the circle of friends on Kronverskaia Street. It had been a long time since I had felt the need to earn my place by entertaining the group. I had become my own person and had the right to listen to and evaluate new additions. One of these was the secretary of Krimer, a man by the name of Radovskii who was witty and always had funny stories to tell. He willingly participated in our impromptu masquerades, nighttime walks, and so on. I could sometimes convince my husband to join us. K.M. did not tell amusing stories but sometimes he would be so eccentric that he made everyone feel lighthearted. He might wear a black suit with a white stripe or a yellowish fluffy suit topped by one of his many crazy ties. He would put together different combinations of clothing and accessories, along with corresponding gesticulations and voices.

Once or twice a month K.M. and I would invite guests to our home. The New Economic Policy (NEP) had begun and private markets had reappeared. We had at this time a housekeeper, Masha Gubanova, who was a good woman and a devoted friend. For our guests, Masha would cook roast beef and bake wonderful savory pies (*kulebiaka*, also known as *coulibiac*). I used my mother's recipes to surprise our guests with Odessan cuisine. There was lots of wine and many rooms for our intoxicated guests to end up in, usually in pairs. K.M. carried out fleeting flirtations, which I had trained myself to ignore. But it was still hard when I would glimpse my own husband behind a door pressing up against some uninvited girl who had come with a guest. He never touched any of our friends. The first time I saw such a "show," it crushed me to see his lascivious smile, the gestures that were not his at all, the undue familiarity. This could not possibly be the same person whom I considered to be so noble and intelligent. After everyone had left, he ridiculed my objections as naïve. He said that I could not understand the simplest things, such "mischief" always goes on with too much alcohol, and he would not have said a word if he had seen me doing it. This insulted me, which made him laugh again, and he pointed out that the real poignancy of a woman lay in her sexual daring, which I was not yet capable of. But K.M. rarely took such liberties and I convinced myself that it was the inevitable result of intoxication. He really did enjoy drinking in the company of people he found interesting.

The Annenkovs[14] were frequent guests, as were the Zamiatins,[15] the Lebedevs, and the Khodaseviches. I was happiest of all when Pavel Eliseevich Shchëgolev[16] came, for he was an amazing person. His book on Pushkin's fatal duel inspired me to reread Pushkin, including his letters, and Petrograd then became even more meaningful to me. Whenever Shchëgolev was there, I would wait impatiently for all of the tipsy guests to disperse into the separate rooms, finally leaving the two of us alone. He reminded me of Nikolai Gogol's character Sobakevich in *Dead Souls*.[17] Pavel Eliseevich was rather corpulent, too big even to get one's arms around, and would sit there nibbling on a still warm *kulebiaka* while I poured him more red wine (which he drank as if it were water and yet never got drunk). Then he would move on to the veal. Finally, I would pick out for him little mini cucumbers from the jar of pickles, he would groan with satisfaction and begin to spin tales of the past and present.

Once after such a reception K.M. invited Mikhail Kuzmin,[18] who was accompanied by Iurochka Iurkun.[19] There was a lot of food left over from the previous night, plus Masha baked fresh pies. K.M. preferred Kuzmin's company in a more intimate setting than our large gatherings. He appreciated Kuzmin's musical talents, especially his chamber music. Kuzmin would spend hours at our piano improvising, then recite his own verses as well as French poetry. Meanwhile Iurochka would be eating and eating, without the slightest embarrassment, since this is exactly what he had come to do. They were living at the time in great poverty.

I am not writing anything at all about my family, but I had not forgotten them. As soon as an opportunity arose, I sent my mother napkins, towels, and sheets to exchange for food. In Odessa there was hunger and privation. I must admit that I often did this in secret. K.M. kept a close account of our expenditures, subtracting them from his share of the inheritance. But I felt that I had a right to send these to my family since I took such care of everything else. In her letters mama kept asking me about our wedding. I filled my letters with descriptions of concerts and museums, as if forgetting such "trifles" as our wedding, which, incidentally, had never taken place. We had registered soon after our arrival from Odessa in one of the civil registry offices, but did not get around to the church wedding that meant so much to my mother. Mama turned to guile and wrote that my father would visit just to see what our life was like. I knew that his real purpose was to confirm our marriage certificate. So K.M. made arrangements with a pastor at the Lutheran Church on Furshtatskaia Street, and we were duly married in a side chapel behind the altar. For this, he took out from hiding the wedding rings of his parents. My father never did come for a visit. Later we divorced according to civil law, but to me this marriage performed in the church remained inviolate.

My friend Ania arrived unexpectedly from Odessa. K.M. had never encouraged her to pursue acting, since in his opinion, she could not articulate half of the Russian alphabet. But he found her face strikingly original. He knew from me that Ania was not a possible conquest, for she was strictly chaste and believed physical intimacy permissible only if there was deep eternal love. Her acting studio had closed down, but she and a fellow student Zoia, whose aunt lived in Petrograd, had decided to try their luck here. Secretly they hoped that my husband would use his connections in the theater world to help Ania become a great tragic actress. So Ania and Zoia spent a lot of time with us. I showed them around the city and took them to museums and theaters. I also took them to see Father Vvedenskii,[20] not realizing the consequences. We went to the Church of Zakharia and Elizabeth, where this priest "performed." He looked more like an actor than a priest, tall and slender with a pale, elongated face and penetrating eyes. His face bore only a hint of a mustache and his wavy black hair lay expertly combed. He spoke freely and easily, playing with his melodious voice, and struck grandiose poses from which his brocaded cassock swayed back and forth like a bell. Well, my fellow Odessans fell in love with Father Vvedenskii. Acting as if possessed, these two Jewish girls did not miss a single sermon. Ania claimed that religion had nothing to do with it, that what was important was not *what* this amazing man said, but *how* he said it … And it seemed to her, no, wait, she was positive that he had looked right at her and was speaking only to her. Fortunately, this preacher of the Living Church went off somewhere for his next public performance, and in the meantime Ania calmed down. But this episode had altered her earlier convictions about love and sex, which amused K.M. One evening Ania remained with us after dinner, resting on an antique sofa while we sat in armchairs. I took the dishes to the kitchen, washed them, and prepared tea. After gathering the cups, I went into the sitting room and, obviously, they had not heard me coming. Ania was lying inappropriately with her body stretched out on the golden upholstery of the sofa. It is true, K.M. was sitting on his armchair, but his hand was moving up the leg of my school friend. My first emotion was fear, because for the first time, I found my husband's actions repulsive. What excuse could I find? There was no lecherous smile, we had not drunk wine, and Ania was not a delirious actress ready to kiss anyone available. I told Ania she needed to leave. "Why should I be the one to leave?" The poor girl had decided that since she had allowed K.M. such liberties, he now belonged to her. Ania looked to K.M. for support, but he just cast his eyes down. "Yes, Ania, you must go," I responded. Ania had to stand up and straighten out her dress. She hunched over even more than usual and left. I said nothing to K.M., for I was completely disgusted. But, for the first time, he was repentant. He claimed that he was simply "conducting an experiment" to see what this sanctimonious person would do. I went to Ania the next day. She greeted me coldly but I could not spare her feelings. I told her that K.M. had told me everything she had allowed him to do. "He told you all that?" Ania uttered tragically. I apologized for hurting her but she needed to see that "Konstantin Mikhailovich is depraved. He does whatever he pleases without any feelings for others." I told her to go back to Odessa. We talked for a long time and parted company, after promising to write. Later her entire family emigrated to Italy.

I could never stay angry at my husband for very long. But I was becoming embittered as I discovered repellant traits behind the thick veil of my adoration for him. I was not jealous, for I understood that such behaviors were the custom in Bohemian circles. Still, some in our group *always* behaved virtuously. But then again, they lacked that versatility of knowledge, talent, and technical genius that K.M. possessed. How could I not admire his ability to fix plumbing, replace expertly the electrical wiring, construct a cooking apparatus, or turn two useless bicycles into one excellent new one and then ride on it, sitting backward on the handlebars? And what about the "Karlsruhe?" Who else could have come up with this? In our apartment we had an enormous two-meter ironing board. K.M. made some calculations and then lay this board on the sill of an open window so that the bigger part of it hung out over the street. He placed the other end on the coffee table. He told me that since we did not have a summer place to go to, this would be our vacation spot, our "Karlsruhe." To convince me that it was safe, he sat on the edge of the board and dangled his legs over the street. During the White Nights we often drank coffee sitting on our Karlsruhe. After all, being in love means you have to know how to forgive almost anything.

But then events took a frightening turn. The poet Nikolai Gumilev[21] was executed. This upset everyone, but it particularly disturbed K.M. He never wrote on any identification forms or applications that he had been an officer in the tsarist army. His theatrical work and his teaching at Zubov's Institute seemed to provide a cover for him. But sometimes on the street or at a public discussion, he would recognize one of his former soldiers. His own appearance was such that once you met him, you could never forget him. K.M. was afraid that someone was going to recognize him and betray his past. Fortunately, during the time of the war, from 1914 to 1917, he had a beard and a mustache, which hid his protruding teeth and reduced chin. But the shape of his skull and the way he walked, with a light step and leaning to the side, remained the same. So he decided to focus all of his energies on emigrating to France, which would also enable him to deliver to his family members all of the valuables we had kept safe. I was the only one who knew this. He left the Mardzhanov Theater and devoted himself anew to sorting through his possessions and figuring out what could be sold. He made calculations and took notes and looked gloomy and anxious.

As in the past, I hung out with my friends on Kronverskaia Street and grew closer to Valentina Mikhailovna. Gorky at this time was preparing to go abroad with Solovei and Titka (Maria Benkendorf), so Valentina Mikhailovna and her husband left the rooms on Kronverskaia. They had received a fine apartment in a town house on the Neva embankment and old friends began to gather there again. It so happened that the artist Vladimir Tatlin[22] lived in the same building as Valentina Mikhailovna. His room was in the attic, along a different staircase. The Lebedevs introduced me to him when they took me to listen to him play the bandura.[23] He played this instrument skillfully and performed the intricate songs of Ukrainian kobza players in a highly unique style. He had even once performed in Germany on a bandura during one of his exhibitions in 1914. Everyone was making a fuss about his design for the projected "Monument to the Third International," but what I liked were his charcoal and Indian ink drawings for the planned production of the opera "The Flying Dutchman,"[24] which, incidentally, never took place.

The turn to the NEP brought back restaurants, cafes, and candy shops, to say nothing of department stores, which one by one opened their doors in Gostiny Dvor and Apraksin Dvor.[25] Private shoemakers also began working. I managed to get money from my husband to purchase gray suede knee boots with a black patent leather toe reaching to the laces designed by the best shoemaker on Morskaia Street, as well as patent leather pumps with French heels that I had dreamed about since my youth. He did not like spending money, but although I sewed all my own clothing, I could not make shoes. One floor below us lived a woman by the name of Emma Ivanovna who had been a lady's maid to a princess who had emigrated. One day, for some reason or another, she dropped by. As she stood in the kitchen, she looked around in amazement at the rows of long shelves crammed with copper plates and dishes. There were items piled up from the smallest saucepan to enormous containers for fish, big enough to corral a sturgeon. Emma Ivanovna had long wanted to open a specialty café-restaurant for a refined clientele offering her famous hor d'oeuvres and hot dishes, and copper cookware was exactly what she needed. Emma Ivanovna took me to her apartment and opened a chest of drawers, which were packed with *sporkami*[26] made from the finest French velvet, lengths of silk and light wool, ribbons, guipure, lace, feathers, and other such items usually associated with the aristocracy. I began to barter. For the frying pans and saucepans I received several pieces of silk, wool, and velvet. Moreover, for two large teapots and a copper boiler with a valve, Emma Ivanovna agreed to make clothing for me from these fabulous fabrics.

K.M. was surprised by my adroit handling of this transaction. No one had wanted to buy copper cookware; the items in demand were the rugs, china, porcelain, tapestries, bronzes, and paintings. K.M. cautiously sold these mainly to Latvians and Estonians whom Zhak would bring to him. The purpose of selling family possessions was to get money, which K.M. could then use to purchase potable valuables to take abroad. Buyers brought the money in suitcases; these were the currency notes issued in notes of one million rubles (*milliony*) and it was my tedious task to count them. Then Zhak would sniff out those who still had family treasures and he would take K.M. to them. But my husband was cautious. He was handling the common property of his family and he did not wish to take any risks. The persons selling treasures would show a few pictures or miniatures and let him keep them, either as a deposit or on trust. They primarily came from the social layers known in those days as "the former people,"[27] and they trusted K.M. as "one of them." Then K.M. would invite the best experts he knew, A. N. Benois and Iaremich,[28] to inspect the items. In return we provided them with a sumptuous dinner. Masha and I worked tirelessly to come up with exquisite treats for them. K.M. gave us the Molokhovets'[29] cookbook and noted what he wanted from it. A. N. Benois turned pink from eating so much of our tasty offerings, all the while chatting contentedly. Yaremich just drank and remained silent. After coffee, the experts went into the sitting room where a painting stood on the easel or a miniature lay on a velvet pillow. They would examine the object, turn it over, and study the wood frame and canvas. Then conferring among themselves, the experts would offer their evaluation as to whether or not it was valuable, whether or not genuine or a copy, and so on. We had several such dinners. K.M. bought the pictures which the experts approved. The eye of A. N. Benois was infallible. One of these canvases K.M. later donated to a museum in The Hague.

It was my job to search out small items such as antique snuffboxes, porcelain, and pendants at newly opened antiquarian shops; I could now identify the time period with one glance. K.M. would follow-up and purchase items I recommended. All of this was very tiresome. His family's possessions held us hostage; they did not belong to us, but we had to sell them. Then we had to buy new items to hide and devise a way to get them to his family. We relaxed by going to the theater, though not in Petrograd. We went several times to Moscow to see the premiers of Aleksandr Tairov[30] and Vsevolod Meyerhold.[31] This was a real holiday for us. But the most remarkable and unforgettable was Evgenii Vakhtangov's show *Gadibuk* performed at the Gabim Theater.[32] Despite our not understanding a single word, we were not only enthralled but literally felt ourselves drawn in and merged with this production. We had never seen anything more talented and that pushed the limits of theater to such a degree. K.M. proclaimed that nothing could ever top it and that after watching it, he felt very insignificant. Since then, more than half a century has passed, and I have attended many theaters in the Soviet Union and Paris. I have watched most of the touring French and English theater performances. Yet, never have I seen such a fabulously staged dramatic pantomime as *Gadibuk*, in which highly pitched voices filled your soul instead of just words. This was an event unsurpassed in the history of Russian theater.

Despite how much we loved to go to Moscow, such trips were rare. Once or twice a month we went to a nightclub called "The Freemasons," which reminded us of the former Comedians' Halt cabaret.[33] It was located on Nevskii Prospekt in the apartment of the artist Nikolai Khodotov. They put up a cloakroom in the entryway, and from there you went into a large hall, where there were tables covered with white tablecloths and a small stage. Actors and singers, still with traces of makeup on their faces, gathered there after their performances, as did masters of ceremony, singers, directors, and artists. The stage was open to anyone, the mood was relaxed, and people enjoyed themselves. Once Zhak brought a man by the name of Derzibashev, a Chekist with a wild Caucasian look to him. He also brought the man to our apartment. I was a bit afraid of him. Derzibashev drank a lot, but hardly ever spoke. He just glared with his dark, malevolent eyes.

It was Derzibashev, though, who helped K.M. get permission to travel to Germany in 1923. For this trip my husband prepared himself very deliberately. He wanted to go to Berlin because his younger brother Vadim was there, and K.M. intended to give him part of the family valuables to pass on to the other siblings. Vadim himself was also in great need. He knew multiple languages, but lacked concrete skills. He had not been trained for a profession, a situation the majority of émigrés faced. K.M. had a shabby shaving brush with a metal handle that could be unscrewed, and because it was hollow, he filled it with large diamonds from his mother's earrings. Then he melted stearic acid mixed with India ink (so as to make it look dirty, he explained) and poured it into the remaining space in the handle and tightly screwed the brush back into it. He hid several other stones in similarly nondescript objects and dressed modestly so no one would possibly think that he could be conveying an entire fortune to his family abroad.

Masha and I remained alone in the enormous apartment and promised that we would guard everything closely. I was bored. Valentina Mikhailovna had been gone for a month and was still away visiting Gorky in Berlin. I had other friends, but I was not as comfortable with them as I was with Rozochka, and I could not drop in without an invitation. But my loneliness soon ended. Our friend Alexander Nikolaevich Tikhonov invited me to a gala party at the offices of the World Literature publishing house. He had always flirted a bit with me and made fun of my loyalty to that "old, severe" husband of mine. Alexander Nikolaevich was charming, intelligent, and an excellent conversationalist, and I sometimes thought that if it had not been for K.M., then maybe ... For this gala event, I enlisted the help of Emma Ivanovna to make a ballroom dress from black tulle fabric. I had a rather low cut neckline and a splendid skirt with flounces all around plus a small sash around the waist formed out of dark glass beads. I wore dark silk stockings and my new pumps, but no jewelry. For special occasions, K.M. allowed me to wear brooches or a string of pearls from the secret stash. But I did not like to wear jewelry that did not belong to me, and truly, not having ever owned jewelry, I had no particular desire to wear it. Besides, with this outfit, jewelry would have been superfluous. In the massive black cloud of my gown, just a little skin was showing, and herein lay the secret to my allure. The dress was inspired by Konstantin Simov's lavish illustrations of French marquises, and thus adorned, I felt especially light, happy, and frivolous.

Alexander Nikolaevich escorted me to the hall. A group of young people clustered around me; I had heard of them—they were all part of the literary association known as the Serapion Brothers.[34] "I have brought with me a black Columbine," teased Alexander Nikolaevich and then left me with them. Besides the Serapions, there were also the Shvarts brothers,[35] their wives, and friends such as Vova Pozner,[36] the enchanting Zoia Nikitina[37] and pretty Dusia, who soon became the wife of Misha Slonimskii.[38] They looked me over and made some jokes, but they were so cheerful and pleasant that I immediately felt at home with them. Zhak came in and declared: "Why, it is Aguti!" From that point on my Kronverskaia nickname was established among the Serapions. Zhenia Shvarts, Levushka Lunts,[39] and Vova Pozner were the wittiest and the liveliest members of the group. They were always coming up with different tricks to amuse one another as well as their friends. I never laughed so hard in my life. When they called us to supper, I ended up between Konstantin Fedin[40] and Mikhail Zoshchenko,[41] and both plied me with wine (I declined the vodka). They competed in paying court to me, which sparked witticisms and impromptu comments from Zhenia Shvarts and Lunts. My cavaliers responded in kind and no one was offended; everyone was happy and having fun. After supper I found myself sitting in a deep armchair in the sitting room with the light dimmed. I almost got lost in this chair, but the flounces of my gown stuck out like a ballet tutu. I knew that I looked beautiful sitting there and I was happy, and I just kept feeling merrier. Zoshchenko was sitting down on a low stool on my right side, while Fedin stood on my left, tall and strapping, with his right hand on the back of the armchair. Their competition continued. They kept interrupting each other as they vied for my attention. They were intense in their rivalry. But over time Zoshchenko grew increasingly morose while Fedin became more animated. The three of us were a sight to behold. As acquaintances kept passing by, they would stop, look, listen, offer a rejoinder, laugh loudly, and then walk away only to be replaced by someone else.

Fedin was well built with broad shoulders and admittedly turned my head a bit with his big, bright eyes, his splendid voice, and precise speech, to say nothing of his remarkable early achievements as a writer. I could see that he was a bona fide celebrity, and I was getting malicious glances. All of this flattered me. Fedin's drab wife was also there, pretending not to notice anything. Only recently he had married the plain and completely unattractive Dora.[42] Fedin excused himself for several minutes and went to get some wine. Zoshchenko spoke quietly, but his speech was choppy, with broken phrases: "Such women should be kept under lock and key," "Where have they been hiding you?," and "Can I see you tomorrow, that is today?," for it was probably around 2:00 a.m. at this point. He spoke these "intoxicated" words with a certain annoyance, and his dark velvety eyes remained melancholy, while his lips curled into a strange smirk. His *Tales of Nazar Ilyich Mr. Sinebriukov* (*Rasskazy Nazara Il'icha gospodina Sinebriukhova*) had captivated me, and I pictured the author as a happy and easygoing person.[43] And now he was sitting here right next to me. Certainly he was handsome, but so tortured and sad. It was probably from this evening on that I developed a special fondness for Mikhail Mikhailovich as well as a desire to tread carefully with his feelings. This gulf between his creativity and his gloomy, pensive outlook made me think that there was some sort of inner turmoil, perhaps a heightened sensitivity or even vulnerability. I was about to make our conversation lighter and more friendly when Fedin returned with white wine, and the finger that was holding the bottle had a handkerchief wrapped around it. "You are wounded? Did you run into a burglar?" Mikhail Mikhailovich asked mischievously. Fedin answered, "A woman bit me because of Aguti, but I have returned nevertheless!" The Shvarts brothers then came up, along with Lunts and Pozner, and they all had wineglasses. Fedin filled everyone's glass, then his own, and taking my shoe from my foot he loudly announced: "I am going to drink wine out of Aguti's shoe." This irritated me. I loved the attention, but did I really want him drinking wine out of my new shoe? Fedin, however, was no fool. Though he acted the part of a knight battling for my affections, he was also squeamish. He put a small glass of wine into my shoe, and grasping the heel and the glass with his large hand, he drank the wine quite imperturbably. His buddies were struck by his quick thinking and applauded him, and I was happy to have my shoe back on my foot, completely dry. Yet, nonetheless, the escapade left a bad taste in my mouth. It was not really about trying to impress me. He just wanted to show off in front of his friends.

It was by now quite late. Both of my "knights in shining armor" escorted me home, which was not far, just down the street. I went in quietly to the large empty apartment and made the rounds of all the rooms. There was no one to whom I could describe my fabulous evening and the "stir" I had made at the party. K.M.'s ancestors looked down upon me disapprovingly from their golden frames. Only one winked merrily at me, and I smiled back at her as I went into my bedroom. That very same evening my cavaliers from the party came together to visit me. But Mikhail Mikhailovich stayed longer than Fedin. The latter's cheerful conversation had not managed to dispel Zoshchenko's gloom. When Fedin left, Mikhail Mikhailovich began to pace about the room and then declared in a rather shrewish voice: "In more primitive times, a man did not have to bother with amusing the woman he desired, he simply seized her by the scruff of the neck and took her off into the bushes." Though taken aback, I responded, "But, Misha, that was in prehistoric times. Besides, I am not sure where women keep their scruff nowadays." We both laughed. I explained to Misha about my three-year friendship with the Khodaseviches and their circle of friends. Having already seen and heard just about everything, it was hard to "put one over on me." Henceforth we conversed naturally, as friends. Misha began coming over nearly every evening. Sometimes he came with other Serapions. I began to attend their meetings, where I met Olga Forsh[44] and the writer Evgenii Zamiatin. The Serapions shared their writings and criticized one another mercilessly, but they also praised enthusiastically. I was happy in their company and was struck by how different they were from the Kronverskaia circle. They had pure, more direct relations with each other; there was no gossip, backbiting, or malicious jokes and no need to be continually amusing. I felt as if I had acquired "my own" genuine friends. I wrote to Rozochka and to K.M. about all of this. Rozochka wrote me long letters in return; she told me that she had read to Gorky my letter about the new dress and the evening at World Literature and that he had sung my praises and said that I should try writing. K.M., on the other hand, wrote only short notes along the lines of "I am bored without a letter from you, K" or "Why have you not written?" I wrote almost daily but it took a long time for my letters to get there.

My husband was in Berlin for two months. On the day he returned, Masha and I cleaned the whole apartment and prepared tasty treats. I was at the station to meet his train one hour before his arrival. I was terribly nervous and happy. As the train appeared in the distance, the sound of the wheels grew louder and my heart beat faster. K.M. jumped down on to the platform, spry and light on his feet. As he ran to me, he pulled out from the inner pocket of his coat a large gray, black, and orange silk scarf and, brandishing it in the manner of "Princess Turandot," he wrapped it around my neck. People were watching us, and several laughed. I was embarrassed by such a theatrically staged reunion. True, this was my first foreign gift, but why the rush? We got into a horse cab and went home. He asked immediately: "So, how are your friends? Have you begun any romances?" From astonishment I lost my voice and whispered, "What do you mean?"

"Oh well, its a pity! It would be easier if you had. You see, while I was in Berlin, I began to see Rozochka in a new light, and I have gone completely crazy over her." Not making a sound, I hunched over, and I must have gone deathly pale. K.M. looked at me anxiously, took my hand, and began to reassure me: "Now nothing happened; I simply worship her, as if she were an icon." This did not help. He had never before prayed to either God or the devil and now suddenly Rozochka had become an icon for him? Rozochka, whom he previously had spoken about indifferently or even cynically? We were both silent. This was not the homecoming I had expected. But then he pulled out presents from his suitcase. There was a lovely summer coat; a black lacquer bag lined in red, Moroccan leather; a suede hat to match the color of the coat; and fringed gloves. Masha and I had never seen such luxuries before, and they spoke volumes about the West. On top of this, there were various liqueurs and weighty bars of Swiss chocolate.

So, he had at least thought about me and had wanted to surprise me. Maybe I was being silly. After all, "nothing" had happened, at least none of "that," and it did not even occur to me then to doubt my husband's truthfulness. So what was I worried about? I had tried endlessly to convince him that Valentina Mikhailovna was a most interesting, unique, and talented woman. Well, finally in that foreign environment he had realized her friendship had much to offer. Besides, Rozochka was still in Berlin with Gorky for another month and a half, and anyway, before he left K.M. had promised we would go to Odessa upon his return. I had not seen my parents in three years, and surely there he would forget this whim. In Odessa we visited areas familiar from my childhood—the Big Fountain, the monastery garden, and my favorite places by the sea. We lay in the fragrant grass beneath my old oak tree and bathed at the deserted shore in and among my beloved rocks. He was more affectionate and even more passionate than he had been in the first months of our marriage. Valentina Mikhailovna did not come up in any of our conversations.

After we returned to Petrograd, I was in the hospital for several days having a second abortion. Just as with the first one, I begged, cried, and insisted on my right to have a child, but K.M. would not relent. We had to focus all of our energies on getting away to France. Plus, we would have little money; the lion's share of the wealth would go to his brothers and sister. A child would only tie our hands and would have to endure hardship as we built a new life for ourselves. Valentina Mikhailovna brought me flowers in the hospital and said that she missed me. Everything seemed to be as it should, given our close friendship. But now, K.M. never refused to go with me to see Valentina Mikhailovna. He even sought out excuses to go to her in the middle of the day, whether to take a book or to fix an appliance. In the evenings, he would sit at the table as if in a state of shock, not listening to anyone, hardly speaking, and never taking his eyes off Valentina Mikhailovna. She took no notice of him, but was always animated, fashionably and coquettishly dressed, and now in the style of women in the West, heavily rouged her cheeks. At home I told my husband that he was making a fool of himself, behaving like a starstruck schoolboy. He said he could not help himself; he needed me to be a faithful friend and understand his suffering. This meant, I thought, that he expected me to console him because she did not return his feelings.

The weeks passed. K.M. continued his feverish preparations for our departure and set the date for the summer of 1924. The endless sale of family possessions continued, as did the purchasing of small paintings and antiquarian items that would have value in a foreign market. K.M. no longer worked with Zhak after he caught him in some nefarious scheme. I was the only one helping him. In the evenings we went to Valentina Mikhailovna's, or to the Krimer's luxurious apartment on the embankment close to us. Sometimes everyone went to the theater and once in a while to a restaurant. Rozochka still paid no attention to K.M. and instead was especially affectionate with me. But Didrikhs grew morose, and everyone began to feel uncomfortable. I was wretched and embarrassed. I decided that I needed to speak frankly with Valentina Mikhailovna. I told her that I was not surprised my husband had fallen deeply in love with her, but it was more than I could stand. I had resolved to leave him, which meant that I could not come to see her anymore. I wanted to assure her that I loved her as before and did not blame her. I myself would have fallen in love with her, had I been a man.

Rozochka hugged me, insisting that Samogon was making all of it up as a joke and that my friendship was more important than this buffoonery. But I said that nothing would change my mind and left. That very day I found a room to rent on Spasskaia Street and in the evening told K.M. that I was leaving him. He said nothing, and I had a funny feeling that he already knew.

In the morning I packed a small suitcase, wrapped my pillow in a blanket, and asked Masha to help me load everything on a handsled. But K.M. carried my things down, laid them all out, and then tied them with a cord. Masha and I pulled the sled to my new apartment. I did not turn around, but I must admit that I hoped my husband would chase after me and seek to take me back home. But nothing of the sort happened. I just stood there in a daze in the middle of my half-darkened new home. What had I done? How was I going to live now? Masha was crying. She made my bed, hung my clothing in the wardrobe, and promised to drop by daily. Then she left. It was cold in the room. The firebox was in the adjoining room, where the woman who had rented the room to me lived. She was a passionate card player and warned that sometimes she would spend entire days at the Vladimir Club. One other woman lived in the apartment, who was unattractive and had a 15-year-old son but no husband. She dropped in and began to chat, but I said that I had errands to run. I went to the World Literature publishing house. Aleksander Nikolaevich listened to me in amazement. At first he thought I was teasing. When he realized that I was serious, he berated me for acting foolishly. The affair with Valentina Mikhailovna would not last long and soon everything would return to normal. But I interrupted him; I had not come for comfort but for advice as to how I should support myself. Alexander Nikolaevich asked if I could translate, but I said no. I had almost forgotten German, and my knowledge of French was very scanty. Then he promised to give me proofreading jobs and to help me make connections with other publishers as well.

Thus began my absurd, restless life on Spasskaia Street. Proofreading jobs were intermittent, so money was tight. Nearby was a tavern where in the morning I would order a half portion of tea and a roll. Everyone looked at me curiously, but I would quickly polish off my breakfast and go. When there was no work for me, I would stroll down Nevskii until I reached St. Isaac's Square, hoping all the while to run into K.M. I stayed away from Mokhovaia Street, though, for fear he might see me through the window and assume I was coming home. I stood for a long time staring into the windows of stores, but we never met, not even once. Masha often dropped in on me to bring a piece of pie and meat cutlets. And she kept me informed about my husband and Valentina: "She came with a dog" or "they drank tea and soon left." I found it insulting that she was visiting him but not once did she drop by to see me. But then I had put myself into this pitiful situation.

The Annenkovs lived very close to me as did Mary, a dear friend, and the Krimers. I frequently dined with each of them and hung out with them in the evenings. But it bothered me that I could not reciprocate. Once people knew my new address, they dropped by without an invitation, which showed their concern, but still irritated me. No one had ever come to our home on Mokhovaia Street without being invited. I tried not to appear unhappy, but obviously I was. So I took to staying out in the evenings. Once Mary's brother and his friend took me to a recently opened nighttime café-cabaret. They snagged a table and ordered tea and pastries. The next thing I knew the Kronverskaia social group came in and took a neighboring table—Valentina Mikhailovna, her husband, my husband, Radovskii, the Krimers, and Zhak. They all nodded their hellos to me, but no one came up to my table. They just settled themselves down and began a lively conversation among themselves. My place had always been there, among them, but now they seemed to be doing fine without me. I felt a lump form in my throat and turned very pale. Alexander Mikhailovich, Mary's brother, looked at me anxiously and asked me if I would like to leave. I could not even answer. I knew that if I tried to speak, I might become hysterical and start shouting the devil knows what. So we left. The following day Shura (Mary's brother) dropped by. He was a devoted friend and realized I was living only in the unlikely hope that K.M. was going to confess his guilt. Either I needed to go and ask forgiveness myself for stirring gossip and making him into a monster or truly build a new life for myself. But how was I to do this? I could not go back to my parents, so I had to find employment. I went to the Labor Exchange[45] and wrote on my application that I knew French. A stern gentleman examined me and said that my knowledge was too limited. I turned to a supervisor and said that I was in extreme need and was willing to do any work. He gave me directions to a factory that needed a timekeeper. I did not even know what this word meant. I went to this factory, located somewhere on the Okhta River, and found the human resources department. I handed my order to a pale-faced woman in a red kerchief who took one look at my hat, fur coat, and shoes and said: "We do not need your kind here." Of course, it had been stupid of me to go dressed like this, but I simply did not have any other clothing. This was the outcome of my effort to find work.

But then everything changed. One day Masha came running and said that K.M. had fallen from a streetcar platform. He had torn off two fingers from his right hand and needed me to return and help him. So I rushed home. K.M. greeted me as if I had been gone for twenty minutes instead of two months. He looked pitiful, with yellowish skin and rust-colored stubble on his face. His right hand was bound up in an old kitchen towel. The fingers had not been completely severed, and it had been stitched back, but his hand hurt badly and he could not use it. He needed someone to help with daily tasks and change the dressings. I tidied up, for everything had been neglected. K.M. would not let Masha touch his things. My room was just as I had left it. I found a piece of black silk in the chest of drawers and made a sling. I washed his left hand with hot water and sent Masha for the barber to shave him. I was back home, K.M. needed me, but I was afraid to believe my happiness would last. Valentina Mikhailovna at the moment was visiting her father in Moscow. We did not discuss her.

I was right: there was no happiness. Rozochka returned and sent a message through K.M. asking me to rejoin their circle. I hesitated, but then the whole group just dropped in on us, and we spent the evening together as if we had never been separated. Everything was just as in the old days. The Freemasons nightclub of Nikolai Khodotov[46] had closed but the *Vaiateli masok* (Maskbuilders) on Basseinaia Street had opened, and we started to hang out there. K.M. no longer looked so pathetic when he was around Valentina Mikhailovna, but he always contrived to sit next to her and was very attentive. She continued as before to ignore him.

At this time the Moscow Art Theater Studio came on tour to Petrograd. At the Annenkovs I met one of the actors, Aleksei Dikii.[47] Almost instantly, Dikii latched on to me; there is no other way to put it. In the mornings he would come in a cab, run up to the fourth floor in one breath, and press me to attend his rehearsal. If I said no, he would threaten to make a scene. So I would go with him for the entire day: rehearsal, dinner at a restaurant or at the Annenkovs, and then in the evenings there were the studio's performances. Sometimes I met K.M. and our whole social set there, and in that case, I went home with my husband. Many days passed like this. Even if there was no rehearsal scheduled, Dikii still came for me. He would get a boat and we would go rowing on the Neva. Aleksei Denisovich would tie up at the Tishkin floating restaurant (across from the Summer Gardens) and we would climb over onto the porch of the restaurant. We ate crabs and drank beer, and then I would return home late. My husband never seemed upset about this. Alright then, if I could not make him jealous, then maybe by parading my own love affair, I could arouse his interest. After all, he said he liked women who betrayed their husbands. But this was not the sole reason for the affair. I did like Dikii. He was a talented actor, he was handsome and charming, and he drew you to him by the force of his own desire. He played wonderfully on the guitar and sang romantic gypsy songs. He just made everyone around him happy. It was impossible to resist him. For the first time I learned about the genuine passion of a virile young man, and this flattered and excited me. But I had been spoiled by K M. Even if physically Dikii was the best, in everything else K.M. would get the nod. Dikii was an actor of enormous intuition and spirit; he had already distinguished himself for his artistry and for his feel for each scene and role he played. But I could not fall in love with a man inferior to K.M. in knowledge, taste, and, above all, culture.

The tour of the Moscow Art Studio lasted for about a month. There was a farewell gathering at *Vaiateli masok*. One of its members was an obscure actor by the name of Gedroyts, though I may not be remembering his name correctly. Everyone knew that Valentina Mikhailovna had once had an affair with this handsome though foppish actor, and then during her long stay in Moscow had renewed it. All evening long, she danced with him, and they were quite intimate, whispering to one another and sometimes even snuggling cheek to cheek. This was quite daring; at the time it was considered chic to dance stone-faced with your partner. But K.M. behaved childishly. As a "third wheel" he followed behind them, as if he were dancing with them, and he kept trying to listen in to their conversation. In his dashing about, he ran into other couples. I was dancing with Dikii and the embarrassment was too much to bear. When the foxtrot ended, I went up to my husband and said that I did not feel well. He wanted to stay longer, but I insisted we leave. As we walked in the early morning twilight of the White Nights, K.M.'s face seemed old and gray, and I felt sorry for him. I took him by the hand and said: "Now, how is it that you hold weak-willed people in contempt, and yet you let yourself become the laughing stock of the entire place, and why? You already know, for heaven's sake, that she has no need for you." He thrust my arm off and stood before me furious and malevolent. "Well, what about you, are you simply playing the fool or are you truly daft? The entire city knows that she is my mistress, and only you do not see anything?" I gasped, "Your mistress? And all this time you have been assuring me that nothing of the kind …" "Of course I did, because while we were still in Berlin, she insisted that you were not to know, and I promised …"

Something snapped inside of me. K.M. revealed himself as being quite petty, which I had never considered him to be, not even when he was acting like an idiot on the dance floor. I had thought then that, oh well, he is lovestruck, he has drunk too much and is acting foolishly, but tomorrow he will come to his senses. His honesty, his distinctive gentleman's conscience—were these just figments of my imagination? How could he have deceived me for an entire year, forcing me to visit her, to accept her in my home, create mouthwatering dishes and make presents for her? It was all just a cover for this banal adultery. Indeed, Didi was well aware of everything, everyone knew about it, but I was such a fool. But she, how could she have done this to me? I just stood there, unable to move; everything in my head was turning upside down. K.M. looked at me with a mixture of bewilderment and perhaps sympathy. "Oh, come on. What's with you? It is not as though you have not had lots of time to consider this possibility …"

I retorted, "To consider what, that you are a liar and a coward?"

"You make too much of such matters …" was his response. K.M. saw a cab and helped me in, and in a few minutes we were home. I decided to say nothing and came up with a plan of action to allow me to leave once and for all.

The next day I wrote a brief but insulting letter to Valentina Mikhailovna. I wrote that I had never considered my husband to be a piece of property I owned, but that what bothered me was how cowardly she had behaved. Just to satisfy her sexual appetite she had lied and had forced K.M. to lie. I still remember exactly how I worded the last sentence: "You disgust me and I will not have anything more to do with you." That evening we were invited to Valentina Mikhailovna's. I asked a friend to drop by for a minute and gave him the letter for Valentina Mikhailovna, saying that I was not feeling well and would not be going that evening. K.M. was out giving a lecture at the institute. I packed a suitcase and left a note on his dresser saying "Going to Odessa." I said goodbye to Masha and headed for the train station. I ran into Dikii on the staircase as he was coming up to see me. I told him that I was going to Odessa to visit my parents. He himself was leaving that evening and had come to say goodbye. He walked me to the station, and we were able to get me a ticket a half hour before the train's departure. He asked me to write, and wrote his address on the back of a photograph of him in some acting role. With this we parted; not once did I write to him.

My parents knew that we were planning to go abroad and thought that I had come to say goodbye. They had already told their neighbors and friends that their daughter was going to Paris with her husband. Mama feared, of course, that she might not ever see me again, but nonetheless she felt proud: I had not betrayed her hopes, I was achieving a brilliant life for myself. So I could not immediately confront her with my tragedy. There was no husband, no Paris, and basically I had nothing. Even my dimly lit room in my parents' wretched apartment was no longer mine; being hard up for money, they had rented it. I had to sleep in the dining room, on that same oilcloth couch that we had when we lived on Uspenskaia Street. The Armenian pillows had been sold, as had the piano, so the apartment seemed half empty to me. Poverty screamed from every corner. They cooked on an old blue kerosene stove, but they used the kerosene sparingly, for you had to wait in a long line to get it. In Odessa there were lines for just about everything.

I had come without telling anyone, so there was nothing in the house, not even sugar. I spent all of the money I brought with me in just a few days, and then I began to sell the few items I had packed. We had already sold our fall and summer clothes along with much else, since we counted on outfitting ourselves in Paris. After all, the application for our passports and visas had already been submitted and we knew that we were going to get permission. Zubov had registered K.M. for a year-long research trip to examine materials in the Louvre library for his second volume on the history of Italian improvisational theater. So I ended up in the market under the blazing sun, holding out in my hands some underclothes, robes, and scarves. My parents did not try to dissuade me. They assumed that I had more such items at home and were only surprised I had brought so little money. More likely they thought with bitterness that I had become a selfish miser. Well, they cannot really be blamed for thinking this. I had never written them about K.M.'s stinginess. To make them happy, I described only my new clothing. They knew nothing of my flight to Spasskaia Street. I decided to confide in Mama's friend, Margarita Genrikhovna, the exceptionally intelligent and kind woman who had been friends with mama since their childhood. I told her everything. Her face darkened, and she asked what I intended to do. I told her that I had to find work, and I had to come back to Odessa. She shook her head: I was not going to find work in Odessa. At the present time a process of all-out "Ukrainization" was going on, and only those who knew Ukrainian were being hired. Moreover, none of my friends were still living in Odessa.

Margarita made me promise not to tell my parents yet. "You should just wait," she said, "and see what your husband does."

"But you do not understand, Margarita Genrikhovna, the scales have fallen from my eyes. I want nothing more to do with him."

"Nonsense! He has fallen from his pedestal? It will be much the easier to deal with him. He got himself into this mess, and he will have to get himself out of it. You need to think about yourself."

I did not have long to wait. By the end of the first week in Odessa, I had received a letter from K.M. He wrote as if nothing had happened. He said that I had been right to say goodbye to my family, but I should have spoken to him first. I should have taken money for the trip and maybe something from our remaining possessions. I answered with a tragic-sounding letter: I had left for good, I had no feelings left for him. But the tears were flowing as I wrote this. He answered with a long letter, saying that he knew he was guilty. But such guilt was redeemable, he was not a scoundrel, and he would not leave without me. We had worked hard to deal with this cursed inheritance of possessions and together we had to try and build our lives anew. He would not demand anything from me; I could live as I wished, but he would not go abroad without me. Along with the letter he sent money, and when I showed it to Margarita Genrikhovna, she was jubilant. She said that he was a decent man, for any other husband would have gotten rid of such an eccentric wife, for all men are unfaithful.

My letter back was dry: I would go with him, on the condition that he no longer consider me his wife. He sent a large sum of money which I used to buy my ticket and gave the rest to mama. My parents and I said goodbye to one another without tears. I convinced my mother that I would definitely come back, that the research trip was only for one year. I went through agonizing self-analysis. I kept wondering about the logic of repeating my situation from four years earlier when I had departed from Odessa with a man completely unknown to me, albeit talented and interesting, but whom I did not love at the time. I went because it was a chance to go to Petrograd and escape from an intolerable situation at home. And what about now? I was in the process of returning to this man, who once more I was not in love with, and now I was doing so in order to get to Paris. But how could I not go after four years spent talking and dreaming about Paris? K.M. had a huge collection of books, guidebooks, and colorful publications, and he knew Paris inside and out. What else could I do with myself? To my great misfortune, I lacked genuine affection for my own family; our relations had always been superficial. My parents loved me, but they were never my friends and I never confided in them. So now there was only one real possibility—Paris, such a tempting and phenomenal possibility. Paris, the epicenter where people from all ends of the earth go to build a new life. Four years ago it had seemed a miracle that I was getting to see Moscow and Petrograd. Now in front of me lay a new wondrous horizon—all of France!

In Petrograd everything was ready for our departure. K.M. had given the apartment to the Radlovs. Everything that had not been sold was still there, along with the family portraits K.M. had not wanted to sell. Several days before our departure K.M. ran into Osip Mandelshtam and his wife; they were getting settled in a new apartment and did not have any furniture. He brought them to the apartment and said that they could take what they wanted. They chose various items and were especially drawn to a gray marble washbasin and a flowery porcelain basin. I wondered whether Osip Emmanuilovich viewed these as fragments of a bygone era or perhaps they brought back memories of his childhood? The steamer was docked at Vasil'evsky Island. On the day preceding our scheduled departure, K.M. had brought the captain all of the valuables and paintings rolled up into tubes. Otherwise we carried very few items on board with us. I was worried most about my Persian case, so beloved to me, which was inlaid with ivory and copper wire; the inside was decorated with exquisite miniatures and had a little drawer with sections for holding trinkets. Fortunately, K.M. had glued cutouts from journals over the miniatures and the customs inspectors did not question the antique value of the inlay. They pulled open the drawer, looked at my makeup and toiletries, and, laughing, handed it back to me. Then for the first time I boarded a large European steamship. This moment marked the beginning of new wonders and discoveries. I ran back and forth from the bow to the stern, for I could not decide the best vantage point for watching the rolling of the waves and the splattering of the foam. All over the deck were lounge chairs and small wicker couches. Our cabin seemed the height of luxury and I felt as if for the first time I was seeing what genuine comfort really meant. Of course, fabulous foreign ships had come to Odessa, but I never got to board one. I felt as if I were in Europe already!

Our relationship was easily recast. We remained devoted friends, with not a word spoken about the recent past. We were in a new environment and talked about what was of interest to us. It was only when we were in Shtettin, awaiting the train to Berlin, that he raised the subject of Valentina Mikhailovna. He said that now, since I did not have any reason to be jealous, I should be friendly if I ran into Valentina Mikhailovna in Paris; she was willing to forget about my childish letter. I retorted that I had not written the letter out of jealousy; I would not accept even the slightest acquaintance with her because she was repugnant to me. He was silent. Rachel Krimer had already informed me that she had overheard a conversation between Valentina Mikhailovna and K.M. in which Valentina Mikhailovna had said in an aggravated tone: "I demand that you tell her that." And K.M. had responded that he would no longer lie to me. What did she want from me? K.M. was not my husband any more, but we would remain friends. She, on the other hand, was unbearable, and I wanted nothing to do with her.

In Cologne we went out to the platform where female vendors in blue kerchiefs were selling different perfumes. K.M. bought a small bottle of cologne. For the first time I understood the literal meaning of "cologne"; it was Cologne water. The French took the word "cologne" for their refreshing eau de toilette with its unobtrusive and pleasant scent. Despite using fine French and English eau de cologne, I always considered the scent of the Cologne water the very best because it was so light. We stayed in Berlin about a week while waiting for our French visas. We walked around the city and dropped in at pubs to drink beer; K.M. warned me in advance that he was going to order beer with different accents, including Bavarian. The people in Cologne had asked him questions as if he were a fellow countryman.

Once in Paris, we lived in the Latin Quarter in a very modest and cheap hotel on the embankment. All around us lay the old city of Paris. On the opposite shore of the Seine was the Louvre, on the right you could see the towers of Notre Dame, and just next door, on the parapets of the Seine, were the stalls of the booksellers and their claims that, of course, many and many a time Anatole France[48] had rummaged through the books here! Only two steps away was the boulevard Saint-Michel with its endless terraces of restaurants, cafes, and bistros where students of all skin colors hung out. We ate at one of the cheapest restaurants at a common table where any meal cost just one franc. K.M.'s younger brother Vadim dined with us. Vadim told K.M. that since it was my first time in France I should be treated to genuine French cooking. K.M. noted dryly that to do that you could not be in a state of limbo, but able to stand on your own two feet. Anyway, I really enjoyed this meal. I had a small but juicy steak with watercress salad, which I had never eaten before, as well as an artichoke, which I was also seeing for the first time. Before tackling it, I had to watch how K.M. and Vadim ate it. The meal finished with a very tasty crème sprinkled with ground-up bits of cookies. A small carafe of light white wine accompanied the meal. The waiters, or as they are called in France, "*garçon*," were like machines, working fast but still smiling cordially, and despite being very crowded, not once did they bump you with their arms or with the obligatory napkin for wiping away crumbs. I could not imagine anything better than this.

5

Homecoming and a New Start in Moscow

Translator's Note: This print edition includes only the chapters covering Ludmila's life in Russia and the Soviet Union. The chapter recounting Ludmila's three years in Paris after she went there with her husband Konstantin Mikhailovich can be accessed in PDF format on the book's web page on the publisher's website. Paris was an exhilarating experience for Ludmila both in terms of the city itself—its architecture, its street life, its cultural heritage—as well as in terms of the people she encountered there. Soon after arriving she and K.M. joined the social circle of Soviet writer Ilya Ehrenburg and interacted with many famous cultural figures including the poet Vladimir Mayakovsky. But Paris also brought a number of personal challenges as she separated permanently from Konstantin Mikhailovich, who gave up his Soviet citizenship and found work in the French film industry. Despite their break, she and Konstantin Mikhailovich remained close friends and he tried repeatedly to get her to allow him to support her financially. After his purchase of a long dreamed of motorcycle, they would go riding into the outskirts of Paris. But determined to make it on her own, Ludmila first tried her hand unsuccessfully at selling fabrics designed by the émigré artist Ksenia Boguslavskaia, married to the famous painter Vania Puni, with whom Ludmila had a brief affair. For two years Ludmila worked for the Soviet Trade Mission in Paris, headed at the time by the old Georgian Bolshevik, Polikarp Gurgenovich (Budu) Mdivani. To make herself a more valued employee, she learned to type, thereby gaining a skill that would play a large role in her life. While working there, she met Bogdan, a mysterious and dashing man with whom she had a passionate but obsessive relationship that was satisfying physically but lacked a substantive commitment. They engaged in a series of trysts in hotels arranged by him in between what he claimed were frequent business trips. His charisma, good looks, and personal charm kept her from breaking off with him despite her growing reservations about the relationship.

Many aspects of French life enchanted Ludmila, and she describes them vividly, from the boisterous and exuberant Paris street fairs, cafes, and markets to the quaint, serene towns and seaside communities she visited outside the city. But she never lost her desire to return to the Soviet Union. In order to keep her Soviet passport and retain her job at the Soviet Trade Mission, she was forced to divorce Konstantin Mikhailovich, now seen as an émigré and traitor to the Soviet Union, and endured a series of unwelcome advances from the Soviet Trade Representative Mdivani. But in 1927, she lost her position there in an administrative reorganization and faced limited prospects of further employment.

A mysterious friend of Bogdan's tried to recruit her into Soviet intelligence and convince her to move to Vienna, but she refused. This upset her, but even more disturbing was his revelation that Bogdan had kept much from her, including the fact that instead of being away on long business trips, he was an addicted card player. Disturbed by these developments, she decided to ask the Soviet consulate to help her arrange a return to the Soviet Union. The kind consul procured for her a paid trip home as an escort for a boy of 10. His parents had been recalled to Moscow but he had stayed behind to finish his school term and now sought to rejoin his family. This chapter begins with her final farewell to Paris and to Konstantin Mikhailovich, who tried up until the end to convince her to stay.

Dusia and Misha Slonimskii went with me to the station. They were staying on in Paris for several days and then returning to Leningrad (Petrograd was renamed Leningrad in 1924 after Vladimir Lenin's death), so we did not know when we might see each other next. K.M. also came to the station. He brought me a marvelous, portable typewriter he had crafted, pleased that now this might finally come in handy. He had devised this special typewriter long ago by replacing the Latin letter typeface with Cyrillic. This brought tears to my eyes. Dusia and Misha stepped aside and I told K.M. that the hardest part of leaving was saying goodbye to him. "Does this mean that maybe you will come back?" he asked. I did not get to answer him. I had to board the train.

My native land, however, greeted me rather ungraciously. At Negorelom (in Belarus) one of the baggage inspectors detected lumps in the old pillow that I had taken with me when we left in 1924.

"Are there jewels sewn into this?," he asked, his eyes boring right through me.

"What do you mean? I do not have any jewelry …."

"Tell that to someone else. It is better to confess, or else things will get much worse. Now slit open your pillow."

I exploded in a rage: "Listen to me, there is nothing in my pillow. I have no idea what you think is in there. I have slept on it for many years and I have never felt anything in it. You do not have the right to cut up my pillow. You can take out the seam, but then you must sew it back; otherwise all of the down will come out." He smirked and began to take out the stitches with a knife. As I watched, I was a bit nervous. What if back in 1917, before leaving for Odessa, K.M.'s mother or sister had shoved pearls or emeralds into the pillow? What would happen to me then? But all that was in the pillow were two lumps that were bits of fluff stuck together. We stood there wreathed in the pillow's downy stuffing. I insisted they immediately sew the pillow back up, but there was no needle and thread, only a string to tie together the unstitched corner. At least the inspector felt so embarrassed that he let the rest of my items pass, despite my having more dresses, coats, and shoes than one person was allowed. But my splendid pillow was now flat as a pancake.

At the Belorussian Station in Moscow, my cousin Sarra met me. She was the daughter of Aunt Nina, my father's sister. She and her husband rented a small room in a communal apartment and they said that I could stay with them for awhile. As I exited the station, I stared in disbelief at what I thought were men's bodies scattered across the square. My cousin was a doctor and so I asked her in horror if there had been some sort of epidemic. Were these the bodies of the dead? She just laughed: "Do you mean to tell me that you never saw drunks in Paris?" When we arrived, I met Sarra's husband Volodia, a gracious and good-natured person who served me tea. I immediately headed over to the Herzen House[1] on Tverskaia, which Ehrenburg had advised me to do. He was sure that I would see people I knew there who could help me find a job and a place to live. These words turned out to be prophetic. I had no sooner stepped on to the veranda of the restaurant when I heard "Aguti, what are you doing here?!" I glanced over, and it was Viktor Shklovskii! He was eating with great relish some sort of meat dish and, without getting up, motioned for me to take an empty chair at his table. A conversation ensued. I was an object of interest to him, for I had just been in Paris and was fresh from the train station. He began to ask me about Paris. Knowing his particular interest in all things eccentric, I recounted some of the more colorful sides of Paris. I described the fake conjurers who entertain crowds with jokes and funny phrases while trying to sell glue. As people gathered they would glue together broken cups, toys, and other sundry household items and assure the audience that only the glue they invented could make something old new again and spare the householder from unnecessary expenditures. Then I told him about the fairs, the nighttime dances I attended with my Czech writer friend, and the peculiar Parisian way of enthusiastically giving detailed directions when you ask how to get somewhere. He listened and laughed quite a bit. I also ordered dinner and then we drank tea. Finally I asked Viktor about finding work. I told him that K.M. had given me a typewriter with Cyrillic type and I wanted to use it to earn money, for I was broke. Moreover, I had to find a place to live, for being the third person in the room of my married cousin was very inconvenient. Viktor Borisovich leaned back in his chair, looked at me as if appraising my value with his clever, bright eyes, and said:

> Now, go home, sit down at your typewriter and write out everything that you have told me just now, only it must be exactly as you told it to me, and I will take it tomorrow to the journal *Circus*. Then I will draw up a contract for a book to be entitled *The Sights of Paris*. Plus, you now have a room. The Nikulins[2] live in the same building as I do, but they are going away for three months to the Caucasus. They will let you stay in their place and three months should be enough time for you to get settled somewhere. Here is my address. Come to me in the morning with your manuscript.

He handed me the piece of paper with his address written on it and then left with the poet Nikolai Aseev.[3] But I could not move from my chair. I could not believe that I had found right off the bat not only a job but also a room. Was I really in Moscow? Everyone had told me that it was nearly impossible to find both work and a place to stay here. I felt as if I were hallucinating. I got up and went to the restroom to wash my hands and powder my face. There I saw an obscene couplet etched on the wall and that reassured me. Yes, indeed, I was in Moscow.

It was the end of August, and in politics the struggle against the oppositionists was underway. Megaphones at all of the squares and tram stops blasted out the names of those who were involved. This was when I first heard the name of Ivan Smilga.[4]

I knew nothing at all about the current situation. In Paris I had not bothered to read the Russian newspapers, and when I read the French press, I preferred local events and trials, not politics. When I got home, I asked Volodia what was going on and what the loudspeakers were blasting. Volodia's answer was evasive: "Oh, we are just the little people; it does not concern us." For heaven's sake, did he really think I was that naïve? Obviously he was sizing me up, suspicious because I had worked for the Trade Mission and had returned at the state's expense. I told him that I would soon be moving to a room on Skatertny Lane, and then I sat down at my typewriter. I wrote about the street vendors' glue, about the sideshow at the fair featuring a woman without a head, about the unpretentious revue in the workers' quarter, and about Mistinguett,[5] the star of the music halls who performed nearly naked but kept her back to the audience, covering almost the entire stage with the train of her ostrich-feather dress. The next morning I climbed the stairs to the fifth floor of No. 22 Skatertny Lane. Shklovskii took what I had written and said that he would read it that evening. He then proposed that we crawl over to visit the Nikulins. I was perplexed and inquired, "What do you mean, crawl through what?"

"Through the attic," he said. "They live on this same floor, but on the other side. Why go down and then back up again when we can crawl through the attic to the door opening on to their landing?" He looked inquiringly at my light-colored clothing, but I gamely agreed. The attic was very long and dusty; the middle of the attic floor was covered in wires so you had to walk along the corners and protect your head from the beams.

I had been slightly acquainted with the Nikulins in Petrograd, where they had lived before moving to Moscow. We showed up at their door in a sorry state: my hair was entangled with spider webs and Shklovskii's bald patch was covered with red earth. But they were happy to see us and greeted us heartily. Lev Nikulin was married to a woman who in my view was the very embodiment of aristocratic elegance and pedigree, the Princess Volkonskaia. Her bright red lips, large flashing eyes, and black hair contrasted favorably with her cold demeanor, her calm manner, and her self-possession. With these qualities she could not only grasp her husband's cynicism but also respond to it accordingly. They were already packed and were leaving in the next two days. They graciously offered me their room and all of their kitchen utensils. They also introduced me to the proprietor of the apartment, Elizaveta Vasilevna Rumiantseva, whose husband had abandoned her. He had been the chief physician of the Moscow Art Theater but chose to stay in the United States while on tour there. Now he sent his two school-age sons postcards with pictures of the New York skyscrapers. This constituted the only child support he provided.

Within two days I moved in and immediately became friends with Elizaveta Vasilevna, a wonderfully kind and friendly woman from the town of Vyshnii Volochok. I savored her old-fashioned way of speaking Russian and the charm of meeting someone with such an open and naïve spirit. Elizaveta Vasilevna was a nurse, but lacked steady employment. She would do night shifts and sometimes had to be away for several days attending to seriously ill patients. I befriended her sons, Alesha and Iliusha, and took them to the Moscow Zoo and once to the circus. When I began earning money, I would bring home rolls and *boubliks* (thick, ring-shaped rolls) for tea. They had very little money and most days did not have cooked meals, but only heated up the samovar for tea. Elizaveta Vasilevna never complained, but was always cheerful and willing to chat for hours about her relatives and their love affairs. Now I could regularly crawl through the attic to visit Shklovskii, who had shown my first drafts to the editors. The latter approved it, but wanted me to focus more on the Parisian working class. I had to scour my memory to comply with this directive, but it was difficult. I was supposed to be writing about Parisian "sights" and "sounds," not about the situation of the working class, a topic I hardly knew. I added a rather long sketch of the July 14 holiday, Bastille Day, and how all of Paris joins in the celebration. I described how in the workers' districts, people dance on the bridges and how the buses, streetcars, and other vehicles wait for the dance to end before moving on. The drivers even get out and join in the festivities. I also wrote about the celebration of St. Catherine's Day and the "Catherinettes." St. Catherine was the protectress of poor brides, and on this day crowds of festive women, primarily working-class and lower-level office employees, stroll through Paris wearing the requisite bonnet of St. Catherine. They are permitted to snatch up men whom they find attractive, dance with them, and have the right even to kiss them. Many of the young women create elaborate costumes and receive prizes. But as with the description of Bastille Day celebrations, I was revealing the quite happy life of the working class in Paris. Shklovskii crossed out a few things, corrected some, and when he had it ready, he took me to the editorial office. The contract was drawn up, and soon I received the copy-edited proofs. But alas, in the end the censor banned my sketches, *The Sights of Paris*, claiming that I had depicted the situation of the French working class incorrectly. My argument that the book was an outsider's perception of the street life of Paris was to no avail. I got to keep the small advance, however.

My writings did find a home, nonetheless. I became acquainted with someone who worked for the Tashkent journal *Seven Days*, which printed several of my Paris sketches. My piece on the Paris fair appeared in the journal *Circus*, and the Tashkent newspaper *Pravda of the East* hired me to write reviews of Moscow shows, exhibits, and so on. My head was spinning from all of these opportunities. I knew my strengths. I could artfully describe my own impressions but I could not do any sort of political analysis, and in general I was not very good at creative writing. The representative of the Tashkent media gave me a correspondent's pass so I went to theatrical premiers and recorded my response and evaluation of the shows. I tried to describe in a captivating style the contents of the new plays. Some of these were published and I received payment for them. One of the performances I attended was a reading by the poet Mayakovsky at the Polytechnic. My heavens, this man had multiple sides to him! It seemed that each time I saw him he was a completely different person. On this occasion, truly for the first time, he cast a powerful spell on me, dispelling my memories of him from Paris as a mistrustful, squeamish neurasthenic standing for hours to play at wall billiards, putting in one coin after another. What I saw in front of me was the giant Gulliver in the land of the Lilleputians, a man engaging not only a noisy audience fully smitten with him but also the entire world. At the end of his recitation someone asked him rather capricious questions, but his caustic rejoinders silenced this person, who just slunk from the hall. I showed Shklovskii my rapturous review. He liked it, for he was a close friend of Mayakovsky. But he advised me not to send it to the newspaper. It seemed more like a letter to a far-off friend who was pining for Moscow and was not suited for a general audience.

Several days later I saw Mayakovsky yet again. The poet Nikolai Aseev asked me to come to his home with my typewriter. Thankfully it was portable and I was able to dash off his new verses as he dictated. For the most part, I was happy to accept such work, for I needed to help my parents. Aseev stood at the window of his large room and declaimed almost under his breath; meanwhile, at the other end, Mayakovsky, Lilia Brik, Osip Brik himself,[6] and one other person whose name escapes me were playing cards at a table. They were arguing noisily, shouting and even swearing at one another. When I had finished typing, Oksana,[7] Aseev's wife, invited me to stay for dinner, which would begin, she said, once "those guys" stopped "squabbling" over their cards. But I politely declined. I did not think that I could bear seeing yet another incarnation of Mayakovsky: he played cards with considerable concentration, but he seemed not himself, but a weaker version. I said goodbye to the card players as I walked past them, but they hardly acknowledged me. In their eyes I was no more than a typist. Lilia was the only one to look at me, and she was interested solely in my Parisian clothing and shoes. But it was impossible to astonish her with anything. She could well consider herself Moscow's leading trendsetter.

Many acquaintances, mostly men, came to see me in Moscow. They invited me to the theater, to parties, and to exhibits. When they introduced me to their friends, they began with "she is just back from Paris." Upon learning this, women would eye my dresses admiringly and the men would become especially attentive. Rather unexpectedly I stumbled on an old acquaintance. Sometimes I frequented a small café in Stoleshnikov Lane where instead of a meal I would order whipped cream. Lo and behold, at one of these "meals," the fellow approaching my table turned out to be none other than my former boss at the Soviet Trade Commission, Budu Gurgenovich Mdivani, accompanied by an older woman who by her clothing, her slicked down hair, and awkward manners was the stock image of the old Bolshevik revolutionary. Mdivani stared at me and uttered, "Is it really you? I was certain you would never return!" He introduced his companion as an old party comrade. I sensed from the introduction that this was not the moment to recall memories of Paris and his unwanted attentions. But I had no desire to reminisce. Mdivani had changed. He lacked the lofty grandeur of his former manner and instead appeared worried: obviously Communist Party members came to this café to talk confidentially on the assumption that no one they knew would be there. Both had briefcases with them. He asked me where I was working. I told him about my efforts to break into journalism and said that I had nearly exhausted my store of impressions about living abroad. But to depict life correctly here at home I lacked sufficient knowledge of it. He took out a notepad and asked where I was living. I hesitated for a moment. The thought crossed my mind—no, surely he did not intend to start visiting me again. He caught the drift of my thinking and quickly reassured me: "I am in Moscow only temporarily, and I am very busy. I will soon be going home to Georgia. But just in case I find something useful for you, give me your address." I gave him the only address I had, that of Elizaveta, and then took myself off, leaving these old comrades to speak privately. The next day I received from the State Publishing House (GIZ) the complete collection of Lenin's writings in twenty-seven volumes. Three stacks of books were tightly bound with string, and one of the bundles had an envelope attached to it. Inside was a note from Mdivani: "Only after you have studied these works can you become a good journalist. Good luck. Yours, Mdivani." This was how my old boss talked the talk in Moscow. In Paris he would not have given me such advice.

The days flew by, week followed week. I inquired everywhere but could not find a room. Many promised to look for me, but nothing came of it. I either would have to pay a huge amount of money, which I simply did not have, or I could only rent a corner in a passage room. Soon the Nikulins would be returning, and I could not go back to Sarra, for she was expecting a child. My wonderful landlady, Elizaveta Vasilevna Rumiantseva, relieved my worries when she proposed that I stay with her. I could sleep on the couch in the dining room, for she had two rooms. She moved into the big room with the boys. But this could only be a temporary solution, for the dining room was in use the entire day, and I could not easily type there. Soon, though, even this couch became unavailable, for Elizaveta Vasilevna's ailing mother came to live with her from Vyshnii Volochok. She had cancer. Liza decided to move with the boys into the dining room and set up her mother in the large, bright room. There was no longer any space for me.

By pure fluke I discovered that near Tishinskii Square on Electric Lane, a female dressmaker was looking to rent a room to a single female. She would only rent to a woman because the space in question could be accessed only through her own room, which she shared with her teenage son. I rushed right over and took it immediately, for I had no other option. But oh, what a gloomy building and what a ghastly room! It was an enormous government building that prior to the 1917 Revolution had been a state-run Widows' Home. There were dark arches, never-ending corridors with cement floors, and one common washroom on each floor that was dark, dirty, and smelly. There was no longer heat in the building. The dressmaker, my landlady, explained to me that before the revolution warm air had passed through vents, but the system no longer worked. It was already December. My room was cramped, it lacked wallpaper, and it had not been whitewashed in a long time. Instead of a door there hung a faded, dirty curtain. Obviously the main room had once served as a living room for some poor widow of an officer or a government official, while my room had been the bedroom. It was empty except for a rusty iron bed and a dilapidated stool.

One of my new acquaintances was a talented young journalist by the name of Boria Lapin.[8] I phoned him and said jokingly that I had decided to move into a coffin. I called him from Elizaveta's, where I was retrieving my suitcase. He dashed over and helped me move. He immediately noted that something was missing—I did not have a table for my typewriter. Two hours later he came dragging in a solidly built, thick drawing board and two pedestals in the shape of goats to serve as table legs. This construction ended up being quite stable. One half served as my work desk and the other as my dressing table. From Sarra Lebedev, newly divorced and now living in Moscow, I got a kerosene heater in the shape of a small tower. I put it in my room, but I rarely got to use it because the woman I rented from appropriated it for herself. She would come and get it as soon as I left to run errands. Then when I returned, she would announce that she had poured in her own kerosene and hence had the right to use it. I could not argue with her, for I had nowhere else to go.

Work at least was plentiful. My friend Mary had moved to Moscow and her husband worked as the commercial director for the *Mezhrabpom-Rus* film studio.[9] A. Ia. Brik headed the literary department for the studio. Mary's husband hired me to do special assignments for Brik. No one at the studio had the time to keep up with the new literature coming out, yet they were always in need of new stories for films. In order to stay abreast of new trends, they hired me to read the latest literary journals, novels, and short stories and provide annotations for Brik, highlighting the scenes that would be best suited for the movie screen. So I read myself into a torpor. I took out books from three different libraries and the Literary Department gave me ones that they considered a priority. I also read foreign novels in translation. I would read the short story or novel and then immediately sit down at my typewriter to dash off the annotations. I would read wrapped up in a blanket with a pillow over my legs, numb from cold. However, it was difficult to find particularly sharp, cutting-edge plots that would successfully transfer to the movie screen. Many books were very similar to each other. Still, I easily filled my monthly quota of thirty abstracts, each of which required about eight to nine hours of reading, and I did not miss a single issue of a journal or a new book publication. In the mornings, since I did not have a teakettle, I boiled water in a small saucepan on my kerosene heater. Then I would commence my reading. When I had money, I would venture out for lunch at the Belorussian train station and then return ruefully, knowing as I did that the kerosene stove had been absconded and moved to the other room in my absence. Oh, I remember how frightening it was to walk along the streets in this area, especially our rumbling, unlit alleyway filled with eerie echoes. A lot of punks lived here; there were stabbings, loud shouting, and wild brawls; and drunks lay sprawled along the walls and across the corridor.

My landlady was an embittered and irritable woman. Her life was hard and her son Kolka caused her problems, sometimes disappearing for days and hanging out with rough street urchins. Sometimes he came home all hyped up and his mother would scream, "look at you, you are drunk again," and Kolka would yell in a heart-rending voice, "My life is broken, Just like those little glass tumblers that fell from the table and shattered into pieces." His mother was unemployed, but received ten rubles a month from the state. She took in sewing, and if the work was light and going well, she would hum pleasantly. I can still recall, though, her sarcastic verse directed at me: "To hell with you and your pretty looks, what your admirers see in you I do not know, but they are good for little more." If she had something more complicated such as a double-breasted jacket, then she could become quite ill tempered. In time I got to know her moods and could anticipate them, but before I had realized the connection between her sewing and her nerves, I unwittingly asked her who had dropped by and left me flowers. She flung her scissors down and shrieked in a frenzied voice, "You have no conscience, you and your flowers, how dare you interrupt my work, can't you see that I am trying to concentrate?" I begged her forgiveness and put the flowers on the window sill in her room. But no matter how ardently I asked my friends not to visit, my newly found admirers would not listen. People kept trying to entertain me because they knew how terrible my circumstances were. I had a lot of friends and was being invited everywhere, but it all seemed so detached from me. My life felt tedious and horrid at times. Everyone else appeared to have their own comfortably arranged life, except for me.

Questions plagued me. Had I acted too rashly? Should I have left Paris and my pleasant life, where I could be living in a quiet, decent hotel. Instead of dining at the noisy, nasty-smelling Belorussian station, I could be sitting at Rouge's restaurant with the chef peeking out from the kitchen as he puts out a plate with homemade noodles covered in tomato sauce and sprinkled with cheese, yelling out to his son, "This is for the lovely Russian lady." And everyone sitting at the table would smile at me. Yes, that pleasant peaceful life could have continued. Konstantin Mikhailovich had offered me full independence and my own bank account. I could have hung out at the café Rotunde, strolled all over Paris, traveled out to Versailles, and gone racing along the roads with K.M. on his motorcycle to the banks of the Loire River, to Rouen, or to anywhere I wanted to go. All K.M. needed was for me to agree, and we would go. Yes, all this would have been possible had I stayed in Paris. But I also would have had to cut off all contact with Bogdan. I could not forgive his duplicity and lies, nor could I forgive my own shortsightedness and gullibility. I was blinded by love and by my own carnal ecstasy. To resist him would have been very hard for me.

Truth be told, I had moved to another Parisian hotel immediately after I had that fateful conversation with Bogdan's friend. My new place was cozy, right by the church of Saint-Germain, and looked out on a small inner courtyard with walls covered in ivy. Paris lacked address bureaus, so it would have been hard for Bogdan to find me, though I knew he could do so if he wished. I was afraid of this, and yet at the same time I longed for him to find me. I told myself it was because I wanted to make him face the truth, but I knew very well that any conversation between us could be cut short by him simply touching my shoulder. Then off he would go for a month or two, and I would vent my grief by riding with K.M. along the beautiful byways of France. I would have to be supported, not by my lover, but by the husband who had rejected me and then fallen in love with me all over again. K.M. was certainly amenable to this, but I could not exist in such a tangled web.

In Moscow I had at least achieved a degree of spiritual equilibrium. I was independent, my work was interesting, and I could even help my parents a little. Yet I was also living amid filth, a putrid stench, savage brawls, and people endlessly swearing in the building and alleyway. I did not have even a corner that was my own, and I was at the mercy of my hysterical witch of a landlady. My friends kept assuring that I was in fact very fortunate to have secured my own separate room in Moscow; others had only corners and were happy. But I remained unconvinced. I was at a crossroads, and the path I was following was not leading me where I wanted to go. At this point the Slonimskiis invited me to Leningrad and I went. I stayed with them less than a week, but managed to meet up with old friends. Everyone was cordial but they all asked me the very same question: Why had I returned, could it really have been that bad in Paris? Women looked enviously at my dresses, gloves, scarves, and various accessories. I went to Mokhovia Street, up to the fourth floor, and stood at the door of our old apartment, now inhabited by strangers. Oh how I wished for everything to be as it had once been, that K.M. would be inside there puttering about and that when I rang the bell, Masha would answer and I would feel at home.

Upon my return to Moscow, I threw myself with renewed vigor into my work. Besides the abstracts, I was working on a calendar for 1929. I had been offered this job by the very same Tashkent journalist who had earlier commissioned my writings. He had originally received the contract to do it, but he was currently swamped with his own work. He lived with his wife on Bolshaia Dmitrovka in a dark one-room basement apartment filled with files, old calendars, newspaper articles, and piles of dictionaries, handbooks, and reference books. For each day of the calendar, there was a sheet to tear off with a text noting the significance of the day. I could not miss a single anniversary, bicentennial, and so on. So I had to compile a long list of mandatory dates and gather material for writing mini-biographies. I would work in the Public Library for part of the day and then go to Bolshaia Dmitrovka. There I spread out on the floor the sheets of paper with dates and sorted through the materials. You were not allowed to use captions from previous years. The work turned out to be very laborious, but it paid well. I needed money for a trip to Odessa, since I had not seen my parents since returning to Russia.

I regularly received letters from K.M. He wrote to me from Sakhar,[10] where he was working on the French film *Napoleon*.[11] He sent me amazing photographs: a camel with her foal, Bedouins on horseback, ancient wells, grubby children, and all of these skillfully taken from the most unexpected angles. These letters were more dear to me at that time than anything else in my life. In each letter K.M. wrote that he was waiting for me and that I absolutely had to return to Paris. In my letters, I described my feverish activities and assured him that I did not need anything. I only noted that I dreamed of finding a nice place to live. I said nothing about returning. There were moments, though, when I desperately wanted to be in Paris again at a table in a little roadside café with K.M., after which we would go flying down the road on his motorcycle. But I was ashamed to be so weak, and I reminded myself that my repaired relationship with my husband would never be what it had been at the beginning of our marriage, when he pushed all people aside for me ....

Konstantin Fedin also wrote to me from Leningrad, and his letters were emotional and amorous. Once he showed up unexpectedly in Moscow. He took me to a restaurant and said that he would be in Moscow for three days, and we were absolutely to spend them together. He teased me for eating oysters, which he claimed were horrid to someone born on the Volga. "Yes," he said, "you truly are a little foreign bird." He took me to see Meyerhold's staging of *Gore Umu* (*Woe to Wit*).[12] After the show, he told me that we had been invited to dine with Meyerhold. I asked him why I would be included. He admitted "I told everyone I was here with my wife, so for these three days I will refer to you as my wife." When I asked how Dora felt about this, he claimed she would never find out so it would be fine. However, she did soon learn what happened and she blamed me, though it was not my idea. It was very interesting, of course, to see this phenomenal show and to go to the Meyerholds' home, where in those days Zinaida Raikh[13] reigned supreme. It reminded me of my earlier trips with my husband to see theatrical premiers in Moscow.

The next day we went to the Bolshoi Theater to see Ekaterina Gel'tser[14] dance in the *Red Poppy*. After the ballet we ended up at an artists' club and Gel'tser herself sat at our table, as did Vasilii Ivanovich Kachalov.[15] This supper has always remained locked in my memory. We stayed in the restaurant longer than anyone else. The waiters kept looking at us plaintively, but with no luck. In the dimly lit dining hall, Kachalov's captivating voice recited the verses of Tiutchev.[16] In my letter to K.M., I described in detail both the Meyerhold play *Gore umu* and Kachalov's recitation at the empty artists' club. He sent back a response that seemed sad and anxious. He said he envied me and wanted so badly to have been there. I had struck a raw nerve. He was satisfied with the work he was doing and loved the opportunity to be in Africa, on the island of Corsica, and in Italy. But the people he now socialized with were more distant and less intimate than the friends he had before. There certainly was no one who could recite Tiutchev in the late hours of the night. For me it was my farewell to the artistic world that K.M. had introduced me to so long ago. I described it to him because I did not think that it would happen again. And I was not mistaken.

After spending several days in Moscow, Fedin left to visit his family in Saratov. From there he kept calling me and promising to show me the city and to even take me for a ride in a troika on the frozen Volga river. So I decided to go to Saratov, if only to escape from the awful Widows' Home for a few days. I took books with me and wrote draft abstracts on the train. Fedin met me at the station and then took me to the finest hotel in town, where he had reserved a room. We dined in the restaurant, strolled around the city, and the next day we really did tear along in a troika across the Volga River to the town of Pokrovsk. The Volga had frozen as if in the motion of a wave, and the whole time it flung us around, tossing and turning. Having warmed ourselves up with vodka, we treated our coachman and returned to Saratov. I left the next day. I had been a fool to come. I knew that Fedin did not have any serious intentions. I was fond of him, but he was not ready to make any changes in his life, although from his letters he made it sound as if he would love me till death. But I did not believe such fantasies. On the day I left I told him that for him, I was simply "the little foreign chick" with whom he could temporarily escape an unhappy marriage. But he had no intention of ending this marriage, for he valued his family, he loved his daughter, and was basically satisfied with it all. He did not even try to dissuade me. Instead he stopped, grabbed me by the arm, and exclaimed, "How shrewd you are, Aguti. You know me very well." I asked him to leave me in peace and, in future, find other candidates for his compensatory flings. I was too lonely and too unsuited for such a role. We parted as friends. Although he promised to write, I did not promise to answer his letters, and our correspondence soon died away.

K.M. asked me again if I would return and promised to send me a visa as soon as I wrote to him. My will weakened, for I wanted so badly to escape from the horrors of Electric Lane. However, it was already 1928. The New Economic Policy was completely dead, and every day the regime grew increasingly strict. I decided that before I wrote to K.M. giving him my consent, I would consult with Sarra Lebedev. She had a close friend whose work gave him insight as to how the authorities would respond to my application to go to France. They listened and then laughed. What made me think they would approve my application? I had divorced my husband, I was even using my maiden name, and now suddenly I am asking to go and visit him? To say nothing of the fact that he was an émigré who had left on an official research trip but never returned and gave up his Soviet citizenship. I asked, "Well, what if I did not say that I was going to visit him, but that I was going for my own reasons?" Suddenly Sarra looked at me with compassion and felt my forehead to see if I had a fever. She did not need to say anything else; I got the picture. I wrote to K.M. that my own desire meant little at this point; no one was going to authorize an official trip for me without sufficient reason. No one was traveling abroad from the USSR now.

Everything was clear to me now: I had to hold on and not sink into despair. I continued to work on the calendar, I read avidly and wrote abstracts, and from time to time I submitted articles to the Tashkent newspaper. Spring arrived, peoples' faces brightened, and the boulevards of Moscow came alive, all dressed up in bright green foliage. But I was still depressed, for there was still the same gloom, stench, and horror where I was living. It was during this time that I walked into the bathroom, which had the only washbasin to be found on the entire floor, and found a woman hanging by the neck from the pipe. Her worn-out slippers had fallen into the toilet bowl and her stockings, full of holes, had come off from her dangling legs. I screamed and ran out into the hallway. People came running and someone called the police. The noise of people shouting and crying was overwhelming and I buried my head in my pillow. I was shivering, but no one paid any attention to me. My landlady joined in the general hubbub and left her door open; I could not escape the noise. The story that went around was that this woman had not hung herself, but that someone had first strangled her, possibly even her son, who was a delinquent and a thief. I was even more frightened than before.

I left and went to see Liza (Elizaveta), whom I had not seen in over a month. I found her in mourning. She had buried her mother the day before, and the boys were whispering in the other room. I told Liza about what had happened at my Widow's Home. She paused for a moment and then said that I was welcome to come back and sleep on the couch in the dining room, and she would move the boys back in with her. I did not dare to show how happy this made me. I hugged her and said that, for old times' sake, we must have tea. I sent Iliusha out for food and Liza set up the samovar. We sat and talked for a long time, and then the boys came with me to get my things. The landlady raised a fuss and claimed that I was obligated to give her two weeks' notice. But I said nothing and simply paid her exactly what I owed. I also left her the kerosene heater since I knew that Sarra no longer needed it. Now it was like heaven. I was living in Liza's tidy apartment, with her gas water heater in the bath and her window sills filled with perpetually green plants. But what I cherished most was Liza herself, who was such a kind, cordial, and caring person. In fact, it is amazing that, as I look back upon nearly seventy-six years of such a hard and colorful life, I can truly say that I never met anyone as kind, as sincere, and as empathetic as Elizaveta Vasilevna. She never judged me, but only listened to me sympathetically, and I could tell her anything. She understood me and tried to help in every way she could. Of course, she was this way with everyone. I put Electric Lane and that horrid building out of my mind and promised myself that I would never go to that side of town.

Still, I never got used to Moscow. Its aging chapels and narrow crooked streets with whimsical lanes moved me, but nothing took my breath away except when I encountered scenes reminiscent of "Piter":[17] I remember coming upon a large building with white columns, unexpectedly rising up from a distant square. I stopped short as if rooted to the ground: this was a genuine Petersburg-like building. I thought for a moment that I had suddenly been transported miraculously to Leningrad. Yes, it dawned on me then that I was still on my journey. I had not yet arrived home. It was Leningrad that I was longing for, with its broad, straight streets, its well-proportioned, harmonious buildings, its organized architectural ensembles, the mighty flow of the Neva! That city had transformed me, and only there would I be able to find spiritual peace. Such were my thoughts as I stood transfixed by this building. There had been none like it in Odessa. Leningrad was filled with them, and Moscow had some, but they got lost amid the preponderance of squat mansions and new commercial buildings. I confessed my "nostalgia for Piter" only to Mary and her brother. They were native "Piterites" and had moved to Moscow only after my own return to the Soviet Union. Admittedly, they insisted that Moscow has its own special character, I just needed to get to know it better. But, oh well, anyone whose soul has been imbued with the harmony of Leningrad cannot be satisfied with any other city's "special character." Her brother Shura took me along the Arbat's alleyways, and we were charmed by its cozy townhouses. We rested in Arbat's Dog Square (*Sobachaia Ploshchadka*) and walked along the Moscow River embankment. But this just reminded me of the Neva, and I again began reminiscing about "our" city.

At the beginning of the summer was Mary's birthday. I bought long-stemmed roses for her, and feeling gay and very smart, I carried them along just like a little girl, in the crook of my arm. But out of nowhere a thunderstorm developed, complete with hail and a lashing downpour. I was in front of the Moscow Art Theater and ducked into the open door of the nearby vegetarian cafeteria. People had already been crowding in here to get out of the rain. I carefully protected my roses from being crushed as I went into the main hall and sat at a free table. I only ordered tea, since I had been invited for dinner at Mary's. As I was sitting there, looking at the roses, I noticed a tall man from a neighboring table get up and come toward me. He seemed embarrassed and was obviously shy, but came right up and asked: "Are you Mrs. Miklashevskaia, that is, I meant to say, are you Milochka (a diminutive form of Ludmila—Translator's note)?" I stared at him, and something vaguely familiar about him jogged my memory, but I could not figure out who he was or how he knew my name. My first name was known only to my closest friends in Odessa, and not only this, he obviously knew that I had been married. I responded, "Forgive me, yes, you are correct, I am who you speak of, but I am sorry, I do not remember your name …" It was embarrassing for both of us. As he stood there, bending slightly over the table, I peered at him: he was a very handsome young man. When and where had I seen his face? No, not that, his face was still young and even more handsome, in fact amazingly handsome. Then I remembered: our Odessan "Dorian Gray." This was Izya, Len Trauberg's friend, who had accompanied him to invite Konstantin Mikhailovich to offer lectures to us. Yes, at that time he was angelically beautiful, with hair that was almost pure gold, though now it was darker in color. His face had a girlish freshness to it, clean and the color of a ripe peach. He had been too young to shave, for he could not have been in more than the seventh form. He still had the same large almond-shaped eyes, the high forehead, and a small, elegant mouth. There was nothing feminine in his face now, and though he was embarrassed and blushing a bit, the wrinkles appearing on his forehead and nose gave his face a serious, worried expression. He was pleased that I had finally recognized him and said that he had obviously aged quite a bit since we last met. I asked him to sit down at my table and we bombarded each other with questions. I learned that he was living in Leningrad and had been there for a long time. He was teaching Russian history and doing graduate studies. He had come to Moscow to consult with his supervisor, professor Mikhail Pokrovskii, under whose direction he was writing his dissertation. I gave him a brief rundown of my work. The rain had stopped by this time and he walked with me to Arbat Square. He asked if I had a telephone and if he could phone me before he returned to Leningrad. I gave him my number.

The next day I was invited to dine with Bora Rosenblum, that same "big" Bora who was the friend of my Odessan youth. Now he had a wife and a son and lived in the building for employees in the People's Commissariat of Foreign Affairs (*Narkomindel*). He was one of foreign minister Maxim Litvinov's advisors and frequently went abroad. He would bring back luxurious outfits for his wife Sonia, whom I knew well. In Odessa we had been classmates in the History and Philology Department of the Higher Women's Courses. I loved spending time with them. Sonia had the finest taste, and the apartment, beginning with the entryway, reflected both her aesthetic sensibility and her exceptional tidiness. Everything was elegant, there was nothing superfluous, and every object knew its place. Sonia always appeared fashionably dressed. Boris's study was a genuine library, full of books, books, and more books. He had a heavy workload that required him to read daily a stack of foreign newspapers and journals, yet he also kept up with our own domestic periodicals and new books. He simply read everything and still loved to talk and to argue.

Boris opened the door when I arrived. He smiled mysteriously and said that he had a surprise for me. I entered the dining room and Izya was sitting at the table. We said hello to each other quite casually. So Boris was the one surprised, since he did not know that we had already bumped into each other the day before. Izya had just arrived five minutes before me and so had not had a chance to tell Boris about our chance encounter. The dinner was very pleasant. Boris had just returned from a trip abroad and had much to tell us. Izya and I left at the same time, and he walked me home. He was scheduled to leave the next day for Leningrad and asked if he could write to me. I said that he could, though I wondered to myself why he would want to strike up a correspondence with me.

His letters began arriving frequently and, in fact, too often for me to answer them. When I said goodbye to him outside of my apartment building, I had told him that in a month or so I hoped to visit my parents in Odessa. I had not seen them since the summer of 1924. So now he wrote that he too would be in Odessa, for he had been given accommodations at a scholars' rest home there. He said that he would like to see me if I did indeed make it to Odessa. I had in truth been planning to go for some time. I had finished the calendar, and work for the film studio *Mezhrabpom* was beginning to dry up. I had flooded them with so many abstracts that they suggested I take a break. So I wrote back to Izya that I was going to visit my parents during the second half of July through the beginning of August. He wrote back with the suggestion that we meet by the statue of Pushkin on such and such a date at noon. He understood that this day and time might not be convenient for me. But he would start going on that day to the designated spot at noon and wait to see if I could make it. If I did not come the first day, he would go the next day at the same time and continue to do so until I arrived. I showed Liza this letter and she laughed. "My heavens, you have not even left yet and already you have a date. This sounds serious." I told her that this was just boyish behavior. I was older than him by three whole years. There was nothing serious, only the renewal of an acquaintance from long ago.

So I found myself back in Odessa in the very same small apartment on Olginskaia Street. My father and mother had aged noticeably and were much thinner. My old semi-lit room had been rented out to a strange pair, an elderly couple who were taciturn and unfriendly. The piano was gone, of course, and there was no money to get it out of hawk nor could one be rented. The kitchen was a mess. They were cooking only on a primus stove that my father feared because he had heard that sometimes it exploded. He handled it carefully and helped mama by pouring the kerosene into it in the entryway. They no longer quarreled with each other. Their long years together and their sufferings had reconciled them. They were lonely. My older brother lived quite close but rarely visited. He had his own family, a wife and a son, and though they did not have much money, they were not lacking in anything. But he showed little concern for our parents. Though I had not seen my parents in more than four years, I had written to them about my life in Moscow. They did not have any questions to ask me, but were more than ready to tell me about themselves. But it was hard for me to listen to their complaints about my brother and about their friends and relatives. I gave my mother the money I had saved for her, which was much needed. My father was working at a cooperative as an accountant, but for low pay. If it had not been for the tenants and the little bit of help I could give, things would have been a lot worse. During the evening, I sat in the open window, just as I had done in my childhood, gazing at the night sky, dazed by the sight of the old acacia trees covered in white clusters of flowers. I looked out at the sky of my childhood, breathed in the heavy aroma of the acacias, and could not decide—had I wasted these past nearly ten years of my life, years that had separated me from the young girl who had decided in a sudden impulse to go to Petrograd with a man I barely knew?

The whole of the next day I spent getting the kitchen in order, as well as the entire apartment. Mama did not have the energy to keep up with the housekeeping and there was no money to hire anyone. She could barely cope with preparing dinner. Her single joy was in arranging flowers to display indoors. She told me that this was her "last great passion." Indeed, their gloomy squalor was hard on her. Two days passed before I remembered that Izya had already been waiting for three days on the boulevard by the Pushkin monument. I was secretly curious to find out if he was truly waiting there, and I definitely would enjoy going to Primorskii Boulevard and looking out at the sea. So, after breakfast, I got dressed and announced that I wanted to go for a walk. Sure enough, on the bench closest to the monument, there sat Izya, reading the newspaper. He immediately acknowledged me and did not either question or rebuke my impolite tardiness. He simply thanked me for not making him spend his entire vacation waiting for me, since he only had two weeks. He asked where I wanted to go, and I immediately said "to the sea." We went to the beaches at Maly Fontan (Small Fountain), and the next day to the Arcadia district. Then we planned a trip to Bolshoi Fontan (Large Fountain), which was my favorite place in Odessa, to see my beloved oak tree. We skipped a day, for I needed to be with my parents. But then I made up a story that I was meeting old Leningrad friends who had invited me to a picnic, and so the very next morning, Izya and I found ourselves on the summer streetcar No. 29, riding shotgun on its two open cars with the wind blowing on all sides. On our way to catch the tram, I had bought food for us. On our previous excursions, Izya had treated me to ice cream and tea with pastries. I knew that a young graduate student does not have money to spare, so I turned down the offer of a second helping of ice cream. Now I was determined to supply everything for the picnic with my own money. With each of our dates, my young admirer grew more confident. He guided our conversations quite skillfully and, what pleased me the most, he recited wonderful poems. But he did not recite as we did in Odessa in bygone years, with emotion and trembling in your voice. No, his voice was calm. He sensed with exceptional delicacy the rhythm of the poem and his recitations were musical. He seemed to know by heart every poem ever written. Or at least he knew a thousand times more verses than I did. As we sat by the sea, watching the waves come in and go out, I heard for the first time the poetry of Innokentii Annenskii.[18] Izya was particularly fond of him and had memorized all of his poems. After this I was allowed to make requests, and so over the sound of the surf flowed the verses of Gumilev, Blok, Mandelshtam, Akhmatova, Khodasevich, Voloshin, as well as classics of the nineteenth century, plus translations of Byron and the sonnets of Petrarch. We organized several more trips as well. I was fascinated by the fact that despite his relative youthfulness, Izya was very knowledgeable about each of these poets. He loved many of the verses of A. K. Tolstoy and knew his biography quite well.[19] He could also recite from memory nearly all of the verses of Prutkov and discourse insightfully on how they were jointly written by Tolstoy and others.[20] Yes, I thought to myself, he is more complex than I thought! He had vast stores of knowledge that went beyond his specialized field of history, which he also knew very well. His main focus of study was the Pskov and Novgorod Republics. He had written and published on them and his lectures were hailed as breaking new ground. Listening to him talk about history was like listening to a detective story. Each time we met the discussions grew more interesting. I found out that he also worked on the Decembrist Movement and had published a book on the agent-provocateur, Ivan Shervud-Vernyi.[21] He promised to send me the book when I returned to Moscow.

Soon I began to feel as if our ages were reversed and that he was older than me. While I had been going to theaters and concerts first in Petrograd and then in Paris, this serious and inspired schoolboy had been relentlessly studying history while finding joy and relaxation in poetry. In fact, it was due to his deep attachment to history that I was stuck having to listen to the boring verses of Karolina Pavlova.[22] I said nothing for fear of hurting the feelings of my enthusiastic historian, who just could not bear to skip over her poems because he claimed they were stories of history. He had an amazing memory. I knew by heart the work of Pushkin and Lermontov, as well as certain poems of Blok, Akhmatova, Gumilev, and Viktor Gofman.[23] But with Izya, all you had to do was recite one line and he could finish the rest of the poem with gusto. He claimed that he could memorize any poem the first time he read it, and he would then know it forever. He had begun to read at the age of 4 and had memorized from newspapers the monstrous doggerel of the celebrated Purishkevich.[24] Amazingly, he stood right there and recited all of these verses, which made me laugh. He even knew the poems of Aleksandr Amfiteatrov,[25] who like many prose writers considered himself at heart to be a poet. This was bad poetry, but Izya had nonetheless preserved them in his memory. He said that his older brother had an even better memory than he and they would sometimes have contests. I had known his brother in Odessa. I met him when I was still in the sixth class; I remembered him as being very tall with ruddy cheeks and a slight lisp. His fellow students avoided arguments with him because he was so smart and well-read. He was now studying ancient literature, which seemed appropriate since he had been famous in Odessa for learning by heart some type of hexameter when he was only 15. He lived in Leningrad as well and was married to the oldest daughter of a noted Odessa pediatrician, Dr Gurfinkel. This doctor was very expensive and mother had called him only once, when Sasha had pneumonia.

So it was that in order for me to meet the adult Izya, I had to leave Odessa for Piter, spend three years in Paris, and then one year in Moscow. It was strange to be back in my old apartment on Olginskaia, living a daily routine just like old times, as if I had never left. And I was going on dates with the schoolboy I had once met, Izya, who had become a scholar-historian and a man of letters. He did not talk about his feelings toward me, but I could tell that he was falling in love. He would quiver if I accidentally touched his arm while we were climbing a steep precipice or if my elbow brushed against his shoulder as I straightened my hat in the wind. He behaved with exceptional propriety, so courteous and reserved, even to the point of seeming standoffish in his conversation. It was only later that I realized how thoroughly steeped he was in the traditions of old Russian prose writers. In his research he had hitherto probed so deeply into the journals, newspapers, and books of the late eighteenth and nineteenth centuries that it was reflected in his speech and conduct. When we became more intimate with each other, however, he revealed that he did indeed know the Odessan manner of speech that I was so familiar with, as well as in the jargon of modern students. He was certainly a man with multiple sides to him.

Our lovely encounters by the sea lasted for ten days, filled with poetry and historical anecdotes. His period of leave at the House of Rest ended and he returned to Leningrad. He promised to write to me in Moscow and asked me for more prompt replies. I had to stay at least another week in Odessa and try to make up for the daily outings with my mythical Leningrad friends. But it was fine. I had felt like a young girl who was defying her mother to have secret assignations. But upon my return there was always watermelon or a plate of sweet-smelling compote. Mama was not pleased, but she always left supper out for me.

In Moscow I had two letters already waiting for me. One was purely business-like. Izya asked if I would type several archival documents he needed for his next project. I agreed and he soon arrived in Moscow. We met on Tverskaia Boulevard by the statue of Pushkin. The next day he took me to the archive where he had made all of the necessary arrangements. They brought out the two "Delo," or files, and for the first time I got to see these thick pages from the past, filled with writing and ink that had turned brown, fanciful letters and flourishes of the pen. I wanted so much to read everything, but it was not allowed. An old typist was watching over my shoulder; I had the right to type everything that was marked, but every fifteen minutes I had to go out with everyone into the hallway. Labor laws required this. Izya asked me how much he should pay me, and I said that he could read to me several poems of Annenskii. There was no way I was going to take money from him. I could not host him or invite him to dinner. Liza had relatives who had arrived unexpectedly and I was again out of a place to stay. I was sleeping on a cot at the Nikulins, but this was uncomfortable for them and for me.

Izya tried to convince me to move back to Leningrad. He said that one could still find nice inexpensive rooms to rent and promised to find something suitable. I did miss Leningrad, but I was hesitant to just abandon Moscow, where I had lots of prospects for employment. He promised to find me work in Leningrad. But I could not rush such a decision. I promised to think about it and to write him with my response. Without even waiting for my letter, however, he phoned and asked me to come just for two or three days. He had already made arrangements for me to stay at the House of Scholars. He wanted me to see a room he had found. This young man worked fast. I had to think: could I really turn down a chance to go to Leningrad and enjoy a quiet accommodation at the House of Scholars? Shouldn't I give Liza and Zina Nikulina a break from my presence and take some time to determine what I was going to do next? All of these thoughts followed one after another as I raced down the stairs and hurried to the train station. I bought my ticket and sent a telegram to Izya. He met me the next day in Leningrad and took me to the House of Scholars on Millionnaia Street where I left my small suitcase. We then went to look at the room, which was located on Kirochnaia Street. I realized that this was the same street that Izya lived on. I knew his address since, after all, I had written him. The room was on the second floor. It was quite spacious and well-furnished and faced onto the courtyard. The landlady was a typical old St. Petersburg seamstress of the middling sort. She was polite and rather sickeningly sweet in her manner, but her small eyes had a look of cunning to them. She had sized me up in an instant and proposed that I take meals with her. I could manage the price of room and board with her only if I found work. My Parisian coat had given the landlady confidence in my means and it did not even occur to her that I did not have a penny to my name. But I agreed to take the room, considering that I could continue to write articles for the Tashkent journal from Leningrad. I gave her a deposit and promised to return in two to three days. I thought that I had better write down the address and so the landlady dictated it—Kirochnaia, building No. 12, apartment 25. I threw a quick glance at Izya, who turned red and looked out the window. When we had arrived, I had not noticed the number, but I realized now that the room he had "found" for me was in the very same building where he lived. When we had been coming along Kirochnaia to look at the room, I had thought to myself, oh, what a relief, at least he had not had to waste time and energy but had been able to find something on his same street. It turned out, however, that the room was not just on his street, but in his own apartment building. When we got out to the landing, I asked him: "Did you do this intentionally?"

"Not really. My landlady's maid had said that in this building there was a nice room with a quiet family, so I took a look at it and thought that it would be perfect for you …"

"Yes, of course it suits me. The main advantage is that I will not have to eat out in cafeterias. Thank you, Izya. Now where is your apartment?" I asked.

"Mine faces the street." He was still embarrassed. We walked along the river and then dined at the House of Scholars. I did not telephone friends, for I did not really feel like seeing anyone. The next day we visited the Hermitage and in the evening I departed for Moscow to pack my things.

6

Love and Marriage in Leningrad

Now began a peaceful, quiet life in this most beautiful of all cities. I did not have a telephone, and no one knew that I had moved back to Leningrad. I spent my first days here walking along the rivers and canals and strolling through the gardens. The leaves were falling, but some of the trees still wore their amber autumnal attire. I sat on the benches in the Summer Garden and in the Tavricheskii and Mikhailovskii Gardens, and as I did, I gazed through the golden foliage at the sky. Though still blue, it was already showing a glint of gray. I thought of how this sky was the same for all people, and that right at this moment, Konstantin Mikhailovich, wherever he was, might be looking at it, perhaps contemplating some work-related matter since he was so deeply immersed in film production. Finding myself on Nevskii Prospekt, I walked to the end of Theater Street. Turning sharply around, I looked at the ethereal corridor of columns. I wanted so badly to have K.M. there by my side, for it had been he, after all, who had first introduced me to this street. From that great love affair, the best still remained alive—my love for his city, for the Hermitage, and for the symphony. I bought two tickets for a concert, for his beloved fifth symphony. I invited Izya to come, but I still remember how he nearly fell asleep. Music did not move him.

Usually Izya came over in the evenings. I made tea for him, and during our walks I tried to find items for supper that would remind us of Odessa: *boublik*, halva, and olives. We would talk to each other about our day and drink tea, rituals that were then followed by recitations of poetry, discussions of ancient history, and stories of my life in Paris. Izya rented a room from the well-known writer Tatiana L′vovna Shchepkina-Kupernik.[1] His room was closest to the kitchen, so that if he wished to use the main entrance, he had to go through her enormous dining room, which was often filled with guests. He asked if he could have a key to the back door and access his room through the kitchen. It turned out that the back door to my apartment was on the same landing as the back door to his apartment. Izya would walk on tiptoe through a small hallway and I would unlatch and close the bolt without making a sound. By the time he left, my landlady and her two children would be sound asleep. Well, I thought to myself, this sly dog had found me a room that was not only on his same street and in his own building but also on his same landing. Now he spoke more openly about his feelings. He told me that he fell in love with me long ago, back in Odessa when he saw me for the first time at K.M.′s lecture. When he found out that Miklachevsky had taken me on into his theatrical ensemble, he had not missed a single performance of "Liula the Musician," in which I appeared in a ridiculous fairy costume. It really was absurd—the wardrobe mistress had draped me in some sort of rose-colored horsecloth with one arm and shoulder exposed. Then she had let my hair down and it covered me like a cloak down below my knees. My melodic recitation was hopelessly bad, but my hair saved me. It was a great success.

After that, however, I had left for St. Petersburg, got married, and then went to Paris. He learned about my movements from Len Trauberg. Over the years he had girlfriends but did not fall in love. At least not until that moment when the pouring rain drove me into the Moscow cafeteria and he saw again the object of his first boyhood crush. He told me all of this in a somewhat ironic and witty tone, but he was looking at me with fear and doubt in his eyes. To myself I thought, you are not as timid as you pretend to be. He had, after all, settled me right next door. But I liked this about him. It showed that underneath his guise of shyness there was a man who was decisive and self-confident. Over the past eight years, the angelic beauty of this "Dorian Gray" had faded, and his face had become more masculine and serious. I was also attracted by the fact that he was something of a novelty. This was the first time I had ever become friends with a man of science, someone who possessed an equal passion for two different fields, history and poetry. I also found his quiet, modest love for me, without any whim or caprice, to be rather charming. There was a certain purity in our relationship, and it brought back memories of something I had read as a child, a moving tale by B. de Saint-Pierre about the love of Paul for Virginia, set on the isle of Mauritius.[2] But I was no longer shy and spoke my mind to Izya without any qualms. Indeed, he said he liked my openness and felt it added a certain piquancy to our relations. Now he was leaving my apartment in the middle of the night, for he had to be back in his own bed when morning came. Every morning the chambermaid liked to bring him a cup of hot milk and a slice of bread and butter. One had to show respect for propriety and the established order of things.

I grew attached to him and put up a wall of secrecy around our evening rendezvous and our relationship in general. He did not ask me to do this, but I sensed that he shared my desire to keep our connection a secret. He was not bothered as I was by the difference in our ages. But I guessed that he was not ready to tell his mother and brother about us. I did not ask him why, though I surmised he had a good reason for this. There were evenings when he had to go to his brother's home, which is where his mother lived as well. On such occasions I would go and visit old friends. I would most often go to Mary's friend, Anna Entina, who lived on Zakharevskaia Street. She was a striking woman of matchless elegance, lively and garrulous. She was narcissistic, but very cordial, and she loved to socialize. She would invite many interesting people to gather around her oval table. Through her and through Zoia Nikitina I got typing jobs and would be pounding away at my machine for days at a time. Otherwise I could not have stayed in my apartment. Finding employment in Leningrad was hard, and there were many who were seeking help at the Labor Exchange in those years.

Then lo and behold a commission came from the Tashkent journal; they wanted me to write a captivating article on Nikolai Chernyshevsky in honor of the one-hundredth anniversary of his birth.[3] I could not refuse, for I had no other job opportunities. But

I knew absolutely nothing about Chernyshevsky. I did not learn about him in school, and no one in K.M.'s social circles on Kronverskaia or in Paris ever talked about him. So I had to hit the books immediately and gather materials to write this captivating article. For the nineteenth century, Izya had in-depth knowledge of little beyond the Decembrists and the reign of Nicholas I. He nonetheless recommended basic books and journals which I needed to examine. So now every morning I went to the Reading Room at the Public Library and immersed myself in works on Nikolai Gavrilovich Chernyshevsky. Thankfully, the article was targeted at young people. I did not have to worry about trying to get into philosophy, aesthetics, or theory, subjects in which I had little background. But I did need to cover his difficult childhood; his close ties with Vissarion Belinsky, Nikolai Nekrasov, and other brilliant contemporaries; and, finally, his horrible incarceration. There were two episodes that really captured my attention: first, Nekrasov's loss of Chernyshevsky's original manuscript of his novel *What Is to Be Done?*, which he had written in prison and which was then found and sent to the poet by some run-of-the-mill bureaucrat, and second, the daring but unsuccessful attempt by Ippolit Myshkin[4] to rescue Chernyshevsky from Viliuisk Prison and transport him through the Bering Straits to America. Izya willingly became my first editor. As it turned out, he knew quite a bit even about this topic. He found several typographical errors and advised me to add in the fact that Karl Marx had highly valued the works of Chernyshevsky and had even learned Russian in order to read him in the original. This detail was of great value to a young Soviet reader. He also came up with the title, "A Beacon of Knowledge Disgraced" or, more accurately, he did not himself think it up, but he knew where, when, and who had referred to him as a disgraced writer.[5] What did he not have stored in that brain of his!

The article came out, but I still kept going to the Public Library. I thought it might be interesting to write a pamphlet on Myshkin. I was intrigued by his bold, heroic journey from Petersburg to Irkutsk and from there to Viliuisk. I did a lot of reading. I felt that I needed to understand the geography of this journey, as well as the way of life, the morals, customs, and speech common to the various provinces and vast territories through which he passed. I did some rough drafts but I found myself getting away from my subject matter. Then, somehow I ran into Samuil Marshak,[6] whom I had met long ago on that memorable evening at World Literature when I looked so beautiful in my black tuille dress. He and his family lived quite near, on the corner of Liteinii Avenue and Panteleymonovskaia Street. I told him that I was thinking of writing a small book on Myshkin, but I was drowning in my material. What was coming out was more a story about Siberia's natural environment. He was happy to talk with me, for he was always pleased to listen to a beginning writer. He could instantly understand and offer advice.

Aguti, what makes a theme important is whether or not someone has written on it, and therefore Chernyshevsky is an important topic, you know this, do you not? You should read Lermontov's prose. It is the best school for a writer. It will teach you to eliminate what is superfluous and to include only the most important facts. When you have done this, call me. You will come and visit us, and I will read what you have written.

I have always admired and appreciated Marshak. I liked his somewhat raspy voice, his sincerity, and his unique, incredible kindness. What was I to him? He had responsibilities for the magazines *Chiz* and *Ezh*,[7] he had a lot of his own work to do, and he had family, friends, and trips to preoccupy him. Yet he nonetheless called me, he listened, and without fail he always helped me. I was puzzled, though, by his advice for me to read Lermontov, who had been my favorite poet when I was a child. The day I turned 8 years old mama had given me a huge volume of his writing. I read it many times, and at age 12 I turned to his prose. I loved best of all his "Princess Mary."[8] But how in the world was this supposed to help me now? I did not have any of Lermontov's writings on hand, but his prose was in my head, as was Pushkin's, and all the other classics. If they had not taught me anything before now, then reading them again for the twentieth time would not help. Such were my thoughts as I pondered his advice.

I did not speak with Izya about my new project. Our intellectual tastes were actually quite different. I deeply respected his erudition, but found his writing to be a bit ponderous. I wanted to write in my own way, even if it was not as good. I burned in the stove all of my materials on geography and folklore and then laid out Myshkin's accomplishments as if I were talking about him to a group of youngsters. Marshak had said that it was best to direct the book at school-age children in the fifth and sixth form. I then phoned Marshak when the first chapter was ready, and he invited me to come to his home. I went on the designated day and found him in the dining room along with his wife Sonia and the writer Ilin,[9] who was Marshak's younger brother. They acted as my audience and seemed to like my writing. They offered critical advice, but all assured me that the book would be a success. They urged me not to lose momentum and to just write and write until I finished. Marshak said that when I had three chapters completed, then the Children's Department of the State Publishing House would sign a contract with me. He would arrange this and serve as my editor. After a month the contract was drawn up and they even assigned me an artist who brought me drafts of illustrations. Unfortunately Izya came over earlier than usual and found me working with the artist. The latter soon left and I had to reveal my secret to Izya, who was hurt that I had not asked his advice or shown him any of it. I reassured him that I had wanted to show him, well more truthfully, I planned to present him with the completed book as a gift with a very tender inscription. But I did not want to bother him with such nonsense as this, for it was not real literature, but merely a children's story done on commission and written in the style of my schoolgirl compositions. He calmed down, but still pouted a bit. He did not like the fact that someone else besides him might be necessary to me.

He had good reason to be confident that he had won my trust and devotion. But his egotistical conceit led him to overestimate my love for him. It never occurred to him that I had been poisoned for life by my love for my first husband and that no one could ever compete with Konstantin Mikhailovich in my eyes. True, I had felt respect and even passion for other men besides K.M. But with them I had been simply trying to switch gears and tear myself away from that higher level of life and being that I had enjoyed with him. But even then I had only found genuine happiness when I was with K.M. Now I lived in anticipation of his letters. I had not yet written to him about my new love affair, but I had told him immediately about my book project. I could not help but share this with him. I wrote to him about working with Marshak, whom he had known personally. We had listened together to Marshak's translations of Rudyard Kipling's poems when Samuil Iakovlevich had visited our home on Mokhovaia Street. I felt as though I were stepping back into my former life whenever I met with Marshak and the young poets who were always hanging about him, both at home and at the editorial offices on Nevskii Prospekt. Members of OBERIU (Association for Real Art) began to visit me, such as Alexander Vvedenskii, Daniil Kharms, and Nikolai Zabolotskii.[10] Marshak brought them to see me, and they would read their verses and tell amusing stories. They would come around midday and I would serve them tea. I chose not to tell Izya about this when he came over in the evenings. I knew that he would be taken aback by these visits, at the very least.

But then the poet Zabolotskii began to drop in more often and without his comrades. He reminded me of a peasant or a little shepherd. He was rosy cheeked, somewhat awkward with a rounded northern accent. His verses were very unusual, dynamic, and innovative. His animal characters spoke so wisely that they seemed more intelligent than people. I listened to his recitations completely enraptured. Since he too came during the day, he knew nothing of Izya, and he interpreted my enthusiasm for his poetry in his own way. So on the third visit he proposed marriage to me. I was speechless. To me he was just a boy, for he was even younger than Izya. I did not share with him my secret romance with Izya, but only said that our difference in age was too great, and it would be better for him to find a young girl to marry. This made him turn sullen, and he said that it would have been better to have just said "no" than to tell him such nonsense. Then he left, and the whole scene left me with an unpleasant feeling. Certainly a young man falling in love with an older woman was as old as history, but why had this amazing poet proposed marriage so quickly, while my refined historian had not so much as hinted at it and preferred to keep our relations a secret? I did not actively want to marry him, and had he proposed at this time, I might have turned him down. He would never have approved of the people I was now meeting, and he was so different from everything that I had known with K.M. and his friends. Plus, if at first I was pleased by the purity of our relationship, I no longer felt the same way. Nonetheless, I was attached to him, nurtured his self-esteem, and was very attentive to him. He had no doubt that I loved him more than anything else on earth, although I had never spoken such words to him.

Izya read through my draft and since he knew Russian history so well, he found mistakes and saved me from the wretched fate of an author who is writing about a topic without really knowing much about it. Thus with the help of Marshak and my dear Izya, I was getting close to completion. At this point Marshak turned me over to the political editor, the writer Alexandr Lebedenko,[11] who was obligated to demand that each book have relevance for contemporary issues. Something would have to be added and something would have to be taken out. I told the editor in all honesty that I did not know how to make it contemporary. He willingly took this on himself, but as a result, I lost interest in the project. Izya, on the other hand, was very satisfied and felt that I was doing the right thing. He offered to help me find appropriate themes. But then we decided to vacation in the Crimea. I was very run-down from working on the book and from the fact that on top of this project, for the past three weeks I had been working for Pavel Eliseevich Shchëgolev two to three hours a session. We had run into each other at the Public Library, and he had asked me to come to his home and make typed copies of archival materials for him. I just could not say no to this very remarkable person. I was curious to visit and see his books and paintings. I had heard much about them from K.M., but Shchëgolev had never invited us over in those days.

The work turned out to be so interesting I could never have refused it. He wanted me to retype the letters of Sergei Aksakov's daughter, which she had written to her friend in St. Petersburg.[12] All of these letters were devoted to descriptions of Gogol: his readings at the Aksakov home and a hilarious episode of preparing macaroni Italian-style. She relayed scenes of Gogol acting in the role of cook, of trips taken with Gogol in the family carriage (*tarantas*), and of a stop at a station for supper where the notorious fried cutlets had long female hairs all over them. Later Gogol himself recreated the latter in his writings as if the cook-husband had been preparing the cutlets while simultaneously pulling out his wife's hair in a fight. Other letters described Gogol's depressed mood, his unanticipated desire for seclusion, and outbursts of irritability. This work captivated me to such an extent that I was oblivious to all that was going on around me, and there were a lot of distractions. Shchëgolev's son Pavlik,[13] a rather chubby and outgoing young man, was always arguing with his father and mother. He spoke with great pathos, as if delivering a public oration, but it was clearly a theatrical game habitual for him. He was married to the most beautiful woman in Leningrad, Irina Ternatseva. Everything about her was stunning.[14] But Shchëgolev had not approved of his son's marriage. Irina lived separately; Pavlik went about with her everywhere but he lived at home with his parents. Pavel Eliseevich praised my work and asked me to do this permanently. But I said no, that I was busy with another project. I did not tell him what it was, because I knew that he would belittle it. Truthfully, it was hard for me to get him to pay me. He did not see any need for rushing the matter. I tried to explain that I needed the money for my mother. He answered: "Well, there you have it. You always seem to have a sick mother, or your papa is dying, but I do not have any money! You will have to come and work for another week and finish this boring job if you want to get paid." Pavel Eliseevich did not like to part with his money.

After this Izya and I went to Sudak in the Crimea. The town itself was unimpressive. We rented a room from a descendant of the Germans invited to Russia by Catherine the Great. It was a single cottage in a shady garden overlooking the Black Sea. In the mornings we would go down a steep, stony path to a grotto where an old Armenian grilled *shashlyk*. We washed it down with a light white wine and then walked to the sea. We would return home for dinner. The meals we had were unbelievable. We took the advice of Frau Zebald, our landlady, and ordered meals from a Tatar woman who lived near Sudak. Every day at three o'clock a whole brood of Tatars would appear at our terrace carrying the food. The price was very reasonable, and there was enough to feed five people. A 10-year-old girl would carry a pot of borsch or fish soup, followed by her younger brother with two baskets, one with a cooked dish and one with various vegetables. Drawing up the rear was a chubby little toddler who had a watermelon or a honeydew in his little wheelbarrow. After giving us all of this food, the children would tactfully withdraw. They played with the Zebald children until we finished and then they would return to take back the crockery.

After such meals I felt the need to go for a long walk. But here is where our desires did not coincide. Izya preferred to stretch out in our stuffy room and doze. What made it so stifling was that during the day we had to shut the windows to keep out flies. This was the first time we lived together, and I learned new dimensions of Izya. He did not know how to do anything except write about history, recite poetry, and have interesting conversations. He did not even know how to use a hammer. The room lacked a closet, and I needed to hang up my dresses. The landlady gave me several nails and a hammer. I showed Izya where I wanted him to put in the nails and handed the hammer to him. He looked at the hammer and, extremely perplexed, asked me why I had handed it to him: "What am I supposed to do with it?" After listening to my rather annoyed explanation, he took the hammer in hand and promptly hit his finger. I had to bathe it in cold water and listen to him whine. I hammered in the nails myself and never again asked him to do such tasks.

As far as walks were concerned, I did not argue with him. I said that each of us was free to do what he or she desired, and if he preferred to lie in that stuffy room, then it was fine. I was going for a walk. And I left. Soon he caught up to me and we went for a fairy-tale-like hike to the "New World" village.[15] This was a rather long walk, but so beautiful that you wanted to take the longest possible path. It was just as magical there as in the bays of the Mediterranean Sea, which I had fallen in love with years ago when hiking with K.M. in the Primordial Alps. Honestly, it was even more beautiful, somehow stricter, a little more severe, and so untamed that it seemed as if these places were completely uninhabited. We went down to the sea and swam, then returned to the ridge and walked as far as the famous Shuvalovskii wine cellars, which still held extremely rare wines. The old caretaker chatted cheerfully with us as he led us along the underground corridor, calling out the names of the wines. When we departed, he treated us to a small glass of the rarest vintage. We offered a donation "for our tea" and this earned us the right to unlimited tastings of the wonderful wines stored in the cool cellars.

But then the northeasterly winds began to blow, and walks became unthinkable. It was difficult enough to get around the garden without the wind knocking you over. The Tatar woman had to bring our dinner herself. I felt terribly guilty to see this tiny, thin woman carrying on her back the heavy bag filled with our food, but she assured us that she was used to these conditions. She said that the summer winds were nothing compared to those in the autumn. Without being able to swim or go for walks it became quite boring. Now Izya spent entire days lying in bed with a book. I would go crawling on all fours down to the Armenian's grotto. In this weather he did not cook *shashlyk* since no customers came to buy it. But at least there was shelter from the wind and I could watch the sea and listen to the waves breaking on the shore. Soon, though, our vacation ended. Izya had to return to Leningrad, and I had promised to visit my parents. I decided to go to Odessa by sea and tour the entire Crimean peninsula. I boarded the ship at Koktebel, and Izya saw me off. I was very happy. My first trip through the Black Sea lay ahead of me, and if truth be told, I was relieved to no longer be hiding anything and to be alone! I will admit that being unable to introduce Izya to my Leningrad friends and his desire to keep our relations a secret had possessed a certain charm initially, but I was growing a bit tired of it all. Even his inexhaustible store of verses from Homer to the present could not relieve my growing boredom. But he could not understand this, for he was satisfied. Now, though, the Crimea offered its charming diversity, and I was alone with the peaceful sea. The steamship rolled gently through the water and this made me even happier.

I spent the entire day on deck and then decided to spend the night there as well. I just could not breathe in that cabin. Two of the younger passengers took an active interest in my desire to sleep on the deck. They dragged out several blankets and a pillow, and tucked me in. Next they wanted to sing to me but I begged them for quiet: I had dreamed all my life of being able to spend the night listening to the sound of the waves. I gazed at the sky and breathed in the sea air as the waves rocked me to sleep. At dawn, against the backdrop of the sky, I glimpsed a familiar profile: a low forehead, a very proper nose, and a long pipe on a thin, straight cigarette holder. I thought that I was still dreaming. "Evgenii Ivanovich," I said, attempting to give my dream-like vision a name. But this "vision" turned around sharply and looked me square in the face. "Aguti, is that really you? Did you fall from the sky?" Oh yes, this really was the writer Evgenii Zamiatin, and with him was his wife Ludmila, who was a rather spiteful woman. I could tell that she did not want to enter into a conversation with me. I barely managed to tell them I had slept on deck and that I was on my way to visit my parents in Odessa. Evgenii Ivanovich said that they had just come out for some fresh air, but were going back for a nap, and they immediately left the deck. At the time I attributed their abrupt departure to the fact that my friend Mary had carried on a rather long and passionate affair with Zamiatin. His wife, who found out about it, obviously blamed me, although I was completely uninvolved in the matter. But soon it surfaced that Zamiatin was seeking to go abroad.[16] He must have been afraid when he saw me, for those who are running are always afraid of everyone. Obviously they were planning to get off at the next port and were embarrassed that I had seen them.

I did not stay long in Odessa, for I was expecting proofs for my book. My parents viewed me with respect, convinced that I had become a genuine writer. I tried to explain that this was not so and everyone was writing books these days, but they did not want to believe me. Mama asked with alarm whether I was planning to marry again, and did I not want to have a family of my own? I said that at present I had no prospects. Life was hard for them, and my father was often ill. I took him to the doctor to check his blood pressure. He naively thought that just getting this measured could cure his hypertension. Such procedures were relatively new in Odessa. I was very sad as I parted from them. I tried to stay cheerful and upbeat, and promised I would soon come again. But I could not help feeling that I was never going to see them again.

After I read the proofs, I was disappointed. I found my book boring and dull, with nothing literary about it at all. It was even worse than some of my school essays. But the Serapions liked it. At that time Leningrad had its own union of writers, and they accepted me as a member. I got together with the Serapions, with Marshak and other friends during the daytime, and the evenings once more belonged only to Izya. After our two-week separation, we were each happy to see the other, and everything went on as before. In December I began to feel sick. Symptoms that I knew well appeared, but I said nothing so as not to frighten Izya prematurely. We rang in the New Year at my place. I prepared duck with apples, hors d'oeuvres, and dessert. But not only did

I not want to eat, but I could not even look at the food. I told Izya that smelling all the food while cooking took away my appetite. He accepted this and dined with pleasure. Then he drank to my health. A week passed, and I went to the doctor, who dispelled all doubt. I had to tell Izya. He turned pale with fright, and his facial features changed. Then he began to state his case. Neither of us were financially secure. He had hoped that in a year or two he would become more firm on his feet, but until then a child was too much to handle. This enraged me and I felt malice rising within me. I sharply assured him that I would not ask him for anything and I would end our relationship that very day. He would not even have to see the child, but I wanted to have it. This upset him. He insisted that he did not want to lose me and that he considered me his wife, but we needed to wait. The impasse lasted for several days. We had to make a decision, though, before it was too late. I finally agreed to an abortion, but I said that this would put an end to our relationship. When I got out of the hospital, I would find myself another room, and perhaps even return to Moscow. He did not believe me and thought it was a final ploy to get him to change his mind. But I meant what I said. I was disgusted with his cowardice and his fear of responsibility.

Then a series of unexpected coincidences occurred. I phoned my Moscow friend Liza Rumiantseva. She had a close friend who was an experienced physician and who had sometimes assisted with abortions. At this time, abortions were prohibited; they could be done only in secret and were very expensive.[17] Liza told me, though, that this doctor was in the hospital with heavy pneumonia. Then I confessed my situation to Anna Entina, whose friend was a gynecologist who worked at the Obukhovskii hospital. We arranged for me to come on the day she was on duty there. She wrote up a fake diagnosis that required immediate surgical intervention to end the pregnancy. On the day designated for the "surgery," I went to the hospital after doing everything at home that you were supposed to do prior to such procedures. I asked for the physician on duty, but instead of the woman I knew, an elderly doctor came and asked me what was wrong. I said that I had an appointment with the regular physician on duty for that day. But I was told that she was not coming in and would not return for several days because her mother had died quite suddenly. There was not much I could do. It would have been foolish to discuss an illegal procedure with this stern woman whom I did not know. I was secretly rejoicing, though, inside. It seemed to me that my unborn child wanted to live. All of its potential murderers were meeting with misfortune while the child continued to live.

That afternoon Izya went to the hospital expecting everything to be in order. He went to the registration desk but was told that no one by my name was there. He rushed back, not knowing what to think. He was perplexed by this second failure. For several days we did not speak about it, but then he again raised the issue. I felt worse and worse about the entire situation. I just did not want to go through with the procedure, and all of the arguing reduced me to tears. I decided to look up the physician who had performed my abortion in 1924. He was quite old now, but worked as an assistant to a surgeon in one of the hospitals. Once again I did everything required and came to the hospital. They put me on an operating table, but the surgeon came in and noticed a small skin blotch on my inner thigh. He said that he would not do the abortion because this could be an indication of streptococcus, which could lead to sepsis. Without listening to any of my pleading, he just left the operating room. But I did not mind. I was overjoyed to take my unborn baby home. Three times I had agreed to this murder, but now there was no one in this world who could force me to do it. Once again Izya went to the hospital registration desk and then rushed back in a disconcerted state of mind. I remained calm and told him firmly that the child was going to be born and that I would raise it on my own. He need not come again. No one would know that he was the father of this child. Finally Izya gave in. He said that he did not want any further attempts at an abortion. We would have the child and everything would be fine.

As it turned out, we did not have to worry about where we would live, for Izya's landlady, Tatiana L'vovna Shchepkina-Kupernik, suggested that he invite me to live with them. Her set of rooms had been transformed by the process known as the reduction of living space, which began in Leningrad during the winter days of 1930.[18] The free and peaceful life people had long enjoyed in their apartments came to an end. Inspectors, caretakers, and other officials arrived with tape measures to climb over furniture and measure scrupulously the area of inhabited space. Tatiana L'vovna, though, had devised a plan: they would give up one-half of the apartment. She proposed to the house management committee that they put up a stone divider to separate off three rooms and the enormous kitchen, where they could install a bathroom. She would keep the other rooms leading out to the street and the dark dining room, which could be converted into a kitchen with a sink and stove and then they could partition off a room for the housekeeper, Maria Petrovna, and her mother, Tatiana Ivanovna, who was the cook. Past the three rooms leading out to Kirochnaia Street, there was a fourth room, large and square shaped, that opened onto the courtyard. It had served until recently as an office for Tatiana L'vovna's spouse, the famous lawyer Nikolai Borisovich Polynov.[19] He had a large practice with two assistants and the room was filled with shelves of lawbooks and law codes stacked up to the ceiling. Tatiana L'vovna offered us this room and one leading out to the street, leaving two big rooms for her and Nikolai Borisovich. Izya was overcome with embarrassment and said that he really was planning to get married, but there was still one more circumstance to explain. Tatiana interrupted him with "I know, I know, even if you have twins it is fine. You have to agree that I would rather have you than the family of a policeman with six kids." For some reason she was positive that they were going to put a policeman's family in with her.

Hence a new life began for me in an old and familiar social milieu. Tatiana L'vovna and her friends, the style of their conversations and their manners, reminded me very much of the social circles frequented by K.M. Tatiana L'vovna and Nikolai Borisovich seemed to like me. They had welcomed Izya into their company from the first days of their acquaintance, for they valued his modesty, self-discipline, and quiet nature. So everything in terms of our relationship with Tatiana L'vovna and her husband worked out very well. What unnerved me, however, was Maria Petrovna, the true mistress of the household. Tatiana L'vovna, in general, did not interfere in what the housekeeper did except to order the menu each evening for the following day. Housekeeper Maria Petrovna was around 50 years of age and worshipped Nikolai Borisovich. She safeguarded religiously his habits, and with a mother's tenderness took care of the suits, dinner jackets, morning coats, and tuxedos that filled his huge wardrobe. She cleaned and pressed them, and even sprayed them with flowery eau de cologne. She performed the same rituals with the linen of the venerable master. In the mornings no one else could use the bathroom before Nikolai Borisovich, for she considered it a cardinal rule that the man of the house be the first to wash and shave. For him she scrubbed the faucets, the bath, and the washbasin until they sparkled. Tatiana L'vovna always got up late, so if we were in a hurry, we would wash up in the kitchen, so as not to disturb this sacred ritual. Some grains of Maria Petrovna's tenderness had fallen upon my Izya as well, but now he became my duty in her eyes. I, though, was a "sly opportunist" who had seduced this handsome young man and gotten pregnant on purpose. In truth, Maria Petrovna even hated Tatiana L'vovna. Of course, she never dared to be rude to her face. But Maria Petrovna would not look her in the eye, but just listened with her face turned away, grumbling all the while. She did this despite the fact that she had worked in their household for nearly thirty years. Tatiana L'vovna tolerated her because she knew that she was not prepared to do even one-tenth of what this woman did for Nikolai Borisovich.

Izya and I moved into the room that opened up onto the courtyard. It was gloomy because it faced north. I wanted the other room, which was sunny, big, and cheerful, to be the nursery. I prepared for motherhood by reading books. I learned that a nursery should contain only the items most necessary for the baby, and objects should not be so high that they cannot be dusted regularly. I bought a cradle shaped like a wicker basket on small legs and a small white cabinet for linen. Tatiana L'vovna gave me a rather large table with short legs which we used for changing diapers. Above it was a small, white shelf that held jars with cork stoppers for cotton, gauze, and various solutions. Tatiana L'vovna happily sold us furniture for our room and we placed a large wardrobe and bookcase as a barrier between the windows so it seemed as if we each had our own half of the room. The large desk and bookshelves stayed put, and Izya soon filled them with his own books and files.

We needed to get our household budget in order. Fortunately at this time the publisher of the series *A History of Factories and Plants* offered me work. The Union of Writers in Leningrad had put my name forward to participate in a labor collective to write the history of the Skorokhod Factory.[20] I did not think twice about agreeing to do it, for huge expenses loomed. Unfortunately, I was assigned the very earliest and dullest part, from the 1880s until 1905. I had to go and work in the library for days at a time, and it was boring. My interest in the story picked up only when Guchkov[21] came on the scene. He was a major stockholder and was, moreover, a bit of a romantic who went off to fight on the side of the Boers in South Africa.[22] I went out to the factory and discovered that several of the old workers were still alive. I arranged to speak with them at the State Publishing House and provided tea and pastries. The old men and women drank the tea, but no one ate more than one pastry. They were very evasive in what they said and looked at me quizzically, not sure exactly what it was I wanted from them. Next I visited two old women workers in their apartments behind the Nevskii Gate. They lived with their children and their children's families. The apartments had vases with paper flowers, crocheted napkins, and tablecloths, and on one of the women's small tables was an old gramophone with a blue trumpet horn. All of these items reminded me of Odessa and the décor of tailors' and seamstresses' small apartments my mother and I visited from time to time. The interviews, though, were unproductive. They did not complain about exploitation, starvation, or the cold. One spoke tenderly about the ends of sausages and ham that you could buy in any shop back then for three kopeks. She lamented that today's sausage bears no resemblance to it, and added that in general there was enough of everything then. When I asked her about the work, she said that well, it was work. You could negotiate with the foreman, and for holidays, of course, you had to entertain him. Another reminisced about tails. I had to ask, "what do you mean by tails?" She answered, "Well, it was quite simple. My husband worked at a tannery, and they would bring skins from the slaughterhouse that still had tails, and they let us have them. I made cabbage soup (*shchi*) from the tails, which had lots of fat." Finding out about the tails was a minor victory for it at least enabled me to discover that in the tannery there was always a horrible stench and all of the tanners suffered illnesses.

These reminiscences, though, offered little material to paint a convincing picture of the impoverished condition of workers in the Skorokhod Factory. I had to turn to newspapers, especially old Petersburg papers from the prerevolutionary period. I usually went through these in the mornings. Then I would meet Izya at the writers' cafeteria on Nevskii Prospekt. He dined there as my husband with a pass in my name. The meals were excellent with a great variety of food. The buffet had different snacks and fancy bread buns. We had very little money then, but the meals we got here were within our budget. This cafeteria was quite unique. Boris Kornilov[23] would recite his new poems in the smoking room so loudly that you could hear him in the kitchen. Aleksei Chapygin[24] entertained everyone with the art of onomatopoeia: he squeaked, he meowed, and he hummed. Then we would walk home along Nadezhdinskaia Street, which is now Mayakovskaia, and this took us straight to our home on Kirochnaia Street. Izya often would have to go and lecture, and I would toil over my manuscript on the history of the Skorokhod Factory. In the evenings we would go for walks, then drink tea, and have the obligatory recitation of poetry. I made the acquaintance of Izya's mother, brother, and sister-in-law. I did not feel any particular warmth from them and I certainly did not display any myself, but everyone was polite. Each projected a decided air of self-importance, self-assurance, and authority. Yet, I hardly took notice for it did not matter to me in those days. All that concerned me was what was going on inside of me.

With the coming of spring I began to feel very sick. I had to go through a series of tests and the doctors put me on a strict diet, limiting my fluids to 100 grams a day—milk, soup, or tea. I chose to drink pure water, which I portioned out into three small glasses. Thirst tormented me. I would drink greedily my morning portion and then would have to wait in tremendous agony until I could drink my second glass in the afternoon. In the evenings Izya made sandwiches that were so tempting. I poured tea for him but had to limit myself to two small rusks and my third glass of water. They frightened me at my checkups, telling me that if this strict diet did not improve my condition, then they might have to induce labor artificially. Fortunately such a situation was avoided, and they stopped scaring me. I studied medical books and regulated my own diet. There was much that I would not let myself eat.

At the beginning of July, Izya went away to Peterhof;[25] he had received leave to stay at the House of Rest for Scholars located there. He promised to phone me to check on how I was doing, but I was quite content to be alone. I had bought all of the baby's layette, and now I needed to boil, iron, and put together the bed with mattress and blankets. The delivery date was drawing near. I was sure that the baby would come at the beginning of August. In a clean sheet I packed everything I would need to take to the maternity hospital. I knew that Izya would never know what to pack and how to lay it out, no matter how many times I explained it. He was due to return August 5. An hour before his return, I began to go into labor, but the pains did not feel normal. I phoned my doctor and he said that this was not good and that I needed to call an ambulance. I decided to wait for an hour, but when the time passed and Izya had not yet returned, I went ahead and phoned for the ambulance. I was all alone in the apartment. Tatiana L'vovna had gone to Moscow and I knew it was useless for me to try and ask Maria Petrovna for any help. Izya arrived before the ambulance and he looked exhausted. I told him that I had had to call the ambulance because my labor pains were not normal, but my words just went in one ear and out the other. He plonked himself down on the sofa and reproached me for being so callous. Could I not see that he was tired from having to carry a heavy suitcase? I had not even given him a chance to catch his breath. I was not surprised by his heightened egotistical self-absorption. I could only blame myself for having encouraged him in this direction. But I was still deeply offended. I was about to respond angrily but the bell rang and a young doctor came through the door. Orderlies followed bearing a stretcher, but I said that I could get myself downstairs. The doctor objected and said that in this situation it was best to be cautious. They were going to have to put me into the surgical ward because an operation was unavoidable.

The doctor's words finally got through to Izya. He got up and led me downstairs into the ambulance. The young doctor continued to paint a vivid picture of the dangers awaiting me. Izya trembled slightly, and I tried to assure him that everything was going to be fine. In fact, everything did go well. I was in labor for about twenty-four hours, but on August 6, around 4:00 p.m., I gave birth to my daughter. Before they took me to the recovery ward, while I was lying in the corridor, someone laid a tiny parcel above my knee. I figured out what it was when it stirred slightly. This was my very first moment of joy, the first in that unbroken chain of happiness that began precisely when I first saw her. They took us to my ward, where the nurses looked at the number of my bed, wrote down the history of my condition and the baby's number, and then took her away from me. They did not bring her back to me for a whole twenty-four hours. But I had anticipated this. Despite feeling tired and weak, I pulled out a postcard and wrote a few lines to Konstantin Mikhailovich. I wanted to share my joy with him first and foremost.

It was only now, at age 31, that my life really began. Everything else around me gave way, everything else became secondary to the invisible but enchanting circle that surrounded me and my Elenushka. No one was allowed to breach this circle. It was bright and joyful; within it we did feeding, bathing, and walks. Everything that involved me with the baby brought me happiness. I understood that this clear and brilliant love had always lived inside of me. I was born with it and now it had broken through, and nothing could destroy or even weaken it. Everything that had happened before now seemed trivial and distant. I felt as if I were looking at the previous thirty years from the other end of a pair of binoculars. To know that only you could do what this tiny person most needed and that as time passed you would be doing even more that was good for her was a joy that I could never until now have imagined. In those first months the sole symbol of life for me was the ritual of looking after the baby. She was to be bathed only in water that had been boiled, her underclothing had to be boiled and pressed and somehow dried, and the oilcloth on the swaddling table was cleaned three times daily with a boric solution. No one was allowed into the nursery, and no contact at all was permitted—no kissing and no tickling on her little cheeks. My devotion to motherhood irritated Maria Petrovna among others. She was not used to me being in the kitchen. Until now we mostly dined away from home and kept an electric teapot in our room. Now all of a sudden I was demanding my right to a corner of the stove, and each day I was taking a load of swaddling cloths into the bathroom. There I soaked them in a large basin and poured out the dirty water into the washstand. I tried to do all of this so as not to incur her wrath, but the very fact that I was engaging in these activities aggravated her. I imagine her thoughts ran like, Good God, it is just a child. Everyone has children and no one else gets so carried away with it.

I paid no attention to Maria Petrovna, but Elenushka's papa also grew irritated and could not cope with the fact that I had, in his words, "tossed him aside." He was used to my constant attention, to our having tea together in the evenings, and to the fact that I listened so avidly to him. But now suddenly I did not need any of this. I remember his reaction the first time I told him to dine alone while I rushed to feed my daughter. I put out on the table everything he needed for supper and turned on the teapot. I told him to go ahead with supper because I was going to feed Elena and then put her down to sleep. He looked at me in bewilderment and said: "Can you really not put off the feeding for thirty minutes in order for us to eat together?" "Absolutely not, the baby's routine cannot be disrupted," I retorted as I hurried to the nursery. This made him angry. True, he did turn off the teapot, but he left everything else the way it was and went out somewhere. At this point I began to sleep in the baby's room. I had not been able to find a nanny; collectivization was going in the countryside.[26] I did not mind. In these early, difficult months, I feared infection and did not want anyone else coming into contact with the baby. Although Izya understood that after a woman gives birth, conjugal relations had to be put aside for about two months (the doctor had told me six weeks, but I added a bit to make it an even two months), it still irritated him that I did not seem to miss his company. But I was not rejecting him; I would have joyfully welcomed him into my new world if he had not been so blinded by his stupid stubbornness and pride.

For the first time ever, I asked him to put out his cigarette before we entered the nursery. He got angry and looked at me with irritation. Then he sat down at his desk and said that he was not going in if this was the rule. I did not invite him into the nursery again. But that very same morning I made sure to drink tea with him and to share with him that our daughter was already smiling. Now, to be sure, he did go in to see the baby, and he even helped me sometimes with the nightly baths. The way we bathed her was to take a jug and pour warm bathwater over her. I would hold Elenka in my arms, face down, while her father took the jug and poured the water calmly, without rushing. Papa was clumsy, though, and either missed her altogether when he poured or, because he was so nervous, dumped it on her all at once. Sometimes Tatiana L'vovna helped with this procedure. She had never had children of her own and had rarely come into contact with them. But she liked my daughter. She always assured me that she could never have imagined that a little baby could have such a well-defined, perfect face, such attentive eyes, and, on top of that, curly hair.

In this way the first months went by. Izya's work took an interesting direction. He was offered a position in the Academy of Sciences Institute of Archeology. He was only 27 years old and had already defended his Candidate's degree dissertation.[27] Such a post set him apart from the ranks of not only other young scholars but the more established historians as well. Moreover, he was working vigorously on the memoirs and correspondence of the Bestuzhev brothers.[28] In the evenings, while our daughter slept, I typed for him, and we talked to one another. But every fifteen to twenty minutes, I would leave to check on her and make sure she was not crying. This always irritated Izya. He would tell me that he was very disappointed in me. He had thought that I was an intelligent woman and an interesting colleague, but he could see now that I was just a typical female, tied to a baby and diapers. I knew that his resentment had deeper roots than irritation over changing a baby. I responded petulantly that after seeing what kind of miraculous human being we had been ready to murder, I would never again agree to abort a child. I would rather give birth each and every year. So if he did not want any more children, it was up to him to do something about it. I knew my words were mean-spirited, but I was obsessed in my devotion to my child. I wanted to belong only to my daughter, to keep my body pure so that no extraneous emotions would get transmitted to her through my milk, and to not let anyone touch me except for her tiny fingers. During these early months, even the slightest accidental touch of her hands to my face when I was dressing her for a walk or while I was leaning over her crib filled me with such joy. This was all I needed, and I truly could not handle other emotions. But Izya did not understand or appreciate my devotion to maternity, which compared to other women came later for me, at the age of 31. Maybe, if he had shared just a tiny bit of my obsession, I would have felt closer to him, and I would have felt that we had truly become a family.

I would catch myself thinking about K.M. and what he would have been like as a father. No matter how capricious he might be, he would have quickly and expertly prepared our meals, and oh what rationalization he would have introduced into our routine. Undoubtedly he would have devised a pulley for bringing down the baby carriage from the third floor, so that I would not have to first take it down to the street and then go back up for the baby. He probably would have picked up the carriage with the baby in it and then run down the stairs. Of course, in other respects, he would have been overprotective. No, no one can be compared to K.M. We continued to correspond. When winter was approaching, I received notice from *Torgsin*[29] that an account had been opened in my name at *Torgsin* stores. K.M. wrote to me that he had set this up because he thought a Leningrad baby would need vitamins and it would be easier to get them through *Torgsin*. Thanks to him, from the age of 3 months, my daughter was greedily devouring apple and orange juice.

For ten days I could not return to writing. It is not just because the pressure is increasing and has made my eyes worse. Even with this happening I have still managed to type several lines a day. Since entering the aura of those bright and singularly happy first years of being a mother, I have been completely engrossed in all of the details, in all of the small, yet so significant moments of celebration, such as her first word, her first steps, and the spiritual bond that so quickly formed between us. I have been ready to describe it all day by day, for it is so clear and vivid in my memory, as if it has not been forty-five years since that time, but only six months at the most. But I realize that I needed to "cool it." This is not a diary. Diaries are written in full ignorance of the future. I, on the other hand, know what is coming and what I am going to have to describe. I simply cannot allow myself the luxury of getting stuck in that "faraway blue nursery." The room really was blue, for it had light blue wallpaper with a slightly noticeable silver pattern. We also had an antique chandelier with crystal pendants that flashed with dark blue and scarlet lights in the evenings. Tramcars went up and down Kirochnaia and the pendants sometimes tinkled from the vibrations.

I breastfed my daughter for thirteen months, until autumn, as I was advised. She was weaned without any problems and with a voracious appetite ate everything offered to her. Once I was finished with breastfeeding, I became more of myself again. I hired a nanny, mainly to take the baby for long walks. She slept in the nursery, so I returned to our bedroom. My husband and I began to eat again at our table, and we once more conversed about many topics. I returned to working, mostly for Izya, but I also earned some on the side. But we had very little money. Iraklii Andronikov[30] would bring work for me to do. At that time he was still very young, and he came over nearly every evening. He was Il'ia Silbershtein's[31] assistant in Leningrad. They were collecting materials for the series "Literary Heritage." Izya wrote articles for it and, in addition, gave them much assistance. He had an exceptional library in our home, and he stored in his head such a volume of information that he had no problem helping Iraklii with his research.

Sometimes I would call on Anna Entina; once a month she held interesting receptions that attracted such personages as Kornei Ivanovich Chukovskii with his "Chukokkala" literary scrapbook in hand,[32] Iurii Nikolaevich Tynianov,[33] and Georgii Vereiskii.[34] Anna was working now at the publishing house known as Soviet Writer. She had completed a degree at a commercial institute in her youth and this enabled her to get the position of bookkeeper for the publisher. She did not need to work, for her husband was a dental surgeon in the military. But she was bored and wanted to be part of a social circle of writers and artists. She had inherited money from her parents, which enabled her to present dinners of such refined elegance and foods so unique and tempting that you never turned down an invitation. Moreover, Anna was a lively, sociable, and witty person. Nonetheless, I did not go every month. If it coincided with the nanny's day off, then I stayed home to bathe my daughter, for I did not trust anyone else to do this. Anna always laughed and called me a crazy mom. I just could not tell her the truth, which was that my daughter's company was dearer to me than anyone else's.

When I was attending such social gatherings, or at the theater or even the symphony, I would be thinking with secret joy that soon I would be returning home. I would sneak into the nursery and without making a sound would look at my daughter's little arms all stretched out and her scattered curls, and listen to her regular breathing. Then

I would quietly tiptoe to the crib, fix the blanket, and perhaps, as sometimes happened, in her dream-like state she would say "Mama" and hold out her hands. I would pick her up, warm and sleepy, and help her sit on the chamber pot and then lay her back down again.

This simple, ordinary procedure had special meaning for us. Our relationship formed amid such love and trust that my daughter was never capricious or deceptive, nor prone to tears. On the contrary, I would tell her in the afternoon that I was going that evening to an interesting concert, or to the theater, or that I was meeting up with friends to have a nice supper, and that I would tell her about it the next day. She would be happy that mama was going to have fun and only asked that I be sure to look in on her before I went to sleep. I always went in at the appropriate time. If she did not wake up, then I would leave a sign next to her pillow that I had been there, such as a little boat with a colorful candy cover or a chocolate figurine. She reached the age of one before I knew it, and after that I gradually developed together with her and at times pushed her against her will. I drew simple pictures for her, and already at the age of three, she could draw animals and flowers very well, with much expression. She was not as good at drawing people; for a long time she drew them in age-old childish fashion, quite primitive. But she could draw wild animals that looked as if they came right out of the fairy tales we read. We had our favorite songs and poems. I did not wish to compete with her father so I conceded poetry to him. He was only a guest performer, though. He woke up while his daughter was out for a walk and came home after she had gone to sleep. On the rare occasions when he did get to spend time with her, he would entertain her with poetry. He did not know how to do anything else. He did not go for a walk with her, put her on his shoulders, or even pick her up. Nor for the most part did they even talk. All they shared was poetry. All I asked was that he not recite Karolina Pavlova and other similarly unknown poets. He was fine with this and limited himself to Pushkin and Lermontov. Elenushka and I knew the majority of these poems, for they often were part of our games. We would speed up the tempo of the verses in accordance with the game. As a consequence, our daughter could fire off many of them quite rapidly. So when her father recited them slowly, and in a melancholic tone, observing the proper break in the rhythm, she would assume that he was pausing because he had forgotten the next line, and she would prompt him. He liked this and viewed it as a family trait. She truly did inherit from her father an ability to memorize very long poems after one recitation. She could also from the age of 4 read her own books effortlessly and soon was reading anything she could get her hands on. She had albums for drawing as well as the usual notebooks for learning how to write letters of the alphabet.

When the nanny had a day off and my husband was home, the three of us dined quite cozily. During one such occasion she amazed both of us by reciting from memory Pushkin's "Monument" (*Pamyatnik*), a poem which neither one of us had recited to her. It turned out that it had been printed on the back of one of her notebooks and though she did not understand the majority of the words, she had nonetheless memorized it without a single mistake.

Finally, Izya did fall in love with his daughter. He had realized that he did not really like children, and during the first year his baby had seemed to him to be more like a lump of meat. He was even afraid of her. But now he loved this little girl, not just because she was his daughter, but because he simply liked her very much. Our little girl attended a preschool group learning English and her father worked at the Academy of Sciences. Sometimes he would work there until late in the evening and then again at his own desk until three or four in the morning. I did the housekeeping and worked in the evenings. I read quite a bit. K.M. sent me good new books to read. Thanks to him we were among the first to get the French translations of Agatha Christie's novels.[35] Izya could not speak a word of French, but could read it fluently. In this way our life flowed peacefully, quietly ....

7

Motherhood in a Time of Terror

The calm of our family life was interrupted by the ill-fated day in December of 1934, when our friend Serezha Gessen[1] arrived with the news that the Leningrad Communist Party head Sergei Kirov[2] had been murdered. We did not want to believe it, but once it was announced officially there was no room for doubt. We did not own a radio since neither of us cared for superfluous noise. We never discussed politics as there was barely enough time for issues that did matter to us. I have to admit, though, that the murder of Kirov upset us. He had been hugely popular and enjoyed respect not only among the workers but also among writers and scholars. Serezha soon left, but Izya continued to sit as if in a state of shock, not moving except that his hands were shaking. I prepared some strong tea and asked him why he was in such a state. I even admonished him to be in control of himself. He looked at me with such a sad and lingering look that I became quite terrified. "This is only the beginning," he said, "terrible consequences are going to come from this." I asked him, "How do you know this? Why talk such nonsense?" He smirked and answered bitterly: "I would not be a good historian if I could not figure this out. The consequences could affect each one of us." I accused him of overreacting and all he said was, "Let's hope you are the one who is right."

Soon we learned that the assassin was some unknown employee at the Smolny Institute by the name of Nikolaev.[3] People said that he did it out of envy, but all kinds of rumors were circulating. I was relieved—it was just an ordinary murder spawned by jealousy. The Paris newspapers had reported such incidents nearly every day. However, they soon began exiling people. In our stairwell they evicted an elderly couple who were formerly of the gentry. Then the arrests began. They took the brother of Nikolai Borisovich (Tatiana L'vovna's husband), Boris Borisovich Polynov,[4] a geologist and a leading soil specialist. Serezha Gessen, who now came to see us nearly every day, told us in the strictest secrecy that he had been summoned "there" (meaning the offices of the NKVD, the secret police—Translator's note), where they pressured him to act as an informer. Serezha tried to tell the story in a humorous vein but the summons had definitely frightened him. He was a decent human being and could not do this type of thing. But the officers were dangerous and threatening. So Serezha decided to play the fool. He burst out laughing at the proposition and said that however much he wanted to help, he would bring them more harm than good. Alas, he confessed, he lacked the necessary qualities—he was talkative by nature, absentminded, prone to forget people's names, and chronically late everywhere he went. Plus, he often had too much to drink, and he might just inadvertently spill the beans. He did love to brag, after all. The conversation went on for a long time, but Serezha stayed in character as an unpredictable chatterbox. They let him go, but suggested that he seriously consider the offer and made him to sign a statement saying that he had refused to act as an informer. Despite the underlying humor, this story could not cheer us up. Serezha himself became gloomy in telling it. He now lived in constant fear of being summoned again and felt as if they were watching him. His name was now registered "there." Izya told him to be careful and discrete. He should cease telling anecdotes, watch every word he spoke, and stop wearing his heart on his sleeve, as Serezha was wont to do. After all, Serezha was not the first person summoned for such a talk, and others were more likely to have agreed to "help." Serezha visibly sagged at this warning, though. How could a man who lived quietly, who was cheerful, who trusted everyone and had a wide circle of friends live like this? But Serezha could never be downhearted for very long. We had supper and after sharing a bottle of brandy, he cheered up and even played chess with Izya before leaving.

Time passed and Izya calmed down. No one summoned him. No other of our acquaintances had any such experience or at least no one said anything about it if they did. We had become good friends with Pavlik Shchëgolev and spent much time at his home and he at ours. He had become a serious European historian, and he worked with the vaunted scholar Evgenii Viktorovich Tarle.[5] Pavel Pavlovich was stout like his father and acted with a bit of comical self-importance. But he had a sharp intellect and was well educated. He and his first wife Irina had divorced and he had remarried, this time to a woman who was a true original. If Irina Ternavtseva had been the most beautiful of all women, then Antonina Nikolaevna Izergina,[6] or as her close friends called her, Totia, was the most charming, creative, and intellectually refined of all the persons I happened to meet in the course of my long life. She was a very attractive woman, elegant, and entirely feminine in her appearance. As far as her tastes go, I cannot say enough here that would do justice to her. She was the most outstanding of the scholars working in the Hermitage. She not only had a deep knowledge of the paintings, but she could always find something new and fresh in long familiar canvases. She also wrote original impressionist poetry. But what amazed me the most about her was her enthusiasm for Alpinism. She was a genuine Alpinist and had completed very difficult climbs. She earned the ranking of First Class Sportsman and even served as an instructor for the Red Army. I have to admit that I was surprised that she had chosen Pavlik as a husband. He seemed so very pudgy and apathetic compared to her. But he moved her somehow, though I think she pitied him more than she loved him. She was impetuous, effusive, and full of life. She could make the most unpleasant remarks to someone directly to his face and then turn around a little while later and be on completely friendly terms with that very same person.

The most amusing individuals gathered at their home, including the Hermitage employee, the elegant and handsome Lev L'vovich Rakov,[7] as well as the witty and rather spiteful Iakov Ivanovich Davidovich.[8] The writer Pavel Luknitskii[9] was often there. He too was an Alpinist and was Totia's partner for her mountain climbs. Totia and Pavel Shchëgolev lived in the same apartment as his father, the same apartment where in the past I had typed the Aksakov letters. It was perfect for these gatherings with its antique furnishings, mahogany wood, Elizabethan lamps, several valuable old paintings, and the Shchëgolev library. There was always a lot of vodka on the table. This group were heavy drinkers, and Totia could keep up with the best of them. This highly feminine blonde in a white billowy blouse, after downing several glasses, would begin to talk in a very uninhibited fashion, so much so that Pavlik, playing the role of the severe spouse, would yell at her across the table, in front of everyone: "Totia, I am going to have to ask you to go stand in the closet and think about what you just said." Totia would then act perplexed, and putting on the submissive demeanor of a naughty schoolgirl, go obediently out the door. A moment later, she would return, drink down the next glass, and then spew forth such virtuoso verbal filth that even Pavlik could not devise an appropriate punishment. This was all great fun. The scene shocked me, though, the first time I witnessed it. Of course, it was particularly disconcerting to me because it happened just one day after I had been at the Hermitage and had seen Totia leading a group of teachers on a tour. She looked so smart, elegant, and aristocratic and her polished use of words was inspiring and literary. She cast a spell over her audience, and several were looking more at her than at the pictures themselves. She was not even aware of this, for she was looking at these canvases, so familiar to her, as if she were seeing them for the first time. She shared with these provincial teachers the great joy that comes from grasping the genius of the artistic masters. But from under the collar of her severe jacket you could see just a frill of this billowy blouse.

These scenes made Izya blush. It was not that such words shocked him. He was very familiar with the earthy forms of the Russian language from ancient times. But he hardly expected to hear coarse words from the mouth of a woman such as Totia. The others were used to it, and they themselves liked to use strong language in their own academic arguments. I grew a bit tired of this. I viewed the use of such words as a sign of a weak vocabulary and lexical deficiency. Because they could not find sufficiently precise and proper words to express their views, these tipsy young scholars blurted out anything that came to mind. But Izya got accustomed to them and even grew attached to this social group. He could not alter his own old-fashioned and flowery language, but he was willing to listen to others speak in a different manner. I hung out with them less often. They all thought I was insanely obsessive as a mother. No one from this group at that time had children. They did not like children and they laughed at my devotion to my daughter, though not unkindly. This suited me, for I did not find this company of people particularly amusing or astonishing.

I was happy to spend the evening alone at home, reading or working, and relieved not to be breathing in tobacco smoke. Sometimes I would go to the Philharmonic or to the Mariinsky Theater for a ballet performance. When this group of friends came to us, I tried to be the best hostess I could be, which led to arguments with Izya, who was horrified by my expenditures. As I ponder these words, remembering the "horror" felt by my scholarly, handsome, and worthy husband, I am reminded of the very foolish and vexing peculiarity of my relationships with men. Was I really just unlucky in this realm? Or is there something in me that facilitates or encourages such behavior? I had rationalized K.M.'s extraordinary economizing and absurd miserliness as being the product of his heightened sense of obligation to his family. I knew he did not want to spend any more than was necessary from their shared inheritance. But still, he was earning his own money. Plus, I was so young, and he had introduced me into a social circle in which all of the women were well dressed. Yet what would I have done without my own resourcefulness and the opportunity to barter the unwieldy copper crockery for fabric and footwear? But K.M. spared no effort nor expense when we hosted the entire social group and provided abundant food and drink. Here his pride really showed—"do not dare disgrace yourself," even if on a day-to-day basis there was constant economizing. At the time this struck me as funny, and even touching. I loved him very much and I knew how to find the good in everyone. But then when we got to Paris, he still carefully calculated all of our expenses for every meal. I was able to dress fashionably only after I started to work. Yet, once he knew that I was not going to come back to him, he spared no expense in taking me for rides on his motorcycle and out to restaurants. Then, my goodness, when I ended up far away from him, he opened up an account for my child at *Torgsin*. Now consider Izya; during the first year of our bucolic love he habitually dined every evening at my table, despite knowing that I had very little money and that I had to help my parents. Yet he not even once proposed to help out in any way. I ignored this and prepared delicious, even if modest, suppers for him.

Several days before I gave birth I had received an honorarium for my work on the Skorokhod factory and it was a pretty substantial sum of money in those days. I put it in a desk drawer that was always open. When I returned home with my newborn, I discovered that the drawer was now locked with a key. Thus it began: Izya declared that I had a tendency to be extravagant, but now it was time to start saving. Therefore, he would henceforth give me an allowance and I was to record all of my expenditures. He himself would pay for the apartment, the firewood, and the electricity. I said nothing in response, for all of my attention at that time was focused on my baby's needs, and I did not want to get upset while I was still breastfeeding. Izya took my silence as meaning I agreed to submit to his direction. But my feelings for him, already not very stable, definitely wavered. Nevertheless, I did not wish to deprive my daughter of her father, and he had many good qualities. I convinced myself that no one is perfect and it was necessary to take stock of the good and not dwell on the bad. So life went on in this vein.

It became difficult now for me to help my poor elderly parents, who were living in a state of near starvation. When I first raised this with Izya, he noted dryly that he did not give anything to his mother, who was being supported solely by his brother. Therefore it would not be fair to give money to my parents. I knew that as soon as I finished breastfeeding I was going to go back to work and earn at least some money, but until that time I developed a plan. I began to pull down books from the enormous glass cabinet, where there were monographs, publications of the Academy of Sciences, albums, and many other literary and artistic materials. The books stood in three rows on each shelf, with even more unbound editions squeezed in on top of them. I did not touch the poetry books, nor the Academy books, but I sold off to secondhand booksellers some from the very back rows or from the unbound albums. The money I received I sent to my mother. Izya did not notice the missing books, for he never had time to go digging in this wardrobe. But when we invited guests for dinner, I insisted on having my own "menu." I argued that we could not be rude to people who had treated us to dinner more often than they dined with us. Izya looked pained, but he relented. The guests always left satisfied and even the next day would phone to say that everything had been delicious. Such dinners came easy to me. I recalled the receptions we had had on Mokhovaia Street, and even here, on Kirochnaia, there was something to be learned from Tatiana L'vovna, who loved to entertain. On Tatiana's day she always invited us, and I would watch all of the cooking and preparations in the kitchen. Tatiana L'vovna's parties were very interesting. The very last vestiges of a fading era would visit her. It was obligatory for the marvelous singer Marina Nizhal'skaia[10] to sing intimate love songs, accompanied on the piano by her devoted Alexei Taskin.[11] The artist Maksimov also attended, whom I knew from Odessa as a magician, but who was now a dramatic actor.[12] The portly Iurii Iurev[13] presided over the table as if petrified in stone; in her day the great Mariia Ermolova[14] had bestowed her blessing on his theatrical career. At Tatiana's the ladies wore corsets, black silk dresses, and puffed-up hairstyles, and their husbands stood to listen to the singing and applauded elegantly.

Twice the eminent historian Evgenii Viktorovich Tarle attended these receptions. Tatiana L'vovna was very good friends with his sister Maria Viktorovna. Often Izya and I felt embarrassed and a bit out of place with these other guests, but not so in the company of Tarle. Like everyone else, this master conversationalist captivated us. His talent forced even the arrogantly languid Maksimov and the solemnly proud Iuriev to listen to Evgenii Viktorovich with their mouths half open. Oh he could tell wonderfully fascinating stories, spiced with historical anecdotes and details about the Spanish, French, and Russian courts that no one else knew. What a speaker he was! Undoubtedly these two famous actors admired his diction and rich intonation. Before leaving, Evgenii Viktorovich came to our room to look at the newest additions to Izya's library. In spite of his economizing, Izya quite frequently bought books on history.

Tatiana L'vovna liked to invite my Elenka over for tea. She loved my daughter, and especially appreciated her composure, despite being surrounded by temptations. In Tatiana L'vovna's enormous room, there were many bookstands and small tables with shelves, all of which were filled to the brim with the most alluring knickknacks—shepherdesses, ballerinas, dogs, cats, and other items from old factories. My daughter's eyes would light up, but not once did she ever dare reach out a hand, even to the Little Red Riding Hood. To reward her, Tatiana L'vovna let her play with the couch pillows. There were no less than thirty of these, from ones made of huge brocade fabrics sewn with beads to small, round lace pillows the size of apples. But the most fanciful feature in this fairy-tale-like room was the collection of butterflies. They were hung on the wall in flat, glass boxes. They were not plain butterflies but enormous tropical ones, some as large as birds. There was one that was cornflower blue and one that was laced with all of the colors of the rainbow. There were also black ones that looked like velvet. Usually Tatiana L'vovna herself brought my daughter back to me, but after thirty minutes, I would go to fetch her, fearful that she was interfering with Tatiana L'vovna's work. Tatiana spent hours during the day at her typewriter working on translations of Shakespeare's plays. But I will admit that this was a pretext to see one more time the lovely butterflies so Elenka and I could then paint them from memory with watercolors.

Life, it seemed, was turning out well for us. Izya was thriving at work, we had interesting friends, and our daughter brought us nothing but joy. She was kind, sociable, cheerful, and willingly shared with everyone. She voluntarily gave her toys to other children within her playgroup. The latter was organized in the following way: Each of the children took turns hosting the playgroup at his or her apartment. The "turn" lasted for one week. The children loved coming to our room most of all. No one had such a large and practically empty nursery—thirty meters. The children would bring their breakfast with them, and the host mother provided the tea. After the meal, the teacher took them out for a walk. This gave me a lot of free time. Izya quite often loaded me with work, but I managed to get extra jobs, "on the side," as well. I wanted to earn my own money that I did not have to report to him. For this work I went to a building that was located inside the Gostiny Dvor. There I met up with old friends, most often running into Mikhail Zoshchenko. He was the only one with whom I still had a genuine friendship. He began to visit me when he found out that I was often at home during the daytime. Once again we began to have incredible conversations. As if he were confessing to a priest, he told me about his passions, claiming he had gotten involved in these affairs not for love but on a whim. He recalled the first time we met, his own amorousness, and reproached me for being cold. But he said all of this in such an amusing way, spontaneous and simple, yet so intimate, as only he could do. He showed me his notebooks, where he had written down themes for future short stories. There was a lot there. But, to my regret, Mikhail Mikhailovich began to write plays and longer books with psychological elements. I insisted that there could not be anything better than his short stories; they were not just his "first attempt at writing." I made it clear that I did not care for his philosophizing; this offended him and made him gloomy. Knitting his brow, he carefully took out a pinch of tobacco from a small antique snuffbox and inhaled in a highly stylized, old-fashioned manner. He got particularly angry when I ridiculed his theories about sex. He insisted that breastfeeding was what awakened erotic feelings in boys and a desire for women, and that he himself had a memory of this. As corroboration, he confided that he courted only full-figured women. I asked him with irritation, "what happens then with girls, do they also get from their mother's milk a desire for other girls?" At this we both laughed, the gloom evaporated, and before he left, we kissed for quite a long time. This became our established practice. No matter what we were arguing about, no matter what we said to one another, we would kiss when it came time to say goodbye.

This was my secret, and it helped compensate for my troubled relationship with my husband. On the surface, our family life seemed perfectly happy. I made sure of this for the sake of my daughter. I remembered too well how troubled my own childhood had been and how difficult it had been for me to endure the discord between my parents. I tried with all of my might to develop in my daughter love and respect for her father. Yes, he deserved this. But his economizing, his insistence that I keep daily accounts of all purchases of meat, vegetables, butter, brooms, and blocks for my daughter, was insulting and killed my former affection completely. He especially irritated me when he said I was wasting money on toys and that it was possible to exist without blocks. He criticized me even when it was my own money I was spending on her. But now I simply ignored his remarks. I had my own secret friend.

There was still another reason for our disharmony. Izya was becoming besotted with Totia. He began to visit her every evening. There was a legitimate and respectable reason for this. At the beginning of 1936, Pavel Shchëgolev died after undergoing a serious operation. All of us attended the solemn civil funeral in the auditorium of the university. Totia was there, surrounded by friends, while the first wife, Irina, wearing a black, tight-fitting dress and a mourning veil, struck a tragic pose as she lowered herself on one knee right in front of the coffin. So it was that Izya, along with all of the other friends of Pavel Pavlovich, found it necessary to make sure the young widow was never alone. They gathered at her place, conversed, drank, ate, and stayed there until very late. Truthfully, Totia did not display any particular preference, but it was clear that Izya had fallen hard for her. This suited me just fine. I asked no questions and responded to his unnecessary explanations that I preferred relationships to be free and to allow each person to act as he or she desired. It did not even occur to him that my words applied to my own behavior as well.

Soon, though, both of our passions ended abruptly. We were brought back together by illness. Elenushka suffered a severe case of influenza, complicated by an infection in the inner ear. There was fever, delirium, doctors, bags of ice, and a constant state of alarm. Now Izya went only to work and then returned immediately home. He would look at me with fear in his eyes, trying to figure out what our daughter's temperature was. It was her first serious illness, and it lasted several weeks. Our daughter grew weak and pale. The doctor advised us to take her somewhere warm for the summer, but not anywhere with extreme heat. We decided to go to the village of Novye Senzhary in the Poltava region (Ukraine). Friends recommended this place to us and gave us the address of a proprietor with whom they had stayed for several years running. I made arrangements with him and we decided to go there at the beginning of May. I no longer sent my daughter to the playgroup, but took her for walks myself. I fed her an enriched diet and we were inseparable for entire days at a time.

Meanwhile, the world around us was becoming nightmarish. Izya was coming home from work very alarmed and our friends were bringing us depressing news. Arrests were happening more frequently, along with ruthless purges. Sons were beginning to turn on fathers, brothers against brothers. The dreadful term "enemy of the people" emerged. People, despite knowing they were innocent of any crime, nonetheless prepared a suitcase with underwear, and their wives cooked hard-boiled eggs for their husbands to take with them when they were arrested. But I remained calm, for I knew that Izya was far removed from politics. True, he had avoided entering the party when he was invited to do so, but he told them he just did not feel prepared for this. At work everyone respected him. He lectured at the university in addition to working in the Academy of Sciences, and the students loved him. What did we have to fear? However, alarming news again came when some historians were arrested. Izya asked me to stop corresponding with Konstantin Mikhailovich. This was not hard since he himself had stopped writing. Obviously, it was clear in Paris what was happening here. May arrived, and I happily took my daughter to Novye Senzhary far away from these rumors and anxieties.

*****I am again in the hospital. But I must continue.*****

I went alone with Elenka to Novye Senzhary. Izya would not be able to join us until the end of June. We rented an entire cottage in an enormous fruit orchard, right next to the Vorskla River. Hearing Ukrainian being spoken unsettled me, reminding me of my childhood. In the evenings the women sang songs familiar to me as they returned home from work, though it would be more accurate to say that they were not singing, but lamenting. My daughter and I went on many walks. Over a small hill and to the side there was a large, overgrown pond. You could hear the toads croaking there and the sound was tragic, and terrifying, much like the sound of an organ. I was never superstitious, but these sobbing toads sent shivers through me. "What horrors lie in wait for me?" I asked myself. Izya wrote frequently. In his letters there was not a single word that was careless. He repeated over and over that his nerves were strained and that he wanted only one thing—to be with us. I could sense his alarm. There had been many arrests before my departure, including writers and scholars whom we knew. I asked my landlord to whitewash the walls and ceiling of the third room and to put a table there for my husband who would soon be arriving with many books. Gala, one of Elenushka's friends from her playgroup, arrived with her mother. I had rented a room for them near us. Everything was working out just fine: the children played in the garden, bathed in the river, and walked with us to the market, which was a happy and boisterous place. Then in June, when we were already counting the days until papa would arrive, a telegram came from Izya's brother: "Come now, Izya is seriously ill." I understood what this meant, but I told everyone that my husband had fallen ill and that I needed to go home for several days. Gala's mother took my daughter to stay with her while I was gone.

At home I saw that our room had a seal on it, but the nursery was open and so I moved in there. I phoned Izya's brother. They asked me to come immediately, though they received me quite coldly. His brother's wife told me that Izya had visited too often with people in Leningrad and Moscow and obviously shot his mouth off, and this was the result. They considered it my duty as his wife to take up his case; they were washing their hands of it. They advised me to go to Moscow, where a longtime friend of Izya's lived, a public prosecutor and a member of the party. I went the very next day and arrived during Maxim Gorky's funeral.[15] The central streets were nearly impassable and it was difficult for me to get to the prosecutor. I knew him well, for he had often visited us. He had spoken openly about everything and sometimes revealed frightening things. I rang the bell. He opened the door, recoiled back, and even turned pale. I asked him whether he knew anything about what had happened to Izya. He seemed annoyed and said that yes, he knew about it but he did not understand why I had come to him. He was completely powerless and he advised me not to poke my nose anywhere. I should just stay at home with my daughter. He was clearly not going to let me cross his threshold, and so I left.

After I had returned to Leningrad, I phoned the NKVD. I said that the room in which I had all of my things, including dishes and clothing, had been sealed. They told me that they would unseal it in the near future, and that I must not go anywhere. After two days an investigator came and removed the seal. He said that he had "taken" my husband, but had not at that time been able to search the library so he was going to do this now. The search went on for several hours, for there were endless numbers of books, mostly on history. He took away with him several works by Izya's mentor, Mikhail Pokrovskii, including those listing Izya as editor. I asked what my husband was accused of, but he answered evasively, saying that the investigation was only beginning and that for the next month or two there would be no information or communication. All of the unpleasantness that had alienated me from Izya vanished from my memory, swept away by my boundless pity for him. I kept imagining him in his lonely cell, thinking about us; I could sense his fear, his complete helplessness.

I had no one I could speak to about what had happened, no one with whom I could share my fears, my despair. Everyone shrank from me. I phoned one of our recent acquaintances and sensed I should not phone again. Everyone was afraid of getting involved in a tragedy that could strike any one of them. I learned that in the Academy of Sciences about two hundred persons had been arrested, most of whom were party members. I felt heartened: maybe these party members were guilty of some form of opposition in the past. But Izya was not in the party, he studied early Russian history, and did not involve himself in contemporary politics. He was a Marxist scholar. My hope was that the investigation would show it was all a mistake and that he had just been swept along in the general stream of arrests. Surely he would be set free once this was cleared up.

Yet, no matter how difficult and frightening this was, what upset me the most was being separated from my daughter. Until now I had not been away from her for even a single day. It worried me that she was far away and staying with strangers so I decided to go and get her. The celebration of her birth was drawing near, the brightest day of my life. I bought presents and headed to Senzhary. My daughter saw me from a distance and raced out to meet me. I told her that daddy was ill and that we needed to be at home. In two days' time we left. We were the only passengers in the train compartment, and I took this moment to tell my daughter the truth. I explained that some people in the Academy of Sciences had done something wrong, they had been arrested, and our papa was among them, though he was innocent. Once everything could be explained, he would be able to come home. But she was not to talk with anyone in our apartment building about papa. I only had to tell her this once. She never forgot it and she never argued about it. We had long ago come to an understanding that I wanted only what was best for her. So yes, this 6-year-old girl was my only friend during these terrible days. She never complained while spending long hours in her room while I was out searching for work. I had to establish an official "identity" in order to transfer a living space, such as our room, to my name and personal account. I also had to earn money because I had no one and nowhere to turn to for help. I tried to find work as a secretary, a proofreader, a typist, or as a translator, but I always had to fill out an application that asked the question about whether I had relatives in prison. Once I responded yes, all conversation ceased. I did not even try to get work at the writers' publishing house; everyone there was shaking in fear. It was Zoshchenko alone who, after running into me on the street, asked what was wrong. When I told him the reason, he was angry at me for not having said anything to him, not even phoning him. He came to see us that very day and met my daughter. After watching her draw at her small children's desk, he said that he had at home a solid Swedish desk that he had bought for his son to use, but now the son had outgrown it. He offered to bring it for Elenushka, if she would like to have it. My little girl looked at me shyly, and I said: "she should speak for herself." She beamed and said that she very much would like to have it. The next day Mikhail Mikhailovich brought a large, bright lacquered school desk that had been made to order during the NEP period. It was a tremendous desk with a seat that could be adjusted as the child grew. The desk had a lid that folded down, and underneath were boxes and different compartments. The desk became like a home to her, and she used it for a long time. I asked Mikhail Mikhailovich not to visit us on a regular basis; a cloud hung over us and he needed to be careful. He said that he was not afraid and that he would not abandon friends who were in trouble. But I insisted. He agreed only under the condition that I take from him a very large sum of money, which I very much needed and which I felt I could take from him without any qualms. I have never known anyone in my life who was equal to him in his nobility and delicacy of feeling. Now I was able to hire a housekeeper who could take my daughter for walks and prepare meals. I was not sending her to the children's playgroup since I knew that the parents of the other children would not like it if I did.

Finally I found work. I went in the late afternoon with my typewriter to a rather strange institution located in the basement of an Industrial Institute in the Lesnoy district.[16] Here artists worked on animated films with production-oriented and scientific themes. There was no requirement to fill out a personal information form. It was a new enterprise and much had been written by hand, so my typewriter was very much prized by the young man in charge. My marriage with Izya had not been registered, and our last names were different. But no one there asked me anything or even knew whether or not I had a husband. I worked quickly. I became acquainted with several of the scientific workers who gave me work to do at home. In the evenings, after I had tucked in my daughter, I worked for several hours in our room.

The time came when it was possible to ask for information about Izya at the NKVD. I had to go to a special building, constructed on the spot of the demolished Sergievskii Cathedral. After standing in line for several hours, I always received the same response, "The investigation is on-going." But each time I would post a letter through the mail requesting information and sign it as the wife of the arrested man. Finally I was told that I could now correspond with him. I was both relieved and frightened by this, for I did not know what it meant. So I went to see Serezha Gessen, whom I could visit without any misgivings. I learned a lot from Serezha: he said that from time to time they did release people. He knew that sometimes they allowed correspondence as a reward for certain services, but we both rejected this possibility, for we knew that Izya was not capable of turning informer. It was also possible that the investigation had ended, or that he had grown so weak that it was necessary to get help from his family to support him. Now began hours of standing in the lines at Shpalernaia Street with heavy bags in my arms. I did not speak to anyone. Serezha warned me that I needed to be careful, for *seksoty* (agents of the secret police) were everywhere.

At the end of December, a phone call woke me up during the night. A male voice told me curtly that my husband was at the prison on Nizhegorodskaia Street. If I wanted to supply him with food and warm clothing, this had to be done during the next twenty-four hours. Packages would only be taken until evening. So I set off with a big basket to the Eliseiev Emporium[17] on Nevskii Prospekt and bought cheese, whole sausages, sugar, etc. As I was leaving the store, I ran into Totia Izergina. She was one of the few who had not acted cowardly. She had phoned often and invited me to come over, though I had no time for visiting her. When she found out why I had bought so much food, she took me by the arm and said that she would be over to help carry the package to the prison. She did come and brought a sheepskin coat and a large bag full of warm clothing, the most notable item of which were her large Alpine knitted stockings. I had already collected quite some time ago a warm hat, gloves, and some other such items. We took all of this to the prison. Among the crowd of relatives one could hear one word repeated, "Solovki."[18]

Very difficult but nonetheless happy days passed. Nothing could overshadow the happiness I felt when spending time with my Elenushka. Soon, I again went to find out information about my husband and was told that Izya had been sentenced by a special session of the Military Tribunal, on the basis of Article 58, points 1, 10–11, and 8, to ten years with a deprivation of civil rights for another five years. Soon they confiscated our possessions and the library; it was only with great difficulty that I was able to hold on to my typewriter and a small work table. Literally the very next day the investigator and his wife moved in to our room. I had to relocate to the nursery. I often had to work at night and it was hard on me knowing that this was interfering with my daughter's ability to sleep. Our housekeeper Maria slept soundly, for the typewriter did not bother her. But occasionally my daughter would say, "Go to sleep, Mommy, you have to get up so early." And I would tell her just to lay on her side and go to sleep because I had promised to finish it by the next day. I would go over to her, she would reach out and hug my neck, and I would bury my face in her thick curls. During such moments I was happy, perhaps happier than I had been before or since ....

The year 1937 came, bringing closer the one-hundredth anniversary of Alexander Pushkin's death. Serezha Gessen was preparing an exhibit for the celebration and would be lost for days at a time at the Pushkin House. Sometimes he phoned and asked whether I had received any letters, but so far there were none. Then one evening the ringing of the phone interrupted my work, and it was Serezha's wife, Zhenia. Her voice trembling, she begged me to come immediately. I ran over, for she lived nearby at the corner of Znamenskaia and Basseinaia streets. The door to her apartment was wide open, and people had already gathered there. I knew from the looks on their faces that something tragic had happened. Serezha had been run over by a bus while running across Palace Square. Now his body lay in the morgue. His wife threw herself at me and began to scream: "Tell me now, which of us is more unhappy? Your husband might come back, but mine never will!" These words terrified me. I was already distraught by Serezha's death, but it was no less frightening to hear her speculating about my husband's fate. I walked at the funeral with Serezha's friend. As we approached the cemetery, he whispered to me: "Perhaps this was for the best? Believe me, they were going to take him. They were going to let him finish the exhibition and then arrest him. We are all on those lists." I shrank from these words—where did he learn about such lists? But sure enough, soon they arrested him.

To say that 1937 was a year of horror is an understatement. Every day and every hour of this year was a nightmare. All of this is quite well known. I have nothing new to say about it. If I had not been expecting my husband's letters, then I would have taken my daughter away to the most remote place I could find. I would have gone somewhere without the newspapers that terrified me with their endless reporting about children torn from their parents, husbands from their wives, wives from their husbands, or where I did not have to watch how someone at any moment would trample into the mud his closest friend. A university instructor by the name of Lev Plotkin[19] called my husband a "fascist thug" in an article he wrote. Then at the beginning of March, a letter finally came from Izya in the Solovki camp. He said that he was living in a common barracks, that he was often outside, and that thanks to slanderous testimony he had been charged with organizing Kirov's murder. He urged that all efforts be made to get his case reexamined so that he could prove his innocence. He was confident that truth would prevail, that he would return to us. He promised that everything would be different and he would again deserve my love. He added that he was allowed one package a month and explained what needed to be included. Now our most important task was to put together the package for papa. Elenka prepared her drawings, and together we packed it up. Then we waited for further letters, but none came.

At the end of July, though, a package was returned with "address not found" marked on it. What were we to make of this? However, there was little time to ponder the question. Several days later they called me in, took my passport, and ordered me to leave with my daughter in forty-eight hours and go to the village of Dvinskii Berezniak in the Arkhangelsk region. "On what grounds am I being exiled?" I asked. The answer was: "As a family member of a repressed enemy of the people!" A functionary in a military uniform opened the door for me, and in the corridor stood a crowd of women waiting with the very same order. I went to Liteinii and did not even know on which side of the street to walk. This monstrous nonsense—"enemy of the people"—hit me with the force of an axe on my head. Now these words would stick not only to me but also to our daughter. In one year Elenka would start school. What awaited her there?

Forty-eight hours! What should I do first? Go and pick up the money owed me for work I had done? I needed to sell some of our possessions and buy tickets. The latter turned out to be quite easy. All over the city there were stalls selling tickets to exiles, for there were thousands of us. As I stumbled home, I sat down on Furshtatskaia Street across from the Lutheran Church of St. Anne, where long ago Konstantin Mikhailovich and I had been married. I had never told my daughter about him, it was still too early for her to know that her father was my second husband. But always, when I would pass by this portico, I would stop and think about him. Now I said goodbye to this amazing building, where I had recently brought my daughter to hear the playing of the organ. Inside the church courtyard there was a school that Elena was supposed to attend. I had been happy that she would not have to cross the street to get to it.

Fortunately, when I got home no one was there; my daughter was walking with Maria in the small public garden at the Spasskii Church. Without anyone watching, I quickly examined our things and picked out what was most essential. But how could I carry our blankets, pillows, shoes? I had very little money and what I had, I would need. I had a large hat box I had brought back with me from Paris. But I needed this to store all the photographs and letters that I did not want to destroy, along with silver spoons and trifles that were valuable to me. I took all of these over to my brother-in-law's apartment on Nevskii Prospekt. I found only Izya's brother at home, for his wife was in Odessa visiting her parents. On the way back I bought traveling bags and straps. As I returned home I was tortured by anxiety. How could I explain to my daughter what was happening? I went into the apartment quietly, and thankfully I encountered only Tatiana L'vovna in the entryway. I asked in a whisper if I could speak with her in her room. She stared, then took me by the arm, and led me to her room. I told her that we had to leave within twenty-four hours. She was a remarkable woman, with an inexhaustible memory and strong work ethic. In her special way of speaking, using diminutives and charming words of endearment, she offered me food and flowers. She sounded like an old-fashioned lady of the manor, but in reality she was a pragmatic woman, decisive and sharp. I explained to her that what I was finding most difficult was figuring out how to explain to Elenka what was happening. How could I do this so that she would not feel as if she were being punished and cast out of Leningrad? Perhaps I could tell her that we must go live in the North to be closer to papa? But what else should she know? "I will explain the rest to her," Tatiana suggested. "You go back to your room, and I will invite her to tea with me."

I went into the nursery. Lenochka was drawing at her desk. Maria was in the kitchen. My daughter jumped up and ran over to me. She immediately asked me why our things were packed in the suitcase. I said that we were going North to the town of Arkhangelsk, and I showed it to her on a map. I said that we would be closer to papa and we might get permission to visit with him. "Are we coming back after that?" "We will see," I answered. "Will I be going to school?" "Absolutely."

"Will I be going to the school here?" I responded, "Probably. But now you must pack your most favorite books and please you can bring only one doll. For now we must make do with less, and then later on we can buy what we need." My daughter stood there, not certain what to do. It was hard for her to take in all of this. But right at this point Tatiana L'vovna came in, all smiles and very merry, to invite Lenochka to have tea. She was with Tatiana L'vovna no more than fifteen minutes, but she came back happy and content. Tatiana had described to her the northern climate and promised to write letters to her. She also asked my daughter to draw pictures and send them to her, for she said that the places we were going to were just like in fairy tales, with very dense forests and many wild animals.

I wrote two advertisements for a quick sale of the desk and dresser and hung them out on Kirochnaia and Liteinii Streets. I had very little money. I knew that I could sell at a good price the antique Elizabethan chandelier with its blue glass and crystal pendants, so I called an old acquaintance who had fallen in love with it long ago. He promised to buy it. After dinner I sent out Elenka on a walk with Maria while I finished packing and waited for potential buyers. I heard the bell and ran to the door, hoping that a buyer had come. But, oh lord, no, it was an NKVD man who had come to confirm that I would be out of the room in twenty-four hours. He looked approvingly at all of the commotion and then cast his eye on the chandelier. He said, "All lighting fixtures must remain where they are!" "But why?" I asked. "This is a very valuable piece and I myself bought it. I need money, and I have people who wish to buy it from me."

"That is of no consequence. Lighting fixtures stay where they are. Do you understand me? I will be back to check on you." It became clear to me that this functionary had an affinity for antiques.

Mikhail Mikhailovich (Zoshchenko) phoned that evening. "Is there something on your mind, would you like to talk?" I asked. "There is." "Alright," I said. "I will come and see you." I left thirty minutes later, for we could not speak in front of my daughter. We walked along Kirochnaia to the Tavricheskii Garden. It was not an easy conversation. Zoshchenko's face was gloomy, even malevolent. He walked me back home, reminded me that I had promised to send him my address, and then put a small package in my hand. "Do not refuse this, Aguti. You do not know what lies ahead for you. Write as soon as you can ..." In the package there were five hundred rubles.

We left the next day, accompanied to the station by Mikhail Mikhailovich and Maria. Zoshchenko gave Elenka candy for the trip—there were chocolate fish, butterflies, flowers, and leaves, enough to amuse her for the entire journey. It was all very tasty and interesting. She determined that she would first eat the flowers and the butterflies and only later move on to the animals. Maria ran behind the train car and sobbed. I was touched by her sympathy for us, since after all she had not been with us for very long. But once we got to Arkhangelsk, when I was digging around in the suitcase, I realized that she had been crying tears of repentance. For two days the suitcases had stood open and now my favorite silk blouse that had been embroidered by hand was missing. I had ordered it while in Paris and I had taken very good care of it. It was my "going out on the town" blouse that I wore with my blue suit. Loyal Maria had decided that I could do without such luxuries in exile, but had obviously repented at the station and wailed out of compassion for me. It reminded me of the time many years ago when we had gone to visit my father in Tiflis and our young nanny stole from a large basket all of my mother's new clothes. So I considered myself fortunate that Maria had limited herself to just one blouse. The next morning we faced a journey of 480 kilometers by boat along the Northern Dvina River. The day was warm and clear. This was my daughter's first boat trip, and everything amazed and pleased her. All around us there were similar women, sitting on baskets, bundles, and packages, with children and with ailing grandparents. Some disembarked along the way.

Many exiles got off at Dvinskii Berezniak, and the rest went on to Shenkursk. We stepped down from the ship onto a dismal, empty pier. There was a small store and a gloomy shack with a red calico stripe, "The House of Collective Farmers." A little to the side there was a one-story, sturdily built wooden hut, the district office of the NKVD. There they wrote our names down, took our paperwork, and told us on what days we were to report. Then they informed us that we were free people and had to find our own place to live and work. We were to look for both in the village of Semenovskoe, about one kilometer away from the pier. We walked through a barren terrain accompanied by two guards. They put us temporarily in an empty school. The school desks were pushed into a corner. You could lay where you wanted, or wherever you could find a space. They wanted us to clear out as soon as possible because they needed to get the school ready for opening day on September 1. There were about twenty persons crowded together in this classroom. Next to us was the Nazarov family, consisting of the mother, sister, wife, and 5-year-old daughter of someone repressed. The sister, Verochka, was so deaf that it was necessary to shout, and even then she did not always understand you the first time. Moreover, she was dwarf-like in stature and somewhat infantile in manner, but was so kind, friendly, and affectionate that people overlooked this. She immediately took notice of Elenka and brought her niece over to us, suggesting we make a bed for the girls to share. We did, and our girls became fast friends.

The wife of a journalist by the name of Iuzhin was among our group. He too was in Solovki. We had figured this out while we were still on the steamer. This lady was spoiled and arrogant. She was accompanied into exile by an Armenian friend, who took on herself the job of making all of the living and working arrangements for her. I am not kidding, but the very next morning this energetic Armenian found a large room and proposed that I rent it along with her Sonia. I agreed, but first the room had to be disinfected and thoroughly cleaned. The Armenian took on this job as well. We had to spend two more days living in the classroom. Elenka and I went on many walks and returned to the classroom only to eat. On the second day, at dinnertime, we witnessed a terrible scene. There was a woman among the exiles, Nina Posylkina, whom I had noticed while we were still on board the ship. She was tall, slender, and pretty, but had vulgar, even brazen manners. She was all agitated and kept talking about how she had ended up in exile by mistake. She went on and on about being a Muscovite and that she had always been true to Soviet power and had herself informed on her husband, an enemy of the people, who was now in prison. She added that she had already been to see the local NKVD boss and had told him everything. He understood her, and guess what else …. She pulled down the collar of her summer dress and showed the blue bruising left by his kisses. "He fell in love in an instant," she declared, laughing triumphantly. He promised to clear up everything and had already arranged a room for her. She looked around with a haughty glance at everyone, but none of us said a word.

Sonia Iuzhina's friend began her conversation with me by reminding that she had been treating us to pies and even to marinated starlet. Then she admonished me for being too affectionate as a mother, for, after all, a child is simply a child, and I was not going to find a better room in this village. She revealed that she had made these arrangements for me in return for my taking care of Sonechka. After all, she explained, Sonechka had grown up in such comfortable surroundings that she could not get her hands dirty. This would be repugnant to her and so all hopes lay on me. She would send us nice packages from Armenia that would take care of all of our needs. But I had to give Sonechka my full attention. Without saying a word, I went out with my daughter for a walk. We dropped in at each house on a street that stretched on endlessly. We made arrangements with a woman to rent her summer cookhouse, which had a separate passageway made of large canopy. On the left was the half belonging to the landlady and on the right, a *povet'*.[20] My daughter and I had not heard of this word. An enormous Russian stove, situated right by the door, took up three-fourths of our room. Along the walls there was barely enough space for two cots. Two small windows looked out to the courtyard and between them stood our table. The landlady promised to sell us some firewood. From there we headed back to the pier and went into the store, where we bought calico for the curtains, a kerosene lamp for the wall, matches, several candles, two buckets, and other such items. We carried all of this to our new home and then went to get our things from the Armenian lady. She gasped and groaned and said that I did not know how to live or how to appreciate a good turn. I thanked her for the tea and the magnificent pies and said that I would not have taken advantage of the treats if she would had clarified from the beginning what was expected of me in connection with this sumptuous room.

We worked hard to organize our new space. I had brought with me an enlarged portrait of Elenka in a ski outfit. We fastened it between the windows, covering up the peeling pier glass mirror that hung over the table. We stored the suitcases in a nook behind the stove. All of our dresses hung over my bed and were covered with a sheet. I quickly put the curtains together and hung them in the window. The room now seemed cozy and smelled of new calico. The landlady gave me several earthenware pots and metal tongs. I confessed to her that I had never used such things before and had never stoked a genuine Russian stove. This kind woman suggested that I get up a bit earlier and watch how she did everything. I grasped the basics but it took me a while to learn where and when to put this or that pot on the stove. It had to be lit very early in the morning. I did not close the damper because it was only the end of July. To get bread and other food we had to go to the pier. The landlady gave us fresh milk from the cow and occasionally a few eggs.

Elena was delighted with the *povet'*. It was an enormous shed that shared the same roof as the house. Next to its entrance was a very primitive outhouse without doors, and further on was a pen for sheep. Next to this was a stall for Chernukha the cow, then a perch for hens, and further along there was a piglet. On the other side there were broken shafts, carts, sleds, and wooden sledges, and piles of shaft bows were lying around. On the walls hung rakes, sickles, and scythes, and bundles of grass hung down from the ceiling beams. Piles of hay and straw took up a large area. There were also old chests, chairs without legs, and all kinds of junk. My daughter's eyes were dazzled, and she could spend entire days here in this area that was part-museum and part-menagerie. But I made her promise me that she would never go there without me. We went when we had a reason to and then lingered a bit, especially in the evenings when all of the birds and animals were settling down. My little girl was thrilled when she got to pet the sheep or hold the yellow chick in her arms. She made it so easy for me. I could have lived anywhere as long as I could be with my bright-eyed, cheerful, and affectionate daughter. We would be eternally happy together, no matter where we ended up. We shared a love for butterflies, for animals, for taking long walks, for reading books about traveling, and for collecting flowers to put into a herbarium.

Now, though, I had to concentrate on finding a job. I frequently ran into other exiled Leningraders on the street, and everyone said there were no jobs. I covered the entire village. They turned me down at the party district committee office, at the district Soviet executive committee office, as well as at the district Financial Department.[21] I went to the Livestock Procurement office (*Zagotskot*), but they told me there were no openings. I saw a hut with a sign identifying it as an office for local production of butter (*Masloprom*) and the thought occurred to me that here, if you worked diligently, you might get to buy butter sometimes. I had seen none in the store. I went back home, picked up my portable Remington typewriter, and went back to *Masloprom*. In the small hut there were several tables, and the room was filled with smoke. Everyone there were smoking *makhorka*.[22] The supervisor sat at a table that was covered in pink paper, with a desk calendar and a glass with pencils. He looked at me inquiringly. I put my typewriter down on the edge of the table, lifted up the typeface, and said: "This is my typewriter. I am a typist. I was sent here with my young daughter and I must find work." He looked at my typewriter. Everyone came and looked at the machine (after making the rounds of all the offices I had seen how no one had a typewriter). "Do you know how to calculate percentages?" the supervisor asked. "Of course I do! I have studied a great deal, and it is easy for me."

"Well, we need a statistician. We need to record milk and butter production for each of our outlets. The information has to be gathered over the telephone." As he said this, he pointed his finger toward a wooden apparatus hanging from the wall. I said that I could, and he offered the position to me on a trial basis, for a month. I did not even bother to ask about wages. I had to begin work at 8:00 a.m. the next morning. I lowered the typeface, closed up the typewriter, said goodbye, and headed for the door. "Hey, wait a minute, where are you taking that?" Won't you be typing reports on it?"

"Of course, but I will bring it with me each day. It is a fragile machine, and it needs to be cleaned and given a rest … I will do all of this at home."

"Well, we will see. We do not need a statistician who does not have a typewriter." I did not have a clue about statistics, but I had decided nothing would stand in the way of my getting this job.

I arrived home elated. I told Elenka that I had found a job and that we would live within our means and be able to send papa fifty rubles. Now began my routine of getting up at 6:00 a.m. to light the stove and prepare hot food on it for the entire day. The first days I was able to rush home in order to dine with Elenka, but soon this proved to be impossible. My conversations over the telephone took up an inordinate amount of time. It took hours to get connected, and the party district committee demanded strict compliance with the dates for reporting on production. It was very stressful for me to not get home until twilight and have to see the sad little face of my daughter pressed against the window pane, waiting for me to return. There was even a look of fear on her face. The days were still quite warm, but she kept the window closed because she was afraid of neighborhood boys who would throw rocks at her and cry out "You're a little Trotskyist, an enemy of the people, that's what you are …" This situation could not continue. I knew that among the exiles was an unmarried woman who had taught English, and I offered her thirty rubles a month and meals if she would come to us each morning by 8:00 a.m. and spend the day with my daughter until I returned from work. She willingly accepted my offer. Now I had to get up even earlier in order to prepare more and better food for the day. I took with me some bread and sugar and worked without a break, no longer distraught about my daughter being cooped up in our room. Now she could go for walks with the teacher and even speak with her in English.

Oh what splendid holidays my days off were for us! We would go to the Dvina River. We got to know little boys who played along the shore, and they would bring us small golden carp, which we put into a large pot-bellied jar that stood in one of our windows. On the other window sill there stood a rather primitive but large cage in which a red-breasted bullfinch now lived. Elenka named him "Red-breast" after his coloring. He was quite tame and when we ate, he would jump onto the table. In such a way, the "three of us" would have our meals.

The summer came to an end. The family brought a bull for Chernukha the cow, as normally was done in the countryside. But my daughter, who saw through the window how the bull mounted the cow, cried out "Mama, call our landlady, he is hurting our Chernukha!" This was a critical moment, for I remembered how my childhood had been darkened by crude and false explanations of the basic facts of life. I had long ago promised myself not to shy away from telling my daughter the truth. But it was difficult to do. My daughter, who was crying, started off to call the landlady, but I stopped her: "It is not necessary. Look, her husband is in the yard and is watching everything. He is the one who ordered the bull to be brought here." But why?" she sobbed. "So that in the spring, Chernukha will give birth to a calf." My daughter was speechless. She sat back down at the table and stared at me intently. I ventured, "Do you understand? You do not have to watch. Everything is fine: the owner knows when to take the bull back, and Chernukha is not afraid of anything, she is calm." This began a long conversation. My daughter now remembered the rooster who had jumped on the hen and the fat mother cat who had given birth to kittens. We worked our way to the point that all animals, birds, and even insects have to be parents. My daughter then asked, "And people too?" I responded, "Yes, but people do not do this in the open. Generally people want to have children and be a family, if they love one another and want to live together for always." All of this encouraged my daughter's inquisitiveness. She wanted to know more, but I felt the need to bring this to an end. I said, "I have told you the most important points. Without this life on earth could not continue, but it is a very serious topic and you must not speak about this with anyone. If your friends in school want to speak with you about it, then you tell them that you already know about it from your mother. Do you promise?" My daughter promised, but it was obvious that this conversation had agitated her. A swarm of questions were swirling around in her little head. I needed to calm her down. The bull had already been removed. We looked at our aquarium. Elenushka watched the carp and asked timidly, "and the fish as well?" I responded by describing the immense schools of fish swimming to spawn and lay eggs. This fascinated her and drew her into her favorite world, that of the animals. Now everything was fine. And for me a very heavy burden was lifted from my shoulders. I had been dreading this moment. But now I knew that my daughter would never suspect that her mother was ashamed by what life required her to do.

Winter's cold began to set in. I had to get up even earlier to heat the stove. Once I started submitting my typewritten reports to the party district committee, the local executive council, and other offices, news spread that a "typist-statistician" was working for the butter production office. So comrades with files came to our office and approached the supervisor, pulling out their papers and whispering to him while looking slyly at me. "Just set it down," the manager would say, "we will take care of it." He then tasked me with preparing instructions for the collective farms along with protocols, orders, and a stack of all kinds of illiterate scribbling. All had to be typed, along with multiple duplicate copies as well. This slowed me down, so I had to take work home so that I could type after my daughter went to sleep. Fortunately, I did not have extra work every day, and then Elenka and I would go for a walk along the dark, quiet street before going to bed. I was terrified of the dogs here, for they were huge and ran in packs. I would quietly hum to hide my fear. But my daughter firmly reproached me: "Mommy dear, do not sing. It will not help. The dogs will sense your fear and know that you are afraid. You just mustn't be afraid!" I was embarrassed. My daughter thought of all dogs as her friends and did not fear them. A 7-year-old child could already teach me a thing or two.

The money I had sent to Izya was not returned to me. This meant that he was at Solovki. I wrote to his brother to let him know. He and his wife were aware that I was working, but that my wages were barely enough to sustain us. Izya's sister-in-law wrote back to say that they would send us fifty rubles each month that I could send on to Izya but in my name. So this is what I did. I sent the money, but there were no letters from Izya. Perhaps he did not get to see the envelope with our address on it. I wondered whether he even knew that we had been exiled to this area. My daughter received several packages from her aunt and uncle. Tatiana L'vovna also sent us various delicacies for the New Year holiday. We had a New Year's tree with homemade toys and a sumptuous feast. As an employee of *Masloprom* I was able to buy two kilograms of excellent butter wholesale, a head of cheese, and a nice piece of pork. We invited our friend the teacher to join us. This was as many guests as we could accommodate, and we did not go to anyone else's place to celebrate New Year. The Armenian woman had left the settlement, and the very attractive and elegant Sarra Kravtsova moved in with Sonia Iuzhina. Sarra came up to me one day on the street and asked if she could drop by just to chat. She complained that she did not have anything to talk about with Sonia. I hated the idea of having to cut short my evening stroll with Elenka for even an hour, but I could not really refuse her. When she came, she was well dressed and wearing expensive perfume. Why did she want to talk to me about her luxurious life in Moscow? She was from so-called high society. She did not know anything about her husband's fate. When I went out for a stroll with her, she told me with great ardor about her affair with a big-shot military boss. His unit had been stationed in Belarus, if I remember correctly, but he came to Moscow frequently, and they shared wild nights together. This apparently was what she had so badly wanted to talk about with me. I did not invite her again; it was a waste of time.

In terms of inviting people over, I made exceptions only for children. Sometimes Vera Nazarova brought her niece to play with Elenka. Two or three times a girl who was two years older than Elenka came to play, though in terms of maturity they were about equal. Her name was Elena Radchenko. She had arrived in the village with her mother after us. They had been exiled from Kiev and it was very difficult for them here. In Kiev the mother had been a teacher, and here she had been happy just to get a position as a janitress. She left her daughter with us when she had to work in the evenings. Elenka and I would walk with her to the other end of the street.

In February of 1938, rumors began to circulate that they were sending some of the exiles away to unknown places. The talk at first was mainly about men. But in March it became clear that in our village two women had been taken away. Fear engulfed me … such horror! There was nothing I would not have done to keep things as they were. Please, I am willing to work nights at *Masloprom* and do what everyone asks me to do. I will light the stove at 5:00 a.m., draw water from the ice-covered well, just let me be able to rush home from work to be with my daughter and forget all of my troubles in the amazing bond I share with her. "This is all that I need!" I repeated to myself over and over as I went back and forth from work to home.

In April Nina Posylkina stopped me on the street. She did not work anywhere, and she talked openly about her relations with the local NKVD boss. Everyone feared and avoided her. "What's that you have, is that a typewriter?" she asked.

"Yes, it is a typewriter, I use it at the office."

"You know, I have a friend, and he needs a lot of typing done. I will bring him over. Where do you live?"

"Thank you, but I am very tired at the end of the day, and I have a child and housekeeping to do. I do not work at home," was my response. But she followed after me, spewing out all sorts of rubbish the whole way back home, and then she wanted to come inside. But I said that I had to feed my daughter her dinner, our room was a huge mess, and so I simply could not let her come in now. She smirked wryly and said brazenly: "Well, another time then!" This encounter left a bad taste in my mouth. She was a repulsive and loathsome woman.

I had the following day off. We went for a walk with our teacher friend, my daughter ran ahead with her toboggan, and the two of us talked about the new arrests. I told her that the thought of such a horrible fate chilled me. What would happen to my daughter? She responded, "Do not think of such things … nothing will happen to you. Why would they arrest you? They need you here; you are doing work for everyone." But I made her promise me that if something did happen, she would take care of my daughter. At the beginning of April, a second letter arrived from Zoshchenko. The first had arrived in autumn. Before leaving I had promised to send him my address. But I wrote only in the fall after I had secured my job and could report that I did not need anything. He had then responded with a brief note in his characteristically large handwriting. I did not write to him again. In the second letter he asked me why I had not answered his letter and inquired whether one could rent a room for the summer in our village with meals provided. He also asked about the local climate and the environment. I quickly responded that it was impossible to find a room and that one could not for a minute expect to be fed because all of the householders are in the fields from dawn to dusk. It would be much better for him to vacation in the south … These letters meant a lot to me, and I kept them. It was not just that they were letters from a loyal friend. They were letters written by a major writer, a man of amazing talent. But how could I have allowed him to come here? People would have known him from the portraits in his publications, and there would be gossip; no, it was an absolutely absurd notion.

We prepared for the May 1 holiday by tidying our room and scrubbing the stove clean. We made red flags, carnations, and even wound strips of red paper around the bullfinch's cage and the fish bowl. My little girl loved this holiday. At the pier I bought her the book *Dersu Uzala* (Dersu the Trapper)[23] and a very comical velvet monkey. For the time being I hid these items, for it was our custom to bring out presents only on the morning of the May Day holiday. At work they had supplied us generously with butter, cheese, cottage cheese, pork, and eggs. We also had flour left from a parcel. We molded bird and fish shapes out of the dough and ended up with cheerful and buttery baked buns. The delicious aroma of roasting pork rose from the stove. Our landlady called for us to go to the *banya* (bathhouse). After steaming ourselves, we ate with a hearty appetite and lay down to sleep in our clean sheets.

At one o'clock in the morning, a knocking at the door awoke me. But I could not imagine anyone coming to see me at this hour. It had to be someone wanting the landlady, for our doors were right next to each other. The knocking continued. Quietly, so I would not wake my daughter, I said that the landlady's door was the next one. "No, it is you whom we want! Open the door!" I threw on a robe and opened the door. There were four men standing there, two wearing the uniform of the NKVD and two peasants serving as witnesses.

"What is it you want?" I asked.

"We have an order here," and they handed me a piece of paper. "Do you have a lamp?"

I switched on the lamp. Then I heard, "Where is your typewriter?"

My god. They had been craving my typewriter for a long time and had decided to arrest me in order to confiscate it. That was what immediately flashed through my head. "If you need my typewriter, then take it! I carry it each day to work, but you can tell them there that you have confiscated it."

"We have come for you, not the typewriter," smirked one of the uniformed men. Elenushka woke up and then sat up. She looked around, not understanding anything. I realized that I had to act quickly if I were to help my daughter. "Alright," I said,

> if you want to make it easier to do what you were sent here to do, then first you must let me send a note to my daughter's teacher, who lives only two houses down from here. She will come and stay with my daughter. Then, you have to let me write two telegrams to be sent tomorrow to my relatives. They will come to get my daughter. If you do not let me do this, then I will raise such a ruckus that it will wake everyone up in this house. I will not give you the key to my suitcase, and I will not get dressed. You will just have to take me as I am, in my nightshirt, and you will have to drag me across the snow.

"There is nothing you can do for your child. Tomorrow they will come and take her to the orphanage."

I retorted back: "Tomorrow is a holiday, and the day after as well. It is now nighttime, and my daughter cannot be left here by herself. Either you take both of us, or you send one of these witnesses with this note." I wrote down on a scrap of paper: "Come immediately." They agreed to take it. They did not really want to have the entire household woken up on the eve of the holiday.

This good woman came right away but was trembling with fright. I gave her all the money that I had, and it was a sufficiently large amount. I had just received my salary the day before; moreover, I had managed to tuck away for a rainy day nearly the whole sum of money that Zoshchenko had given me. I told the teacher that the oven had enough food in it for several days, and Lenochka would know where our other provisions were. I asked her to please keep Lenochka with her at all times, to go for walks, and to use the money to buy everything that they needed. If there was any money left over, then she should give it to whomever it was that came for my daughter. "But who will be coming?" she asked timidly, looking fearfully at the Chekists. I explained that I would write telegrams to our closest relatives, but I needed her to send them first thing the next morning. I tore two pages out from Lenochka's checkered notebook. I wrote a telegram to her uncle: "Elena has been left all alone." Suddenly a thought flashed through my mind. What if at this very same hour he was being arrested in Leningrad?! As a safeguard, I addressed a similar text to Tatiana L'vovna. She knew the telephone number of my relatives and could get in touch with them. I addressed the two telegrams and repeated: "Send these as soon as you possibly can. It is absolutely vital that they come for her!"

"Alright—enough of this! Open up your suitcases!"

There were two suitcases, one with my things and one with my daughter's. At the bottom of my suitcase lay the two letters from Zoshchenko, which they took. With this the search ended. They confiscated my passport and typewriter and then ordered me to get dressed. I said that I would not get dressed in front of them; they had to go out and stand outside. They grumbled that this was not standard procedure but went out nonetheless. I went up to my daughter, who was shaking all over. I held her in my arms and told her that this was all a mistake, that we were good people, that I could not have done anything that was bad, and that I would probably be returning home soon.

"Oh mommy, papa did not do anything bad and he hasn't come back yet! …" Her words sent a chill through me. These midnight visitors had aged my child by at least five years …

I pulled out from under my pillow the book I had gotten for her and the monkey. I gave them to her, and for a minute she was calm and smiling. She liked the monkey very much. But then she looked at me again and began to sob as she cried out, "What will I do without you, mommy?"

> Please do not cry—you must be brave for me. This is so hard for me. Think how I will feel to be away from you! I give you my word that I will return. I do not know exactly when that will be, but I will return and we will be together again. Until then you must take my Tiutia and safeguard him; keep him with you, and this will be my pledge that we will be together again.

This Tiutia had been given to me while I was in Moscow by my friend Boris Lapshin, who had brought it back from Chukotka. It was a tiny walrus that had been carved out of a tusk by a little Chukchi girl. Boris had lived there and brought back several of these amazing handcrafted items. My daughter adored Tiutia and loved it when I allowed her to play with him. This present shocked her: she knew that I was giving her something I cherished deeply. Now she was in charge of taking care of tiny Tiutia. She stopped crying, she clenched the walrus in her hand, and put her arms around me. It would have been easier for me to die at this moment than it was to let go of her. But I gathered my strength and told her that either her uncle or Tatiana L'vovna would be coming for her. She would get to go to her Leningrad school, and she would be much happier there than here. I would write long letters to her and would return as soon as I could.

The guards yelled for me to hurry up. I dressed quickly and shoved into the small suitcase (I still had my suitcase from Paris) a change of underwear, a dress, and a brush. I asked Lenochka if she would give me her little blue mug for brushing teeth. This made her happy. She jumped up and put it into my suitcase.

I still have to this day that little blue mug and my tiny Tiutia.

8

Into the Vortex of Suffering: Ten Years in the Gulag

The prison regime was severe. We went to the toilet once in the morning and then again in the evening. There was an open chamber pot in the stuffy, overcrowded cell that everyone had to take turns emptying. At first the cell was quite bright and well ventilated due to the large and open *fortuchka* (a hinged pane for ventilation in Russian windows—Translator's note). But soon they put "muzzles" on the outside of all the windows: high fences built from planks fit tightly together that slanted upward at an angle of about 30 degrees and that were higher than the window. The *fortuchka* was open night and day, but no air came into the cell. The summer was sultry with no breezes. We saw the sky only when we were taken out in groups for our brief exercise. We walked in single file within a small enclosure. On one of these walks, I noticed that someone had carved the name "Elena" on the fence. I could not possibly stop, for the guards in the tower were watching our every step. In the course of several laps, I read the entire sentence "Elena has been taken to Leningrad." I knew this already, but the message also told me someone else had been arrested from Semenovskoe village. Who was it?

Two months went by, but they did not call me in for questioning. The composition of our cell was constantly in flux, with some being sent away or transferred and new people coming in. One was a colorful person, a descendant of the Pomors who had left Novgorod and settled on the coast of the White Sea. She was a strict Old Believer,[1] tall and lean, and she immediately reminded me of the Boiaryna Morozova in the painting by Surikov.[2] When she came in to our cell, she was clenching a silver goblet in her hands. The guard tried to pry it from her hands but she hit him with her elbow and said contemptuously: "Leave me alone, I will not drink from your unclean cups." The fellow recoiled and left her alone. For two days she sat on the floor in the corner, like a plucked eagle. It was so hot in the cell that we all were half-naked, sitting close together and drenching each other with our sweat. She still wore her ingeniously tied *povoinik* (a traditional headdress of a Russian married woman) over her gray hair braided high on her head. Her dark linen sarafan[3] was tightly clasped above her chest, and she clung to her goblet. On the third day, I threw a towel on my shoulder and sat down next to her. She asked me where I was from, and I answered "Leningrad." "Well you are from a city of Lenin and I am from Kanin Nos." She began telling me about her husband, a noted fisherman who died while rescuing drowning sailors. She also talked about her grandson who had joined her in jumping from ice floe to ice floe, spearing the fish with a harpoon. This is how they made their living. Then lo and behold she learned to write, and she wrote to Stalin asking about her husband's "pension." Other people wrote as well, and somehow, after a year, the "pension" started arriving. When the elections began, she went to vote, but did not recognize the names. She demanded a new ballot so that she could vote for Stalin, since he was a just man and had given her a "pension." Her shouting brought soldiers who arrested her, saying that "you do not have the right to disrupt the process of the elections. You must vote for the deputies who are listed on the ballot." But she refused and threatened to keep shouting. For the two weeks she was in our cell, she drank only boiled water from her goblet and ate only from the middle of the bread, because "unclean hands" had not touched it there. Then they came and took her away. Did they send her back to Kanin Nos or into exile somewhere? The latter is more likely. She was about 80 years old. Her story did not make any sense to me. But the day before she left, she whispered to me that her real fear was for her grandson; they had enemies back in Kanin Nos who were jealous because of their two strong boats. "They have probably made off with my grandson." This made me think. Perhaps if I had not thought to take my typewriter into exile, then I might still be with my daughter. But no, let her go to school in Leningrad, away from here!

Finally in August I was summoned to my first interrogation. A red-haired investigator by the name of Kalinskii began with the customary line used with everyone:

"Talk to me."

"Talk about what?" was my response.

Kalinskii: "When and whom did you recruit for your terrorist organization?"
Me: "What do you mean, what organization? I was charged with not informing on my husband ..."
Kalinskii: "Shut up! Here you are not Dostoevsky. We will shoot you and there will be no monument."
Me: "I could care less about a monument, but why would you shoot me?"
Kalinskii: "You know perfectly well why; we have all the facts at our fingertips. It is better to confess, if you wish to make it easier on yourself."
Me: "What evidence? I do not understand."

Promising I would now hear it, Kalinskii made a phone call and ordered the duty officer to bring in the witness. In came Nina Posylkina, the very same siren who had immediately started an affair with the district NKVD boss and then showed us all her "love bites." She did not work anywhere and constantly let everyone know, "I always get what I want." Of course everyone tried to avoid her, but how can you do this when the village only has one street? Posylkina sat down confidently on the chair at the other end of the table. Smiling, she looked at the interrogator. Kalinskii asked me, "Do you know this citizen?" I responded, "Yes, I know her. We were sent into exile at the same time."

Kalinskii:	"Do you socialize with her? Are you friends?"
Me:	"Not, not really. From time to time she greeted me on the street, but I always tried to avoid her."
Kalinskii:	"Is this so? Witness Posylkina, remind the defendant of your meeting at the post office. Obviously she has a poor memory."
Posylkina:	"It was in October. She had to go to the post office to claim a general delivery letter and I was standing behind her in the line. She read me the letter she received."
I cried out:	"That cannot possibly be true! The post office in the village closes at 3:00 pm, and I work until 6:00 pm. Furthermore, the office of *Masloprom* is more than a kilometer from the post office, but this is beside the point. I never received a general delivery letter at that post office."
Kalinskii:	"Silence! I'm the only one who can ask questions here. Continue," he nodded at Posylkina. "Whom was the letter from?"
Posylkina:	"The letter was from the writer Zoshchenko. He told her that they were arresting writers, and that it was impossible to live like this, and now all of their hopes lay on her," and at this point Posylkina pointed her finger at me, "fulfilling her promise."

I looked with horror at Posylkina: what was she doing, how could she make this up, and how did she even know that Zoshchenko had written to me? The blood was pounding in my ears, and I would have screamed had a spasm not seized my throat.

| Kalinskii: | "What did the defendant say after she read this line from Zoshchenko's letter?" |
| Posylkina: | "She said, 'Now my hand will not tremble to kill Yezhov!'" |

This was so absurd, so stupid, and improbable that I snapped back into consciousness and even laughed. "You find this funny?" the interrogator said ominously. "Do you know what these words are going to cost you?"

I responded, "But I never said these words, and besides, I would never read such a letter aloud in the post office to Posylkina, everybody knows about her. I do not know what has made her libel me, but I never received any such letter from the writer Zoshchenko."

Kalinskii:	"How can you say that you never received it, when you read it to the witness Posylkina!"
Me:	"But that is a lie. I ask you to bring in the daughter of my landlady, who works at the post office and can confirm that I did not go there. She herself brought me my letters because she knew I did not get home from work until after the post office was already closed."
Kalinskii:	"We do not need you to tell us whom to call as witnesses. Continue," he nodded to Posylkina.

She again began to chirp away, claiming that she was repeatedly with me at my apartment where my followers gathered to carry on anti-Soviet conversations and where we formed an organization for carrying out terrorist acts. "Do you deny this?" gloated Kalinskii. I adamantly denied all of it. "Posylkina has not even once crossed my threshold, there were no meetings at my home; since arriving only one or two women have visited, and they came separately and at different times. My landlady can confirm this."

Kalinskii: "So, it turns out that everyone is lying. Only you are telling the truth."

I responded, "Who do you mean by everyone? Posylkina is lying, and I am telling you how it really was …."

He finished the report and gave it to Posylkina to sign and then handed it to me: "Sign this."

I retorted, "What do you mean? I will not sign my name to such slander."

Kalinskii: "You may write that you do not agree with it."
Me: "No, I do not want to touch it."
Kalinskii: "As you wish, but you are not helping yourself."

They took me back to the prison. It took me awhile to recover. I was shaking not only in my arms and legs, but everything inside was trembling as well. The women in the cell were sleeping, but several of them raised their heads and asked "Did they beat you? Why are you trembling?" I said that no, I had not been beaten but I did feel feverish and my teeth were chattering. "I am just a bit feverish." The stuffy air, the snoring, the yellowish faces overwhelmed me. I kept seeing in my mind the image of the interrogator, his cold office, the opened window, the soft armchairs, and the bottle of mineral water on the table …. It was not enough to have exiled me and my daughter from Leningrad, depriving me of my customary way of life in a large city. It was not enough that I was living with a child in the summer kitchen of a village hut and that I worked myself to the bone. No, they had to arrest me, tear me from my child, and accuse me of not having informed on my husband, as if he had actually done something to report. Oh, but what sort of wife would inform on her husband anyway? Even this was not enough for them. So over the course of four months they worked to invent a charge for me—the murder of Nikolai Yezhov (head of Stalin's secret police, the NKVD until November 1938—Translator's note). But how and where in this godforsaken place, in a village 480 kilometers from Arkhangelsk, where the rivers are frozen with no navigation possible from October to May, and where I reported regularly each day to the commander? And why would I want to kill Nikolai Yezhov? What was Yezhov to me? I never even thought about him. It would have made more sense to have put me on trial for being totally disinterested in Yezhov, rather than for seeking to kill him.

I just stood there, pressed against the door. The peephole opened up and the guard asked why I was not sleeping. "I feel sick, please let me go to the bathroom." I must have looked wretchedly pale for she immediately opened the door. I barely managed to make it to the washroom before I vomited. I washed my face and head with cold water and laid my head on the thick copper faucet. The attendant took me back to the cell. Two women were sleeping on my bed. I sat down on the stool and pressed my head against the round iron stove. The attendant could not see me from here. Gradually my thoughts cleared. What most frightened me was that they were dragging Zoshchenko into all of this. Why were they doing this? How did they even know that we were friends? It was quite simple, actually. They had not found in my home or on my person any documentation beyond Zoshchenko's two brief and completely innocent letters. The few other letters I received I destroyed and I did not keep a diary. There were only my daughter's notebooks and albums with her drawings. If Misha had not signed his letters with his full name, but only with the letter M., then these letters would not have drawn such attention. So now they have invented a mythical third letter and are brewing this nasty, absurd stew of lies. Obviously they were trying to create a conspiratorial case involving a famous writer. Maybe even now Misha was sitting in a fetid cell crowded with people. I could drive myself insane with such thoughts. Why did I not destroy those two letters from him? If it had not been for those two letters, they would have settled for the charge that I had not informed on my husband.

There was nothing else for them to use. Anyone could have confirmed that no one ever gathered at my home. The idea of an "organization" was absurd. Such nonsense! What horrified me, though, was that I had brought misery upon Misha. How could I live with such a burden on my heart? Morning came, and I barely made it to the lavatory. I had begun suffering from an "irritable bowel," which meant I had diarrhea and bloating. I knew that it was just stress, but the attendant called the nurse and they put me in the hospital. In the morning I received a slice of white bread and half a glass of thick milk curd, and for dinner I was given bullion and white sugar. This fabulous food lifted my spirits a bit. It was nice to be in the hospital even if only for a week. On the third day I developed a toothache and was sent to a dentist. She was an elderly Jewish woman, very kind and gentle. While she was washing her hands, I looked at her table, and right next to her bag lay a small green book with Zoshchenko's portrait framed in a large white oval. Under the portrait was the very same signature as in my letters. What did this mean? Were his books not banned, or did this woman simply not know? She asked me to open my mouth and began to prepare my tooth for the filling. I was suffering from the pain, but I was ready to endure anything if I could only find out what this meant. When she finished with the filling, I asked her, "Are you fond of Zoshchenko?" She smiled, threw a glance at the book, and answered cheerfully, "Who doesn't love him? He writes such amusing stories. I always read on the way to work. In fact, I only bought this book today, it is fresh off the press."

"Do you know whether anything has happened to him?" I asked.

"Something has happened? But what could have happened. Do you know him?" she asked.

"Yes, I am from Leningrad. We were friends when we were young, and last night I had a nightmare …"

"Surely you do not believe in dreams? You should stop such nonsense. He recently received a medal, and everyone adores him, so what could have happened to him?

I understand how people in your situation begin to believe in dreams, but you are a cultured woman. Nothing has happened to him. He is now a wealthy man ..." I wanted to throw my arms around her and kiss her on the cheek, but I did not dare. A simple tooth repair does not merit such enthusiasm. Nothing could have happened to Zoshchenko if they were selling his books and awarding him medals. My illness passed and they discharged me from the hospital. But I was able to return to the cell with greater peace of mind that I had not brought misery upon anyone else.

I decided not to think any more about the investigation but only focus on my daughter and find something to occupy my time. Women in the cell practiced divination. They threw pieces of coal into water and chanted something unintelligible. Others broke off pieces of brick from the stove, shook them like dice, then tossed them on the floor to interpret. I decided I would make checkers out of bread. I divided each piece of bread into two parts. I topped one-half with crushed pieces of coal to make the black checkers, and the remaining halves were the white checkers. We played till we felt stupefied. I liked kneading the bread, since after my illness I would not eat this sticky, half-baked doughy pulp. So I began to sculpt toys, pretending that I was making them for my daughter. We had often created toys out of modeling clay. From my prison bread dough rabbits and people came to life, and then I made a vase and decorated it with tiny leaves and roses. The women were impressed and exclaimed that I could not possibly be a novice. Next I fashioned several flowers, and both petals and stems looked natural. Soon I had a collection of two different vases, two bouquets of flowers, and many figurines. They stood on a stool in the corner near the stove. During one of his regular inspections, the head of the prison noticed them and asked who had fashioned bread into toys. I identified myself and said that I could not eat the bread right now because of a problem with my stomach. A miracle then happened. He ordered that my toys be included in an exhibit of prisoners' work and that instead of my allotted 600 grams of black bread, I would be given 300 grams of bread in the form of rolls. I ate every last crumb of these rolls and never again did it cross my mind to sculpt with my bread.

***January 5, 1976

I have not been able to work on this manuscript for three weeks. The previous pages were all written at TsNIRRI (Central Research Institute of Radiology and Radiophysiology); this notebook with its pink cover is lying next to me on the table. I have not been able to bring myself to pick it up or to type from it. It is not only that my eyes are poor. I am simply afraid of it.

When I had reached the village of Semenovskoe, I was already feeling wounded spiritually. I was suffering at this time from so much, yet little did I know the tragic fate that each day was bringing closer to me. I had my daughter with me, and our friendship, our excitement at seeing each other when I returned from work each day, brought us joy and light. This enabled us to bear the dark absurdity of our life in that village. But writing this now, I know everything that happened after the night of May 1, and I have spent four decades in a state of shock. I cry at night and when I walk, and I can now barely control my emotions in the ward and in the cafeteria. Maybe this is why my eyes have become worse. I must not cry.

This time they did not give me a radiation treatment. They used tomography to take endless X-ray pictures and then concluded that there was nothing to irradiate. Nothing remained from the small tumor. So, they discharged me, which is a good thing. This cobalt therapy, or as they called it, "Cobalt surgery," is torturous. And I have nowhere else to go. GIDUB cannot come up with any other treatment. I swallowed a pill and decided to force myself to work a bit more to help get my mind off my eyes.

I must hurry, though, because my condition is getting worse. I have to be succinct. I can remember everything down to the slightest detail from May 1, 1938, to the present, but I will try to highlight the main moments in my life as a prisoner. I did not know then that I shared the fate of millions of people. I was naïve and thought for sure that I could prove my right to return to my daughter. I was determined that I would be such a dependable worker that the district party committee, the executive council of the local soviet, and all other such organs would affirm how I had unselfishly served them in the sowing and harvesting campaigns. This is what I told myself, as I tried to calm myself down and stop reproaching myself. But my despair was infinitesimal. I felt so guilty with regard to my daughter. How could I have forgotten the words of Izya, speaking after the Kirov murder: "This could affect the fate of all of us." When the telegram came telling of his "serious illness," why did I have to make helping him my priority, instead of thinking about our daughter and about my obligation to take care of her? We had never registered our marriage, and our last names were different. We should have left immediately from Senzhary and gone to Odessa. I could have thought of something there, perhaps burying ourselves in some inconspicuous small town, maybe in Siberia, the Far East, or the devil knows where, and in this way we might have escaped from such misfortune.

Translator's note: Ludmila here goes back in her narrative to the very first days after her arrest on May 1. What she described in the first paragraphs of the chapter took place not immediately after her arrest but after she had been transported to Arkhangelsk for interrogation.

After my arrest, what tore me apart was my fear that they had taken my daughter to the NKVD child distribution center (I had heard about this already, since in the village mothers of preschool-aged children had been arrested before me), that I would never find her, or that she had fallen ill, tormented by fear and grief at being alone. They initially put me in a wooden lockup, where I could not even take a step. Broad plank beds, about three or four in number, lay across the threshold. The ceiling was low and there was a narrow little window covered with bars. When they brought me in, I had noticed that there were similar rooms on each side, but they were empty. I could not sit down on the beds without feeling as if I were being bitten. I ran my hand down my leg and shuddered from the disgusting smell of crushed bedbugs. I was in this bug-infested place for three weeks. During the day I discovered that the bedbugs filled up all of the cracks in the logs, the planks, and the ceiling. I told the guard about this in the morning when he brought me a rusty mug of boiling water and a piece of black bread. He laughed and said, "A bedbug is not a bear, he will not hurt you, drink your tea!" I broke off two pieces of wood from the rotting beams and killed as many as I could.

I was not taken out for interrogation. I spent entire days standing on the plank beds and looking out the narrow window. In front of my prison there was a huge clearing covered by dirty, melting snow and further along was a fence sitting on tall posts.

I heard a siren on May 4 and 5. Navigation had opened up in the river. Had anyone been able to come for my Elenushka before they took her away to a children's home? How could I find out what had happened to her? Who was going to tell me? The next day, however, I saw a woman in a dark coat fall down in the snow on the other side of the fence. She cried out quickly: "Listen to me, they have taken your daughter away, Dunia took her away from here!" The window did not have any glass, and I had taken out the dirty rag that had been there the very first day. I recognized the voice of my landlady. Oh what joy! They had been able to get Elenushka away from here. Dunia was a maid, a wonderful, kind woman. My daughter was in Leningrad, she was living on Nevskii Prospekt, in a fine, spacious apartment, with lots of books. Her aunt was fluent in three languages. What joy!

The empty, dismal days dragged on. They did not take me out anywhere for interrogation. Had they arrested me for no reason? Near the end of the second week they finally came for me. The head of the district branch of the NKVD quickly filled out my biographical form after getting the necessary information from me: nationality, age, education, and so on. Then he commanded: "Talk to me."

"What do you want me to talk about?" I responded.

"You know what I mean."

"But what interests you?" I asked.

"There is no use pretending. Talk." Nearly an hour of this went by. He had a lot of patience. Certainly more than I did. I was sick of this ridiculous farce and blurted out in exasperation: "So which would you like me to tell you, a fairy tale or a play in my own words?"

"Enough. Tell me why you did not inform on your husband when you knew about his counterrevolutionary activity?" This was unexpected. I could not imagine anything more absurd. I said that he had never taken part in any such thing so there was nothing for me to report. At this he began cursing, calling me an accomplice of an enemy of the people, and then at the end of his tirade added: "Fine, it is a good thing that your son is now in our hands. We will be sure to make an honest man out of him." I said nothing. Let him think that it was my 7-year-old son whom he had thrown in prison without any one to look after him, for I knew that my daughter was already safe in her aunt's apartment on Nevskii Prospekt.

They did not call me out for any further interrogations. Apparently they had no other charges against me. At first they had exiled me as a wife of an enemy of the people, and now they had arrested me. How was this going to end? Even though my heart felt lighter knowing my daughter was safe, I was still worried about her. Her new family would be very different from ours. After all, I had not been close with either Izya's brother or his wife. My sister-in-law, who desperately wanted to have a baby but could not, had always avoided seeing Elena. We usually celebrated my daughter's birthday with a party on February 6 rather than August 6 because everyone was on vacation then. My friends typically would arrive well before the supper in order to see my daughter, give her a present, and talk with her. But her aunt would just come late and drop off her presents; she did not even want to see the child. During all of the happy years before Izya's arrest, we visited them with our daughter only twice. Somehow during a rare moment of intimacy, my sister-in-law revealed to me that they had decided finally to adopt a child. Then sometime after this a kitten of theirs died. She told me that this had made her afraid and she no longer wanted to adopt. "When our kitten died, we just got another one. What would it be with a child? I just think that if you cannot have your own, then it is better not to have children at all." This unexpected conversation took place on their large, broad couch, which stands even now in that same room, by the lamp and the window next to the telephone, along with the grand antique bureau, covered with books and files. I probably remember these words of her so well because they were unexpected. We were not friends but this openness touched me. I began to understand her natural envy toward me, the mother of this charming little girl.

This is why I was concerned over what would happen to my daughter in their household—would they welcome her as one of their own or treat her as an outsider? Her uncle was dry and very stern, while her aunt was intelligent and effusive, but highly principled, authoritative, and insistent. My daughter had been raised in an atmosphere of friendly and equal relations between parent and child. She was smart, mature, observant, and very self-conscious. All my hopes rested on good, kind Dunia. The uncle and aunt would be at the university all day, so it would be Dunia taking my daughter to school in the mornings and then bringing her home, feeding her, and taking her for walks. Over and over again I would map out in my head her daily schedule and her time in school, and I concluded that the old adage "with every cloud there is a silver lining" is true. How I had feared the schools in Semenovskoe! It would not have been easy for Lenka there, for she would have been the only literate student in the first class and probably read as well as the teacher. But now she would go to school in Leningrad. So, there was no reason to reproach myself for not having taken my daughter to Odessa from Senzhary. There was no one there for me to turn to, and how would I have gotten money? My parents were dead by this time. My older brother lived with his family in Voznesensk, but they were poor. He had even demanded money for our parents' funerals. Plus, all of our clothing and my typewriter were at our home in Leningrad so we would have had to go back there anyway. I should not feel guilty. This calmed me.

At the end of May, they took me under guard on a steamer to Arkhangelsk. Happily I got to sit next to the window. I gazed at the flowing water of the Northern Dvina and watched the wagtails running about on the rocks along the shore. The guard frequently went out to smoke and I took advantage of this to strike up a conversation with the gentlemen sitting across from me. I asked them for a piece of paper and a pencil and quickly wrote a letter to my daughter, telling her how I was and that I was going to Arkhangelsk. I assured her that everything would be fine and I drew her a flower with a butterfly on it. On the other side of the paper I wrote down the address and then slipped it to the men. I told them that they had to rewrite the address on an envelope and mail it in the city. They were surprised to learn that I was traveling as a prisoner under guard. I told them that they were taking me to prison as the wife of an exile. Their faces darkened, they exchanged glances and whispers, and then they slipped money into my coat pocket. Later, while I was in prison, I often recalled these boys. I had not even thought about money the night I was arrested, but there was a shop in the prison. I used this money several times to buy sugar and sweet bread (*sushki*).

In the Arkhangelsk prison, I was put into a cell filled with women whose husbands had been arrested or exiled. Mostly they were wives of sailors or of district party secretaries and other such officials. They treated me with indifference and even hostility. I felt very out of place. They talked about dresses, shawls, stockings, and all the different luxuries their husbands had brought back for them from faraway voyages. They gossiped unmercifully about other wives who for unknown reasons had not yet been arrested. Then when one ended up in our cell, they greeted her as an old friend and would gossip about those still at liberty. It went on like this until our cell was filled to the brim. At the beginning of September, they took me once more for interrogation. The day was cold and I was wearing a coat, my old one, but it was my Paris coat, still lovely with its necktie collar. A lightweight, open car stood waiting at the gates of the prison. A well-dressed young man opened the door and invited me to sit down next to him. We drove in the open car to Arkhangelsk. The young man had a smile on his face, as if we were good friends driving together. My companion said not a word, and I did not know what to expect. Perhaps they were going to let me go; up until now they had always driven me in the Black Ravens.[4]

"So, how about it? Have you thought about your situation and decided to confess everything and give us the names of those you recruited?" he asked.

"I have nothing to confess. I had hoped that you would talk to the people whom I had identified and who …"

"Witnesses? Oh yes, I have brought in your witnesses." He made a phone call, and they brought into the room Verochka Nazarova, the nearly deaf, infantile dwarf. He asked, "Are you acquainted with this citizen?"

I answered, "Yes. We came at the same time from Leningrad, and her niece played with my daughter." The interrogator shouted, "Citizen Nazarova, do you affirm the testimony you have given?"

"I affirm it," Vera babbled, failing to pronounce several letters.

The interrogator began to read her testimony in a normal voice, no longer shouting, since he knew that I was not deaf. Vera sat doubled up, her tiny arms clasped together. She looked at me with pity and grimaced strangely. They obviously lacked sufficient evidence for the claim that I had formed an organization to murder Yezhov, so they had forced this unhappy person to come and provide absurd statements. Her testimony claimed that she and I had gone together to see the film *Under the Roofs of Paris*,[5] and while watching I had continuously extolled the bourgeois life in the West and said that people there lived better than we did. These statements were signed by Vera.

"Vera," I turned to her and raised my voice, "You know very well that I never left Lenochka alone during the evenings. We were never there together at that film." She was silent.

The interrogator asked in an insinuating manner, "Are you denying that you watched this film?"

"No," I answered. "I saw this film about two years ago in Leningrad. I can prove that I would not have gone to see it a second time, since I had very little money. Have you even seen this film? It shows the sordid lives of thieves, prostitutes, and drug addicts, and offers little basis for celebrating bourgeois life."

"You probably like that sort of life," he continued his verbal jabs.

"Good lord! Look at what you have to do here to make yourself heard to Nazarova. You have to shout, so do you really think I would have screamed out in the club, in front of all of the people there, and interfered with the movie?"

"You said 'Good lord' ... are you by any chance the daughter of a rabbi?"

"I am the daughter of an accountant. But, write what you want, what does it matter." I felt I was going to vomit from these filthy lies. Yes, I felt as if they were covering me with clumps of putrid filth and there was no way for me to get it off and cleanse myself. I refused to sign the report of this confrontation with the witness. The interrogator yelled and threatened, but I remained adamant: you can write whatever you want, but I will not touch it.

My case ended with this interrogation. I was fortunate, though, for others talked of being beaten or of being forced to stand for hours. I had awaited this with horror, but all of that passed me by. They were so satisfied with what they cooked up, and with their ability to coerce witnesses, that they had no need to deal with me. They just gave me a long senseless prison term. After several weeks they took me out into the prison corridor, where some sort of military functionary was waiting for me. Still to this day I cannot figure out what this was about. We went into a small, bright room, and there he handed me the indictment and reported that the investigation was completed. I now had the right to write a letter to relatives, if I had any, and could receive a package. I asked whether I could receive a reply to my letter. "Yes, but you should not write too much." The indictment lay on the table, but I did not look at it. Instead I implored him to allow me a postcard. He snickered, but gave me one and suggested that I prepare it right there in front of him, since writing in the prison cell was prohibited. I wrote to my daughter, informing her that I was well, but needed a food package, a change of underwear, soap, and other sundry items. I asked her to write to me about her school and what she was studying. He smiled again as he took my letter and handed me the indictment, which I had forgotten completely. Nothing else mattered. They had allowed me to correspond with my daughter!

In the cell I read the indictment, which was printed on thin tissue paper. Nothing more absurd could possibly be imagined than what it stated. They had charged me with Article 58, sections 10–11 and 8 through 17. I, it claimed, had organized a terrorist group to murder Yezhov. I had tried to stir up people by reading Zoshchenko's letter at the post office and by extolling life in France at the movies. There was no need of a confession or my signatures; they had plenty of idiotic statements fabricated by the dirty fingers of an investigator who had decided to transform me, a wife who had not denounced her husband, into a major criminal-terrorist. In our cell at this time there was an elderly educated woman, an old party member whom they had also cooked up to be a terrorist. Sighing, she claimed that the more ridiculous the charge the better, for when you got to court it would be clear that this was complete slander. She said that I was very fortunate to be tried in a military court, because this meant that I could defend myself. I said nothing in response for I did not feel that I could fully trust her. I could not bring myself to tell this well-intentioned woman that my husband had also been tried by a military court, that he was better equipped than I to defend himself, and that he unquestionably had not participated in the murder of Kirov. Yet he had nonetheless received a ten-year sentence and now was either alive or dead in Solovki.

I silently pressed her hand and buried myself in the pillow. We slept side by side. I had to push out of my mind any thoughts about my trial or about the future. I was cheered only by the knowledge I could now be connected with my Elenushka; I could see her handwriting and press to my lips the same paper that her dear hands had touched.

I saw from the formal charge that my trial would involve a whole group of people. Sarra Kravtsova and Elena Radchenko would be tried with me. They were probably here in this same corridor. But guards made sure not to let us run into anyone when they were taking us to the exercise area. During a walk, however, I managed to see on one of the walls that someone had etched out with a broken piece of glass the name "Sarra." I had to respond. In my coat I had hidden a piece of coal, and in the course of two rounds, I scratched out the first letter of my name. The biting cold of the northern winter set in, so they lit the iron stove that was fixed into the wall. Many toasted their slices of bread on the red-hot damper. This was the only delicacy, for otherwise our food was quite wretched. In the morning there was bread and hot water, then for lunch we had a soup of putrid *sauerkraut* that sometimes included a fish bone with rounded joints that we could suck for a drop of sweet-tasting juice. There was also sticky *kasha* made from finely ground barley. In the evenings we ate this same *kasha* and hot water. The Arkhangelsk women received parcels and many of them had money. They would buy cookies, butter, candy, and gingerbread in the prison shop. Sometimes they shared their treats with me, such as a candy "lollypop" or a piece of gingerbread. Once the orderly offered us boiled cod in the evening if we would wash all of the benches, washtubs, and the hair-cutting area in front of the bathhouse. We zealously threw ourselves into this job. I chose to tidy up the hair-cutting area, since no one seemed to be there. I began to wash the basins and wipe off the chairs when I noticed in the mirror a woman who was wearing the same dress as I was. Where had she come from? I looked her over: sunken eyes, taut cheekbones, a bluish tinted face with a forehead covered in a small red rash. Good God, I suddenly thought, it is me, this is what I look like! That very morning I had felt this rash. We had in our cell a doctor from the Far East. After the Soviet Union sold its rights to the Chinese Eastern Railway, she had returned to the USSR. At first her homeland had welcomed her, but then it arrested her as a spy. She diagnosed this rash as a sign of a vitamin deficiency and advised me to eat garlic. But where was I to get garlic? I looked at myself in horror. Only my hair looked anything like it did before my arrest. To my dismay, though, all prisoners with long hair had to get their hair cut, due to lice. I did not have lice but they cut my hair anyway up to my neck.

An 80-year-old aristocratic woman, a princess, joined us; she was tall and so thin that it was easy to find space for her in our crowded cell. She hardly spoke to anyone, but the whole time just moved her lips without making a sound. Her face was small and wrinkled, but she still held her head and her gray, disheveled hair proudly. She wore a black, close-fitting dress that went nearly to the floor, with the bodice fastened on small hooks. It reminded me of dresses I had seen in my mother's photograph albums. This elderly princess often unfastened the upper clasps and furiously scratched her body. From the side I could see the gray calico lining of her dress, which also reminded me of my childhood. At that time wool had to have a lining. So why was she scratching herself like this? I wanted to speak to her and find out her story, but I held myself back.

Everyone in the cell always laughed at my curiosity, for I was always eager to speak with each newcomer about what was going on in the free world. But I knew I needed to protect myself and not enter into conversations lightly.

Others, though, did ask her questions. Her few abrupt comments revealed that she had been in prison for a long time. She had been in a different cell, where two old women had beaten her, and after this they had brought her to our cell. She sobbed when speaking about this. Then she declared that she was unmarried and a princess and that her coachman always wore a top hat. These last words she spoke in French. Part of me was tempted to speak with her, for I am sure that it would have made her happy to converse in French. But I was afraid to do so. In the cell there was a young trollop who was always whispering to the warden on the way to the toilets. I could just imagine what she could drum up about me if I said even one word to this princess in a foreign language. I had enough to cope with, so I kept silent.

But sadly, who approached her but this very same tart. She took one look at her dress and began to yell: "Oh come and look, they are swarming all over her, fuck it, they are all over her!" and she banged her fists on the door. The woman on duty was Baradulina, an extremely violent, ill-natured creature. I can recall only the last name of this unspeakably vicious witch. She noisily unlocked the door and then opened it up, yelling as she did "What is all this banging about?" The tart whispered two words to her and pointed her finger at the old woman. A nurse entered the cell a few minutes later. Every evening she came to us to dispense cough powder, ointment, and so on. I received half a tablet of luminal for the insomnia that plagued me from the time of my arrest. But to come in the middle of the day was unexpected. She went up to the old princess, examined the decorative patterns of her dress, and then ordered her to undress. It turned out that she did not have any underclothing on, only a worn-out flannel blouse that at one time had been white. The nurse looked at the collar, recoiled in horror, and called for the orderly to burn everything. Soon the orderly came in dressed in a gray smock and rubber boots. "Undress, right now, quickly!" he said to the old woman. The old woman just clenched herself tight and angrily shook her head. He held in his hands a large iron hoop, and he repeated: "Do it quickly, right now—Lay on this ring your dress, your underwear, stockings, everything" and then turned his face to the door. The princess did not move, and Baradulina barked: "What's with you? You are just standing there, take off your clothes or they will throw you and your nits into the fire." The princess remained paralyzed. Only her eyes moved, as if searching for something to put on. Several women pleaded with Baradulina to give her some clothes, for it was cold, or take her right to the bathhouse. One went straight up to the old woman and began to undress her, which took time. The only way to get the dress off her was to pull it over her head, but it was impossible to do this without her cooperation. Eventually everything was stripped off her right down to her worn-out fur boots and then carted away. The woman was naked. Through her darkened, wrinkled skin you could see her emaciated skeleton and count every rib and every vertebra. Her dark, sunken stomach seemed stuck to her spine.

I was later to see many people pushed to the breaking point. But this long emaciated body of the old woman, shivering from the cold and pressed against the wall, was tragically horrifying. The women sitting at the stove would not let her come near it.

Everyone expected they would take her to the bathhouse. But one hour passed, then another. There was nothing to cover her with, for her coat had also been taken out for burning. It was agonizing to look at her. Many just turned away. Suddenly a scream rang out. "Look, ladies, see what is crawling out from her!" Everyone looked. The princess was holding one arm up to the wall and looking down across her shoulder. A tapeworm was crawling out from her onto the floor. The miserable woman sobbed and was shuddering nearly to the point of convulsions. Anger, disgust, and shame were all there on her face. The worm just kept crawling and crawling, and there seemed to be no end to him. At this point some began to bang on the door and yell in fright. Baradulina opened the door, looked, and began to scream at the old woman: "You see, the bitch would not even ask to be taken to the bathroom!" She ordered her to leave the cell. So, still naked, the old woman dragged herself along, staggering, with the tapeworm stretched far behind her. Baradulina was seething with fury, mainly because the cell doors had been left open for an inappropriately long time. We never found what happened to the princess and her clothing or whether they ever took her to the doctor. She did not come back to our cell.

A feeling of fear, repugnance, and shame haunted me for several days. Never had I witnessed such unfathomable humiliation and degradation as this poor old woman, half out of her mind, endured. I reproached myself for staying silent, for not demanding that the head of the prison be summoned, or for not organizing a genuine revolt. But what would have been the use … The women in the cell just sniggered at what happened and made guesses as to the length of the tapeworm. With their coarse language, they made fun of her pitifully wrinkled body. The majority thought it had been great fun. The old Bolshevik looked at me sympathetically and made a gesture of helplessness with her hands. Later she whispered to me, "It is better that you did not say anything; there was nothing you could have accomplished except to end up in the punishment cell with a second charge tacked on to you." This woman was fully devoted to the party. She was convinced that we had fallen into the hands of a horrible scoundrel, who was trying to compromise the party and Soviet power in general. According to her, Stalin did not know anything about this and that when he did find out what was going on, everything would again be good. He would fix it all. I responded, "Oh please, do you think he does not know about the shooting of Tukhachevskii and all the other generals, as well as the other trials?" She looked at me sadly, shrugged her shoulders, and said: "What do we really know about such people? Maybe they were really enemies … But, I beg you, do not raise such questions." It was strange. We shared much in common, for she had grown up in Odessa in a very poor Jewish family. But she had joined the Bolsheviks even before the revolution and her greatest sorrow was that they had taken away her party card. I understood how hard it can be to lose everything that you are proud of. But I did not know how to respond to her. I had never known anyone like her. In the years ahead I would run into them quite often—collapsed in a swamp, getting burnt while putting out fires in the woods, in hospital beds with broken legs and ribs, starving, suffering from pellagra. Yet they still spoke with pride about their devotion to the Communist Party. I concluded that this must have been their first love. My first love had been different, but I understand—to this day I draw Konstantin Mikhailovich's profile on the margins of newspapers and on every sheet of paper I can find. Soon my companion left the cell. They called her out with her things, but where she was going we did not know.

After several days, I received a package. Oh, how happy I was! There was no letter, but it contained a list of the contents written in Lenochka's handwriting, with painstakingly large letters. The sugar, the cookies, and the candy were in linen bags. My daughter had remembered how we had packed the boxes to her father. There was butter, cheese, bacon, and excellent smoked sausage. In a pillowcase there were stockings, dresses, linen, and a piece of French soap. My sister-in-law had a sister who lived permanently in Paris and who sometimes managed to send her such luxuries. For the first time in my life I felt wealthy. Everything smelled so heavenly! There was so much food! The first thing I had to do was treat everyone. Then I knew I had to divide up these treasures. I would eat small portions, but do so frequently throughout the day so that I could build back my strength and rid my face of the bluish color and the rash.

The day of my trial arrived—December 14. They drove me to the courtroom in a "Black Raven." I only caught sight of my "co-conspirators" Radchenko and Kravtsova in the corridor. They had been arrested about three months after me, when this terrorist organization had been dreamt up by the investigators. Elena Radchenko was cold and sullen. Sarra threw herself on me with tears streaming down her face and barraged me with questions. But this was not really a suitable place for a conversation. All along the corridor were military personnel and two armed Red Army soldiers guarded us. The questioning began. Radchenko and Kravtsova testified that they had never met at my home, that they had never heard anything about an organization, and had never discussed such topics. Kravtsova said that she had come to my home once. When she was asked what we had talked about, she minced slightly and said "Only physiological topics." Radchenko also told the truth. She said that she had dropped by two or three times for several minutes to pick up her daughter, who had been playing with my daughter while Radchenko was at work. Then they called the witness Posylkina. She claimed to have attended many of our gatherings where we three discussed plans to murder Yezhov. They asked Radchenko and Kravtsova whether or not Posylkina had been present at our gatherings, and they both reiterated that there were no meetings of any kind and that they had not even once seen Posylkina at my home.

I asked for and received permission from the court to question Posylkina: "You keep insisting that you were at my home many times. Tell me, what stands out in my room, what distinguishes it from the majority of exiles' homes in this village?" She responded, "Well, it is a room like any room, there are stools, a table ..." Then I asked permission to ask this same question to Vera Nazarova, who was also present in the courtroom. Vera Nazarova looked pleased as she began to describe: "Oh my, well there was a corner for animals with birds and fish, over Lenochka's bed there was a large geographic map, over the table there was a big portrait of Lenochka in a ski outfit and everywhere, everywhere there were her drawings, even on the stove ...."

"And were there stools?" I asked. "No, there were no stools of any kind. There were blocks, well, I should say there was firewood covered with various cloth napkins ..." The witness was ordered to sit down. I asked whether the testimony of Nazarova would be entered into the record. They responded that the trial was being conducted according to law and I did not need to ask such questions. But I had not seen the court secretary writing anything down from her testimony.

Then women whom I did not know testified that Radchenko and Kravtsova had made anti-Soviet statements in the store and in the streets. All of this was tediously slow, and the witnesses stumbled over their words and got visibly confused. All of these invented conversations supposedly took place in private without witnesses, so that all the accused could do was deny that they ever took place. The chairman of the court glanced at his watch and declared our hearing in recess until the following day. I returned to my cell with a light heart. Now I felt as if my reading of all those Agatha Christie novels without stopping to catch my breath had paid off. I had gotten right to the truth of the matter. Getting Vera to describe our home had been a skillful tactic to expose Posylkina's lies. Now no one could believe her and all of her idiotic statements would lose their impact. Vera would still be testifying about my statements during the film *Under the Rooftops of Paris*. But the court had already seen that she was nearly deaf and could not possibly believe that I would shout out such nonsense in an auditorium overflowing with people. I now felt fortunate that my case was being tried in a court, for this way everything could be made clear. Plus, no one had yet said anything about the letters of Zoshchenko.

The next day they made us wait for a long time in the corridor. Radchenko again said nothing, but Sarra assured me that everything would be fine. Then the chairman of the court walked past and cast a dark, malicious glance at us, which destroyed my optimism and filled me with a sense of impending doom. The trial resumed. Again they called Posylkina to the stand, and this time her testimony was exclusively about the letter from Zoshchenko. Obviously they had decided to drive me into a corner with this evidence. But I asked why there was no letter entered in as evidence and why not even once had I been allowed to see this letter. The only response was "why would I need to see it; I had already read it and knew very well what the contents were."

I objected,

> This is a lie, it is the slander of this loathsome woman, who from the first days of our arrival in exile began bragging about her affair with the local NKVD boss. I avoided her. Why in the world would I have read her any of my letters? I never went to the post office. My landlady's daughter would bring my mail to me, because she worked at the post office and knew that I could not get there myself, for my work was very far away.

One of the military judges cut me short. "That is enough. We already know this from your confrontation with the witness. But you have no right to slander the witness, she could not have made all of this up. How could she have known otherwise that you were corresponding with the writer Zoshchenko?"

I responded: "I have asked myself this very question many times, but in reality, except for one very innocent letter about whether or not there were places available for summer rental in the village of Semenovskoe, which was confiscated from me during the search of my residence, nothing in the handwriting of Zoshchenko has been presented …"

"What are you insinuating?" barked the second military judge, who was sitting on the other side of the court chairman.

I retorted: "I am not insinuating anything, but I know that such a letter does not exist, consequently this is a filthy slander against one of our finest writers. He could never have written such letters as she describes."

"However he did write it," the chairman asserted maliciously.

"If you are all so firmly convinced of this, then why is he not sitting here on the bench for the accused?" I asked.

"Do not worry, there is no need to try him here." Even though I knew that Zoshchenko's books were still coming out, my heart still sank. What was I to do? They were very fond of the phrase invented by the investigator, "my hand will not tremble to kill Yezhov!," which was supposedly my response to the nonexistent letter of Mikhail Mikhailovich, a man who was intelligent, prudent, and careful and who unquestionably, like myself, had never even thought about Yezhov, let alone plotted to kill him. Over the long months I had spent in prison, I had seen how women from the Far East and even the wives of sailors who sometimes had hosted foreigners in their homes received as a rule point 6 of Article 58, which was for espionage and brought shorter terms of imprisonment. When it came my turn to have the "last word," I forgot myself and raised a protest against the point 8 of Article 58 I had been charged with, which would bring a longer term. Why, I said, had they decided to make me into a murderer? I had admitted that I had worked for three years in Paris. Of course I was not engaged in spying there, but why did I not receive this charge? Why out of the blue have you accused me of terrorism, I asked, and then burst into tears. "We received nothing but positive accounts from abroad; your behavior there was irreproachable," the chairman answered, and the court adjourned. This statement raised new hope in me. If my three years in France had been irreproachable, then how could I have become a terrorist in the village of Semenovskoe? But the court was in recess for less than ten minutes. They acquitted Radchenko and let her leave a free woman. Kravtsova was given a five-year sentence but only on point 10 of Article 58. They convicted me, however, under points 10, 11, and for the "totality of acts committed," point 8, as if I had actually carried out a terrorist act. I was sentenced to ten years in a strict regime labor camp, with the subsequent loss of civil rights for five years.

What could I do? Call everyone back and ask why they had drummed up this "totality of acts committed?" What had I done? Radchenko was free, Sarra was convicted only on point 10, and if I alone made up an organization, and the totality of actions came from this, then what did I do? My legs stuck to the floor and my knees shook. A lawyer approached me. Oh yes, I had forgotten. The court had assigned a state lawyer to me. He had not done anything except to mumble at the end about leniency. He said that in the next seventy-two hours I had the right to appeal to the Supreme Court. He offered to help but I just brushed him aside. Two guards standing over me rushed me along; they had to get the room ready for the next trial. The lawyer thrust several sheets of paper into my hand: "Write the appeal yourself if you do not want my help, but do not miss the deadline. You have seventy-two hours." They then shoved me into the dark recesses of a "raven." It rattled and it rolled. Fine! I would have liked to have stayed there all day and all night, not having to see anyone or answer any questions. At this point what frightened me was returning to my prison cell.

Fortunately, they did not take me back there, but instead I was put with others who had been convicted and were awaiting transport to the camps. Now Sarra was beside me, telling me about how after me many more had been arrested, and Posylkina had been the chief witness against all of them. Having exhausted her store of news, she returned to the sweet memories of her affair with the general. They sent her away quite soon, after about three weeks, but once again it seemed as if they had forgotten about me. On my very first day in this new cell I had written my appeal; they locked me up in a square room with a table, a stool, and an enormous high-wattage lamp that blinded me. I thought that I laid out my case very convincingly and these judges would be made to answer for their injustice. But two, then three months went by before I received an answer, and it affirmed the sentence as correct. Time dragged on. More weeks went by until finally they took me away in a "Stolypin wagon"[6] to the Vologda prison. I spent the entire journey arguing with the guard who considered it his duty to keep me in his sight even when I had to use the toilet. He would not allow me to close the door, and it was only with great difficulty that I was able to get him at least to turn his back to me. I felt a sense of pity for this young lad, a bit of a dolt, whom they had brainwashed to believe that I was a dangerous criminal.

In Vologda it was frightening. The walls of the cell were painted in black oil paint, there was a vaulted ceiling, and even the blue light that was barely visible in the gloom turned black. The Finnish War[7] had begun and everywhere it was semidark. Here I began encountering women from the most remote towns and villages who similarly had "tried to kill Yezhov." At first I was enraged, but I soon calmed down, comforted by the fact that if there were so many such "terrorists," then no one could take it seriously. Next I went to the Kirov prison where the cells were so overcrowded that the corridors were filled with a constant din, despite all of the locked doors. I ended up next to a woman I had known in Paris. She worked in Berlin, but came for some reason to our Trade Mission. I learned from her that both Bogdan and his friend, who had offered me a comfortable apartment in Vienna, had been shot. "But weren't both of them party members?" I asked indignantly. "All the more reason for them to be shot," she said with a smirk. She held a bundle in her arms, for they had already called her for a transit to the camps. Sometimes all you had was a single minute to try and find out as much as you could.

They sent me to Viatlag[8] at the end of summer in 1939. After all of the prisons I had been in, for the first time I had the boundless sky above me. There were about twenty of us, with most being "*bytovki*" or, more accurately, "*urki*," or criminals.[9] The camp was a big rectangle, enclosed in barbed wire—there were barracks and barracks and more barracks …

No, I am not going to describe the camp. Others have done this and I have little to add. I will limit myself to several episodes in my camp biography.

There, in the woman's barrack, the horror of my situation seized me—I would be spending nearly ten years in this environment filled with stuffy, poisonous air, constant clatter and screaming, foul language, and smelly foot bindings hung out to dry on ropes. Along the walls ran two rows, top and bottom, of continuous plank bunk beds. They put me in the lower row between two women who thereupon raised a racket. They shrieked that it was already too crowded, everyone else had three planks per person, but they had to make do with only five for the two of them. And now what is this! The old orderly reassured them that after the impending transport I would be relocated. My bunkmates, who were rather lively young gals, quarreled back and forth over me with a virtuoso command of obscenities. I said nothing. I was trying to get my bearings. In this barrack there were many of us who were arrested under Article 58 (meaning they were political prisoners as opposed to the *bytovki* and the *urki*—Translator's note), but everyone kept to themselves. This was understandable, for nothing else connected us except for that frightful Article 58. None of us cared about "politics." Coming from countless villages, towns, and hamlets across the country, we knew only our own private sorrows. We were also afraid of each other because while in prison we had been warned by those who had already been in the camps that there were many informants there who helped construct "new cases" that tacked on additional sentences to prisoners.

The following day they gave me a padded quilted jacket (*telegreika*) that was filthy and full of holes. I also received enormous shoe covers (*bakhili*) that had been somehow pasted together from scraps of rubber. They fell off my feet. This was a logging camp, and in addition, prisoners were building railroad branch lines and runners for carting out timber. I ended up in a brigade that dug ditches. I had never used a shovel before this. The brigade leader, a criminal prisoner, handed me a shovel, which right away felt very heavy to me. The soil that we had to dig in was like clay. Alongside the ditch were platforms, and we had to throw our "ballast" (meaning the dirt) up onto them. I failed miserably at this. When I stood in the ditch the wheels of the platform were higher than my head, and I still had to throw the dirt up onto the platform itself. The clay clung to my shovel. A gray-haired man was working next to me, and he said: "You must be stronger with the shovel. Here everything sticks completely ...." Seriously, only a good knife could have pried that dirt from the shovel. At the end of the workday they drove us on top of the wet dirt about three kilometers. It was no less than five kilometers to the zone. The small steam engine with its pipe shaped something like a toilet bowl kept gasping, smoking, and spitting out large sparks. We lay down next to each other and dozed, but the sparks kept falling all over our padded jackets. The dirty padding smoldered and many cried out in pain from the burning. A strong blow along my back woke me up. I jumped up and almost collapsed again. A young dark-eyed man was holding me up. Laughing, he explained to me in mangled Russian that I could have been burnt alive. He had pulled off my padded jacket, which still had smoke coming from it. My savior turned out to be an Italian communist and movie producer. He had come to the Soviet Union expecting a comradely welcome, but instead was arrested as a spy. The next day we ended up working side by side in the ditch. We spoke to one another in French. He said that as soon as he could get back to Italy, he was going to make a film about the work we were doing, the burning jackets, and so on. It was not likely, though, that he ever returned to Italy. He was very worn down ...

I worked in the ditches for several days and received only penalty norms, which provided me only 300 grams of bread per day. I could not achieve even one-fourth of my work quota. I had only one source I could turn to for help—I wrote a letter to my daughter pleading for sugar and fats. I sent the letter through someone who could go in and out of the camp without an escort, and so it bypassed the censors. In one month's time I received my first package. By this point I had come down with boils (*furunculosis*) and was released from regular manual labor. One night I climbed up to the top bunks, where my place was now. My bunkmates were not there, for they worked in the kitchen. I could see our orderly, an old Volga German by the name of Shmidt, sitting by a barrel of water, and he looked very drowsy. In a far corner, by the door, a rustling sound came from the top bunk. This was Aisha; she was Chechen and the day before had beaten this orderly mercilessly. It was the orderly's job to prevent men from coming in to our women's barrack, but Aisha had a friend who had disguised himself as a woman by tying a scarf on his head and pulling on a skirt. But as he was climbing up the bunks toward Aisha, the orderly realized who he was thanks to his chrome leather boots. The orderly tried to pull him back down, and Aisha screamed out in her guttural language. She raised her fists at Shmidt and spit in his face. Now, just like a cat, she jumped down, grabbed up the axe that was standing next to the barrel of water, and hit the old man hard on the head with it. One more leap, and she was back on her bunk. But she saw that I was awake and glared at me. I quickly hid in my blanket; in such matters you could not be a witness if you wanted to survive, and I was determined to survive, no matter what it took. I had to keep my promise to my daughter that I would return to her. Soon someone came from the night shift, let out a scream, and they carried out the old man. All that was left was a pool of blood on the floor. They tried Aisha for the crime, but because she was pregnant, they sent her to a special camp that had a maternity ward.

Good fortune in the camps never lasted. The office I had begun working in was transferred outside the camp zone, and I could not get a pass because I had been convicted as a terrorist and thereby was considered a dangerous criminal. I was again assigned to general work, and this time it was timbering. Once more I had to pull on flimsy galoshes, which I had to tie up with a rope across the sole just to keep them from falling off. The path to the work site was about ten kilometers and went through a swampy forest where controlled burning had taken place. All around us were the sharp, scorched trunks of stunted firs. It was difficult to make your way through here— you had to step on tree roots and if you fell into the muck, you would be afraid one of the limbs would pierce your eye. Meanwhile, the guard followed behind you, cursing you mercilessly, pushing you along and threatening you with his rifle. When we had been in transit, they warned us that anyone lagging behind could be shot for trying to escape.

On the first day of this work I fell to my knees. I clutched at the scorched trunks but they crumbled in my hands. The VOKhR guard[10] threatened to shoot me. I retorted angrily, "Either shoot me, or give me your hand! You can see that I am stuck." He barked back, "Look at what they are sending to us now," but he held out his rifle butt for me to grab and pulled me up. It was exhausting just to make our way along this path. But ahead of us there still loomed a long day of work. I was given a scraper, and I climbed up onto a high stack and went to work. But I did not have the strength to turn over this enormous tree trunk, and there was no one to help me. Each of us had our own stack. I tackled another, but again lacked the strength to turn it over. By the day's end, I had scraped six tree trunks, but only on one side. The norm output was sixteen. So again I was receiving penalty rations—a small portion of bread and a bit of thin soup only in the morning. It was a dark-colored unpalatable slop that smelled of rotten cabbage. Packages arrived only rarely. I always had to be sure and "treat" the person delivering it with sausage or a piece of suet. Otherwise, on the pretext of examining the contents, he would deliberately pour out the buckwheat, the tea, and the sugar as he made his way to the tobacco at the bottom of the box, which I had requested in order to give it to the orderly.

I was rapidly losing strength. But my comrades from the construction office remembered me. At a smaller branch camp (*lagpunkt*), there was a construction division, and they demanded that I be sent there. I had to work twelve hours a day, but I got to stay within the camp zone, and this spelled happiness for me. I was paid fifteen rubles a month, which meant that I could buy sugar and stale cake from the camp store. But as always, my good fortune did not last long. The construction division was liquidated, and the office relocated outside of the zone, where I was not permitted to go. Once more it was back to general labor. Now I was uprooting tree stumps. And of course, I ended up with penalty rations. Blotches and sores appeared on my legs—I had scurvy. Now I was transferred to the "weak" category, which meant I would be assigned to jobs in the camp zone. They selected various forms of "light work" for me, such as washing the floors of four enormous male barracks. I had to carry water from the far end of the zone, scrape the long dirty tables with a piece of glass, and scrub the uneven, trampled-on floor. Plus, all of this had to be completed in two to three hours, before the next shift returned and dragged in more mud. The sanitary inspector, an enormous red-haired Georgian, would step in and yell that I needed to make it cleaner. This work saturated the bandages on my legs with dirt, but the doctor's assistant (*feld'sher*) would not replace them.

One day when I was carrying water, I noticed a group of newly arrived prisoners approaching the bathhouse. It was a convoy of men, and they looked jaundiced and worn out. But it was obvious from their faces that they were intelligentsia. While a guard was detaining the convoy, I managed to ask them where they had come from, and they told me it was Solovki. I scanned them quickly but did not see my husband. I called out his name, and they told me that he had left with another contingent. Because of the war with Finland, the Solovki camp had been liquidated and all of the prisoners were dispersed to separate places. Probably, they said, my husband had been sent further north. They had heard his name before, a while back; they thought maybe he had served as a translator. This was all that I could find out from them.

Soon other prisoner convoys arrived, from the Baltic states.[11] Many were brought in on stretchers straight to the hospital. In order to create reception centers for these new arrivals, all of whom were starving and debilitated, the administration expelled healthy working prisoners from the barracks. The doctors to whom I had been assigned as a "weak" prisoner convinced the head of the Sanitation Division to place me at one of these reception centers. Thus began my work in medicine. My duties at first did not demand specialized knowledge or skill: I took temperatures, dispensed powders and drops, and supervised the distribution of food. The beds were lined up in two rows, top and bottom. The Baltic prisoners lay close to one another, still clad in their own clothing, on top of old, worn-out mattresses full of dust. The flat pillows were not any better. There were no sheets or pillow cases, and there were not enough in the hospital either. The weakest lay on the bottom bunks. It was difficult for me to look at them, and even harder to listen to their stories. Among them were people who only recently had been property owners, physicians, and lawyers. There were also farmers. Their families had been evacuated, along with all of their valuables, such as sewing machines and motorcycles. They had to load these items onto baggage cars, for individually they could only take one suitcase with linen and underclothing. Then came transport after transport, one transit point after another. At night, during one of these transits, the women had been separated from the men, and in the panic of the moment, as they moved in the darkness, many picked up the wrong suitcases. Now many of the husbands and sons had ended up with the clothing of their wives and mothers. So some Estonians and Latvians alleviated their starvation by offering up lovely blouses and nightshirts in exchange for pieces of bread. Likewise the women had with them amazing men's shirts, the likes of which we had never seen. But they had no idea where their possessions had ended up. The strongest ones were assigned to general work, while the others had to saw firewood or work as carpenters. The weakest ones were sent to the hospital, and most of these ended up in the camp cemetery …

At night I would return to my barrack. But I was not getting any rest, thanks to the bedbugs and the rats. Only rarely did any disinfecting occur and then all they did was burn sulfur. This was horrible. We would have to be evacuated out of the zone with all of our things and forced to sit on our bundles whether it was raining or snowing, always under the barrel of the guards' rifles. Such disinfections did not occur more than once a month. The camp authorities never even tried to combat the rats. We kept above our heads the packages sent to us from family, complete with bread and other foods. At night the rats crawled into the boxes, but it was best to lie quietly and ignore them. One woman learned this the hard way when she pounded on the box with her fist, and the rat jumped out and got tangled up in her hair … During such sleepless nights, I would tell myself over and over: I will return to Leningrad and I will tell all of this to my family. I would not be looking for pity or for empathy, but rather to make my prosperous brother- and sister-in-law understand what we had to do here to survive. My neighbor was a Georgian. I learned from her that Budu Mdivani had been shot back in 1937. She also named other Georgians and Armenians who had been executed. I was all confused in my mind: why were they killing Old Bolsheviks?

The war with Germany had begun and our food situation grew even worse. There was no sugar, and the bread was like a sponge—you could squeeze water from it. Transports of prisoners kept arriving. Starving prisoners died after filling themselves with the hot soup, for no one had warned against giving them so much food all at once. When this happened in my barrack, I went to our doctors and begged them to take me on as a nurse in the hospital. Soon an opportunity presented itself, and they gave me night duties. I learned to give injections and to apply cupping glasses to patients (this is an alternative medical therapy that involves creating suction on the skin to promote healing—Translator's note). I mastered quite quickly the required knowledge. An elderly Kharkov doctor noticed my diligence and suggested that I come to the morgue for the autopsies. Here this frantic old man worked with enthusiasm, but longed for an audience. I was scared. Naked, dead bodies lay one after another along the wall, and it was impossible to avoid touching them in the cramped shed serving as the morgue. The autopsies themselves frightened me, especially when the doctor began to saw open the skull. But I could not allow myself to show my fear. I had to earn the respect of the doctors. They gave me books and took time to explain much to me, and soon I was allowed to work day shifts. There were many sick prisoners but nowhere to put them all. They had to put two rusty berths together and lay three sick patients down on top of them. There were few pillows, and you frequently had to put logs covered in old rags at the head of the bed. I was assigned two wards, male and female, each with about twenty-three persons. I had much to do and slept only three to four hours a night. We did not have any medicine. You were lucky if in a single ward you could find even two tubes of camphor. Our elderly physicians had to determine which of the patients would receive these valuable treasures. If a patient was too infirm to drink the half glass of milk prescribed by the doctors, I would give it to a prisoner still fighting to live. The weakest prisoners received an additional 200 grams of wheat bread. I would take such slices and toast them in the kitchen, then hide them. Before the unfortunate individual had uttered his last groan, everyone in the ward who could still eat looked at me. I laid a sheet over the body and carried it out. After about twenty minutes I would return with a bag of the secreted toast and distribute them equally. But I knew that some who now were greedily seizing the dried crusts would soon be bequeathing their shares to others.

It was difficult to treat the sick under these conditions, and the doctors felt demoralized and ashamed that they could do nothing to help them. In the most extreme cases, they had to focus attention only on those who still had a chance to live. With the coming of winter in 1941, the situation became catastrophic. Prisoners were working in severely cold temperatures dressed only in torn padded jackets. The beds and the hospitals were almost completely filled with pneumonia patients. The death rate exceeded twenty prisoners a day in our hospital alone. When a prisoner entered the throes of death, others in the ward would get upset. They wanted us to try and save the patient even if we knew it was hopeless. The doctors ordered me to fill a syringe with distilled water and quickly approach the dying prisoner, letting everyone see that he had not been abandoned. I would sit down on his bed, try to make the rags under his head more comfortable, and wipe off his mouth with gauze. The doctor would come and take his pulse and, with the movement of his eyes, direct me to yet another patient who needed this injection. The patients who died had to be kept for two hours in the ward, after which we would tag the big toe of the left leg, indicating the number of the prisoner's case history and family name. Two nurses had to carry the dead body to the morgue. One night events took a bizarre turn. The nurses had no sooner gone out with their load when they returned and called me into the corridor. They were trembling from fear. I heard them say that there were people in the morgue still alive! A chill ran through me. There had been several deaths that evening. Had I accidentally sent live prisoners to the morgue? All three of us ran to the morgue. The stretcher with the dead body lay on the snow, and the door to the morgue was open. I went in and heard the sound of raucous breathing. I turned on the light and saw a pair of "lovers" lying on the trestle bed where the autopsies were usually done. Without even waiting for me to yell at them, they crawled out of the morgue.

How did I not go mad from such horrors? Probably because everything I experienced was subsumed in my own personal grief. During the first days of the war the bosses shut off radios and banned correspondence. Up until this point, it was only my daughter's letters that offered me an escape and gave me strength. Now, though, this was taken away from me. I learned about the blockade of Leningrad from prisoners who worked outside the camp zone. My mind reeled—was my daughter alive, and where was she? Who was taking care of her? Then a purely accidental happening came to my rescue. A young woman who worked as a courier for the camp *kum* came into the dressing station.[12] She asked if we could cauterize a wart on her arm. She was carrying a big heavy bag with a newspaper sticking out from it. I inquired, "Do you have a lot of newspapers?" "No," she answered, "these are letters." Thus it was that I discovered what was happening to letters—they went to the *kum* who then gave them to the courier to burn. I always carried around with me the latest letter from my daughter, so I took it out and gave this girl the envelope. I told her that if she would keep her eye out for letters from my little daughter and bring them to me, then I would give her a nice present for each letter she brought me. I still had in my possession silk shirts, blouses, stockings …

In this way I began to receive letters again. This sharp girl adroitly figured out how to pass on letters to me without anyone noticing. Now I was able to learn what had happened to my daughter. She had been evacuated from Leningrad at the very beginning of the war along with other children and wives of writers. Her letters arrived from the village of Chernaia in the Perm district. My little girl was living with the wife of G. A. Gukovskii on equal terms with his daughter Natasha.[13] She was missing my letters and worried that she would never be able to find me again if we lost touch. I responded to each of her letters and my savior, the courier, mailed each of my responses. Everything had worked out, and then in 1942 official correspondence was restored.

Try to imagine that all I have written above was being narrated by me in a train to a fellow passenger, but that the ride was now coming to an end. Yet the most significant, the most frightening part now had to be crumpled up, squeezed into a tight fist, and I had to try to finish telling this story in an extremely short time. Maybe what will happen is my fellow traveler, who is getting off before me, will have to run along after it as I stand holding on to the handrail of the platform and shouting out the final words.

Within the region of Viatlag, they began to admit wounded relatives of the camp administrators in the city hospital.[14] The hospital polyclinic was now very busy, and it was too much for the free nurses to cope with, so our department head recommended me to assist them. In spite of the fact that I had been arrested under Point 8 of Article 58, I received a twenty-four-hour pass, and so I began work in the polyclinic set up for the free personnel of the camp. My immediate supervisor, Zonochka Pochtar, was the wife of our camp security officer. At first she allowed me to treat only the armed guards from the camp and their wives and grandmothers, but soon she came to trust me and would take the whole day off when I was working. After two or three months, she left this job and I ended up doing all of the bandaging. I had to leave early from the zone, even before the required morning count of prisoners (*razvod*). The city was about five kilometers from the camp, and I had to be at my job by 7:00 a.m. in order to prepare everything. Admissions started at 8:00 a.m. and lasted until 3:00 p.m. After this I had to sit at the registration desk while the free employees went on break. I took telephone calls, ran errands to apartments with jars and syringes, and after 5:00 p.m. worked again in the dressing station as long as was necessary. Before my appointment, two people had handled this workload, but now they decided I could handle it all by myself. If those same employees that I took care of in the daytime needed to have injections at night, then I had to sit at the desk with a syringe ready to go when the phone rang. This was the doctor's order.

Working at the clinic was hard, yet it brought me great happiness when in the summer of 1946 and 1947, my daughter was able to visit me. I could send letters through unofficial channels, bypassing the censorship, and caution her how to act and with whom to stay. She arrived several days early, before the officially designated time for the visit, and got in line in the corridor of the polyclinic. She came in after everyone else and then sat with me at the registration desk for two hours. I did not tell her anything about my sufferings in the camps. I did not want to ruin these precious minutes with her, and I could not bear her leaving me with a heavy heart. These were always happy, joyous reunions. I could not take my eyes off her beautiful face, her long, thin fingers, and her wavy hair with its strands of gold.

9

Release, Exile, and Rehabilitation: The Bittersweet Taste of "Freedom"

The reward for my good work at the clinic was a reduction in my sentence by four months. I was to be released not in May, but in February. I was counting down the days. But my job at the polyclinic came to an abrupt end even before my release, thanks to Zina Pochtar. She had long since stopped working there, but still acted as if she owned the place. She would come in, open up boxes, take any powders she wanted, even pour out alcohol, and I never tried to stop her. But then one day she came and demanded instruments for an abortion, saying that she did not want a third child with her husband. This I refused to do. I would not give her the key to the cabinet. "What right do you have to deny me this key?" she demanded. "You know very well that abortions are illegal, but I have someone who can take care of this for me."

I responded that "I am not permitted to dispense these instruments. You have plenty of friends in the hospital who are free employees, ask them." She threatened to take the keys from me but I told her that she would have to break down the cupboard. I would not give them up. She turned blue from her anger and spite. "Don't you understand who you are talking to? Don't you realize the hellish pit my husband can dig for you?"

"Oh I know well what he can do. But if your expert at abortions causes you to get an infection, then your husband would dig my grave. So I think it best for me to obey the rules."

She ran out of the dressing station in a state of fury. I was trembling all over. I knew that if I did not get my release, it would kill me. This entire scene took place between two admission periods. The chief of the camp Construction Department (*OKS—otdel kapital'nogo stroitel'stva*) was due to come in for his regular intravenous infusion of calcium. When he arrived, I had to tell him that I could not risk doing his injection because my hands were shaking so badly. He was a good and earnest man, and although we never conversed, I sensed that he felt sorry for me. He asked what had happened, and I told him everything. He was silent for a few minutes and then he said: "I will take care of this. If they try to pull any tricks to harm you, then I will have you transferred to work as my typist." He knew that I could type because his wife also came to me for glucose injections, and I had chatted more freely with her. By the end of the following day, the head doctor sent for me and asked what had happened. He had received an order to fire me. After I told him the story, he said, "You acted correctly. But I cannot disobey an order." I sat in the camp for two days and then a senior duty officer dropped in to tell me that I was to report for work at the OKS.

So, at the beginning of February 1948, I got to return to Leningrad, though I did so illegally. I still had five years in which I was stripped of my civil rights and therefore not allowed to live in major cities. Upon my release I had designated the city of Cherepovets as my intended residence, mainly because I would have to travel through Leningrad in order to get there. Elena and her aunt met me at the station. We had barely gotten in the door of their apartment and sat down at the table before my sister-in-law, whom Elena called "Aunt Musia," said: "We do not want to know or hear anything about your camp life. You must forget all that happened and think only about how to live from this day forward." And henceforth, she always spoke to me with this commanding tone in her voice.

How was I going to live my life? Where was I going to live? After several days they found a way out of my dilemma. My in-laws' housekeeper had a brother who was a guard at the Bol'shaia Vishera Railway Station, located in the Novgorod region, about 130 miles from Leningrad. Armed with two bottles of vodka and various treats, the housekeeper and I went to this station. I still had to pay a certain sum of money, but I did get registered to live in Bol'shaia Vishera. Now I had to acquire a "social position," meaning I had to find employment. There was nothing there except a glass factory destroyed by the Germans during the war. Only the hot shop was working. Glassblowers stood at the red-hot stove and crafted miracles, while a half-destroyed wing served as a "diamond" shop, where master craftsmen applied patterns to carafes, glasses, etc. They hired me to work in the packaging department, which was housed in a dirty, damp basement. Here labored three old women, who reminded me of the witches in *Macbeth*. They were almost always inebriated as they packed the glass products in straw. Their crude language as well as their creepy stories and anecdotes evoked fully the atmosphere of the camps.

My only escape were my trips to Leningrad to see my daughter. I could not go and come back in twenty-four hours, and it was not easy to arrange for an extra day off with the foreman. For this I had to bribe him. I only managed this once every two to three months. My daughter's new "parents" were none too pleased the first time I showed up at their apartment on Nevskii. Her aunt immediately declared that I could not spend the night—what if there was a sudden search, and it was discovered that I was not registered in Leningrad? She phoned a common acquaintance of ours, the widow of "little Boris," Izya's school friend (like Izya, Boris died in the camps); she lived with her daughter in a small room in a communal apartment, but they welcomed me with warmth and tenderness as a guest for the night.

During the summer of 1949, Lenochka came to visit me in Bol'shaia Vishera. I showed her the hot room, and in the evenings as we walked in the woods, she confided her secrets to me. She was a university student now, and there were already both passions and disappointments. She told me that she had never told anyone any of this except for me. After work, a scrumptious supper was waiting for me, for Lenochka was an excellent cook (she had learned to cook during the evacuation). Then on one of these idyllic summer days, while we were eating our supper, we heard a knock at the door and in came the NKVD boss. He looked at my daughter with both amazement and admiration, and even seemed embarrassed. "Excuse me, but I have an order for your arrest," he stated. So once again, my daughter was forced to watch as I was taken away.

This time there were no interrogations of any kind, but rather, it was I who was asking the questions: "Why have you arrested me? I have already served ten years and I am employed; I have not spoken with anyone. My references are good, and I was even given a reduction in my sentence ..."

"Well now, you need to understand that when we liberated all of you, you spread out like cockroaches, and now we need to gather all of you into one place." That was it. There was nothing to talk about.

I was taken to the prison in Novgorod and here I spent three months. The prison authorities interpreted my spotless camp record in their own special way. They started calling me out during the night in an effort to pressure me to act as an informer. As they put it, I had worked honestly in the camps and therefore they knew I could be trusted. If I cooperated, I could get a single accommodation. I was an educated person and could find out what they needed to know and then pass the information on to them. In exchange for this, they would not exile me faraway, and my daughter would be allowed to visit me. But I did not fall for the bait. I became hysterical and played the role of an effusive and cantankerous lady who was afraid to be alone in a cell. I was sick and tired of them, and so they got me to sign a statement of noncompliance and sent me to a transit prison in Leningrad. From there I went once more to the Vologda Prison, and then to Kirov Prison.

There were many of us "cockroaches." They pushed me into a cell so dense with bodies that it reminded me of trying to board an overcrowded bus. I had to just stand there with my back to the door until the time for inspection came. Finally they transported us. I had already survived much, but I could not have imagined the horrors that awaited us. It was a damp winter. We were loaded onto a cattle car lined on both sides with three rows of planks, situated so that you had to sit all bent over. We lay like sprats in a box, and there was no heat. In the mornings, wherever they could find room, the guard put a barrel of boiling water covered by a board with our bread rations spread out on it. Supper was a barrel of terrible-tasting soup. Right next to it, just a step away, was the hole in the floor that served as our toilet. The train ride was bumpy, and as many of the women said, you had to be a trained sniper to get your aim right. As a result, an ice-covered mountain of excrement formed around it. The temperature was over 20 degrees below zero. Our breath hung down in snowy threads from the ceiling of the cattle car, and all of the walls were covered in hoarfrost. It felt as though we were in a stalactite cave. There was no light, for the narrow, barred windows were at the very top of the railcar.

Finally we arrived at the Krasnoiarsk Prison and were taken immediately to the bathhouse. We were so happy to have warm water and to be able to wash our underclothing. We came back to our cell all nicely steamed out and with our hair wet only to find—oh how horrible it was!—nothing but a cement floor. We had no choice but to sit there, holding our wet underclothing in our hands. After several days, they took us out into the corridor and made us line up. A woman in a fur coat with a shabby fox collar accompanied by a foppish young man came up to us. They sized up our muscles and told us to open our mouths (just as in *Uncle Tom's Cabin*, I thought to myself). The prison had basically sold us to Sibleskhoz, a Siberian timber operation. We were taken first to the city of Kansk and then they drove us in open trucks despite the subfreezing temperatures to Dolgii Most (the Long Bridge). Fortunately, the truck driver stopped outside every teashop and one of my fellow travelers, an elderly Armenian architect from Leningrad, insisted I down a small glass of vodka with him at each stop. At Dolgii Most, they transferred us to the NKVD and said that we were now free people. We had to make this place our home and work honestly. We would not be going anywhere else. The next day they sent us to the place where our honest labor awaited us—extracting resin from the snow-covered taiga. I could write a long story about this work, but I do not have the time. Everyone looked back with longing at the time in the camps, where you at least had bread, boiling water, and a place to live. Here we were free but we had to live off our own earnings.

A woman whom I had met in the Novgorod Prison helped me to escape this torment. She had been transferred out here earlier than me. We became close on the basis of our shared fate as mothers. Her daughter had grown up in the family of a friend of hers, and when this woman returned from the camps, she too had met with a stern welcome. During our whispered, nighttime conversations I told her a lot about my daughter and had mentioned Lenochka's address. Having already arrived in exile before me, also in Krasnoiarsk region, she sent a note to her daughter asking her to find out where I was. Then when I was nearly dead from extracting tree sap, I received a transfer to the Ministry of State Security's (MGB)[1] State Farm in the Sukhobuzinskii District. This was where my friend from the Novgorod Prison was; she worked as a free person in the system of the MGB. I knew it was she who had arranged this. But they were not expecting me in the state farm because it had taken so long to process my reassignment and I had not given advanced warning of my arrival. My savior greeted me cordially but I got the feeling that deep down, she was annoyed. The situation quickly became clear to me. Her husband, an old Chekist, had also been in the camps for ten years, and then, as a fellow "cockroach," had been exiled to this very same state farm. But the reunion of the married couple had been far from joyous, for her husband was seriously ill. He suffered a series of heart attacks. She had to miss work to care for him, which aggravated her boss, the state farm director. Plus, caring for her husband exhausted her. It was at this point that she had remembered that I was a nurse and, with great efficiency, had arranged for my transfer. But I had been delayed, and her husband had already died. Thus, I was no longer necessary to her.

It was one thing to have conversations on prison beds, but quite another to end up in a single room with your benefactress, who highly valued her position and so watched your every step and was constantly making comments. Not wishing to be a freeloader, I wrote to my daughter and she and her aunt began to send me lots of packages. But even this did not help. I continued to feel like a parasite. Yet, I just could not find work anywhere. Only at the end of the summer did I finally get taken on as a temporary hire to help with counting the harvest. I worked around the clock, from time to time grabbing a nap on the sun-warmed grain. I received money for this work as well as 40 kilograms of flour. But my life did not get any easier, and the sharp temper of my "landlady" forced me at the beginning of winter to seek other accommodations. I found a place about twenty kilometers from the state farm, in a so-called model or teaching (*uchpedkolkhoze*) farm for those training to become collective farm directors. They hired me as a poultry woman; the hens were sickly and not laying, and it was my job to fix this situation. I had no other option. They put me in a narrow, semidark storehouse filled with the rotten smell of decaying onions. I began my employment. The basic workforce in this woeful state farm consisted of exiled Volga Germans. They lived inside dugouts, which they managed to make unusually tidy and even attractive. The adobe slabs were striking with their geometric precision, and in the small windows there were coquettish curtains with little flounces. Over the beds hung traditional linen envelopes for night clothes,[2] and on each one the obligatory words in German, "Good Night," were embroidered. I often had to go into these dwellings, for the girls who lived there took turns helping me.

Several dozen hens were kept in a dilapidated barn littered with dung. The white hens were filthy and exhausted. Here in this muck, amid these mountains of excrement, I had to find a way to increase egg production. One conversation with the director showed me that I was dealing with an illiterate petty tyrant who knew nothing about the enterprise he was running. I could not immediately put everything in order: I had no prior experience with poultry. I needed books so that I could read up on the subject. I asked the director about this, and he promised to send me for a day to the Atamanovo State Farm, where they had a model henhouse. "But for now," he said, "let's get going, give me some eggs!" And he moved his arms as if he was going to take the eggs from me, one after the other.

Emma, one of the German girls, helped me start shoveling away the dung. As we worked, one of the hens sat down in the corner and her cackling announced that eggs were forthcoming. Several other chickens stood before her in a semicircle, as if they were admiring this solemn ritual. But as soon as an egg appeared, the onlookers would peck at it. Emma said that they had not been providing much feed for the hens, and they were hungry, and so this was what happened every day. In the middle of the barn there was a stump in place of a stool. I sent Emma to get some feed and then I got up on the stump, where I stood as still as I possibly could, turning myself into a statue. The hens did indeed take me for an inanimate object and they roosted on my shoulders and my head, dung pouring down all over me. Only my eyes moved. I watched every hen that was laying and managed to snatch at least one egg from each before the hungry hens could get to it. Then I would return to my frozen posture as a statue. On this first day I succeeded in snatching six eggs. Oh, but how dismayed I was to see what sort of eggs they were! Instead of the egg shell there was only a soft film. I took these eggs to the director and told him that even without reading any books I could see that the hens were starving and required vitamins. I could put the henhouse in order but without feed not much could be done. He hemmed and hawed and said he would think about it. Right next to the henhouse was a small, half-lit barn for the geese, which housed eighteen females and four males. The director complained that last spring none of the goslings had survived and that I was expected to "deliver him a flock."

It turned out that the problem was not with the quantity of feed. As soon as Emma brought it to the little kitchen area in front of the henhouse, women with bags in their arms appeared. But when they saw me, they scattered. The simple fact was that the hens and the geese were being robbed of their food. But you could not blame these thieves. The state farm had not been producing any sort of profit, and wages had not been paid for months. Every mother was simply trying to get grain to make a little bit of kasha for her children. Several days later I got to visit the Atamanovo State Farm. A fellow exile was in charge of the model henhouse there. He willingly showed me everything and explained what they did, then he gave me two textbooks to read. Now I could get down to work. My assistants and I put both the henhouse and the little kitchen area in order. I insisted that carpenters construct experimental nests for the hens that would protect the laying bird—wooden boxes with folding doors that would slam shut as soon as the laying hen entered to roost. The hen could not turn around in the nest and I could always get the egg she had laid. Thirty such nests were built and they ran along the wall contiguously, forming a solid cabinet. I made sure that each hen got her feed without it being snatched away, and the birds began to revive. They started laying eggs with fully formed shells and their number grew with each day.

The geese were a more complicated matter. I had to tag them and then put the corresponding number on the eggs. Emma's father thankfully was a jack of all trades. He made eighteen metal bands with numbers on each and fastened them himself on the feet of the geese. The geese had also not been averse to feeding on the eggs that were laid. Each of them had their own basket for laying eggs. I would not leave until I had in my possession a large warm goose egg and I had put a number on it. I held on to these eggs until one or another of the mother geese stopped laying, then began to fluff out feathers from her abdomen and lay them down in the bottom of the basket. I would place the eggs she had laid into the ready-made nest and she would anxiously sit down on top of them. Out of the eighteen female geese, fifteen sat on their eggs. For the first time in my life, I observed these remarkable birds and their daily patterns. There was one pair which were white with black heads. I designated them the king and queen. She sat regally on her eggs, and he would not leave her side. Sometimes they exchanged delicate moans.

Warm spring days arrived. I opened the doors of the goose pen to let the sitting birds walk around a bit. They knew this was good for them. They plucked out feathers, covered the eggs they had laid and hurried over to the nearby pond. They swam about, washed themselves, poked about in the silt, and then returned and sat stock-still on their nests until the next day. When the "queen" went out for a walk, the "king" remained on the nest until she returned. Only then did he go himself to have a swim. I went to a lot of trouble to facilitate the birth of new goslings. Up until now they had been so weak that they could not break through the thick eggshell. I had to help with this and immediately placed them directly from the egg shell into a basket lined with cotton. Thus it was that I became a midwife for goslings. I brought ninety-four chicks into the world. The day came for their first walk outdoors. The entire flock left the goose pen. The "royal" family kept themselves aloof, while all of the rest waited in expectation. Three ganders fought for the right to be leader. Finally the strongest one led all of them to the pond, and the two defeated geese brought up the rear.

But the most difficult challenge still awaited me. There was a Kalmyk specialist in animal sciences who worked at the state farm. He was an angry man who screamed at me in a shrill voice, insisting that I take the newly born goslings at dawn to a certain field where there was good grass for grazing. He yelled at me in front of the director, who listened to him approvingly. So now I had to get up at 5:00 a.m. and go out into the mist to take the geese to the meadow and allow them to wander about in the dewy grass for several hours. There was nowhere for me to sit down, and I had to do this every day during the entire summer. I would return to the state farm to get the feed, for I could not entrust this to anyone. I considered it a great blessing that the birds were inclined to bed down for the night whenever the sun set. I was not paid any money to do this. I received either millet or linseed oil, and then later I even got bitter camelina oil, which I had never heard of until now.

Trainees came to the state farm—future collective farm chairmen. The director took them around for a tour and boasted about the experimental nests in the henhouse. With the coming of fall, the director said that now my workload would be lighter and so I could help him. I was to report first thing in the morning and type long reports to the district executive committee. In them he made reference to specific line items from various orders and policy statements, demanded money, and insisted on the need for more specialists. But he pronounced the word for "line" in an incorrect way when referring to a specific order or statement: instead of saying "line such and such," he would say "date" (instead of *stroka*, line, he said "*sroka*"—genitive form of the word meaning term or date—Translator's note). I would type the correct word, "*stroka*," but once, when I was typing, he noticed that I had added the letter "t," which he had not pronounced, and he chewed me out in his earthy, native Russian. I said that I would not be treated in this way and that I could not work under such conditions. "You will not have to because I am going to kick you out—you are obviously a saboteur, you are changing my words." That very same day I got a ride in a car heading to the district center, the village of Sukhobuzino. Here lived a very nice young woman from Kharbin. She had sometimes visited us when I was living on the MGB state farm; she had met my roommate in prison. This young woman, Alechka, had been arrested as a spy. She was not even twenty years old when the authorities tore her nursing child from her breast and threw her into a camp. The child soon died in a child distribution center. I knew her address in Sukhobuzino and went to her directly. She was very happy to see me. She needed a roommate: she was renting half a house and it was difficult for her to cover all of her expenses.

Alia (diminutive for Alechka) worked in a tailoring shop and had become skilled at sewing men's pants. She worked with exceptional care and thoroughness, but did not make very much money because it took her too long to complete her quota. She earned extra money in the evenings doing private sewing. Village fashion plates ordered all sorts of needlework and Alia's clientele grew. I got a job pretty quickly in the office of the Butter Production firm. Bypassing all other institutions, I went straight to this office at the end of the main village street. I approached the director's desk and said that I had experience as a statistician. He looked at me incredulously, then nodding his head at the neighboring desk where sat a typewriter, he asked, "Do you know how to use this?"

"Give me a piece of paper and judge for yourself."

I sat down at the machine and it began to rattle off like a machine gun as I typed away. The director beamed. "Show up tomorrow morning at 9 am for work." So I became not only a typist-statistician but also a cashier in the office of the Butter Production firm.

Twice a month I had to pick up money from the bank, nearly twenty thousand rubles in total, and without anyone guarding me, I had to bring it to the office in an old canvas briefcase. My heart sank into my boots: there had been cases of theft here. I had to store the money in a small iron box locked merely by the most ordinary small key. I would be so relieved when all of the foremen gathered and took their share of the money. It was very frightening to go home and just leave such large sums of money overnight without a security guard on the premises. The director proved to be an unsurpassed cad: when I asked him to hire a guard or buy a secure safe, he answered with a flowery stream of obscenities that I had not heard even in the camps. But I had to put up with it because there was no other work to be found.

Our life proceeded monotonously and with little cheer. I lived only to receive the next letter from my daughter. My Elenushka had grown up; she was now a mature young woman finishing up her studies in Italian within the Philology Department of the university. Family influence steered her in that direction. But I knew that with this degree she would not find work; I advised her to take another path, but to no avail. Letters, though, arrived very rarely. There were many exiles here, but only a few were from the intelligentsia. Two of these became our great friends. One was a talented, sympathetic doctor, who would have put both of his hands into a fire to uphold his Hippocratic Oath. He was an expert surgeon, but did not limit himself to just this specialty. At his clinic he never turned anyone away and did whatever it was that people needed him to do, whether it was delivering a baby or treating cardiac patients. He was incredibly charming, he knew literature and music very well, and he could carry on a conversation about virtually any topic. The hospital was near to our room, for we lived at the very beginning of the main road. Our good friend the doctor lived at the opposite end of the road. We would see him going into the hospital as we were getting ready for work. Sometimes, if it was late in the evening and he saw our light was on, he would knock and ask for some hot tea. We were always overjoyed to see him. We would put out on the table everything that we had at the moment. He would tell us about the difficult operations that had kept him at the hospital so late. The second dear friend that Alia and I had in our exile was a man of letters whom I had known while living in Leningrad. He worked as a poultry specialist on a local collective farm and lived in the attic above the henhouse. Sometimes we would visit him though it was difficult for us to get up the stepladder leading to his room. We did not get together with him that often, but when we did it was a happy occasion. There was also a movie theater in the district center and Alia and I did not miss a single film that was interesting. We particularly made an effort to see the films adapted from theatrical plays. I was deeply grateful for such films as *Dance Teacher*,[3] *School of Scandal*,[4] and those based on plays of Anton Chekhov and Alexander Ostrovsky. These were my substitutes for the theater. Our quiet life was disrupted twice a month, when we, the so-called free people, were obligated to report to the local police commandant. There they were rude and routinely tried to extort information, sometimes by threatening us.

In 1952, my daughter informed me that she was getting married. Our correspondence perked up as I asked her an endless stream of questions. I learned that her husband-to-be was a physicist, very intelligent and a good man. I asked my friend Alia to turn down all of her private orders and focus her attention on sewing presents for my daughter. She embroidered a large tablecloth, made patterns for lovely blouses and men's shirts, and sewed divan pillows. These gifts were a success. I soon learned that my daughter was pregnant. This put me into a state of constant fear, especially when my daughter wrote to me about unbearable nausea, vomiting, and her aversions to various foods. Then a letter came that was more happy: she had felt the baby move, bleeding had begun, but then it had stopped, and now she was no longer feeling nauseated.

I showed this letter to our doctor friend. He thought about it and then said, "There is something here that bothers me ..." The next letter brought the news that my daughter had suffered a miscarriage, but that the doctors did not want to intervene surgically to remove the fetus. I rushed to see my friend and when he read the letter he said: "Telegraph them that they must not let her carry the fetus; they must do surgery." But my letters and telegrams were useless. My daughter responded that the doctors in Leningrad certainly knew as much as the doctors in a remote Siberian village, there was nothing to worry about, everything was going to be fine. Unfortunately, matters did not turn out as well as she predicted. Several months later, she had to have her labor induced, and only after two days did they remove the fetus. The Otto Gynecological Institute's clinic thereupon discharged her as though she were perfectly healthy.

The year 1953 came. Living through the "Doctors' Plot"[5] was stressful. We not only felt terrible for the innocent victims of this anti-Semitic campaign but were also afraid for ourselves. Alia was the only one in our circle who was not Jewish. People immediately began looking at me and our two friends, the doctor and the poultry man, with suspicion and ill will. At one point, a policeman suffered frostbite and our doctor friend had to amputate two of his toes. The authorities demanded to be admitted into the operating room, since "this Jew might just cut off his whole leg." Our friend only found out about this later from the head doctor, because in the end they did not post anyone to observe the operation. The death of Stalin in March, though, saved the doctors implicated in the Doctors' Plot. The entire village and settlement was plunged into mourning; everything that was red (the official Communist Party color— Translator's note) now had black added to it. We felt as if we were being watched. Time passed. Rumors circulated that cases were being reexamined and that some of the exiled were preparing to go home. Then, however, they began to release people even without any judicial review. Our settlement got its turn as well. We saw our friends off, then Alia saw me off, and soon she too got to leave and return to Moscow.

Elena, her new husband, and my sister-in-law met me at the station. I greeted my son-in-law very cordially, but could not help thinking to myself: "He is not the type of husband I had wanted for my daughter." He lacked a man's strength of character, and his face revealed a weak will. But they loved one another and were happy. When we arrived home, Elena led me into a room or, more accurately, into a section of her uncle's study partitioned off by books. I had not even managed to take off my coat before my daughter blurted out hurriedly: "Mama dear, I must warn you: Aunt has a serious form of angina pectoris. She mustn't be upset; there is no cure and we have to protect her." After dinner my sister-in-law said: "We have already determined what you will do next: we will rent you a room privately, buy you a typewriter, and provide you with clients. In your situation you cannot count on getting a job. You will have to work for yourself." I was stunned. Typing at the moment was very difficult for me.

I was 56 years old, and when I sat for a long stretch my lower back ached, and at night I suffered from leg cramps. I had hoped to relax for a bit at first, spend time with old friends, and then think about what I would do: maybe proofreading or editing.

But, angina pectoris …. We must take care of our Aunt …

I responded with gratitude. "Yes, this a way forward for me. But I still have a black mark against me in all cities. No one is going to register me to live in Leningrad." My sister-in-law then announced that they would find a place where I could register. They would also pay for my registration and for me to rent a room here in Leningrad. So I was registered in the village of Volosovo, where I went once a month to pay my money. I was able to find a room on Maiorov Avenue. This is when my hard labor (*katorga*) began. The clients my in-laws sent me were professors, some even corresponding members of the Academy of Sciences, and they were very demanding. In addition to manuscripts they loaded me down with books, sometimes very heavy ones, from which I had to copy out entire pages. It was difficult for me to climb up on to the streetcar loaded down with these books, manuscripts, and files of paper. Such assignments always had a quick turnaround time. I had to type until two or three o'clock in the morning and then take it to the person who had ordered it at the precise time that had been designated and, of course, with all of the materials and books in tow.

I liked my work and the number of my clients grew in number. But there was no way that I could even think about taking a break, let alone any extended vacation. I took a half-hour for lunch at a nearby cafeteria and the remaining time I worked, worked, worked …. My daughter phoned, but rarely visited me. When my son-in-law's office missed all of its deadlines and then had to have an article finished by the next day, the two of them would come and sit with me while I typed it. Both of them were working. My daughter taught literature at a school in Leningrad. They would have supper and then come to me no earlier than 10:00 p.m. My daughter, obviously trying to hearten me, would say, "Mummy always rescues us." What else could I do to help them? They received much from my sister-in-law, who loaded this young family with unending gifts. Her sister who lived in Paris was able to send fabulous packages. They had the finest clothing, several subscriptions to the symphony, and they frequently dined with Elena's aunt and uncle. On top of everything else, they received from them a thousand rubles a month just so they would not suffer any hardships.

There I was without a penny to my name, a person who by some miracle had survived my arrest. Still I was a mother and as a mother, I had to find ways to help them in their time of need. But I felt distressed. Sometimes I would go out for a breath of fresh air before going to sleep. I looked with envy at the lighted windows on my street and thought of how there were families living there, people connected by love and by warmth. I often thought that I had been happier in the camps. What had enabled me to survive all of the horrors was my hope of being reunited with my daughter. After all of our meetings while I was in the camps I never doubted that we would again be close, that we would be genuine friends once more. Now I had nothing to look forward to, and I felt a great emptiness inside of me. Yes, even in my beloved Leningrad, I felt a great void. My old friends were less fearful of me now, but nothing remained of our former relations. My in-laws did not invite me to family holidays, though their dates were imprinted in my memory. At best, they would invite me for a different day and offer me what was left of the food. Yes, time had worked against me, and nothing would ever be the same.

Even before I had left the Krasnoiarsk region, I had petitioned several times to have Izya's and my cases reexamined. After my release, I had traveled to Leningrad through Moscow, where I got off the train for several hours in order to speak with someone at the office of the Military Procuracy.[6] They received me there quite cordially and their manner suggested that I could expect good results. But then came the terrible day when I received a phone call from my in-laws asking me to come to their apartment as soon as possible. Elena was also there. Her aunt handed me a letter that stated my case had been reexamined and the sentence remained in force. "It is clear that you did something wrong," my sister-in-law said, "they are rehabilitating everyone now." I could barely stand. "Mama dear, we are just leaving. Come out with us. We have to go and get measured," my daughter said. So these two prosperous ladies headed to a seamstress' shop, but I did not know where to go. I walked along Nevskii Prospekt, then turned onto Karavannaia, where I saw a poster for the film *Snow White and the Seven Dwarfs*.[7] I bought a ticket, and this charming film calmed my nerves. I knew that I had not done anything wrong. I also knew that I had to take action and pack my suitcase for a trip to Moscow. And that is what I did.

First of all I went straight to the investigator who supposedly had reexamined my case. I asked him, "Seriously, if you reexamined my case, then how could you possibly believe that I killed Yezhov? Why must that point 8 (of Article 58) be hung around my neck?"

"In this office, I am the only one who asks the questions," he answered in that rigid, unyielding tone so familiar to me. I started to interject but he simply stated "Your case has been reexamined, the sentence stands. Is that clear?" Then he showed me the door with a nod of his chin.

This left me my one last resort I had hoped not to use. I had to appeal to my old friends for help, those who were now deputies to the Supreme Soviet. I went to see the writer Ilya Ehrenburg, after speaking first on the telephone to Liuba, his wife. She greeted me in a very friendly manner, but I felt immediately that she sought to keep a definite distance between us. There could be no talk of our old friendship. She suggested that I wait in the living room. Ehrenburg was busy at the moment. She put a bunch of dark grapes on the table and left the room but I left them untouched. I walked along the wall and admired the drawings of Picasso hung there. Finally I was summoned. I told Ilya Grigorevich about my recent trouble.

He laughed bitterly and said,

What is happening is that Molotov and his comrades are frightened by the growing number of rehabilitated prisoners. They had not expected so many and have given orders to be more selective. You are not the first to be denied. It is clear that they are simply not rehabilitating those people whom no one makes a fuss about. But I will write in your behalf.

He jotted down the information he needed. I thanked him and then left. Liuba met me in the doorway with my coat and hat, and offered to drive me where I needed to go. In the car, I asked her when she had last seen Konstantin Mikhailovich. Her response devastated me:

> You mean that you do not know what happened? He killed himself. It was an altogether strange affair. It happened back in 1939;[8] the Germans had just taken over Paris. We were awaiting departure for Moscow and ran into Konstantin Mikhailovich near our embassy. He lived close by and invited us back to his attic place. He treated us to a sumptuous supper. We thought that you were dead. Before we had come to Paris, Olga Forsh had told us that you had been shot. So we told Konstantin Mikhailovich what we had heard. Then the next day we learned that he had killed himself with carbon monoxide.

Even now I cannot come to terms with his tragic death. Of course he could not forgive himself for having let me go, and of course he thought that I had been targeted because I had lived abroad for so long. But I was still alive, and he was not. I was so grief-stricken that I could not go that day and see Samuil Marshak. It had to wait till the next day. Marshak gave me a book of sonnets with a sweet inscription, and he wrote on a large sheet of paper my character reference, which he addressed, as I had requested, to the USSR Military Collegium. He gave it to me and said that he would undoubtedly lose it if it were left in his hands. The next visit was to Konstantin Fedin. He did not receive me at his home, but at his Supreme Soviet deputy's office. He had known from the Serapions about my imprisonment and exile. He did not ask me about anything; he just smiled in a friendly manner and repeated several times: "Aguti, Aguti, Aguti …." He spoke this name with his inherent artistry, as if wanting to revive in my memory a time long since passed. My mind, however, was elsewhere, and I briefly explained to him about the catastrophe that had again engulfed me. I told him that I had been to see Marshak and Ehrenburg, and I wanted to ask him in his capacity as a deputy also to plead for my rehabilitation. He wrote down what I dictated, to whom and where it had to be sent, and then I left. I made it to the Military Collegium's public prosecutor's office just at the very end of the reception period. A plump, round-faced colonel brought me into his office (whom I christened "Mr. Pickwick"). I told him what I had been accused of, how long I was imprisoned, and I showed him the notice about my sentence being correct. He screwed up his eyes and slyly asked me, "And why on earth didn't you kill him?"—and then he laughed.

"Maybe because I was at that time 480 kilometers from Arkhangelsk, on the shore of the frozen Dvina River …."

"Alright, yes, we will look into this."

I put on his desk the reference given me by Marshak. "Aha," he said, "who else is going to write a reference for you?" I gave the names of Ehrenburg and Fedin. "Are you also a writer," he asked. "No," I said, "they are just old friends." He wrote several words on a sheet from a notepad, handed it to me, saying, "Have them send it directly to this address, and to my name." At the station I sent a letter to Ehrenburg and Fedin with the address he had written down. The next morning I sat down again at my typewriter and typed out a petition addressed to "Mr. Pickwick" about my husband, whom a military court had convicted of taking part in the murder of Kirov and sentenced to ten years. I asked for my husband to be rehabilitated, who, most likely, was no longer alive. The cheerful and kindly face of "Pickwick" had made me feel optimistic. I had no doubt that he was one of those who opposed Molotov's faction. I was hopeful.

The following Sunday, when I was dining, as was the custom, at my sister-in-law's apartment on Nevskii, I told them about my trip to Moscow. Lenochka was upset. "Mummy, why didn't you let me know that you were going, and when you returned why did you not call?!" I said since she had not phoned these last three days, I figured she was busy. My sister-in-law interrupted our conversation. "Well, may God grant you this. But I doubt that Izya will be rehabilitated. He was up to something, he went so many times to Moscow ..." I said nothing. I knew that Izya and his sister-in-law had not cared for one another. After supper Elena and her husband set off to a concert, Izya's brother went off to his study, and my sister-in-law and I were left alone together, just the two of us. She noticed that I was not in a good mood and so she decided to lift my spirits: "You know that I have a weak heart. I have made out my will, and I want you to know that I am leaving to you all of the photographs of Lenochka." I could barely restrain my laughter. I knew all of these photographs; I had copies of all of them. Elena had sent all of the new photographs to me while I was in the camps and in exile.

In the same building as my brother and sister-in-law's apartment on Nevskii Prospekt was a large consignment shop. One day I went there and bought a suit and a dress for myself. I took it upstairs to their apartment because I knew that Elena was there. I modeled the jacket in front of their large antique mirror, but my daughter thought that it needed alteration. But where could I get this done, I wondered? She and her aunt had a good seamstress for alterations, but she seemed hesitant to suggest this. Then, on some pretext or another, my daughter led me into a room at the other end of the apartment and said to me, "Mummy dear, I can take you to her now, but I am going to have to introduce you to her as my aunt, because she thinks auntie is my mother." I said it was alright and I went with her. The seamstress was a sweet elderly woman who cried out the moment she lay eyes on me: "Elena, look at this, you look so much more like your aunt than your mother! You do not look a thing like your mother ..." Elena turned beet red, but I just said calmly that yes, that happens sometimes. As we went down the staircase, Elena spoke to me with tears in her eyes: "Forgive me, mummy, but what could I do? Aunt is so jealous, and she has done so much for me!" But I understood it all; I was like that biblical mother who would rather give up her child and keep her whole, than to have her cut in two.

Two months passed, and I was summoned to Moscow. I stayed with my cousin Sarra and her daughter Nina. They treated me like family. This time I was in Moscow for an extended period of time, for I had a lot of running around to do. First off, I picked up the posthumous rehabilitation of my husband. Before my departure, while still in Leningrad, I had received a document informing me of Izya's death; on it was written the following: "Diagnosis—heart attack. The place of death is unknown." Still to this day I do not know how in the world they dreamed up that diagnosis. Ten days later I received my rehabilitation, and even without my having requested it, they rehabilitated me for my time in exile as the wife of a repressed person. They promised to send it to me in Leningrad. Above all, what made me the happiest was that Elena now had a completely clean record. She was a graduate student at the university and it was frequently brought up to me in the apartment on Nevskii that having parents who had been repressed was an impediment to a child's career. Elena was very happy, and she began to drop in more frequently to see me and together we began making plans for my new life.

I was supposed to receive compensation for our confiscated possessions and housing. All of this, though, took a lot of time and energy to accomplish. They had readily enough exiled me out of Leningrad as the wife of someone repressed, but when it came time to compensate me for our confiscated library of books and all of our possessions, they demanded that I show proof of our marriage. To do this I had to stand in line at the People's Court and present witnesses to confirm that we had been genuinely married. Eventually I received a room in my most favorite section of the city, not far from Mokhovaia, where so long ago my Petersburg life had begun. The compensation I received allowed me to buy what I needed, but I still had to keep working. I did, however, stop typing for the "elite" academic clients; I took on instead new, younger clients—graduate students, diplomats, archeologists, and physicists. New friends came into my life, whom I enjoyed spending time with, and every year my lovely friend Mary came from Chelyabinsk to visit. Our friendship had remained strong through all the years. I often went to the Leningrad Philharmonia for concerts and to the Capella for choir performances. I would walk to the concerts along my beloved old bridges, past the Engineer's Castle (also known as St. Michael's Castle, across from the Summer Garden and the Field of Mars—Translator's note). Sometimes I met Elena and her husband there. I would be lost in my admiration of Elena; she was tall and shapely, with hair of gold and stunning in her open black velvet dress. Even without any makeup at all, she was easily the most beautiful woman present.

Then, during the winter of 1956, Elena fell ill. At first we thought it was flu. I went to see her every day. She had a slight cough, but it was not the type of cough that you get from the flu. After a week she recovered enough to return to work, yet she frequently complained of exhaustion and seemed uncharacteristically lethargic. Suspecting she might be pregnant, I began to ask if she had been having regular periods. "You know, mama, something strange has been going on. I also have thought sometimes that I was finally pregnant again, but then it turns out that I am not, and this has happened several times this year."

"Do you mean that you are not having your regular cycle?" I asked.

"No, I am often late by two or three weeks, and sometimes by a month" was her response.

"This is not good. Let me take you to see Professor Figurnov.[9] It is hard to get in to see him, but Totia Orbela can help us. She is very good friends with him. There is no finer gynecologist in the city than he."

"Mama, what are you talking about? Are you suggesting we go behind aunt's back? She would never forgive me. Moreover, I already know that she does not like this particular doctor."

"So we simply will not tell her!"

She remonstrated with me, "How can we hide such a thing from aunt? What if he gives me a prescription will we also not tell her about that?"
I could not breach that wall.

My older brother Grisha got in touch with me. I had thought that he had died in Odessa during the war, but even before the war he had been arrested and sent North to a camp. After his release he had stayed on in the city of Pechora and remarried. Each summer he went to Odessa for vacation, and there he learned from relatives who had heard from our cousin Sarra that I was alive. On his way home he stopped off to visit Sarra and got my address from her. He invited me to come for a visit, and so at the beginning of the summer of 1957, I went to Pechora. Elena and her husband were going to spend the summer in Estonia, in the town of Elva. Her aunt had rented a luxurious dacha there.

But I did not like being with my brother's family, nor did I care for Pechora. My brother was in his seventies and his family situation was not a happy one. After his release from the camps, he suffered from loneliness; his first wife had died during the evacuation in wartime, and his son was living in Western Ukraine. He visited them from time to time, but he never felt welcome. His friends in Pechora arranged for him a match with an awful woman—she was an uncultured, malicious peasant woman and an alcoholic as well. She greeted me, as one might say, "with her teeth bared." It irritated her that I had brought my brother two bottles of light Hungarian wine, along with the olives, khalva, and other delicacies we had loved when we were kids. "Why throw your money away on all this rubbish; you could have just bought us Russian vodka," she sputtered venomously. My brother lived in the area once encompassed by his former camp. All one could see were endless lines of shacks, sheds, and basically former barracks that now served as dormitories. Across from each building, about ten steps away, there stood a wooden outhouse. In the evenings, dogs roamed about, and drunks howled disgracefully into the night. There was nowhere to go. I could not believe that this was how I was spending my first summer vacation since our trip to Poltava in 1936. My brother's wife made me feel as if I were back in the camps again. In despair I wrote to Lenochka and asked her if she could possibly look around for a place that I could rent in Elva. I not only could not relax here in Pechora, but I was completely exhausted and fed up. On the very same day I also wrote to my friend Mary, who was visiting a cousin in Leningrad.

It was my sister-in-law who sent me a response from Elva. She wrote that it made no sense to come to Elva. It was impossible to find a room, there were hardly any outdoor markets, and one had to rise at 5:00 in the morning if you wanted to buy something. Plus, the only functioning cafeteria had such a stench from the toilet that it was simply impossible to eat there. Two days later a letter came from Mary, who was also now staying in Elva. Mary had received my letter on the same day she had departed for Estonia. She and her cousin had rented a nice room and they had found a neighboring room for me, which they kindly put down a deposit on. The place was wonderful, they gushed, and the pristine cafeteria they ate in always had a favorite treat of mine, whipped cream. They urged me to come as soon as I could. My brother knew how hard it was for me to bear the company of his wife, and he drove me to the train station. Before my departure from Pechora, I had written to my sister-in-law that I had been terribly disappointed to hear about their dismal experiences in Elva, but that, fortunately, I had received a letter the next day from my friend, who painted the place in much brighter colors. I told her that my friend had managed somehow to find a room for me as well, and so soon we would be seeing each other.

The beauty of Elva took me by surprise: the woods, the lakes, the suspension bridge, the well-kept gardens, and the charming houses all reminded me of provincial nooks in France. On the eve of my departure I sent a telegram to my daughter and asked her to meet me. But she was not there when I arrived. I found out later that she was at the other end of the train greeting their dentist's family. Her aunt had found them a lovely room. Mary's dacha and my room turned out to be located on the very same street where Elena was staying. So, we did see each other soon after my arrival. My daughter seemed anxious and embarrassed. She took me by the arm and whispered to me: "Mummy, everything has worked out well … But you must understand. At the dacha everyone thinks that aunt is my mother. All of this is absurd and so hard to bear, but what am I supposed to do?"

I responded, "Nothing can be done … Something could have been done when it all began, but now it is too late. Do not worry about it. I am here with friends, and when you want to see me, you can come to me."

"No, no! You must come and see us. Aunt will be cross otherwise. You mustn't talk like this! Our dacha is only three places down from you, don't you see!" I assured her that I knew very well where their dacha was, since I had written to her there and thus knew which number the building was.

My time with Mary and her charming daughter, who was three years older than Elena, was a genuine holiday for me. I had only been able to dream of such a vacation since returning from exile to Leningrad. I was surrounded by individuals who were worried about me and who fussed over me. Mary cooked hot meals for me. I had to work hard to convince her to let me share the costs. She was fully prepared to treat me for the entire month. A couple of teachers were staying at the neighboring dacha, and they were friendly and intelligent. We became friends and enjoyed many interesting walks and excursions together. Of course, since we were staying on the same street, we inevitably ran into Elena, her husband, and her "parents." We would all stop, converse in a friendly way, and then disperse in different directions. Elena sometimes would drop by for a few minutes, and I visited them, though not on anything approaching a daily basis. I could tell that Mary was outraged by this situation. But she was extremely tactful and spared me her feelings about it. Elena was remarkably healthy that summer. She often played ping-pong on a lawn near our dacha. I admired her from afar, hidden behind the shrubs of our garden. The month of August flew by. Elena had to be back in Leningrad for the beginning of the school year. She whispered with her aunt for a long time on the platform, while I stood off to the side. After the second whistle she ran up to me, kissed me on the cheek, and then jumped on to the train. She stood next to her husband at an open window, and I could see how her eyes beamed. But I was surprised to see how pale her lips were. Why on such a hot day did this healthy young woman have such pale lips?

I spent two days more in Elva and then went for three days to Tallin. How was it possible that I had lived in Leningrad without knowing that such a wonderful place existed and was so nearby! I walked along its narrow, medieval streets, visited all of its museums, and frequented its tiny cafes, where they sold incredible coffee, whipped cream, and sweet rolls. I flew home in an airplane, and that same evening Elena called up to me through my open window. She and her husband had come to see whether I had returned. I served them tea but I could not take my eyes off of my daughter's face. She noticed this and asked why I was looking at her in this way. I replied, "I am looking at your lips." "Yes, I know, I also have noticed that my lips resemble a dead person's." I pulled down her lower eyelid and saw that it too was bloodless. I turned to her husband and told him to not let Elena go to work the next day. "You must take her to the clinic to get a blood test. This is very serious. You must do this immediately." But he just looked at me fearfully. Elena tried to turn all of this into a joke, and they left soon afterward. Early in the morning a telephone call awoke me. It was my son-in-law speaking. "Come to us at once! Elena cannot stand up. It is urgent. Her hemoglobin is 23. The regular doctor has to come and see her in order to get her admitted to the hospital."

I do not have the strength nor the time to describe the six months of suffering and torment that followed this. Blood transfusions over the course of two to three days revived her, but then everything reversed. For a long time they could not diagnose her condition. In the hospital they discovered a pulmonary infiltration on her lungs. Her aunt was outraged. "How can she have an infiltration on her lungs? Elena has not been coughing." As a teacher, every year Elena had to get chest x-rays done. I went immediately to the lab and ordered copies of my daughter's x-rays for the past three years. On each one of them you could see a dark spot at the top of the left lung. Back in 1952 when she was at the Otto clinic, where they had done a blood test on her, it had been determined that she was RH-negative.[10] I, however, was not able to speak with the physicians. Sparing no expense, Elena's aunt had summoned doctors for a consultation, but I was not permitted to participate. My sister-in-law was considered to be her mother. I spoke about Elena's condition to a new friend of mine who was a biologist. She said that we needed to check her urine for prolan levels.[11] I brought to her laboratory a urine sample and white mice. They conducted an experiment but did not get positive results.

Lenochka's condition worsened day by day. I asked Totia Orbela to set up an appointment for me with Dr. Figurnov. He met with me and I told him everything that I knew. He said that it was necessary to test again for prolan levels, and he sent me to the laboratory. The next day I showed up there and they told me when to come back for the results. I stood on the iron staircase of the old building of the Military-Medical Academy and waited for the answer. I was trembling with fear. The department head called me in and, without looking me straight in the eye, spoke carefully to me. "I do not want to alarm you prematurely, but there is reason to propose that this could be chorionepithelioma."[12] I told the family about this. None of us had heard this term "chorionepithelioma" before, and it meant nothing to us. But my daughter was scheduled for an exploratory diagnostic operation. At home I phoned my dear friend the physician, with whom I had shared my Krasnoiarsk exile. He was living and working in Moscow. I asked him whether he knew what "chorionepithelioma" was. He replied, "Of course I know what it is, but I cannot bear to hear this. It is inconceivable." From my letters he knew that my daughter was in the hospital. His anxious tone sounded ominous. I knew nothing about this condition, so I went to the Public Library and read an article in a medical dictionary. Now I understood what he meant: this was worse than cancer. Back in 1952 a piece of placenta from the miscarried pregnancy had settled in my daughter's lung, multiplied there, and gradually metastasized through all of her organs. The operation to remove it lasted more than four hours. The surgeons came out gloomy. In response to the persistent, imploring look on my face, the surgeon said: "If only we could have gotten to it one year earlier ..."

The period after the operation was frightening. The nurses were on duty twenty-four hours. Specialists were called in, but Elena's condition just worsened. I rose at dawn and prepared mousses and creams that were easy for her to swallow. At 6:00 in the morning, her husband would come by, not even bothering to phone first, for he knew that right at this appointed time I would open the door for him and give him the package of food for Elena. He would take Elena her breakfast, and then I would take lunch to her and stay until her husband came to the hospital after work. I could always tell from Elena's face that he had arrived, for I sat with my back to the door. Upon seeing him, Elena's face would break out into a smile and her eyes would light up. When I was at home I occupied myself with my work. Although my sister-in-law bore the lion's share of the expenses, I nonetheless needed money to buy fruits and to shove three-ruble notes into the pockets of all of the nurses. This catastrophe brought me and Elena's aunt closer together. No one was keeping tabs on maternal rights when our daughter was dying right before our eyes.

The fateful day of March 10, 1958 came. I brought lunch a little earlier than usual. I met a nurse in the corridor, and she told me that Elena had suffered through a bad night. The doctor came into the ward, took her pulse, gave her an injection, and, without looking at me, left the room. I examined her face. God help me, I had had so much experience with death. I phoned my son-in-law, for he was at home that day. I told him that he had to come. But he was so frightened that he did not come directly, but took the long way to the hospital. He did not arrive for nearly an hour, though he lived nearby. I was sitting at her bedside, holding on to my Elenushka's hand, and not letting go. My brother and sister-in-law sat at the foot of the bed. When she began to breathe abnormally (Cheyne–Stokes respiration had begun, a sign of heart failure— Translator's note), they all started fussing about, calling the nurse and demanding that she give Elena an injection. I did not stir, for I knew what this pattern of breathing meant ...

Afterward, friends and acquaintances kept streaming into the apartment on Nevskii to express their condolences to my sister-in-law. To them, she had lost a daughter. I felt rather superfluous in that setting. But it did not matter, for I had little need of their condolences. I found myself drawn there only because this had been where my daughter had spent her schooldays and where she had gone to university. I let go of my resentment and forgot all of the hurt I felt. I was grateful to these people because they had not been afraid during that terrible time to take my daughter as their own. They had made her short life so happy. My friends dragged me out to the symphony and to the ballet, and I did not say no. My soul was in mourning and will be so until I draw my last breath. But life goes on, and there is no point in just lying limp.

Matvei Aleksandrovich Gukovskii,[13] whom I did a lot of typing for, arranged for me to spend my summer vacation in Estonia, in Pärnu. His wife's sister lived there in a small individual apartment, but spent the summer with the Gukovskii family outside of Leningrad. I went and thus began my new life. I would work with all of my energy for nine months of the year in order to travel for three months to new places. All three of the Baltic states, the Carpathians, my own native Black Sea at the outskirts of Odessa, Karelia, Ladoga, voyages down the Volga to Astrakhan and to Perm—I have been to so many places! Voyages by steamer took two to three weeks. I spent the rest of my time in picturesque locations, always alone, and I roamed along lakes and rivers or entered deep into unknown forests with the fervor of a path-breaking explorer. Once, while roaming near Sortavala, I stumbled upon driftwood, smoothly polished by the waves of Lake Ladoga, which resembled the head of a dog. So I began to look more closely at everything I encountered, and each fall I returned with similar "booty."

Until I reached old age, I never tired, and my daily long walks were all that brought me joy. I worked heartily and energetically through the fall and winter, then in the spring my spirit and strength would flag, but I would fortify myself with the thought of the coming summer vacation. The thought often crossed my mind that fate had decided to take pity on me and I was going to enjoy an easy old age. But this was not to be so! I began to suffer tormenting pain in my eyes. Specialists congratulated me: "Fortunately, you only have *myasthenia* in your eyes. It can be much worse, you know!" and would tell me about the harsher forms of this disease. One neuropathologist assured me that the eye form of *myasthenia* never morphed into the general type, and I was glad because then I could somehow keep taking care of myself.

But now this has come to an end. The eye form has mutated into the general form. The disease is progressing.

1976.

Notes

Introduction

1   St. Petersburg was renamed Petrograd in 1914 after war was declared against Germany. The idea was to give the city a name derived from Russian rather than from German. The German suffix "burg" was replaced by the Russian "grad," both of which mean city and "Peter" was replaced by "Petr."

2   Information on Konstantin Miklachevsky and his family along with historic family photographs can be found in several online biographical sites. See the *Alexander Palace Time Machine*, Romanov, Russian History and Royalty Discussion Forum, Topics: Photos of Noble Families, http://forum.alexanderpalace.org/index.php?PHPSESSID=023fad49db6ef4722c276ec4545e057a&topic=1005.msg312295#msg312295 (accessed April 17, 2019); "Miklashevsky, Konstantin Mikhailovich," *Konstantin Vikhliaev I Iuta Arbatskaia predstavliaiut sait semeinogo tvorchestva*, http://kajuta.net/node/1027 (accessed April 12, 2019).

3   Mikhail Nikolaevich Pokrovskii (1868–1932) was a government official and public figure and the most prominent Marxist historian in Russia during the 1920s. He played a major role in shaping early Soviet academic institutions, including the Institute of Red Professors, which he headed from 1921 to 1931 and which trained the first generation of Soviet historians, economists, jurists, and so on. He was elected to the USSR Academy of Sciences in 1929. His work, which evaluated Russian imperial history through the lens of class struggle, was subsequently repudiated by the Stalinist regime, which sought to revive a more nationalist assessment of Russia's past. Pokrovskii had been critical of tsarism and downplayed the role of the individual in history, whereas Stalin was seeking to restore to prominence the unique accomplishments of such tsars as Ivan IV and Peter I. After his death he was accused by the Stalinist regime of "vulgar sociologism."

4   Isaak Moiseevich Trotsky (1903–1937) is considered to have been a very promising scholar and recently has received greater biographical attention from Russian historians. He is seen as having had an influential impact of the historiography of early Russian history and on the history of the Decembrist movement. See V. S. Brachev, "Istorik Isaak Moiseevich Trotsky (1903–1937)," *Noveishaya istoriya Rossii*, 3 (2015), 69–76, http://docplayer.ru/47257618-V-s-brachev-istorik-isaak-moiseevich-trockiy.html (accessed September 7, 2018).

5   *A History of Factories and Plants* (*Istoriia fabrik i zavodov*) was a major publishing venture launched in 1931 on the initiative of writer Maxim Gorky. It not only involved mobilizing multiple authors to write the histories of individual factories but also gathered stories and testimonies by ordinary workers throughout the Soviet Union.

6   Brachev, "Istorik Isaak Moiseevich Trotsky," 70. He taught a seminar on the Decembrists at the Leningrad Institute of Philosophy, Literature, Linguistics and History (LIFLI), which was merged with Leningrad University in the mid-1930s.

7   Brachev, "Istorik Isaak Moiseevich Trotsky," 76.

8   After the publication of Ludmila's memoir in Russia, some who knew her published accounts of their friendship with her or commented on her life. See "Pro Lyudmilu Eizengardt-Miklashevskuiu," *Livejournal*, November 4, 2009, https://taanyabars. livejournal.om/15779.html (accessed September 7, 2018); also see a biography of her written earlier, before publication of her memoir: Anatolii Ferapontov, "Zhizn' minus sorok let," *Chest' I Rodina*, 12, no. 14, July 7, 1999, http://www.memorial.krsk.ru/ Public/90/199907142.htm (accessed September 7, 2018).

9   Iakov Gordin, 'Predislovie," in Ludmila Miklashevskaia, *Povtororenie proĭdennogo* (St. Petersburg: Zhurnal Zvezda, 2012), 3. The phrase *vek-volkodav*, or "century of the wolfhound," is from a poem written by Osip Mandelshtam in 1933 in response to the horrors of Stalin's forced collectivization of the peasantry. It may have contributed to his arrest in 1934. See Igor Aleksandrovich Mel'cuk, et al., *Dependency Syntax: Theory and Practice* (Albany, NY: SUNY Press, 1988), 136.

10 The already extensive historiography of the Russian Revolutions has continued to grow with the one-hundredth anniversary in 2017. For insight into the events of 1917, among the many excellent studies to consult are Rex Wade, *The Russian Revolution, 1917*, 3rd ed. (Cambridge: Cambridge University Press, 2017); Sheila Fitzpatrick, *The Russian Revolution*, 4th ed. (Oxford: Oxford University Press, 2017); Sean McMeekin, *The Russian Revolution: A New History* (New York: Basic Books, 2017).

11 Neil Faulkner, "The Russian Civil War," *Military History Monthly*, 86 (November 2017), https://www.military-history.org/articles/the-russian-civil-war.htm (accessed July 30, 2018).

12 Nicholas V. Riasanovsky and Mark D. Steinberg, "The Stalinist Revolution," in *A History of Russia*, 9th ed. (Oxford: Oxford University Press, 2019), 465–81.

13 The literature on Stalin and Stalinism is vast. For recent assessments see Stephen Kotkin, *Stalin: Paradoxes of Power, 1878–1928* (New York: Penguin Press, 2014) and *Stalin: Waiting for Hitler, 1929–1941* (New York: Penguin Press, 2017); Oleg V. Khlevniuk, *Stalin: New Biography of a Dictator*, trans. Nora Seligman Favorov (New Haven, CT: Yale University Press, 2015); Robert Service, *Stalin: A Biography* (Cambridge, MA: Belknap Press, 2005); J. Arch Getty and Oleg V. Naumov, *The Road to Terror: Stalin and the Self-Destruction of the Bolsheviks, 1932–1939*, trans. Benjamin Sher (Annals of Communism Series) (New Haven, CT: Yale University Press, 2010); J. Arch Getty and Roberta T. Manning, eds., *Stalinist Terror: New Perspectives* (Cambridge: Cambridge University Press, 1993); Chris Ward, *Stalin's Russia* Second Edition (London: Hodder Education, 1999).

14 Cathy A. Frierson and Semyon S. Vilensky, *Children of the Gulag* (New Haven, CT: Yale University Press, 2010), 171; Alter L. Litvin, *Writing History in Twentieth-Century Russia: A View from within*, trans. John L. H. Keep (New York: Palgrave, 2001), 91.

15 V. S. Brachev, "Istorik Aleksandr Il'ich Malyshev (1902–1936)," *Obshchestvo, Sreda, Razvitie*, 2 (2015), 38–40, http://www.terrahumana.ru/arhiv/15_02/15_02_06.pdf (accessed September 7, 2018).

16 Brachev, "Istorik Isaak Moiseevich Trotsky," 75.

17 Litvin, *Writing History in Twentieth-Century Russia*, 90.

18 Ibid., 87–92; Riasanovsky and Steinberg, *A History of Russia*, 479; see also Kees Boterbloem, *A History of Russia and its Empire*, 2nd ed. (New York: Rowman & Littlefield, 2018), 218–20.

19 Litvin, *Writing History*, 90.

20 Oleg V. Khlevniuk, *The History of the Gulag: From Collectivization to the Great Terror*, trans. Vadim A. Staklo (New Haven: Yale University Press, 2004), 148–61.

21 Brachev, "Istorik Isaak Moiseevich Trotsky," 75.

22 See Galina Mikhailovna Ivanova, *Labor Camp Socialism: The Gulag in the Soviet Totalitarian System*, trans. Carol Flath (Armonk, NY: M.E. Sharpe, 2000), 25–32.

23 Ibid., 23 and 186–7; Khlevniuk, *The History of the Gulag*, 9–12.

24 See Ivanova, *Labor Camp Socialism*, 186–7; Litvin, *Writing History*, 86.

25 Ivanova, *Labor Camp Socialism*, 187–8; Litvin, *Writing History*, 86. Also see N. G. Okhotin and A. B. Roginsky, *Sistema Ispravitelno-Trudovikh Lagerei v SSSR, 1923–1960: Spravochnik* (Moscow: Zvenia, 2000).

26 Ivanova, *Labor Camp Socialism*, 187; Edwin Bacon, *The Gulag at War: Stalin's Forced Labour System in the Light of the Archives* (New York: New York University Press, 1994), 28–38; Anne Applebaum, *Gulag: A History* (New York: Doubleday, 2003), 291–2. Other estimates of Gulag prisoners are higher. A. N. Iakovlev, who chaired Yeltsin's commission on political rehabilitations, said that between 1923 and 1953, 42.5 million persons passed through Soviet prisons and camps. See Litvin, *Writing History*, 87–92.

27 See Litvin, *Writing History*, 93. Only established in 1938, Viatlag became one of the largest complexes of camps and prisoners in the Gulag. See V. A. Verdinskikh, *Istoriia Odnogo Lageria (Viatlag)* (Moscow: Agraf, 2001); Ekaterina Loushnikova, "Vyatlag: the Gulag then and now," Open Democracy, November 9, 2012, https:// www.opendemocracy.net/od-russia/ekaterina-loushnikova/Viatlag-gulag-then-and-now (accessed September 8, 2018); more information on Viatlag can be accessed at the website of the Memorial Society, Krasnoiarsk, at http://www.memorial.krsk.ru/eng/index.htm (accessed October 7, 2018).

28 Khlevniuk, *The History of the Gulag*, 10.

29 For a comprehensive analysis of death in the Gulag, see Golfo Alexopoulos, *Illness and Inhumanity in Stalin's Gulag* (Yale-Hoover Series on Authoritarian Regimes) (New Haven, CT: Yale University Press, 2017). As scholar Dariusz Tolczyk notes, there was never the admitted goal of annihilating prisoners, but over the years the conditions under Stalin reduced the chances of survival to a bare minimum, "often to zero." See Dariusz Tolczyk, *See No Evil: Literary Cover-Ups and Discoveries of the Soviet Camp Experience* (New Haven, CT: Yale University Press, 1999), 197.

30 Frierson and Vilensky, *Children of the Gulag*, 336.

31 See Riasanovsky and Steinberg, *A History of Russia*, 516–20.

32 Robin Bisha, et al., compilers, *Russian Women 1698-1917: Experience and Expression* (Bloomington: Indiana University Press, 2002), 11–13; Barbara Alpern Engel, *Women in Russia 1700-2000* (Cambridge: Cambridge University Press, 2004), 5.

33 By 1845, there were thirty-six schools and educational institutions for women, and the Orthodox Church began at mid-century to open up schools for the daughter of clergy. Bisha, *Russian Women*, 163.

34 Ibid., 8, 19–20, 160–1.

35 Barbara Engel, "Women, the Family and Public Life," in Dominic Lieven, ed., *The Cambridge History of Russia*, Vol. II, Imperial Russia, 1689–1917 (Cambridge: Cambridge University Press, 2006), 306–25, at 314; also see Bisha, *Russian Women*, 13 and 164.

36 In 1869 the first women's higher course institution was established in St. Petersburg, the Alarchinsky Courses, and in Moscow, the Lubianka courses.

37 Bisha, *Russian Women*, 164.

38 Engel, "Women, the Family and Public Life," 317–18.

39 Bisha, *Russian Women*, 164–5.

40 Engel, "Women, the Family, and Public Life," 314–15.

41 Bisha, *Russian Women*, 12 and 302.

42 Engel, "Women, the Family and Public Life," 322–3.

43 Ibid., 323–4.

44 Ibid., 324. Engel points out how the new consumer culture "tended to promote individual indulgence over family values."

45 Engel, *Women in Russia*, 129–31 and 135; Engel, "Women, the Family and Public Life," 319.

46 Engel, "Women, the Family and Public Life," 325.

47 *Svod Zakonov Rossiiskoi Imperii* (Collection of Laws of Imperial Russia (1914), V, pt 1, art. 107, cited in Alice Ehr-Soon Tay, "The Status of Women in the Soviet Union," *The American Journal of Comparative Law*, 20, no. 4 (Autumn 1972), 662–92, at 666.

48 Engel, "Women, the Family and Public Life," 328.

49 Engel, *Women in Russia*, 133.

50 Ibid., 134.

51 Ibid., 139; also see William G. Rosenberg and Diane P. Koenker, "The Limits of Formal Protest: Worker Activism and Social Polarization in Petrograd and Moscow, March to October 1917," *The American Historical Review*, 92, no. 2 (April 1987), 296–326, at 305.

52 There were twenty thousand women in medical service. Engel, *Women in Russia*, 141. Also see Barbara Evans Clements, "The Birth of the New Soviet Woman," in Abbott Gleason, Peter Kenez, and Richard Stites, eds., *Experiment and Order in the Russian Revolution* (Bloomington: Indiana University Press, 1985), 220–37, at 220.

53 Clements, "The Birth of the New Soviet Woman," 225–6.

54 Ehr-Soon Tay, "The Status of Women in the Soviet Union," 668.

55 Beatrice Farnsworth, "Village Women Experience the Revolution," in Gleason, Kenez, and Stites, *Bolshevik Culture*, 238–60, at 243.

56 Ehr-Soon Tay, "The Status of Women in the Soviet Union," 666.

57 Ehr-Soon Tay, "The Status of Women in the Soviet Union," 669–70; Greta Bucher, *Women, the Bureaucracy, and Daily Life in Postwar Moscow, 1945–1953* (Boulder, CO: East European Monographs, 2006), 9; Lynne Atwood, *Creating the New Soviet Woman: Women's Magazines as Engineers of Female Identity, 1922–1953* (New York: Palgrave, 1999), 42.

58 Sergei Zakharov, "Family Policy," in Irvin Studin, ed., *Russia: Strategy, Policy and Administration* (London: Palgrave Macmillan, 2018), 319–30, at 320.

59 Wendy Goldman, "Women, Abortion and the State, 1917–1936," in B. Evans Clements, B. Alpern Engel, and C. D. Worobec, eds., *Russia's Women: Accommodation, Resistance, Transformation* (Berkeley: University of California Press, 1991), 243–66, at 243; Ehr-Soon Tay, "The Status of Women in the Soviet Union," 674, Engel, *Women in Russia*, 161–2.

60 Atwood, *Creating the New Soviet Woman*, 73; Zakharov, "Family Policy," 320.

61 The quotation is from Engel, *Women in Russia*, 141–2; also see Clements, "The New Socialist Woman," 222.

62 V. I. Lenin in Karl Marx, Friedrich Engels, V. I. Lenin, and Joseph Stalin, *The Woman Question* (New York: International Publishing, 1975), 56, quoted in Mary Buckley, "Women in the Soviet Union," *Feminist Review*, no. 8 (Summer, 1981), 79–106, at 89; Alice Schuster, "Women's Role in the Soviet Union: Ideology and Reality," *The Russian Review*, 30, no. 3 (July 1971), 260–7, at 261.

63 Leon Trotsky, "From the old Family to the New," *Pravda*, July 13, 1923, quoted in Marie Frederickson," Women Before, during and after the Russian Revolution," March 10, 2017, http://www.bolshevik.info/women-before-during-and-after-the russian-revolution.htm (accessed February 20, 2019).

64 Engel, *Women in Russia*, 143.

65 Ibid., 153.

66 Ehr-Soon Tay, "The Status of Women in the Soviet Union," 662; Atwood, *Creating the New Soviet Woman*, 46.

67 Clements, "The New Soviet Woman," 221.

68 Atwood, *Creating the New Soviet Woman*, 65.

69 Buckley, "Women in the Soviet Union," 80–1.

70 Gail W. Lapidus, *Women in Soviet Society. Equality, Development and Social Change* (Los Angeles: University of California Press, 1978), 99; Buckley, "Women in the Soviet Union," 83.

71 Engel, *Women in Russia*, 210.

72 Schuster, "Ideology and Reality," 263.

73 Engel, *Women in Russia*, 164; Barbara Clements, *Bolshevik Women* (New York: Cambridge University Press, 1997), 250.

74 Engel, *Women in Russia*, 175.

75 Schuster, "Ideology and Reality," 263.

76 Atwood, *Creating the New Soviet Woman*, 104.

77 Buckley, "Women in the Soviet Union," 100.

78 Engel, *Women in Russia*, 173–4.

79 Ehr-Soon-Tay, "The Status of Women in the Soviet Union," 676.

80 Atwood, *Creating the New Soviet Woman*, 2–3.

81 Ehr-Soon Tay, "The Status of Women in the Soviet Union," 668.

82 Engel, *Women in Russia*, 182.

83 Clements, "The Birth of the New Soviet Woman," 232. Domesticity now took on a newly progressive value, rather than enslaving women; housework became "socially useful labor." See Ehr-Soon Tay, "The Status of Women in the Soviet Union," 674; Atwood, *Creating the New Soviet Woman*, 14.

84 The cost of divorce went up by the 1944 law from 500 to 2000 rubles. See Buckley, "Women in the Soviet Union," 134; Atwood, *Creating the New Soviet Woman*, 115–16.

85 Those performing abortions could face up to three years in prison; a woman having one would be "censured" and fined if it happened again. Husbands could get two years in prison for their wife's abortion. Ehr-Soon Tay, "The Status of Women in the Soviet Union," 674; Atwood, *Creating the New Soviet Woman*, 116.

86 Engel, *Women in Russia*, 181; for discussion of contraception in the Soviet Union in the 1920s and 1930s, see Goldman, "Women, Abortion and the State, 1917–1936," 243–66, especially 243–7; Atwood, *Creating the New Soviet Woman*, 45.

87 Ehr-Soon Tay, "The Status of Women in the Soviet Union," 677; Bucher, *Women, the Bureaucracy, and Daily Life*, 14–15; Buckley, "Women in the Soviet Union," 94. If you bore and raised ten or more children, you were a Heroine Mother, while mothers of seven, eight, and nine children received the Order of the Glory of Motherhood. The Motherhood Medal went to mothers of five or six children. The 1944 law as well as subsequent legislation in 1949 taxed persons based on how many children they had, coming down especially hard on small families and childless couples. See Bucher, *Women, the Bureaucracy, and Daily Life*, 13; Zakharov, "Family Policy," 321.

88 Bucher, *Women, the Bureaucracy, and Daily Life*, 52 and 59.

89 Atwood, *Creating the New Soviet Woman*, 104 and 172.

90 Soviet studies recorded women spending up to twelve hours per week preparing food, six hours shopping, and six hours doing laundry, while men spent, respectively, on these same tasks, ninety minutes, three hours, and thirty minutes. See Buckley, "Women in the Soviet Union," 93. Rural peasant women had even less access than urban women to basic health care, maternity homes, childcare facilities, and had to cook and clean without running water, indoor plumbing, and electricity. See Engel, *Women in Russia*, 172.

91 Buckley, "Women in the Soviet Union," 90.

92 Bucher, *Women, the Bureaucracy, and Daily Life*, 70.

93 Engel, *Women in Russia*, 173–5.

94 Buckley, "Women in the Soviet Union," 88.

95 Although women predominated in the medical field, over half of the chief physicians were men; similarly, 71 percent of women were teachers, but 69 percent of secondary school directors were men. Buckley, "Women in the Soviet Union," 88.

96 Buckley, "Women in the Soviet Union," 98; Ehr-Soon Tay, "The Status of Women in the Soviet Union," 682.

97 Ehr-Soon Tay, "The Status of Women in the Soviet Union," 680.

98 Buckley, "Women in the Soviet Union," 80.

99 Clements, "The Birth of the New Soviet Woman," 221; Atwood, *Creating the New Soviet Woman*, 166.

100 Atwood, *Creating the New Soviet Woman*, 126–8, 169–70.

101 Khlevniuk, *The History of the Gulag*, 147; see as well Golfo Alexopoulos, "Stalin and the Politics of Kinship: Practices of Collective Punishment, 1920s–1940s," *Comparative Studies in Society and History*, 50, no. 1 (January 2008), 91–117.

102 Emma Mason, "Women in the Gulag in the 1930s," in Melanie Ilič, ed. *Women in the Stalin Era* (London: Palgrave, 2001), 131–50, at 131–2; J. Arch Getty, Gabor T. Rittersporn, and Viktor N. Zemskov, "Victims of the Soviet Penal System in the Pre-War Years: A First Approach on the Basis of Archival Evidence," *American Historical Review*, 98, no. 4 (October 1993): 1017–49, at 1025; Getty, Rittersporn and Zemskov record women as 24 percent in 1945 but other studies show a higher percentage. For higher estimates, see Applebaum, *Gulag*, 311 and 315–16; Wilson T. Bell, "Sex, Pregnancy, and Power in the Late Stalinist Gulag," *Journal of the History of Sexuality*, 24, no. 2 (May 2015), 198–224, at 206.

103 The following year Beilis and his family emigrated to Palestine and then to the United States, where Beilis died in 1934. In 1911, the writer and public commentator V. G. Korolenko published a protest which he entitled, "To Russian Society (on the matter of the blood libel charge against Jews)." Among the eighty-two well-known writers and public figures who signed this were Alexander Blok, Maxim Gorky, Feodor Sologub, Leonid Andreev, and Viacheslav Ivanov. For more information on the case, see Robert Weinberg, *Blood Libel in Late Imperial Russia: The Ritual Murder Trial of Mendel Beilis* (Indiana-Michigan Series in Russian and East European Studies) (Bloomington: Indiana University Press, 2013).

104 See Oleg Budnitsky, *Russian Jews Between the Reds and the Whites, 1917–1920* (Philadelphia: University of Pennsylvania Press, 2012), 9–34.

105 Frierson and Vilensky, *Children of the Gulag*, 348. For more information, see Joshua Rubenstein and Vladimir P. Naumov, *Stalin's Secret Pogrom: The Postwar Inquisition of the Jewish Anti-Fascist Committee* (New Haven, CT: Yale University Press, 2001).

106 See Jonathan Brent and Vladimir P. Naumov, *Stalin's Last Crime: The Plot Against the Jewish Doctors, 1948–1953* (New York: HarperCollins, 2003).

107 Barbara Heldt, *Terrible Perfection. Women and Russian Literature* (Bloomington: Indiana University Press, 1992), 64–5; Beth Holmgren, "For the Good of the Cause: Russian Women's Autobiography in the Twentieth Century," in Toby W. Clyman and Diana Greene, eds., *Women Writers in Russian Literature* (Westport, Connecticut, London: Praeger, 1994), 127–48; see discussion in Maria Rytkönen, "Women's Histories: Autobiographical Texts by Contemporary Russian Women," *Aleksanteri Papers*, 1 (2001), 2–5, at http://www.helsinki.fi/aleksanteri/english/publications/contents/ap_1-2001.pdf (accessed August 15, 2018).

108 Heldt, *Terrible Perfection*, 102.

109 Jochen Hellbeck, *Revolution on My Mind: Writing a Diary under Stalin* (Cambridge, MA: Harvard University Press, 2006), 7–8; Rytkönen, "Women's Histories," 18; Marianne Liljeström, Arja Rosenholm, and Irina Savkina, eds., "Introduction," in *Models of Self. Russian Women's Autobiographical Texts* (Saarijärvi: Kikimora, 2000), 5–14.

110 Rytkönen, "Women's Histories," 5–6; see Beth Holmgren, *Women's Works in Stalin's Time. On Lidiia Chukovskaia and Nadezhda Mandelstam* (Bloomington: Indiana University Press, 1993).

111 In this respect Ludmila's memoir could be compared to Elena Bonner's 1994 memoir *Mothers and Daughters*; see discussion in Rytkönen, "Women's Histories," 14–15.

112 Rytkönen, "Women's Histories," 7–8; also see for extensive analysis of Gulag survivor memoir and their tropes, Leona Toker, *Return from the Archipelago: Narratives of Survivors* (Bloomington: University of Indiana Press, 2000).

113 Rytkönen, "Women's Histories," 8.

114 Brachev, "Istorik Isaak Moiseevich Trotsky," 69.

115 Gordin, "Predislovie," 4–5.

1 An Odessa Childhood

1 Alexander Sergeevich Griboedov (1795–1829) was a famous Russian poet and playwright most famous for his satirical play *Woe from Wit*, which is considered to be one of the most significant works in Russian literature. He died in 1829 in Iran while on a diplomatic posting.

2 Georgii Dziubin was the father of the poet Eduard Bagritskii (Dziubin).

3 Ludmila is probably referring to the shop of the well-known textile merchant and haberdasher, V. T. Ptashnikov. The writer Valentin Kataev recorded fond memories of going annually to Ptashnkov's shop for school uniforms and supplies. See Marjorie L. Hilton, *Selling to the Masses: Retailing in Russia, 1880–1930* (Pittsburgh, PA: University of Pittsburgh Press, 2014), 80, 151.

4 *Odesskie novosti* (The *Odessa News*) was a daily literary, commercial, and informational newspaper (1885–1917).

5 The Russo-Japanese War was fought during 1904–5 between the Russian Empire and Japan and was a product of their imperial rivalry over territory in Manchuria and Korea. It was primarily a naval conflict and after several major defeats, including the near total loss of the entire Baltic fleet, Russia had to sue for peace. The Treaty of Portsmouth called for Russia to turn over Port Arthur to Japan but did not award reparations to Japan.

6 On October 17, 1905, a tsarist manifesto granted civil liberties to the Russian population. The very next day pogroms against Jews broke out. The Odessa pogrom that lasted from October 19–22, 1905, was particularly vicious, more violent, and lasted longer than all of the preceding pogroms put together. During this time Russians, Ukrainians, and Greeks killed over 400 Jews and damaged over 1600 properties belonging to Jews. See Robert Weinberg, "The Pogrom of 1905 in Odessa," in *Pogroms: Anti-Jewish Violence in Modern Russian History*, ed. John D. Klier and Shlomo Lambroza (Cambridge: Cambridge University Press, 1992), 250–1.

7 Jewish self-defense brigades emerged in Russia as a response to the wave of pogroms that swept across the country between 1903 and 1905. In 1905 the Jewish Self-Defense included more than two thousand persons, the main organizers as well as the backbone of which were Jewish students. Butchers, cargo drivers, and craftsmen also took an active part in the self-defense movement. It was in fact in Odessa that for the first time the Jewish self-defense brigades were able to deliver a decisive repulse to perpetrators of the pogrom.

8 Aleksandr Vasil'evich Kaul'bars (1844–1925) was a baron and a general in the Calvary. In 1901 he was the assistant commander of the troops in the Odessa military district, and then in 1904 he became the commander. He served as Odessa's governor general. He died in emigration in France in 1925.

9 Lustdorf was a former German village on the shore of the Black Sea near Odessa.

10 Charles-Louis Hanon (1819–1900) was a French pianist, composer, and piano pedagogue. He was the author of instructional songs and etudes for piano. Hanon's *The Virtuoso Pianist in 60 Exercises* enjoyed widespread distribution and is still used by students worldwide.

11 A song from the repertoire of opera singer Iurii Morfessi (1882–1957). Revivals of this song were famous during the period of the First World War ("My mother loved me, she worshipped me" about the return home of a crippled soldier). The song had come out before the war and was already popular in the prewar period.

12 This romantic song was recorded for the first time in a 1912 songbook. The songwriter, Iakov Prigozhii, was a pianist and arranger for the Moscow restaurant Yar. It was a popular song throughout Russia and many versions of it were sung.

13 This is an old choral song based on games played from Easter to Petrov Day. In the song various motifs rotate from themes of labor and love to the symbolism of the ritual of transition for St. Thomas's Sunday (the first Sunday after Easter). The course of the game marks symbolically the transition of a recently married girl into the circle of married women.

14 This is the hill where in 1812 more than four thousand victims (about one-fifth of the city's population) from a Middle Eastern plague were buried. The word "*chuma*" means "plague" in Russian. It is located on Vodoprovodnaia Street. See *The Odessa Guide* (accessed September 2018), http://moscowamerican.com/odessaguide/CEM1_Plague_hill.htm.

15 To sit Shiva (the word stems from the old Hebrew word for seven) means to carry out the Judaic custom of a seven-day period of mourning following the burial. The first one is mentioned in the Book of Genesis (60:10) and was carried out by Joseph after the death of Jacob. In accordance with the Talmudic tradition, after the Great Flood the Lord mourned over the destruction of the human species for seven days. Shiva is observed by the closest relatives of the deceased and involves obedience to a series of ritual prohibitions.

16 Observations and reflections of the author regarding prostitution are at the center of Alexander Kuprin's (1870–1938) novel *Yama* (The Pit, 1915). The story is based on documentary materials, newspaper reports, and several memoirs such as, for example, *Notes of a Singer from a Café Chantant* by Z. Vorontsova.

17 Aleksander Mitrofanovich Fedorov (1868–1949) was a poet, writer of fiction, playwright, and friend of Ivan Bunin and of Alexander Kuprin, both of whom were guests at his dacha near Odessa.

18 The Sibiriakov was the first permanently functioning Russian dramatic theater, and it was established in 1903 thanks to the resources of the Odessa entrepreneur Alexander Illiadorovich Sibiriakov. Many artists and musicians from around the world performed here, such as Maria Savina, Isadora Duncan, and others. The building today houses the Odessa Academic Ukrainian Musical Drama Theater of V. Vasilko.

19 The Odessa National Academic Theater of Opera and Ballet opened in 1810. In 1873, the building was almost completely destroyed by fire and it was not until 1881 that the Venetian architects Fel'ner and Gel'mer built a new theater in its location. Within its walls, Nikolai Rimsky-Korsakov, Sergei Rachmaninoff, and Peter Tchaikovsky performed their compositions, Fedor Chaliapin and Leonid Sovinov sang, and Anna Pavlova danced.

20 Sergei Ivanovich Utochkin (1876–1916) was a pioneer in the sport of bicycle racing in Russia and was also one of the first Russian pilots.

21 The dacha of Kovalevskii was located in the suburban districts of Odessa. Several legends surround the building of this dacha, which featured a tall tower supposedly built by a merchant by the name of Kovalevskii. According to legends he committed suicide by jumping from it.

2 Growing Up during War and Revolution

1 Vladimir (in Hebrew Ze'ev Jabotinsky) Evgen'evich Zhabotinskii (1880–1940) was a journalist, writer, poet, orator, and soldier who became a prominent leader in the modern Zionist movement. He was a founder of the Jewish Self-Defense Organizations that sought to fight back against pogroms.

2 The Bestuzhev courses were one of the most prominent of the women's higher education programs established in late imperial Russia. The courses were named after the first director, Konstantin Bestuzhev-Riumin, and opened in 1878 as a privately funded institution. In 1889 with Bestuzhev-Riumin's retirement, the courses were renamed the St. Petersburg Higher Courses for Women but informally many continued to refer to them as the Bestuzhev courses.

3 Vera Vasil'evna Kholodnaia, whose maiden name was Levchenko (1893–1919), was an actress in silent films.

4 Natalia Andreevna Lisenko (1880–1969) was an actress. She performed in the Korsh Theater in Moscow and began acting in films in 1915. From 1920 onward, she acted in films abroad. She was the partner and wife of Ivan Mozzhukhin.

5 Ivan Il'ich Mozzhukhin (1889–1939) was a theater and film actor. He began acting in films in 1908. He appeared in more than one hundred films in Russia and abroad. He wrote scripts and was a poet (published in the Russian film press). He emigrated in 1920 and made films in France as well as in Hollywood under the name of Moskin. He died in Paris.

6 Ol'ga Vladimirovna Gzovskaia (1883–1962) was a theater and film actress.
7 Vladimir Vasil'evich Maksimov (1880–1937) was an actor who worked in numerous theaters including from 1919 to 1924 in the Bolshoi Dramatic Theater in Petrograd. After 1924, he was a teacher in the Leningrad Institute of Performing Arts.
8 Vitol'd Al'fonsovich Polonskii (1879–1919) was an actor in the Maly Theater until 1916. He was one of the most popular actors in prerevolutionary Russian cinema.
9 Osip Il'ich Runich was an actor in Russian silent films. He acted in several dozen films of leading directors. In 1939 Osip Runich moved to South Africa where he worked in the troupe of the Jewish Artistic Theater.
10 Francesca Bertini (1888–1985) was an actress, director, and producer.
11 Konstantin Dmitrievich Bal'mont (1867–1942) was a Symbolist poet, translator, and essayist.
12 Aleksandr Aleksandrovich Blok (1880–1921) was a Russian poet and dramatist and a leading figure in the Symbolist movement. Mysticism and musicality characterized his poetic style. He married Liubov Mendeleeva, the daughter of the famous Russian chemist Dmitry Mendeleev, and he made her famous through the poetry he wrote for her as a symbol of "Eternal Femininity."
13 Igor' Severianin, whose real name was Igor' Vasil'evich Lotaryov (Lotarev) (1887–1941), was a poet of the Silver Age. He was proclaimed the "King of Poets" in a performance at the Moscow Polytechnic Museum in 1918.
14 Rabindranath Tagore (1861–1941) was an Indian writer and public figure. He was a major figure in Bengali literature and music and in 1913 became the first non-European to win the Nobel Prize in Literature. His name is written as Rabindranath Thakur in Indian languages.
15 The Savage Division (the Caucasian Native Cavalry Division) was a cavalry division formed in 1914 by Muslim volunteers born in the Caucasus and Trans-Caucasus regions.
16 Both of these towns were north of Odessa. Zhmerinka is about 195 miles from Odessa and Berdichev about 302 miles.
17 Petr Alekseevich Kropotkin (1842–1921) was an anarchist theorist, geographer, historian, essayist, and man of letters. As a determined opponent of any form of state power, Kropotkin did not accept the concept of the dictatorship of the proletariat.
18 Aleksandr Fedorovich Kerensky (1881–1970) was a leading politician and political figure; he was a minister and then prime minister in the Provisional Government in 1917. In 1918 he went abroad to seek negotiations to organize intervention against the Bolsheviks. He lived the rest of his life in emigration and taught at Stanford University. He died in New York.
19 Consuelo and Tot were characters in the play by L. Andreev, *He Who Gets Slapped*. It premiered on October 27, 1915 in the Moscow Art Theater.
20 Vasilii Vasil'evich Rozanov (1856–1919) was a religious philosopher, literary critic, and public affairs commentator.
21 Pavel Aleksandrovich Florensky (1882–1937) was a philosopher, theologian, mathematician, and engineer. In 1910 Florensky was ordained into the priesthood. In 1933 he was arrested and convicted and from 1934 onward was a prisoner in the Solovki camp system. He was executed on December 8, 1937.
22 Elena Petrovna Blavatskaia (1831–1891) was a religious philosopher of Russian birth but whose main work was done in the United States, England, and British India. She was the founder of the Theosophical Society that was based on Indian philosophy, Hinduism, and Buddhism.

23 Annie Besant (1847–1933) was a prominent activist for women's rights, a prolific writer and orator, and a follower of Blavatskaia. She was a leading orator for the Fabian Society in Britain and for other socialist organizations. After Blavatskaia's death she headed the Theosophical Society and began to work for Indian independence in the aftermath of the First World War. She became prominent in the Indian National Congress Party and died in India.

24 Theosophy, derived from the Greek words *theos* (God) and *Sophia* (wisdom), meaning "divine wisdom," is a religious philosophical movement founded in the United States in the late nineteenth century by Russian émigré Elena Blavatskaia. There is disagreement over whether or not it should be considered a religion or a philosophy. Based largely on the writings of Blavatskaia, it blends elements drawn from multiple sources, including Neoplatonism, Hinduism, and Buddhism and posits spiritual emancipation of the soul as a primary goal of life.

25 In Dostoevsky's novel *The Devils*, the character of Nikolai Vsevolodovich Stavrogin is central to the story. He is a strong, handsome, and intelligent aristocratic landowner who exerts an extraordinary, though malicious influence over the other characters. Through the eyes of the narrator he is presented as repulsive because of the way he can manipulate his charismatic hold over people and the sadistic pleasure he derives from their torment. He is complicit in illicit acts including rape and murder.

26 Boris Vasil'evich Varneke (1874–1944) was a scholar and teacher of classical languages, a professor and historian of the theater. He taught at Odessa University.

27 Mikhail Il'lich Mandes (1866–1934) was a philologist and professor at Novorossia University. He was also one of the leading specialists on Greek source studies.

28 Evgenii Nikolaevich Shchepkin (1860–1920) was an historian. In 1897 he was appointed professor at the Prince Alexander Bezborodko Nezhin (Nizhyn) Institute. Beginning in the fall of 1903 he gave lectures at the Women's Pedagogical Courses.

29 Petr Mikhailovich Bitsilli (1879–1953) was a professor at Novorossia University and the University of Sofia, an historian and cultural theorist, literary scholar and critic, and specialist on the European Middle Ages and Renaissance. After 1920 he lived in emigration.

30 Eduard Georgievich Bagritskii, real name Dziubin (1895–1934), was a poet. He was born in Odessa to a religious Jewish family. In 1915 he began publishing his poems in Odessa literary anthologies and he became a well-known figure among the young Odessa literary mavericks of the day. From 1920 onward, Bagritskii worked in Odessa for the southern section of the Russian Telegraph Agency (Rossiiskoe telegrafnoe agentstvo, IugROSTA). He edited the literary page for the Odessa *Izvestia* newspaper.

31 Nikolai Fedorovich Baliev (1877 [other sources cite 1876 or 1886]–1936) was a theater actor and director. He helped found the Moscow Artistic Theater's "cabbage parties" [*kapustniki*], from which emerged in 1908 the basis for the satirical cabaret theater known as "the Bat." The cabaret existed until the October Revolution and then was reborn in Paris in the 1920s. "The Crooked [or the distorting] Mirror" was a satirical theater created by theater critic Aleksander Kugel, which from 1910 onward was a permanent theater with daily performances. The director of the theater was N. Evreinov. The theater existed until 1918 and then revised its work after the period of the New Economic Policy (NEP), operating from 1925 to 1931.

32 Konstantin Mikhailovich Miklachevsky (1886–1944) was a St. Petersburg actor, director, theater historian, and author of the much-talked-of book *Commedia dell'arte, or the Theater of Italian Comedy in the 16th, 17th and 18th Centuries*.

33 The play "Menekhmy," or "Bliznetsy," is known in English as "Menaechmi" and translated as *The Two Menaechmuses or The Brothers Menaechmuses*, or *Gemini, The Twins*. It was a comedy by Titus Maccius Plautus, a Roman writer believed to have lived from 250 to 184 BC. It was staged by Miklachevsky in 1919 in the Odessa Chamber Theater.

34 *Commedia dell' arte* was an early form of popular theater based on improvisation, the use of masks, and stock characters. It originated in Italy but spread throughout Europe between the sixteenth and eighteenth centuries. It was very popular in France and in England it inspired such forms of theatrical entertainment as pantomime and Punch and Judy shows.

35 Leonid Zakharovich Trauberg (1902–1990) became a well-known Soviet director and scriptwriter. He studied at the comic opera studio and worked in theater in Odessa and Leningrad. In 1919 he organized a theater-studio in Odessa, and in 1921 together with G. Kozintsev set up the Factory for Eccentric Acting (FEKS). Beginning in 1924 Leonid Trauberg worked as a director for the movie studio Lenfilm.

36 Isaak Moiseevich Trotsky (Izya) (1903–1937) was an historian. In 1924, he completed his studies at Petrograd University and in 1935 became a professor in the university's Department of History. He specialized in the history of the Novgorod Republic, as well as the history of the Decembrist Movement and the tsarist secret police.

37 Dorian Gray was the hero of a novel by Oscar Wilde, *The Portrait of Dorian Gray* (1890). He remained eternally young and handsome, while at the same time his portrait grew old, becoming increasingly deformed as a reflection of the genuine inner character of the outwardly beautiful personage depicted in the painting.

38 *Na Kanune (On the Eve)* was an émigré newspaper published in Berlin from 1922 until 1924. It was published by members of the émigré political movement known as the *Smenovekhovtsy*, who had come together through their joint work on the periodical publications entitled "Smena Vekh" (Change of Landmarks).

39 Maksimilian Aleksandrovich Voloshin (1877–1932) was a poet, critic, and artist who played a prominent role in the Symbolist Movement in Russian literature.

40 Boris Sergeevich Glagolin (1879–1948) was an actor, producer, and playwright. He worked in the People's Theater in Odessa. In 1927 he went on a theatrical tour to Germany and from there to the United States, where he stayed and became a filmmaker.

41 This was a play by G. Polianovskii devoted to the life and works of Jean-Baptist Lully (1632–1687), a famous seventeenth-century French composer and founder of French opera.

42 Konstantin's father was Mikhail Il'ich Miklashevsky (died 1917) and his mother was Olga Nikolaevna (Troitnitskaia) Miklashevsky (1852–1919).

43 Princess Tat'iana Mikhailovna Gagarina (1875–1967) was married to Prince Anatole Gagarin (1876–1954), who like Il'ia Miklachevsky was an officer in the Chevalier Guards Regiment and the son of Prince Anatole Evgeneevich Gagarin (1844–1917).

44 Il'ia Mikhailovich Miklachevsky (1877–1961) was a commander in the Chevalier Guards Regiment. In 1919 he was the commander of the second Caucasian Division of Denikin's army.

45 "The Ceremonial Meeting of the State Council" was commissioned in 1903; the session portrayed took place on May 7, 1901, on the day of the one-hundredth anniversary of the founding of the State Council. It was the largest painting done by Il'ia Repin. He completed it in 1903 with the assistance of B. M. Kustodiev and I. S.

Valerskii. The canvas, which he painted from life, was exhibited in the rotunda of the Mariinsky Palace in Petersburg, then transferred to the Museum of the Revolution, and from there in 1938 to the Russian State Museum.

46 In her manuscript, Ludmila referred to two small children, but the couple had three when they left, according to a family member: 10-year-old Nadezhda, 5-year-old Giorgi, and newborn Pavel, only several months old.

47 Vladimir Nikolaevich Davydov was the stage name for Ivan Nikolaevich Gorelov (1849–1925); he was an actor and he taught theater at the St. Petersburg Theater School.

48 *Hofmeister* was a high court rank, borrowed from German court practice by Peter the Great, with responsibilities for administering court staff and managing ceremonial functions.

49 A comedy by Lope de Vega. The play ran on the Russian stage under this specific title until 1930, when M. L. Lozinskii decided to replace this more literal translation of the title with the now standard version, *The Dog in the Manger*. The widow Quinn was the heroine of the play *The Playboy of the Western World* by the Irish playwright John Millington Synge (1871–1909).

50 Vasilii Vasil'evich Davydov (1898–1941) joined the Russian Communist Party (Bolshevik) in 1918. He was a department head in the second Section of the Red Army Intelligence Staff. He was arrested in 1938 and shot in 1941.

51 Mariia Fedorovna Andreeva, whose real name was Iurkovskaia (1868–1953), was an actress. She first went on the stage in 1886. She joined with Maxim Gorky and Alexander Blok to create the Bol'shoi Drama Theater (Petrograd, 1919), and she performed there until 1926. She was the common-law wife of the writer Maxim Gorky.

3 A New Life in Petrograd

1 Argo's real name was Abram Markovich Goldenberg (1897–1968). He was a satirical poet, playwright, and translator.

2 Natan Isaevich Altman (1889–1970) was an avant-garde artist, Cubist painter, and book illustrator. He was one of the founders of the "Jewish Society for the Promotion of Art." He took part in a number of late imperial art exhibitions, and in the 1920s worked on stage designs for various Jewish theaters. He lived in Paris between 1928 and 1936, then he returned to St. Petersburg and spent much of his remaining life working in the theater and writing about art. His 1914 portrait of the poetess Anna Akhmatova hangs in the Russian Museum in St. Petersburg.

3 Moisei Il'ich Frumkin (1878–1938) was deputy commissar for Foreign Trade.

4 The Miatlev mansion formerly belonged to the Naryshkin family and is located at 9 St. Isaac's Square. See Alexander M. Schenker, *The Bronze Horseman: Falconet's Monument to Peter the Great* (New Haven, CT: Yale University Press, 2003), 354, note 87.

5 Maria Gavrilovna Savina (1854–1915) was an actress.

6 Petr Petrovich Kriuchkov (1889–1938) was an employee of the State Security forces. He worked as Maxim Gorky's secretary for many years, and his main responsibility was to keep an eye on the writer. After Gorky's death he was accused of being involved in "harmful methods of medical treatment" leading to the death of Gorky and his son, M. A. Peshkov. He was shot in 1938.

7 Sergei Ernestovich Radlov (1892–1958) was a theatrical producer, playwright, theoretician and historian. He helped establish the theater known as the People's Comedy. During the Second World War, Radlov's theatrical troupe was taken prisoner by the Germans. Upon their repatriation to the Soviet Union, Radlov and his wife, the poetess Anna Radlova, were arrested and sent to the Gulag camps. Anna Radlova died in the Gulag, and her husband was released in 1953.

8 The comedic novel, *The Twelve Chairs*, by Odessan natives Ilf (Ilia Arnoldovich Feinsilberg) and Petrov (Evgenii Petrovich Kataev), was published in 1928 and introduced the character of Ostap Bender, inveterate trickster and conman. The plot centers on Bender and other characters trying to get ahold of jewelry that had been hidden from the Bolsheviks in one of twelve chairs from a wealthy family's dining room set.

9 Viktor Borisovich Shklovskii (1893–1984) was a writer, literary scholar, critic, film historian, and movie writer. In 1916 he helped found the "Society for the Study of the Theory of Poetic Language (OPOYAZ)."

10 Valentina Mikhailovna Khodasevich (1894–1970) was a painter, watercolorist, and decorative artist. She designed stage sets for the theater.

11 Ivan Ivanovich Manukhin (1882–1958) was Maxim Gorky's personal physician and had a private practice in St. Petersburg.

12 Jules Verne (1828–1905) was a French writer of many popular and now classic stories such as *Twenty Thousand Leagues under the Sea* and *Around the World in Eighty Days*. Mayne Reed (1818–1883) was an English writer and author of adventure novels.

13 Gustav Emar (1818–1883) was a French writer and author of adventure novels.

14 Lidia Alekseevna Charskaya (1875–1937) was a children's writer. Her real name was Lidia Alekseevna Churilova, and her maiden name was Voronova.

15 Dmitry Sergeevich Merezhkovskii (1866–1941) was a novelist, poet, critic, and religious philosopher. He is considered to be a cofounder of the Russian Symbolist movement. He was married to the Russian poetess Zinaida Gippius and with her went into exile after 1917. For his prolific output of novels, plays, poetry, and essays he was nominated for the Nobel Prize in Literature nine times but never won. He died in Paris in 1941.

16 Maria Valentinova Chaliapina, maiden name Pittsol'd. She was the wife of Feodor Chaliapin.

17 "The Last Bourgeois" (also known as "A Museum of the Old Order") was an agit-satire (meaning agitational satire, a satirical story infused with topical political meaning, with the purpose of political education for the mass audience) written by K. Miklachevsky and staged in the open air at the Zoological Garden in the summer of 1920.

18 George Delvari, whose real name was Georgii Il'ich Kruchinskii, was a circus artist, clown, and acrobat. From 1920 to 1922 he worked in the People's Comedy theater in Petrograd.

19 The play "The Bedbug" (*Klop*) was a comedy by Vladimir Mayakovsky (1928). The play was staged at the Meyerhold State Theater. The director was Vsevolod Meyerhold and the musical score was done by Dmitri Shostakovich. "The Bedbug" is a satire on Soviet bureaucracy and the philistine main character leads a bourgeois life while on the surface adhering to Soviet maxims.

20 *Samogon* is a Russian version of moonshine, an alcoholic drink distilled from a variety of ingredients including grains, corn, beetroot, and potatoes. It appeared as early as the thirteenth century, predating vodka, but has been considered illegal

throughout much of its history. Some types of *samogon* can be deadly if made from such toxic ingredients as methanol or car radiator fluids. See Tom Burton, "Of Russian Origin: Samogon," *RT Russapedia*, https://russiapedia.rt.com/of-russian-origin/samogon/ (accessed April 18, 2019).

21 Maxim Alekseevich Peshkov (1897–1934) was the son of E. P. Peshkova and Maxim Gorky.

22 Maria Ignat'evna Benkendorf (1892–1974), also known as Moura Budberg, Countess Benkendorf, and Baroness Budberg. Her maiden name was Zakrevskaia, and she was first married to Count Johann von Benkendorf and then briefly to Baron Nikolai von Budberg-Bönningshausen. She was the personal secretary and mistress (some sources refer to her as his common-law wife) of Maxim Gorky. She became the mistress of H. G. Wells in 1920 when he visited Russia and then again in 1933 when she emigrated to London. She was a famous adventuress and worked simultaneously for three secret intelligence services: Soviet (the Cheka), English, and German.

23 Pepekriu was the nickname of Petr Petrovich Kriuchkov.

24 Vladislav Felitsianovich Khodasevich (1886–1939) was a poet, prose writer, and critic. In 1925 Khodasevich emigrated to Paris.

25 Anna Ivanovna Khodasevich, maiden name Chulkova (1887–1964), was the second wife of V. F. Khodasevich, the sister of the poet G. I. Chulkov and the heroine of the collection *A Happy Little Home* (*Schastlivyi domik*).

26 Friedrich Eduardovich (Fritz) Krimer (1888–?) before the revolution was an economist and a major figure in banking. He was friends for many years with Gorky and worked on the latter's newspaper, *Novyi Zhizn'* (New Life). He was executed during the Stalinist terror.

27 This is a dig at the Provisional Government in 1917 and Alexander Kerensky's issuing of large amounts of ruble notes, known as Kerensky bills or Kerensky rubles.

28 Leonid Osipovich Utësov (1895–1982) was a popular variety performer, singer, and film actor. He was one of the founders of the Russian music hall and gained fame as a jazz musician. He was reportedly Stalin's favorite singer.

29 Herbert George Wells (1866–1946) was an English writer, social commentator, and journalist. In 1914, 1920, and 1934 he visited Russia, where he met with Lenin and Stalin (see his books, *Russia in the Shadows*, 1920 and *An Experiment in Autobiography*, 1934).

30 The Villa Rode was a winter café-chantant (a type of nightclub; these were establishments serving alcohol and food but also featured popular and often vulgar singing and dancing shows) in the district of Petrograd known as Novaia Derevnia (New Countryside). The restaurant was in the style of a dacha (country home or estate), set in a garden. Inside there was a common dining room and separate suites. One of these was always reserved for Grigory Rasputin.

31 The St. Petersburg Court Capella, also known as the Court Chapel, is a long-standing musical institution founded in Russia in the fifteenth century. Over time it came to consist of a choir, an orchestra, and a concert hall.

32 The author may be mistaken in saying that she became his wife. Most sources claim that she remained his mistress and refused to marry even when Wells asked her.

33 George Phillip Wells (Gil) was the oldest son of H. G. Wells, and he accompanied his father on his trip to Petrograd in 1920.

34 E. Lopukhova and A. Orlov were a dancing couple who first performed in 1910. They choreographed and performed the number "Ryazan dance (Ryazanskaia pliaska)." They were part of the artistic troupe of the Mariinsky Theater.

35 A bayan is a type of accordion invented in Russia in 1907 and named after an eleventh-century poet Boyan who was mentioned in the classic epic chronicle of the early history of the Slavs, *The Lay of Igor's Campaign*.

36 Vladimir Vasil'evich Lebedev (1891–1967) was a painter and graphic artist. He worked for the journals *Satirikon* and *Novyi Satirikon* (the *New Satirikon*).

37 The People's Comedy Theater, founded by Radlov in 1919, operated only until 1922. This may have been one of the last productions Konstantin Mikhailovich worked on for this theater.

38 Basargina's real name was Liubov' Dmitrievna Mendeleeva-Blok (1881–1938); she was also called Busen'ka or Bu. She was an actress and a scholar who wrote on the theory and history of ballet. She was the wife of A. A. Blok and the inspiration for his poetry—she came to represent the "Eternal Feminine," the ideal image of womanhood, but this proved an impediment to their marriage because it made Blok reluctant to engage with her sexually.

39 Aleksandr Nikolaevich Tikhonov, who also used the pseudonym A. Serebrov and N. Serebrov (1880–1956), was a writer. He managed the publication known as *World Literature* and from 1930 to 1936 he headed the Academia publishing house.

40 Petropolis was a private publishing house in Petrograd founded in 1918 by Iakov Noevich Blok, and it lasted until 1922.

41 Nadezhda Zalshupina came from an educated Petersburg family. Her father, Aleksandr Semenovich Zalshupin, published the weekly judicial and criminal journal *Life and Court*. Her brother, Sergei Aleksandrovich Zalshupin, was an artist.

42 The journal *Stolitsa i usad'ba* (*The Capital and the Manor*) was published from 1914 to 1917 in St. Petersburg by V. P. Krymov (1878–1968). A total of ninety issues came out, with a print run of up to one thousand five hundred copies. It was a journal about St. Petersburg mansions and townhomes. The journal *Starie gody* (*Old Times*) came out from 1907 to 1916 and was published by the "Circle for Lovers of Russian Fine Publications" under the chairmanship of the bibliographer and bibliophile Vasilii Andreevich Vereshchagin (1861–1931).

43 Georgii Kreskent'evich Lukomskii (1884–1952) was an art historian and an artist. He was connected with the "World of Art" exhibits and publications. From 1908 he published his articles in the journals *Old Years*, *Architect*, *The Capital and the Mansion*, and *Apollon*. After 1920 he lived in Paris. His book about Jewish art in European synagogues, *Jewish Art in European Synagogues—From the Middle Ages to the Eighteenth Century … With 281 Illustrations*, published in 1947, increased scholarly interest in Jewish art of the Middle Ages.

44 Sergei Nikolaevich Troinitskii (1882–1946) was an art historian and scholar, a specialist on heraldry. He worked in the Hermitage beginning in 1908, and in 1918 he became its director. He was fired in 1935 from this position, and on March 4 of that year, S. N. Troinitskii and his wife Marianna Epidiforovna Borisova-Musatova were sentenced to exile in Ufa.

45 Aleksandr Nikolaevich Benois (in Russian, Benua) (1870–1960) was a painter and graphic artist, illustrator and book designer, a master of theatrical decoration, director, author of ballet librettos, leading historian of Russian and West European art, a theorist and a publicist, and an expert on theater, music, and choreography. He was one of the organizers and theoreticians of the association known as "The World of Art" and founded a journal of the same name. In 1918 Benois became head of the Picture Gallery of the Hermitage. In 1926 Benois emigrated and settled in Paris.

46 Konstantin (Kote) Aleksandrovich Mardzhanov, whose real name was
Mardzhanishvili (1872–1933), was a director. He was a reformer in the Georgian
theater. Beginning in 1897, he worked in Russian theaters and in the Moscow Arts
Theater. During the 1920s, he worked in the Rustaveli State Georgian Theater as well.
In 1928 he established a drama theater in Kutaisi, which is now the Mardzhanishvili
State Georgian Theater (Tbilisi).

47 *The Abduction from the Seraglio* is an opera in three acts composed by Wolfgang
Amadeus Mozart and first staged in 1782. It featured a story set in sixteenth-century
Turkey involving the attempt by the hero Belmonte to rescue his love from the
Seraglio (the inner living quarters of the harem women) of Pasha Selim.

48 Mayakovsky finished the poem "The 150 Millions" at the very beginning of 1920. He
wrote it during the time of the Civil War, inspired by his faith in the victory of the
revolution. His first title for the poem had been "The Will of the Millions."

49 Lili (Lilia) Iur'evna Brik (1892–1978) was Mayakovsky's lover. He dedicated to her his
early love lyrics as well as the long love poem, "That's What" (Pro Eto).

4 Gathering Clouds: Marital Storms and Emigration

1 Nikolai Nikolaevich Evreinov (1879–1953) was a dramatist, director, producer,
theoretician, and theater historian. He directed in 1911–12 the theater of V. F.
Komissarzhevskii, known as "The Merry Theater for Aged Children," as well as
the theater The Crooked Mirror from 1910 to 1917. He participated in the artistic
performances and activities of the Stray Dog Cabaret and The Comedians Halt
Cabaret. In 1925 he went to Poland on tour for The Crooked Mirror and then
emigrated to Paris.

2 Leonid Borisovich Krasin (1870–1926) was a high-ranking Soviet and Party official
(Commissar of Trade and Industry and of Railroads) and a diplomat.

3 Grigory Mikhailovich Kozintsev (1905–1973) was a movie producer. In 1921
Kozintsev along with L. Trauberg and S. Iutkevich organized an avant-garde creative
association known as FEKS (The Factory of the Eccentric Actor). He began to work in
movies beginning in 1924.

4 Sergei Iosifovich Iutkevich (1904–1985) was a director, artist, and film theorist. He
made classic biographical films about Lenin, including one that won a Cannes Best
Director Award, *Lenin in Poland* (1966).

5 Vladimir Kazimiovich Shileiko (1891–1930) was an Assyrian specialist and scholar.
He introduced into scientific circulation many Sumerian, Assyrian-Babylonian,
Hittite, and other ancient written inscriptions and manuscripts. He was also
a poet who was part of the circle of friends around Gumilev, Akhmatova, and
O. Mandelshtam. He was the second husband of Anna Akhmatova.

6 "Else paler seems my saddened face/Above the silk of lilac glaring/Eyebrows can
almost be embraced/by the long bangs, uncurled and daring"—from a poem of
A. Akhmatova, "My Neck Is Shaded by the Beads," 1913, included in her volume of
poetry published in 1921, *Plantain* (*Podorozhnik*). Translator's note—I have referred
to the translation of this poem by Yevgeny Bonver, published on the Poetry Lovers
Page, http://www.poetryloverspage.com/yevgeny/akhmatova/my_neck_is_shaded_
by_beads.html (accessed June 5, 2016).

7 Vadim Mikhailovich Miklachevsky (1890–1963) was Konstantin Mikhailovich's
   younger brother, and after finishing the Alexander Lyceum in 1911, he worked until
   the February Revolution in the Office of the Ministry of the Imperial Court. After
   emigrating he married Maria Vladimirovna Okhotnikova (1897–1983).

8 Valentin Platonovich Zubov (1885–1969) was an art scholar. He was a count and the
   creator-director of the St. Petersburg Institute of the History of Art (from 1912 to
   1924). From 1925 he lived in exile.

9 Alexei Mikhailovich Remizov (1877–1957) was a Russian modernist writer who
   emigrated from Russia in 1921. He was fascinated by medieval Russian folklore
   and superstitions and incorporated them into his writings; he also was skilled at
   calligraphy. His writings in emigration focused on dreams and on demons but he
   could not find a publisher until late in his life. He died in Paris in 1957.

10 Fyodor Sologub was the pen name of Fyodor Kuzmich Teternikov (1863–1927). He
   was a poet, novelist, playwright, and author of essays. He was part of the Russian
   Symbolist movement in literature and is best known for his novel, *The Petty Demon*.

11 Anastasia Nikolaevna Chebotareskaia (1876–1921) was a writer, translator, and the
   wife of writer F. K. Sologub, whom she married in 1907. She committed suicide on
   September 23, 1921; the couple had been seeking permission to emigrate for over
   two years and only in the summer of 1921 received notice that they could leave. It is
   thought that the strain of their difficult living conditions and worries over emigration
   contributed to her jumping from the bridge.

12 From 1921 to 1923, poetess Anna Akhmatova and the actress Ol'ga Afanas'evna
   Glebova-Sudeikina (1885–1945) lived in Building 18 on the Fontanka embankment.
   Back in 1910 this had been the family apartment of the Sudeikins. Akhmatova moved
   in with her in 1921 at the time of her friend's tour to Vologda. Even after the return of
   Sudeikina she remained there until 1923.

13 The quote "And why do these myrrh-bearing women invite us" is an expression
   that was commonly used in the Silver Age and later was applied rather ironically to
   describe those who were the most obsequious admirers of one or another of the poets
   or charismatic figures of the period. The term *zheny—mironositsy*, literally "myrrh-
   bearing" or "holy wives," referred to Mary Magdalene and the other women who
   brought myrrh to anoint the body of Christ on the third day in the crypt.

14 Iurii Pavolovich Annenkov (1889–1974) was a painter, graphic artist, a theater and
   film artist, a director, and writer (his literary pseudonym was B. Timiriazev). From
   1913 to 1924 he lived in Petrograd and Moscow. He put on shows for the cabaret
   The Crooked Mirror and the Comedians' Halt, as well as others. After 1925 he lived
   in Paris.

15 Evgenii Ivanovich Zamiatin (1884–1937) was married to Liudmila Zamiatina
   (1883–1965). Zamiatin was a Russian journalist and writer of short stories and novels
   in genres such as science fiction and satire. He is most famous for writing what is
   arguably the first dystopian novel of the twentieth century, *We*, which depicted a
   future police state bearing many similarities to Soviet Russia. His increasingly critical
   and sarcastic writings on the Soviet Union made it hard for him to get published.
   He was given permission by Stalin to emigrate in 1931 and died in Paris only six
   years later.

16 Pavel Eliseevich Shchëgolev (1877–1931) was an historian, literary scholar, a collector
   and publisher of ancient manuscripts, and a publicist. In 1916 the first edition of his
   book *The Duel and Death of Pushkin* came out. He published extensively on the life
   and writings of Alexander Pushkin, A. S. Griboedov, and Mikhail Lermontov.

17 Mikhail Semenovich Sobakevich is one of the landowners who sells dead serfs to Chichikov in Nikolai Gogol's classic satirical novel *Dead Souls*. In his physical appearance he is depicted as resembling a bear and a glutton when it comes to food. His powerful and authoritarian manner are mirrored in the furnishings of his solidly built estate, adorned with massive furniture and portraits of Greek military generals.

18 Mikhail Alekseevich Kuzmin (1872–1936) was a poet, prose writer, and composer. He studied at the Conservatory in St. Petersburg, where he was a pupil of Nikolai Rimsky-Korsakov and performed as a composer and pianist. In 1906 he published his first verse cycle, *The Alexander Songs*, and his first novel, *Wings*. In 1908 he published a book of verses entitled *Nets* (Seti).

19 Iurii Ivanovich Iurkun (1895–1938) was a fiction writer and a friend of Mikhail Kuzmin.

20 Aleksandr Ivanovich Vvedenskii (1888–1946) was a leading figure in the Russian Orthodox Church. He was one of the leaders of the Renovationist Movement in the Russian Orthodox Church. After the split of the so-called "Living Church" in 1922, he became the head of his own group known as the Ancient Apostolic Church.

21 Nikolai Stepanovich Gumilev (1886–1921) was a Russian poet, literary critic, and a cofounder of the Acmeist movement in Russian poetry. He was the first husband of Anna Akhmatova and the father of historian and Gulag survivor Lev Gumilev. He fought in the First World War and was decorated for his bravery. He opposed the Bolshevik regime and in 1921 was arrested by the Cheka, who accused him falsely of participating in a supposedly monarchist organization, the Petrograd Military Organization. He was shot on August 26, 1921.

22 Vladimir Evgrafovich Tatlin (1885–1953) was a painter, graphic artist, artistic designer, and theater artist. He took part in the exhibits of the World of Art, the Union of Young People, the Jack of Diamonds, and The Ass' Tail. During 1919–20 Tatlin constructed a model for the monument dedicated to the October Revolution, "Monument to the Third International," which was displayed at the eighth Congress of Soviets in December 1920. This model for a "Tower" was not preserved; it was supposed to have been the tallest building in the world (its planned height was approximately four hundred meters), but the monument was never constructed.

23 The bandura is a Ukrainian stringed folk instrument similar to a lute and the balalaika. It is also referred to as a "kobza."

24 In 1913 Tatlin completed sketches for the Richard Wagner opera "The Flying Dutchman," which was in production in 1915 but was never performed.

25 Gostiny Dvor and Apraksin Dvor are two shopping arcades and markets built in the eighteenth century that housed different shops and vendors. Both still operate today. Gostiny Dvor is located on Nevskii Prospekt and Apraksin Dvor (also known as Apraksin Yard) is on Sadovaia Street.

26 Sporok, sporka were thin coat covers or linings for outer wear.

27 The "former people" included disenfranchised groups such as the aristocracy, the upper middle classes, clergy, tsarist military officers, and so on.

28 Stepan Petrovich Iaremich (1869–1939) was an art historian and painter. He took part in the exhibitions of the World of Art. Beginning in 1930, he was the head of the Hermitage museum's restoration workshop.

29 Elena Ivanovna Molokhovets (1831–1918) was the author of the book *A Gift for Young Housewives* (1861). During her lifetime this book went through twenty-nine editions,

and the print run for each was approximately three hundred thousand copies. It contained over four thousand recipes. It was banned by the Soviet government in 1917 for being too "bourgeois" and decadent. She also authored the book *Rules for High Society, Etiquette and Good Manners.*

30 Aleksandr Iakovlevich Tairov (1885–1950) was an actor and director. During the 1906–7 season, he was an actor in the theater of V. F. Komissarzheskaia in St. Petersburg. In 1914, Tairov joined with Alisa Koonen and a group of young actors to create the Kamerny (Chamber) Theater.

31 Vsevolod Emil'evich Meyerhold (1874–1940) was an actor, acting teacher, and director. He was one of the reformers of the Russian theater. From 1920 to 1938 he headed the theater in Moscow (from 1923 it was known as the Meyerhold Theater) and the acting school that was connected with it. He died a victim of Stalin's repression.

32 On January 31, 1922, on the stage of the Gabim Bible Studio (Jewish Theater) in Moscow, the premiere of the show based on the play of the Jewish writer-philosopher S. Ansky (S. A. Rapoport), *Gadibuk*, in the translation from Hebrew of Kh. Bialik took place. Director Evgenii Vakhtangov produced it, and young Jewish actors performed the roles. After the triumphant world tour of the Gabim theater from 1926 to 1930, the show received recognition as one of the most outstanding theatrical achievements of the twentieth century. It received enthusiastic reviews from Nikolai Evreinov, Viacheslav Ivanov, Albert Einstein, Sergei Eisenshtein, George Bernard Shaw, Rabindranath Tagore, Mark Chagall, and David Ben-Gurion.

33 The Comedians' Halt was an artistic and literary cabaret that existed in Petrograd from 1916 to 1919. Its creator was Boris Pronin, a director, actor, and participant in a number of Meyerhold's theatrical initiatives. It opened its doors on April 18, 1916, in the basement of the House of Adamini, which stood at #7 Field of Mars, on the Moika canal embankment. Pronin's project was intended as the successor of the famous Silver Age artistic cabaret known as The Stray Dog, which had closed the previous year. The artists B. Grigor'ev, A. Iakovlev, and S. Sudeikin painted the walls with decorative panels on themes drawn from the Italian playwright Carlo Gozzi and the German Romantic writer E. T. A. Hoffman. Many representatives of the Silver Age Bohemian set were regular guests.

34 The Serapion Brothers was an association of writers (prose writers, poets, and literary critics) formed in Leningrad on February 11, 1921. The name came from a cycle of novels written by E. T. A. Hoffman, *The Serapion Brethren*, which centered around a theme of individualism and nonconformity in the pursuit of art. Members of the group were Lev Lunts, Ilia Gruzdev, Mikhail Zoshchenko, Veniamin Kaverin, Nikolai Nikitin, Mikhail Slonimskii, Viktor Shklovskii, Vladimir Pozner, Elizaveta Polonskaia, Konstantin Fedin, Nikolai Tikhonov, and Vsevolod Ivanov.

35 Evgeny L'vovich Shvarts (1896–1958) was a writer and dramatist, the author of more than twenty plays as well as screenplays for eight films. He lived in Leningrad beginning in 1924. During the time period depicted here, he was closely connected with the Serapion Brothers.

36 Vladimir Solomonovich Pozner (1905–1992) was a Russian and French poet, translator, journalist, screenwriter, and literary critic. He was born in France but in 1910 he came with his family to St. Petersburg. He worked in the literary studio connected with the publishing house World Literature (1919), which became later a studio run by the House of Art. He was a member of the Serapion Brothers.

37 Zoia Aleksanderovna Nikitina (1902–1973) was the wife of the writer Mikhail Emmanuilovich Kozakov. She worked for publishing houses except during the time of her two arrests and two prison terms.

38 Mikhail Leonidovich Slonimskii (1897–1972) was a writer. In 1920 he became a resident in the House of Art, and he studied at the literary studio of E. I. Zamiatin. At the beginning of the 1920s, he joined the Serapion Brothers literary association.

39 Lev Natanovich Lunts (1901–1924) was a writer of prose, a dramatist, and political commentator. During the period 1918 to 1922, he studied in the history–philology department at Petrograd University. He knew Spanish, Italian, English, French, old French, and classical Hebrew. He joined the Serapion Brothers. In 1923 Lunts went to Germany for a cure but after one year, he died from a brain disease. He was the author of the article "Why We Are the Serapion Brothers," which was considered to be the manifesto of the group. It was this article in particular that A. A. Zhdanov quoted in 1946 to prove the anti-Soviet tendencies of the writer M. M. Zoshchenko and of the Serapion Brothers in general.

40 Konstantin Aleksanderovich Fedin (1892–1966) was a writer. Beginning in 1921, he participated in the Serapion Brothers literary association. In 1934, he became a member of the Presidium of the SSP (Union of Soviet Writers).

41 Mikhail Mikhailovich Zoshchenko (1894–1958) was a popular Soviet writer during the 1920s and 1930s who specialized in short stories that were humorous, witty, and satirical in their exposure of the foibles of human life and the problems of bureaucracy and corruption. He came under attack along with Anna Akhmatova in 1946 with the Zhdanov Decree issued by the Communist Party Central Committee. His works were banned from publication and he was expelled from the Writers' Union. Only after Stalin's death in 1953 could he again be published. He died in Leningrad of heart disease on July 22, 1958.

42 Dora Sergeevna Aleksander was the wife of the writer Konstantin Fedin.

43 Mikhail Zoshchenko's first published book was *Tales of Nazar Ilyich, Mr. Sinebriukhov*, which came out in 1921. It was a cycle of stories narrated by an ex-soldier from the First World War. The stories abound with Zoshchenko's ironic sense of humor and were very popular.

44 Olga Dmitrievna Forsh (1873–1961) was a prose writer. Her main work was an historical novel, *Odety kamnem* (*Palace and Prison*, 1924–5).

45 The Labor Exchange (Birzha truda) was the government-run office that handled both matters of employment and unemployment. Individuals seeking work were supposed to report to these offices and find employment through them. During the 1920s, though, many employers hired workers without going through the Labor Exchanges. See William J. Chase, *Workers, Society and the Soviet State: Labor and Life in Moscow, 1918–1929* (Urbana: University of Illinois Press, 1990), 137–8.

46 Nikolai Nikolaevich Khodotov (1878–1932) was a theater actor, dramatist, and memoirist. He worked in the Alexander Theater.

47 Aleksei Denisovich Dikii (1889–1955) was an actor and a director. In 1910 he joined the Moscow Art Theater. K. S. Stanislavsky and Vl. I. Nemirovich Danchenko were his teachers. In 1936 Dikii was arrested and spent five years in a corrective labor camp, but nonetheless went on to portray Stalin in several films.

48 Anatole France (1844–1924) was a French novelist and literary critic.

5 Homecoming and a New Start in Moscow

1 The Herzen House was the birthplace of the famous Russian radical writer
   Alexander Herzen. The Soviet state took over the building and gave it in 1920 to
   organizations of Russian writers. Some who lived there or who performed public
   readings of their work there included Osip Mandelshtam, Andrei Platonov, and
   Maxim Gorky.
2 Lev Veniaminovich Nikulin (1891–1967) was a noted Soviet writer whose works were
   translated into foreign languages and who received numerous state awards including
   the Stalin Prize in 1952. He wrote adventure novels, historical novels, travel essays,
   and biographical studies of leading cultural figures such as Fedor Chaliapin, Chekhov,
   Ivan Bunin, and Aleksandr Kuprin.
3 Nikolai Nikolaevich Aseev (1889–1963) was a poet. He was particularly close to
   Velimir (Victor Vladimirovich) Khlebnikov and to Vladimir Mayakovsky.
4 Ivar Tenisovich Smilga (1892–1937) was a professional revolutionary and a Bolshevik.
   He served as a party and state official and was a supporter of Trotsky. He was executed
   in 1937.
5 Mistinguett (1875–1956) was a French performer, cabaret singer, and actress. Her real
   name was Jeanne Florentine Bourgeois and from humble origins she became one of
   the most popular and celebrated female entertainers of her day. Her flamboyant style,
   unique voice, and charisma were legendary.
6 Osip Maksimovich Brik (1888–1945) was a literary critic, publisher and editor, and
   a scholar of poetic theory. He was one of the organizers and leaders of such Soviet
   artistic circles as *Kom-fut* (Communist-Futurists), LEF (Left Front of Art), and REF
   (Revolutionary Front of Art). He was the husband of Lilia Brik.
7 Oksana; her full name was Kseniia Mikhailovna Siniakova (1893–1985). She was the
   wife of N. N. Aseev.
8 Boris Matveevich Lapin (1905–1941) was a writer and a journalist. In his youth he
   wrote expressionist poetry and traveled extensively. He was the brother-in-law of Ilya
   Ehrenburg. While working as a military correspondent, he died at the beginning of
   the Second World War.
9 *Mezhrabpom-Rus* was a joint venture shareholding company between the USSR and
   Germany. It formed the Soviet film studio *Mezhrabpom-Rus* in 1924 by merging with
   producer Moisei Aleinikov's studio known as Rus.
10 This must be a location in Egypt, possibly Saqqara or Jurf al-Sakhar, though it is not
   given as one of the official locations where the film was made, possibly because the
   Egyptian scenes did not make it into the final version of the film, and director Abel
   Gance was never able to raise the money needed to make the five additional films he
   originally planned. It is also not clear whether these were scenes shot for the version
   of the film that debuted in April of 1927. Ludmila does not give the precise date when
   she received these letters.
11 The film *Napoleon* was one of the greatest films of silent and world cinema. It was
   directed by the French director Abel Gance who was called "the Victor Hugo of
   French cinematography" for his innovation. The first version of the film debuted on
   screen in 1927.
12 *Gore umu/Gore ot uma, Woe to Wit/Woe from Wit* was a play put on by V. E.
   Meyerhold in 1928. He adapted the play from the 1823 play of Alexander Griboedov,

Woe from Wit (*Gore ot uma*) and renamed it *Woe to Wit* (*Gore umu*), and essentially rewrote much of the play.

13 Zinaida Nikolaevna Raikh (1894–1939) was an actress. In 1921, she joined the State Experimental Theater Workshops run by V. E. Meyerhold. From 1928 to 1938 she was an actress at the Meyerhold Theater. She was the wife of Meyerhold and in 1939, when her husband was arrested, she was stabbed to death in her apartment by a person thought to be an agent of the NKVD.

14 Ekaterina Vasilevna Gel'tser (1876–1962) was a ballet artist. In the 1920s, thanks to the efforts of her husband V. D. Tikhomirov, her repertoire acquired new ballets, *La Esmeraldo* and *The Red Poppy*.

15 Vasilii Ivanovich Kachalov (1875–1948) was one of the leading actors of the Moscow Art Theater and well known for his public readings of poetic works and of prose.

16 Fedor Ivanovich Tiutchev (1803–1873) was a Russian poet and diplomat, an ardent Pan-Slavist. As a poet his works were not well known during his lifetime but the Russian Symbolists, including Alexander Blok, were inspired by his poems. He is now considered to be one whose works are most often quoted and memorized.

17 "Piter" is an affectionate abbreviation for St. Petersburg used by those who live in or who feel a fondness for the city. It continued to be used during the period when St. Petersburg was officially named Leningrad (1924–1991).

18 Innokentii Fedorovich Annenskii (1856–1909) was a Symbolist poet, translator, and literary critic. He was a precursor and teacher of the Acmeists.

19 Aleksei Konstantinovich Tolstoy (1817–1875), was a poet, novelist, and historical dramatist.

20 Prutkov was a fictional poet created by A. K. Tolstoy and used by him as a vehicle for satirizing poetic conventions and life in the Russia of Nicholas I; Tolstoy wrote these poems with the Zhemchuzhnikov brothers.

21 Ivan Vasil'evich Shervud (1798–1867) was a noncommissioned officer of the Novomirgorod Lancer Regiment and an agent-provocateur. He was the son of an English machinist sent to Russia in 1800. Shervud infiltrated one of the Decembrist groups, the Southern Society, several months prior to the Decembrist Uprising and wrote a detailed denunciation. In 1826 he was transferred to the Guards and received the right to go by the hyphenated name "Shervud-Vernyi," or Shervud the Loyal.

22 Karolina Karlovna Pavlova (1807–1893) was a poet, prose writer, and translator. She is best known for her novel in verse and prose, *A Double Life*, and though her work was highly criticized in her lifetime, the later Symbolists praised her poems and she is considered by some to have been unfairly evaluated due to the fact that she was a woman in an age when poetry was dominated by men.

23 Viktor Viktorovich Gofman (1884–1911) was a Symbolist poet, prose writer, critic, and translator. In 1911 Gofman moved to Paris where he committed suicide.

24 Vladimir Mitrofanovich Purishkevich (1870–1920) was a far right wing Russian political leader. He was one of the leaders of the first nationalist organization, "The Union of Russian People" and the "Union of the Archangel Mikhail." He took part in the murder of Rasputin.

25 Aleksandr Valentinovich Amfiteatrov (1862–1938) was a publicist, a literary and theater critic, a dramatist, and prose writer. He also wrote satirical verses and satirical, entertaining newspaper features known as feuilletons.

6 Love and Marriage in Leningrad

1 Tatiana L'vovna Shchepkina-Kupernik (1874–1952) was a writer, dramatist, poetess, and translator. She was the granddaughter of the famous Russian actor Mikhail Shchepkin, and her first publication was a poem she wrote at age 14 in memory of Shchepkin. She translated the work of Shakespeare and Moliere as well as Lewis Carroll's *Alice in Wonderland*; she is credited with translating more than sixty plays into Russian in addition to writing her own works such as *Happy Women* and *Lady with Violets*. For a discussion of her literary contributions and colorful private life, see Donald Rayfield, "The Forgotten Poetess: Tatiana L'vovna Shchepkina-Kupernik," *The Slavic and East European Review*, 79, no. 4 (October 2001), 601–37.

2 Jacques-Henri Bernarden de Saint-Pierre (1737–1814) was a French writer. His novel *Paul et Virginie* (Paul and Virginia) brought him fame across Europe.

3 Nikolai Gavrilovich Chernyshevsky (1828–1889) was a nineteenth-century radical publicist and writer whose legacy as a revolutionary was much celebrated during the Soviet period. He was the chief writer and editor of the influential journal *Sovremennik* and a harsh critic of Alexander II's Great Reforms. He looked to revolution as the only way to eradicate the evils of serfdom and social and economic inequality. Arrested in 1862 for his radicalism, Chernyshevsky wrote in prison his most famous work, the novel *What Is to be Done?*, which argued for socialism, women's emancipation, and depicted characters fully committed to revolutionary activism. This novel was widely read and inspired multiple generations of radical youth, including Bolshevik leader Vladimir Lenin. Chernyshevsky was sentenced to hard labor and spent the years from 1864 to 1883 in Siberia. He returned broken in spirit and health and died in 1889.

4 Ippolit Nikolaevich Myshkin (1848–1885) was a Populist revolutionary. In 1875 he tried to free Nikolai Chernyshevsky from his Siberian exile. He put up armed resistance to his arrest. He was sentenced to ten years of hard labor. He was shot for protesting against prison conditions.

5 The phrase "A Beacon of Knowledge Disgraced" is from a verse entitled "Na Smert' Mezentsov" (To the Death of Mezentsov) written in the 1870s by A. A. Ol'khin lamenting the continued imprisonment of Chernyshevsky. The lines of the verse are "Ugasaet v dalekoi iakutskoi taiga, Iarkii svetoch nauki opal'noi …" (Fading away in the far off Yakut taiga, A bright beacon of knowledge disgraced …). See V. G. Korolenko, *Stat'I, retsenzii, ocherki* (Directmedia, 2014), https://books.google.com/books?id=qh2IDwAAQBAJ (accessed April 19, 2019), 42–3.

6 Samuil Iakovlevich Marshak (1887–1964) was one of the most prolific and popular Soviet writers for children as well as a poet, dramatist, translator, and literary critic. He was particularly well known for his translations of Shakespeare's sonnets and poets such as William Blake, William Wordsworth, Rudyard Kipling, and Robert Burns. He won numerous awards including four Stalin prizes. He reportedly was nearly repressed in 1937 but had his name removed from a list of targeted victims by Stalin himself.

7 *Ezh* and *Chiz* were children's magazines established in 1928 and 1930. The title "*Ezh*" was an acronym for *Ezhemesiachnyi zhurnal*, or *Monthly Journal*, and was directed at schoolchildren and members of the Pioneer movement. It is also translated as "Hedgehog." *Chiz* was an acronym for *Chrezvychaino interesnyi zhurnal*, or *Exceptionally Interesting Journal*. It was intended for young children. It is also translated as "Siskin" or "Siska."

8 "Princess Mary" is the longest of the tales told in Mikhail Lermontov's classic novel *A Hero of Our Time*. It relates the story of the hero Pechorin's courtship and seduction of Princess Mary in Piatigorsk and is considered by some critics to be the most important of the five linked adventure tales told in the story.

9 Mikhail Il'in, whose real name was Il'ia Iakovlevich Marshak (1896–1953), was the younger brother of Samuil Marshak. He was an engineer-chemist and writer. He wrote books for children that sought to make complicated scientific topics accessible to them. He liked telling the story of simple, ordinary items that everyone used in daily life and also wrote on the development of technology.

10 OBERIU (Association for Real Art or Union of Real Art) was a group of poets, writers, and other cultural figures that existed from 1928 to the beginning of the 1930s in Leningrad. Vvedenskii and Kharms were leading figures in this closely knit authors' collective. It considered itself an avant-garde group, rejected traditional forms of art, and cultivated the grotesque as well as the poetics of the absurd. After 1930 they found it impossible to get work published, which forced some of the members to move into the "niche" of children's literature. Many participants in OBERIU were repressed and died in prison.

11 Alexander Gervas'evich Lebedenko (1892–1975) was a writer of prose. From 1926 to 1931 he worked as a journalist and editor for a publishing house. He published his first book in 1917 and mostly wrote on revolutionary and historical themes including the First World War and the Russian Civil War.

12 Sergei Timofeevich Aksakov (1791–1859) was a nineteenth-century Russian author. He is mainly known for his autobiographical writings about his childhood growing up on a noble estate (*Years of Childhood, A Russian Schoolboy*, and *A Russian Gentleman*). He became a close friend of the writer Nikolai Gogol, author of *Dead Souls*, and Gogol visited him at his home in the village of Abramtsevo. Aksakov's daughter Vera (1819–1864) also became a writer and is most noted for her diary written during the Crimean War and for her memoirs about the writer Gogol.

13 His full name was Pavel Pavlovich Shchëgolev.

14 Irina Valentiovna Ternatseva (1906–1993) was the wife of P. P. Shchëgolev and later of the artist Natan Isaevich Altman.

15 Originally it was named New Light village by its founder Prince Golitsyn, but was renamed at the request of Tsar Nicholas II; the location is noted for its wine making.

16 The memoirist is mistaken here. It was in 1931 that Zamiatin was allowed to leave for France legally, thanks to the entreaties of Maxim Gorky.

17 Here the memoirist is mistaken, for abortions were not made illegal until 1936. But growing restrictions were being put upon abortions due to government unease over the high numbers of abortions being carried out, especially in urban areas. She seems to suggest that she had to have a doctor declare the abortion to be medically necessary in order to have it done.

18 The memoirist writes of the process known as densification (*uplotnenie*) as beginning in Leningrad in 1930, but in actuality this process of assigning two or more families to a single apartment space began in 1918. Already Tatiana L'vovna had been sharing part of her apartment with Izya but new regulations were making further division necessary.

19 Nikolai Borisovich Polynov (1873–1939) was a lawyer and the husband of Tatiana Shchepkina-Kupernik. Before the 1917 Revolutions he was an editor of the journal *Iurist* (The Lawyer) and afterward became a defense lawyer noted for being willing to

defend victims being prosecuted by the secret police. See Rayfield, "The Forgottten Poetess," 620.

20 The Skorokhod Factory was founded in 1882 as the factory of the Association of Mechanical Footwear Production and until 1896 was located at 130 Obvodny Canal Embankment. It is now located on Zastavskaia Street. It made footwear for men, women, and children and, during the First World War, soldiers' boots. Workers from the factory played a role in the events of 1917 and formed a Red Guard unit. See "Skorokhod Factory," *Saint Petersburg Encyclopedia*, http://www.encspb.ru/object/2855695127?lc=en (accessed April 19, 2019).

21 Aleksandr Ivanovich Guchkov (1862–1936) was a Russian politician active in the prerevolutionary State Duma who became minister of war in the Provisional Government of 1917. During the First World War he headed the Central War Industries Committee. He was the son of a factory owner and studied history at Moscow State University. He was adventurous and took to traveling after university, which is how he ended up volunteering to fight for the Boers for the Anglo-Boer War (see next note).

22 The Boers were the descendants of the Dutch, French, and German colonists in South Africa. The Boer settlers founded the Orange Free State, the South African Republic, and the colony in Natal. After the Anglo-Boer war ended, the Boer republics were annexed to Great Britain and in 1910 became part of the Union of South Africa.

23 Boris Petrovich Kornilov (1907–1938) was a poet. He joined the group known as VAPP (the All-Union Association of Proletarian Writers) under the leadership of V. M. Saianov and was considered one of the most talented young poets in Russia. In 1937 he was arrested, and he died in prison on November 21, 1938.

24 Aleksei Pavlovich Chapygin (1870–1931) was a prose writer and author of the historical novels *Stepan Razin* and *Itinerant Folk*.

25 Peterhof is a town that is part of the larger municipality of St. Petersburg, located about 20 miles from the city center on the shores of the Gulf of Finland. Peterhof is famous as the place where Peter the Great built palaces and gardens intended to rival Versailles in splendor.

26 The memoirist's connection of her inability to hire a nanny due to collectivization is somewhat surprising in that the upheavals of collectivization led many peasant women to leave the villages and therefore become more available to work as nannies and maids.

27 The Candidate's degree is roughly the equivalent of a master's degree in the Western system, but many consider it the equivalent of a first Ph.D. because of the length and the extent of research and writing required for it. In 1935, Izya's application for a doctoral degree was supported by the well-respected historian and academician B. D. Grekov on the basis of Trotsky's two books and other noted publications, but the onset of the terror and then Izya's arrest in 1936 meant that it was never approved in Moscow and never awarded. See Brachev, "Istorik Isaak Moiseevich Trotsky," 72–3.

28 The Bestuzhev brothers were Nikolai, Paul, Alexander, and Mikhail, sons of a liberal member of the gentry, a writer, and civil servant Aleksandr Fedoseevich Bestuzhev who guided his sons into military careers. They each were participants in the 1825 aborted Decembrist Uprising and were sentenced to terms either of exile in the Caucasus or to hard labor in Siberia.

29 This is the acronym for *Torgovlia s inostrantsami*, Trade with Foreigners, which were special state-run stores operating in the Soviet Union between 1931 and 1936 open to those with access to hard currency.

30 Iraklii Luarsabovich Andronikov (1908–1990) was an historian, philologist, art historian, and a leading figure in the Soviet media. In 1928 he began performing at the Leningrad Philharmonia and was a brilliant mimic. He wrote multiple books on Lermontov and beginning in 1952 began to appear on Soviet television.

31 Il'ia Samoilovich Silbershtein (1905–1988) was a well-known literary scholar, art historian, art collector, and a doctor of art history. Beginning in 1931, he was one of the founders and editors of the series *Literaturnoe nasledie* (Literary Heritage). Over his lifetime he published almost 100 compilations of archival materials and edited almost half of them.

32 Kornei Chukovskii (1882–1969) was a poet, publicist, critic, a translator, and a literary scholar. In 1906 Kornei Ivanovich went to the Karelian town of Kuokkala, where he developed a close friendship with the artist Repin. He lived here for about ten years. From the combination of the words "Chukovskii" and "Kuokkala" came the word "Chukokkala" (reportedly an invention of Repin), which Chukovskii used as the title for the humorous handwritten almanac that he maintained from 1914 until the last days of his life. It was first published only in 1979 and contained a miscellany of autographs, notes, puzzles, and various sketches of famous people, both literary and artistic.

33 Iurii Nikolaevich Tynianov (1894–1943) was an historian and literary theorist, and a writer of historical novels.

34 Georgii Semenovich Vereiskii (1886–1962) was a graphic artist and painter. He was best known as a portraitist and was a member of the World of Art group.

35 Agatha Christie, whose maiden name was Miller (1890–1976), was an English writer. She was one of the most famous authors worldwide of detective novels and one of the most widely published authors in the whole of human history (after the Bible and Shakespeare).

7 Motherhood in a Time of Terror

1 Sergei Iakovlevich Gessen (1903–1937) was an historian. He was the author of works on Pushkin and on the history of the Decembrists.

2 Sergei Mironovich Kirov (1886–1934) was the popular Communist Party boss of Leningrad. He was a participant in the Russian Civil War and had headed the Azerbaijani Communist Party organization before being appointed to the position in Leningrad in 1926. He was a strong supporter of Joseph Stalin and close friends with both Stalin and Serge Ordzhonikidze.

3 Leonid Vasilevich Nikolaev (1904–1934) was a petty Communist Party functionary. On December 1, 1934, he killed Kirov. He shot him in the head a few steps from Kirov's office in the Smolny Institute. He was arrested immediately, sentenced to death, and shot.

4 Boris Borisovich Polynov (1877–1952) was a soil scientist. He was elected a corresponding member of the Academy of Sciences in 1946. At the time of his arrest, he was the director of the Soil Institute of the Academy of Sciences. He was arrested on May 11, 1937, in Moscow, where he was taken to the Lubyanka Prison and accused of being a secret British agent. He was transferred to Kresty Prison in Leningrad. He was freed from prison on March 28, 1939, with the dismissal of "Case 23283."

5 Evgenii Viktorovich Tarle (1874–1955) was an historian and was elected in 1927 as a member of the Academy of Sciences. He was arrested and exiled as part of the so-called Academic Affair fabricated by the secret police (the OGPU) in 1929–31. Later he received the Stalin Prize three times, in 1942, 1943, and 1946.

6 Antonina Nikolaevna Izergina, referred to in the text as "Totia" (1906–1969), was an art historian and scholar, a specialist in Western European painting. She worked in the Hermitage in the sector devoted to the Study of West European Art (OIZEI—Otdel Izucheniia Zapadno-Evropeiskogo Iskusstva). She became the wife of Academician I. A. Orbeli, the director of the Hermitage.

7 Lev L'vovich Rakov (1904–1970) was an historian and museum specialist. During the Second World War he created the Museum of the Defense of Leningrad. He was arrested twice, in 1938 and in 1950. The second arrest was in connection with the Leningrad Affair. His "crime" was that he had established the Museum of the Defense of Leningrad. He was sentenced to twenty-five years imprisonment and the loss of civil rights for five years and loss of property. He was interned in Vladimir Prison, from which he was released in 1954 by the very same tribunal "for the absence of any crime."

8 Iakov Ivanovich Davidovich (1899–1964) was a lawyer and a specialist on military customs. He was famous for his collection of artistically rendered toy soldiers, including the full complement of the Russian and French armies that met at the battle of Borodino. He kept them in numerous boxes and sometimes would bring them out. He set them up in historically correct formation, fully knowledgeable of the minute details of their movements across the battlefield.

9 Pavel Nikolaevich Luknitskii (1900–1972) was a Soviet writer of poetry and books on Central Asia based on his extensive travels in the region. He also amassed a vast archive of materials by and about the poet Nikolai Gumilev, which has subsequently been published by his widow. He also wrote a biography of Anna Akhmatova whom he met and interviewed as a young poet in the 1920s when he was researching his hero, Gumilev.

10 Marina Nizhal'skaia was a singer. She was the wife of the operetta star and idol, Mikhail Antonovich Rostovtsev.

11 Alexei Vladimirovich Taskin (1871–1941) was a pianist, a composer, and the concert maestro for Fedor Chaliapin.

12 The memoirist may be referring to Vladimir Vasilievich Maksimov (1880–1937), a Russian stage and silent film actor. He is known for his role as Tsar Alexander I in the 1927 film *The Decembrists*.

13 Iurii Mikhailovich Iurev (1872–1948) was an actor and teacher who got involved in the work of the theater. Beginning in 1893, he worked in the Alexander Theater. In 1919, he was one of the founders of the Bolshoi Dramatic Theater (now named for G. A. Tovstonogov).

14 Maria Nikolaevna Ermolova (1853–1928) was an actress. She was an honored artist of the imperial theaters, and in 1920 was named a People's Artist of the Republic. In 1871 she was assigned to the dramatic troupe of the Maly Theater. The power of her talent as a tragic actress was most clearly revealed in her role as Joan of Arc (in the play *The Maid of Orleans* by Friedrich Schiller). In 1921 she left the stage.

15 Maxim Gorky died on June 18, 1936 in Moscow and was buried in Red Square.

16 This is an area in the northern section of the city that includes parks and a number of important scientific research institutes.

17 Located at the corner of Nevskii Prospekt and Malaia Sadovaia Street, the Eliseiev Emporium was built in 1902–3 by the wealthy Eliseiev merchant family, which already

operated five such shops in St. Petersburg. The building style was Art Nouveau, and although its lavish and sumptuously decorated interiors drew criticism from some, it became a very popular place for city residents to shop for food. After 1917 the Bolsheviks nationalized it as Gastronome No. 1, but like the memoirist, people in St. Petersburg still referred to it as the Eliseiev Emporium. It is still a flourishing retail complex today.

18 Solovki Special Prison Camp was first established in 1923 in the Solovetskii Islands as a place of detention for opponents of the new Bolshevik regime and served as a prototype and foundation for what came to be referred to as the Gulag.

19 Lev Abramovich Plotkin (1906–1978) was a literary scholar. He was one of the active participants in the persecution not only of Izya but also of Mikhail Zoshchenko and other writers.

20 This is a difficult word to translate. It seems to refer to a shed with a canopy or awning typically found in peasant yards.

21 Soviets were councils that existed at each level of government; in this case the Soviet was the local village council.

22 This was a native form of tobacco, strong and high in nicotine typically smoked by peasants in Russia.

23 *Dersu Uzala* (Dersu the Trapper) was a book published in 1923 by explorer Vladimir Klavdievich Arsen'ev (1872–1930), who was an ethnographer as well as a writer and researcher of the Far East. He wrote this book about his travels and described the natural flora and fauna he encountered. The book is named for the man who served as his guide, Uzala the trapper, helping to immortalize him along with the two feature films later made that were based on the book.

8 Into the Vortex of Suffering: Ten Years in the Gulag

1 Old Believers (*starovery*) are Orthodox Christians who maintain the rituals and beliefs of the Russian Orthodox Church as they were prior to the Great Schism (*Raskol*) of the period 1652–66 when Patriarch Nikon introduced reforms intended to bring Russian Orthodox practices in line with modern Greek practices. Old Believers refused to adopt the changes and were persecuted severely throughout the period of imperial Russia.

2 Vasilii Ivanovich Surikov (1848–1916) was a painter. In 1881 he became a member of the Society for Traveling Art Exhibitions. In 1893 he became a full member of the St. Petersburg Academy of Art. The painting "Boiaryna Morozova" (now hanging in the Tretriakov Gallery in Moscow) was completed by Surikov in 1887. It shows the defiant Old Believer Morozova being arrested and holding up two fingers, indicating Old Believer resistance to altering the practice of making the sign of the cross with two fingers as opposed to using two fingers and the thumb as prescribed by the reforms of Nikon.

3 A sarafan is a long, trapeze-shaped jumper-style dress that is part of traditional Russian folk costume. It dates back to the fourteenth century; the word sarafan is of Persian origin but the dress may have been brought to Russia from Europe. It was mainly worn by peasant women after the reforms of Peter the Great altered the styles of dress for upper- and middle-class Russians to follow more contemporary European fashion.

4 This was the nickname for the secret police cars under Stalin, which typically traveled at night and were associated with death because many of those taken away in them never returned.

5 The film *Under the Roofs of Paris* came out in 1930 and was the first sound film of director René Clair. It was made in France. The film was one of the first French sound pictures, but it was restrained in its use of spoken words and instead told much of its story through music and striking visual shots. When the film debuted, it was hailed as the "most beautiful film in the world."

6 The Stolypin wagon (Stolypinskii vagon) was a special type of railcar used to transport large numbers of prisoners to the far reaches of the Gulag. It was named after the Russian Prime Minister, Petr Stolypin, who in the aftermath of the 1905 Revolution carried out mass arrests and deportations of thousands of peasants convicted in summary trials for taking part in the unrest. The car was specially designed to transport these prisoners and had two parts to it, one compartment for the peasant family and the other for the livestock and tools. After 1917 the Cheka and then the NKVD adapted it for conveying their prisoners, whom they crammed into the livestock compartments for long journeys without water or cots and with minimal toilet facilities.

7 The Finnish War, also known as the Winter War or the Russo-Finnish War, was a military conflict that began with the Soviet invasion of Finland on November 30, 1939, and ended with the Moscow Peace Treaty signed on March 13, 1940. The Soviet Union had demanded Finland cede territory in western Karelia to help strengthen the security of Leningrad as well as several islands. When Finland refused the USSR invaded on the pretext of a border dispute. The poorly equipped Red Army suffered unexpectedly large losses against a determined Finnish army, but with no outside assistance coming, the Finns had to concede after three months. The peace treaty forced Finland to give up 11 percent of its territory and allowed a Soviet naval base to be built on the Hanko Peninsula. The military reputation of the USSR was tarnished by the war, however, and may have encouraged Hitler to believe the Red Army could be easily defeated.

8 Viatlag was a large complex of forced labor camps in the Viatka region, Kirov Oblast, one thousand kilometers northeast of Moscow. Here a reported number of eighteen thousand prisoners died between 1938 and 1956. This was a marshy area filled with swamps and forests. Uprooting tree stumps, as Ludmila describes, was one of the major forms of labor done here. Famous prisoners included memoirist Dmitri Panin, Soviet actress Tatiana Okunevskaia, and Japanese film star Yoshiko Okada. See Ekaterina Loushnikova, "Vyatlag: the Gulag then and now," openDemocracy, November 9, 2012, https://www.opendemocracy.net/od-russia/ekaterina-loushnikova/vyatlag-gulag-then-and-now (accessed September 8, 2018). Also see V. A. Berdinskikh, *Istoriia Odnogo Lageria (Viatlag)* (Moscow: Agraf, 2001).

9 The terms *bytovki* and *urki* are prison slang for different categories of prisoners: neither referred to political prisoners but rather to common criminals. The *bytovki* were less violent ones accused of violating some aspect of the civil code, while *urki* were regular criminals often convicted of crimes of violence. One of the greatest sources of torment for the political prisoners was being mixed in the camp population with criminals, many of whom were given positions of privilege and authority by camp bosses and guards.

10 In Russian, *Voenizirovannaia okhrana*. These were militarized security guards attached to most Soviet ministries, including the Gulag camp administration.

11 Soviet annexation of Lithuania, Estonia, and Latvia occurred in 1940 as a product of the Molotov–Ribbentrop Pact signed in August 1939 between the Soviet Union and Nazi Germany, assigning the Baltic states to the Soviet sphere of interest. The deportations of thousands of persons from these three formerly independent countries took place in 1940–1 and targeted those suspected of being opposed to Soviet rule by virtue of their past political affiliations, economic standing, religious beliefs, and so on. Many who were farmers were deported in preparation for the collectivization of agriculture.

12 The *kum* was the camp security officer who managed the network of informers.

13 Natalia Grigor'evna Dolinina (1928–1979) was a philologist, writer, dramatist, and teacher. She was the daughter of G. A. Gukovskii, a noted historian and literary theorist.

14 In her text, Ludmila referred to this hospital as a "sotsgorodok" hospital, which means that this urban settlement may have been an example of a "specific form of industrial communally-oriented new town," examples of which did exist in some places in the Soviet camp system. But she makes no other reference to this town nor does she explain anything more about its character. For more on Soviet town planning and the difference between "sots-gorod" and "sotsialisticheskii gorod," see Carola Hein, ed. *The Routledge Handbook of Planning History* (New York: Routledge, 2018), 198.

9 Release, Exile, and Rehabilitation: The Bittersweet Taste of "Freedom"

1 The Ministry of State Security (*Ministerstvo gosudarstvennoi bezopastnosti SSSR*) was the name given to the Soviet state security apparatus from 1946 to 1953, the functions of which included administration of the Gulag and key economic enterprises employing prisoners and exiles.

2 Also referred to as a "night-dress case." According to the 1870s magazine *Cottage Hearth: A Magazine of Home Arts and House Culture*, it would be in the shape of a large envelope and was often ornamented with lace or embroidery. See Kesiah Shelton, "The Household," *Cottage Hearth: A Magazine of Home Arts and House Culture*, vol. XI, no. 1 (January 1885), 203, https://books.google.com/books?id=SWshAQAAMAAJ&pg=RA1-PA203&lpg=RA1-PA203&dq (accessed August 25, 2018).

3 The film *Uchitel' tantsev* (*Dance Teacher*) was made by director Tatiana Lukashevich for Mosfilm in 1952. It was a filmed performance of the Central Theater of the Soviet Army based on a play by Spanish playwright Lope de Vega.

4 The film *Shkola zlosloviia* (*The School of Scandal,* also known as *The School of Calumny*) was a film based on a theatrical performance. The director was Abram Matveevich Room, and the film was made in 1952 for Mosfilm. It was a performance of the Gorky Moscow Art Theater and was based on the comedy of the same name by Richard Brinsley Sheridan and produced by N. Gorchakov and P. Largin.

5 During 1952–3, a group of Moscow doctors, most of whom were Jewish, were arrested on trumped-up charges of conspiring to murder Soviet leaders. It is believed that this was intended as a prelude to a new purge of the leadership as well as a wave of terror against Jews. Stalin's death halted the proceedings and the arrested doctors were released.

6 The Military Procuracy was part of the office of the Procuracy, one of the most powerful institutions in the Soviet system of justice, with a wide range of functions regarding investigation and prosecution of criminal cases. The Military Procuracy was in charge of reviewing rehabilitation applications for cases that had been brought before Military courts and tribunals, which applied to both Ludmila and Izya.

7 The film *Belosnezhka i sem' gnomov* (*Snow White and the Seven Dwarfs*) was an American film made in 1937, directed by Walt Disney and David Hand, based upon the stories of the Brothers Grimm. It was the first full-length animated feature film and marked the debut of Walt Disney on the "big screen." It won many awards, including an Honorary Oscar for its innovative quality. It was not shown in the Soviet Union until after the Second World War and was in distribution from 1955 to 1959.

8 The year 1939, given here as when Konstantin Mikhailovich died from carbon monoxide poisoning, conflicts with existing biographical information on him. Most biographical entries and sources give his date of death as either 1943 or 1944 in Paris.

9 Konstantin Mikhailovich Figurnov (1887–1961) was a gynecologist and obstetrician, a corresponding member of the USSR Academy of Medical Sciences (elected 1946) and a major general in the medical service. He was the head of the Department of Obstetrics and Gynecology at the Leningrad Military-Medical Academy.

10 It is not clear why Ludmila brings up this fact, although it may be because being Rh-negative is much more rare than being Rh-positive and if in her earlier pregnancy the fetus had been Rh-positive, this could have caused a problem for Elena and maybe this was a factor being discussed as possibly responsible for her illness. It also may be related to difficulties with blood transfusions.

11 Prolan is a hormonal protein.

12 Chorionepithelioma is a rare tumor consisting of cells from the placenta that appear in the mother after pregnancy.

13 Matvei Aleksandrovich Gukovskii (1898–1971) was an historian and art scholar. In 1948 he was named the deputy director of the Hermitage Museum's Scientific Department. In the summer of 1949 he was arrested, and sentenced to ten years in the camps by a decision of the OSO (the Special Council of the State Security Ministry) on August 5, 1950, under Article 58, point 10. His conviction was overturned at the end of 1954, and in 1955, he returned to Leningrad and was appointed deputy head of the Department of the History of Western Art. From January 1960, he headed the Scientific Library of the Hermitage. He was elected as a member of international institutes in Amboise (France) and in the Italian cities of Milan and Mirandola.

Further Readings

Adamova-Sliozberg, Olga (2011), *My Journey: How One Woman Survived Stalin's Gulag*, trans. Katherine Gratwick Baker, Evanston, IL: Northwestern University Press.

Adler, Nanci (2002), *The Gulag Survivor: Beyond the Soviet System*, New Brunswick, NJ: Transaction.

Alexopoulos, Golfo (2017), *Illness and Inhumanity in Stalin's Gulag* (Yale-Hoover Series on Authoritarian Regimes), New Haven, CT: Yale University Press.

Applebaum, Anne (2003), *Gulag: A History*, New York: Doubleday.

Atwood, Lynne (1999), *Creating the New Soviet Woman: Women's Magazines as Engineers of Female Identity, 1922–1953*, New York: Palgrave.

Barnes, Steven A. (2011), *Death and Redemption: The Gulag and the Shaping of Soviet Society*, Princeton, NJ: Princeton University Press.

Bertaux, Daniel, Paul Thompson, and Anna Rorirch, eds. (2004), *On Living through Soviet Russia*, London: Routledge.

Bonner, Elena (1993), *Mothers and Daughters*, New York: Vintage Books.

Bucher, Greta (2006), *Women, the Bureaucracy, and Daily Life in Postwar Moscow, 1945–1953*, Boulder, CO: East European Monographs.

David-Fox, Michael, ed. (2016), *The Soviet Gulag: Evidence, Interpretation, and Comparison*, Pittsburgh, PA: University of Pittsburgh Press.

Figes, Orlando (2012), *Just Send Me Word: A True Story of Love and Survival in the Gulag*, New York: Metropolitan Books.

Frierson, Cathy A., and Semyon S. Vilensky (2010), *Children of the Gulag*, New Haven, CT: Yale University Press.

Getty, J. Arch, and Roberta T. Manning, eds. (1993), *Stalinist Terror: New Perspectives*, Cambridge: Cambridge University Press.

Gheith, Jehanne M., and Katherine R. Jolluck, eds. (2011), *Gulag Voices: Oral Histories of Soviet Incarceration and Exile*, New York: Palgrave MacMillan.

Gregory, Paul R. (2013), *Women of the Gulag: Portraits of Five Remarkable Lives*, Stanford, CA: Hoover Institution Press.

Ilič, Melanie, ed. (2000), *Women in the Stalin Era*, London: Palgrave.

Ivanova, Galina Mikhailovna (2000), *Labor Camp Socialism: The Gulag in the Soviet Totalitarian System*, trans. Carol Flath, Armonk, NY: M.E. Sharpe.

Joffe, Nadezhda A. (1995), *Back in Time: My Live, My Fate, My Epoch*, trans. Frederick S. Choate, Oak Park, MI: Labor.

Khlevniuk, Oleg V. (2015), *Stalin: New Biography of a Dictator*, trans. Nora Seligman Favorov, New Haven, CT: Yale University Press.

Shapovalov, Veronica, ed. and trans. (2001), *Remembering the Darkness: Women in Soviet Prisons*, New York: Rowman & Littlefield.

Slezkine, Yuri (2017), *The House of Government: A Saga of the Russian Revolution*, Princeton, NJ: Princeton University Press.

Toker, Leona (2000), *Return from the Archipelago: Narratives of Survivors*, Bloomington: University of Indiana Press.

Vilensky, Simon, ed. (1999), *Till My Tale Is Told*, Bloomington: University of Indiana Press.

Index

CPSIA information can be obtained
at www.ICGtesting.com
Printed in the USA
LVHW080306181121
703569LV00014B/95